A Time of Silence

GW00671964

The years 1936–45 in Spain saw catastrophic civil war followed by fierce repression and economic misery. Families were torn apart and social relations were disrupted by death, exile and defeat. Society became traumatised so deeply that people avoided talking openly of these years for decades.

This study attempts to show how the Civil War was understood and absorbed, particularly by those who could claim themselves as 'the victors', during and in the immediate aftermath of the conflict. It does so by exploring the interchanges between violence, ideas and economics during a period in which liberalism was seen as a foreign contagion that infected carriers of impurities, such as freemasons, regional nationalists, the working class, non-Catholics and women. This was the context of the internal colonisation that confirmed Franco's victory, concentrated economic power, and left executions and starvation in its wake.

MICHAEL RICHARDS is Lecturer in European History, University of the West of England

Studies in the Social and Cultural History of Modern Warfare

General Editor
Jay Winter *Pembroke College, Cambridge*

Advisory Editors
Paul Kennedy *Yale University*
Antoine Prost *Université de Paris-Sorbonne*
Emmanuel Sivan *The Hebrew University of Jerusalem*

In recent years the field of modern history has been enriched by the exploration of two parallel histories. These are the social and cultural history of armed conflict, and the impact of military events on social and cultural history.

Studies in the Social and Cultural History of Modern Warfare intends to present the fruits of this growing area of research, reflecting both the colonization of military history by cultural historians, and the reciprocal interest of military historians in social and cultural history, to the benefit of both. The series will reflect the latest scholarship in European and non-European events from the 1850s to the present day.

Titles in the series

1 *Sites of memory, sites of mourning*
  The Great War in European cultural history
  Jay Winter
  ISBN 0 521 49682 9

2 *Capital cities at war: Paris, London and Berlin 1914–1919*
  Jay Winter and Jean-Louis Robert
  ISBN 0 521 57171 5

3 *State, society and mobilization in Europe during the First World War*
  Edited by John Horne
  ISBN 0 521 56112 4

4 *A time of silence*
  Civil war and the culture of repression in Franco's Spain, 1936–1945
  Michael Richards
  ISBN 0 521 59401 4

A Time of Silence

*Civil War and the Culture of Repression
in Franco's Spain, 1936–1945*

Michael Richards

CAMBRIDGE
UNIVERSITY PRESS

CAMBRIDGE UNIVERSITY PRESS
Cambridge, New York, Melbourne, Madrid, Cape Town, Singapore, São Paulo

Cambridge University Press
The Edinburgh Building, Cambridge CB2 2RU, UK

Published in the United States of America by Cambridge University Press, New York

www.cambridge.org
Information on this title: www.cambridge.org/9780521594011

First published 1998
This digitally printed first paperback version 2006

A catalogue record for this publication is available from the British Library

Library of Congress Cataloguing in Publication data

Richards, Michael, 1961–
A time of silence: civil war and the culture of repression in Franco's Spain,
1936–1945 / Michael Richards.
    p.   cm. – (Studies in the social and cultural history of modern warfare : 4)
Includes bibliographical references (p.   ).
ISBN 0 521 59401 4 (hb)
1. Political persecution – Spain – History – 20th century.
2. Messianism, Political – Spain – History – 20th century.
3. Nationalism – Spain – History – 20th century.
4. Power (Social sciences) – Spain – History – 20th century.
5. Spain – History – Civil War, 1936–1939 – Influence.
6. Spain – Economic policy.   7. Autarchy.   I. Series.
JC599.S6R53   1998   946.082–dc21   98–3444   CIP

ISBN-13 978-0-521-59401-1 hardback
ISBN-10 0-521-59401-4 hardback

ISBN-13 978-0-521-02506-5 paperback
ISBN-10 0-521-02506-0 paperback

For Nancy, Anna and Eve

'Aquí la flama de l'esperit és un record vague, una història perduda, una arruga fossilitzada.'

Agustí Bartra, *Tercera elegia*

'Estarás así un tiempo esperando en silencio, sin hablar mal de nadie. Todo consiste en estar callado. No diciendo nunca nada de eso. Todo el mundo, poco a poco, verá como eres de bondadoso, de limpio, de sabio . . . Estoy desesperado de no estar desesperado.'

Luis Martín-Santos, *Tiempo de silencio*

Contents

List of illustrations   *page* x
Acknowledgements   xi

Introduction   1

Part I: The context of self-sufficiency

1 Civil war and self-sufficiency: the Francoist reconstruction
   of nation and state   7
2 Purifying Spain (I): the elimination of dissent   26
3 Purifying Spain (II): degeneration and treatment   47
4 The 'verticalisation' of Spain: the state and work   67

Part II: The practice of self-sufficiency

5 The politics and economics of autarky   91
6 The wages of autarky (I): self-sufficiency and industry   110
7 The wages of autarky (II): the myth and reality of rural life   127
8 Austerity and resistance   147

Conclusion   170

Notes   175
Bibliography   270
Index   309

Illustrations

1 *Fresco de la Destrucción*   *page* 8
2 Nationalist troops saluting Christ   12
3 Saint Teresa's Day, 15 October 1941   51
4 'A sad memory of Red Madrid'   63
5 An image of 'ideal womanhood', according to the official
   ideology of the Sección Femenina   63
6 'The Cross of the Fallen' at the ruins of El Alcázar, Toledo,
   1940   69
7 Rafael Aburto and Francisco Cabrero, *Monumento a la
   Contrarreforma*, 1948   70
8 Flags offered by the Sección Femenina to the Army Corps
   during the Field Mass at the National Rally of the SF at
   Medina del Campo, Valladolid, May 1940   72
9 Franco's visit to the Barcelona industrial suburb of Sabadell,
   January 1942   119
10 The Escuela Mayor, Málaga, 1940   149
11 Prayer to 'The Fallen' in the 'shelter of rest' (*albergue de reposo*)
   of the Sección Femenina, August 1942   154
12 Confirmation Day, July 1939, Plaça de San Jaume, Barcelona   155

Acknowledgements

I am pleased to acknowledge the indispensable financial support provided during the gestation of this study and to offer my gratitude. The British Academy awarded the fellowship during which I was able to complete the work. The Cañada Blanch Foundation provided urgent financial support at an early stage. The Generalitat de Catalunya, granted a Batista i Roca fellowship that enabled me to spend much needed time in the archives of Barcelona. I have also benefited from the assistance of the administration and staff of the following institutions: The Biblioteca Nacional and the Archivo Histórico Nacional, both in Madrid; the Archivo General de la Administración, Alcalá de Henares; the Cámara de Comercio, the Sociedad Bilbaína, the Civil Governor's Office and the Centro Industrial de Vizcaya, in Bilbao; the Biblioteca de Catalunya and the Archivo del Tribunal Superior de Justicia de Catalunya, in Barcelona.

I would also like to thank several people who have generously given time to discuss the subject matter of this book or assisted in other practical ways. It was begun as a PhD thesis under the supervision of Professor Paul Preston, whose unrivalled knowledge of Spain and of the Franco years have been at times daunting but always enormously stimulating. His immense enthusiasm has been infectious and his support and encouragement have been unfailing. During the early stages, Helen Graham showed enormous patience in discussing the issues and in making me see the breadth of the historical problems that the early Franco years presented. Professor Ian Kershaw, at the University of Sheffield, where much of the final version of the book was written, provided a stable and stimulating environment in which to work, as well as always being ready to give his personal encouragement and advice. Thanks are also due to my other colleagues at Sheffield. Martin Blinkhorn and Sebastian Balfour kindly provided invaluable advice, at several stages, as well as examining the original thesis. Paul Heywood and Mary Vincent have provided a Hispanists' haven in Sheffield offering encouragement, advice, hospitality and conversation, mainly of things Spanish, during many evenings. Joseph Harrison, Sheila Travis, Mary Vincent, Chris Ealham, Julia Merritt, Sebastian Balfour and Mathew Thomson all contributed their thoughts and criticisms after kindly finding time to read earlier drafts of sections of the final product. Tim Rees provided advice and respite during spells in the Madrid archives. None of the above bears any responsibility for the judgements of this book or the errors that may occur in its pages. Finally, the support of several other friends has been inestimable. Sue Parsons, as always, continues to offer friendship and encouragement, as have Diane and Ken Richards. Clara Pasqual, Raquel Mardomingo and Francisco Romero have provided support, hospitality, kindness and much needed diversion at various moments.

Introduction

This is a study of Spanish society during and after the Spanish Civil War. More specifically, it focuses on ideology and forms of repression in the period 1936–45, the first decade of what became the Franco dictatorship. In doing so it addresses two fundamental themes: first, the meaning of the concept of 'the Nation' in the wake of a catastrophic and bloody civil war, and, second, the significance and purpose of political economy where a whole section of society is defeated and its culture prostrated by a military authority.

These are very broad areas of discussion and, indeed, some parameters need to be established at the outset. What this book does *not* aim to do is to provide a typology of political violence in Spain. Neither is it a study of Catholicism and the Civil War, though religion enters substantially into the analysis throughout. Nor is it a fully elaborated account of agricultural crisis and industrial policy in the first Franco years. It is also beyond the remit of the study to analyse systematically the language of dictatorship and repression, and still less is it a social history of women in the 1940s. Each of these vital areas of historiographical interest would require a distinct treatment in its own right, a considerable task which has hardly begun in the case of Spain in this period. What it does attempt is an examination of the reconstruction of the nation by looking at how violence, religion, gender, language, psychiatry, economics and the state came together in the idea of *self-sufficiency*. It sets out, then, both a thesis about the nature of Francoist nationalism and power, and a suggested research agenda for the future.

Its conclusion is that nationalism and economics were both a major part of the repressive confirmation of the defeat of the democratic Second Republic. The idea of *purification* and a reality of *closed space* pervaded the regime's highly moral construction of the reordered nation and informed triumphalist economic relations. These two ideas signified a repressive silencing both of alternative concepts of the nation and of a humane vision of political economy.

Popularly, both in Spain itself and abroad, Franco has become known for three things: first, victory in the Spanish Civil War, second, bringing about a so-called 'economic miracle' during the 1960s, and, thereby, thirdly, preparing the way for the transition to democracy in the 1970s. The substantial mythical elements of this image are now being systematically undermined by historians.[1] However, a great deal remains unexplained. The apparent void in the course of Spain's contemporary history between the Civil War and the tourist boom of the 1960s remains frustratingly present. Collective memory in Spain has been formed through an attempt by the dictatorship to extirpate the sense of history once possessed by those who became 'the defeated'.

The Franco dictatorship was established by the victory of a coalition of right-wing social, political and military forces, united as what Franco called 'the national soul', in the Spanish Civil War of 1936–9.[2] The dictator's regime lasted for nearly four decades. During this period Spain became a modern industrialised society.[3] The study of Francoism has tended to concentrate upon comprehensive 'definitions' of the regime in the light of this development.

The purpose here is to analyse the interaction of the ideological, social and economic aspects of Francoism's establishment in power during and immediately after the Civil War as a way of grounding these theoretical contributions historically. Hence, in large part, it is a study of the brutalities of everyday life as lived by substantial sections of the population in the course of the Civil War and in its aftermath, and an attempt to suggest some ways in which they may be explained.

This study of the genesis and early years of the Franco regime began as a search for the concrete links between economic elites, war and the politics of the dictatorship. In this investigation the notion of *autarky*, or self-sufficiency, ostensibly the economic strategy of the regime, as developed during the conflict, was absolutely central.[4] How could autarky be explained when its postulates seemed irrational in economic terms? Gradually it became evident that self-sufficiency was much more than an economic precept. Economic autarky was only part of a broader desire to seal off society, to enclose Spain. The conflict was deemed to have revealed a national 'collective psychology' to be protected, nurtured and encouraged by an essentialist ideology related to everyday life and violence. An imposed quarantine or silencing signified the continuation of war as a work of cultural destruction in the broadest sense.[5] The orthodox view of economic self-sufficiency as 'irrational' therefore becomes a problem as self-sufficiency is more broadly understood as a whole culture of repression.[6]

Economic autarky under Franco, a concept which affected millions of Spaniards' everyday lives in this period, has always been explained, in some measure, by reference to the Second World War although the roots of self-sufficiency are actually to be found in Spain's own Civil War. The traumatic crisis and war of the 1930s determined the nature of economy and authority in the post-war period. The existing political organisation of society had been threatened at the same time that a multitude of cleavages opened up, centred on class, nation, religion, beliefs and mores, generations and gender. The leading Falangist intellectual Ernesto Giménez Caballero reflected pathologically on the Republic and its defilement of his vision of the nation:

They had destroyed the very substance of our being. The very soul of us as Spaniards and as men [sic] . . . The Catholic in Spain had lost his God. The monarchist his king. The aristocrat, his nobility. The soldier, his sword. The employer, his capacity for initiative. The labourer his opportunity to work. Woman, her home. The child, respect for his father. And even the Spanish language – compañera of the empire – as Nebrija described it . . . – was a spittoon for all kinds of regionalist filth . . .[7]

Any Civil War is a struggle between competing visions of the nation, and the Spanish Civil War was no different in this respect. The Francoist side, however, had a more coherent and durable nationalist vision than the Republicans. That Francoist nationalism clashed with alternative ideas is plain in the extent of the violence which was employed in justifying and imposing this vision. In looking at this violence, at ideas, and at economics it is possible to get closer to Francoism as a nationalist regime and as a form of totalitarianism.[8]

'Degeneration' had for decades been associated with the threat posed by 'the City', harbinger of 'foreign contagions' like liberalism leading to moral decay. Calls for 'surgical' treatment in order to regenerate Spain – both morally and 'physically' – by returning to economic, political and cultural 'essences' were frequent.[9] Rightist regenerationists had previously conjured up the equation of degeneration and violence in terms of national immortality:

When dealing with the spiritual ruin of Spain, we must turn our hearts to stone and be willing to sacrifice even a million Spaniards to the wolves if we wish to avoid having ourselves thrown to the pigs.[10]

The regenerationist symbolism of essential Spanishness coincided with the ascetic regimen that Francoism imposed.[11] Communism was 'the gravedigger of history'.[12] A whole way of life, culture, tradition itself, was at stake. By the time of the Civil War these essences had almost been lost – 'the people no longer knew itself'[13] – and were only to be recovered at the expense of an enormous sacrifice. One of the founding principles of the Falange, the Spanish fascist party, was a 'revaluation of violence'.[14] War was seen as an 'element of progress' and violence as ascetic, as 'creative and purifying'.[15]

Francoism instrumentalised Spain's disaster: it was from this that its understanding of 'progress' and 'the nation' sprung. It was in this institutionalisation of victory (and defeat) that silence was imposed.[16] A cultural and economic barrier was erected around Spain and around Spaniards. The monopolisation of public memory and the public voice by the victors occupied the space enclosed within these barriers. Not for nothing were the internalised mental strategies of survival and redress, privately articulated by 'the defeated' and the exiled, shaped by a desire to see those who spewed forth the official line *ad nauseam* consigned to a place where they too had no language, a place where communication, or culture, was denied: to reverse the imposed reality by sending the dictator to a strange land, to silence him.[17]

This book, then, is an analysis of what the government itself called moral and economic reconstruction during and after the Civil War. The opening chapter explains, first, the historiographical vacuum of the 1940s itself in terms of nationalism, violence and suppression and second, relates the reconstruction of nation and state to the ubiquitous idea of self-sufficiency: the 'reimagining' of 'purified' subjects within 'purified' political space.[18] The rest of the first half of the book provides the all-important context of social and economic relations in the years of autarky by looking at the 'moral reconstitution' of Spain, according to 'the victors' – a merging of public and private spheres in the 'purification' of an isolated society through the expunging of 'Anti-Spain', understood as individuals, ideas and cultures.

The second half of the book looks at how this environment of closed space and reordered morality affected economic relations, broadly understood. Particular ideas of purity and nationality were the backdrop of sacrifice and social control, the basis of a kind of internal colonisation[19] which was the essential condition for Spain's 'resurgence' during Francoism.

Part I

The context of self-sufficiency

1   Civil war and self-sufficiency: the Francoist reconstruction of nation and state

When the Spaniard finds himself totally united with his essence, adhering to it through an intrinsic way of understanding, his life will return to its pristine essential glory.[1]

Recuperating the history of the 1940s

For nearly four decades, during the Franco dictatorship, history was manipulated by the regime as it cultivated a particular memory.[2] A closure of the past, and, in a sense, of time itself, was imposed from above.[3] The decree of April 1940 announcing the foundation of Franco's gigantic monument to the Nationalist victory, the Valle de los Caídos, stressed that 'the stones . . . rise up . . . (to) challenge time and forgetfulness'.[4] This closure through the repetition of myth was stultifying for much of society but deeply reassuring in the maintenance of traditions, of the possession of history, for particular groups.[5] Time was reordered according to the understanding of policemen, soldiers, state functionaries and priests in writing the history of the 1930s.[6]

Issues of class and regional identity were played down as diagnoses of the 'sickness' of the national character and were cast in religious, psychological or medical terms. According to this state version of the past, 'the defeated' had no history apart from their 'violation of the Motherland'. The country was to be remade in the image of the myths of the Spanish essence, encapsulated in the 'Crusade of Franco' to save Christian civilisation as represented by reconquering Catholic Spain.[7] In defence of this essentialist conceptualisation of the *Patria*, the idealised division of the people into 'Spain' and 'Anti-Spain', 'good' and 'evil', was exacerbated by the regime.[8] The sin of association with the ideas and organisations of the Republic was not only to be confessed but recanted, suppressed and negated at a personal level. An associated dualism between the spiritual self and the 'evil body' to be punished was also imposed as a daily psychological torture, 'with the deliberate purpose of transforming the Spanish masses into a herd of mutilated beings'.[9]

7

Figure 1 *Fresco de la Destrucción*, showing a 'broken' Spain and the 'Red terror', Exposición de la Reconstrucción de España, Madrid 1940. (Biblioteca de Catalunya.)

According to Franco, the Spanish war was 'no artificial thing': it was 'the coronation of an historic process, the struggle of the Patria against the anti-Patria, of unity against secession, of morality against crime, of spirit against materialism, and there (was) no other solution than the triumph of the pure and eternal over bastard, anti-Spanish principles'.[10] The war had signified the triumph of light over darkness, of truth over error, health over sickness.[11]

Spain was seen as having experienced distinct historic periods: from the middle of the seventeenth century she had 'isolated herself, closed within herself, and struggled at all cost to save herself from the threatening contagion' that none the less 'infected' her during the eighteenth and nineteenth centuries. This isolation was seen as essential to the recovery of Spain's 'life', 'being', 'personality' and her permanency 'in time and in space'.[12]

The symbols used by Francoism were borrowed from the fifteenth-century era of Ferdinand and Isabella, when Spain had before 'triumphed over malignant foreign powers', when Islam was defeated and the Jews expelled. The verification of a common past was seen as essential in achieving a shared sense of national immutability after the Republic's attempt to 'annihilate the . . . soul of immortal Spain'.[13] The Civil War 'condensed the history of twelve centuries'.[14] This vision was to be pursued by the elaboration of a set of ideas based on the notion of Spain's historic destiny as a people, as a 'living entity', chosen by Providence as a source of good. Each day that passed 'signal(led) the realisation of a prophecy'.[15] The conquistadors of the fifteenth century were portrayed as the ideal of Spanishness against which various 'Others' – indigenous peoples, Republicans, the Spanish working class – were to be measured.[16] 'Isabel [was] the national spirit against foreign annexation'[17] and the idea and experience of expulsion was again to be important, in several ways, during the Franco era. Francoism enforced both the physical expulsion of hundreds of thousands of Republicans and a kind of expulsion of thought through the proscription of 'foreign ideas'.[18] Symbolic renewal meant 'purification' and destruction. Falangists were charged with 'the obligation of persecuting and destroying judaism, freemasonry, Marxism and separatism . . . Destroy and burn their newspapers, their books, their magazines, their propaganda.'[19]

Writing the history of Francoism with any claim at all to objectivity was hardly initiated until the 1980s.[20] Forgetting the recent past in post-war Spain was both enforced by authority and employed as personal and collective strategies of survival.[21] A kind of tacit agreement to forget was entered into. This 'pact of oblivion', as it was known in political circles, became an important condition of the process of the peaceful transition to democracy in the 1970s and 1980s.[22] However, the internalisation or evasion of the relatively recent past has been one of the factors which has led to a belief, both in Spain and elsewhere, that Francoism quickly legitimised itself through the more or less painless creation of a modern consumer society.[23] One of the symptoms of the control of memory has been a collective partial blindness. Moreover, as Manuel Vázquez Montalbán has written, 'very little of this hidden memory has been recovered in the new democratic Spain'.[24]

The press in Spain, throughout the Franco years, was firmly controlled by the state. The regime's Press Law, promulgated in April 1938, supposedly as a provisional wartime measure, remained in force for more than a quarter of a century. Thousands of executions were carried out behind this barrier of secrecy. Until the late 1960s journalism as such did not exist: 'journalists' were, in effect, state functionaries charged with maintaining the regime's monopoly of ideas.[25] Moreover, the sheer longevity of the Franco regime has affected the state of archival collections which hold material on the Civil War and dictatorship. The dictatorial authorities were able to 'clean up' the evidence of the regime's crimes in a way which was not possible in the same systematic manner in Germany and Italy where the brutal regimes of Hitler and Mussolini fell as chaos reigned around them. Rigidly restricted access to records favoured particular historians, sympathetic to the state, employing a methodology which eschewed explanation.[26]

Darkness and modernity

Thus, the 1940s, '*los años oscuros*', remain shrouded in darkness. Images are blurred by layers of obscurity and obstacles in the way of illumination have been difficult to overcome. The post-war decade has been portrayed by historians as an aberration or a deviation from the road to modernity. But the meaning of modernity itself was at stake. Daily life was shaped by the culturally constructed forms of repression effected during the war itself. The period 1936–45 witnessed a brutal repression simultaneous with a rapid reclamation of power by social elites. These elites both supported violence and had a vision of the future, albeit one which re-cycled a great deal of the past.[27] The regime ultimately oversaw profound economic change and development, but was established through violence and suffering. The Civil War and the early post-conflict years were deeply marked by an inexorable self-pruning of extermination and expulsion: an 'impossible exorcism' in the pursuit of purity'.[28]

The Spanish malady was 'treated' through a violent political economy which, in reality, reproduced sickness and suffering. As many as 200,000 men and women were executed by the regime in the wake of the war.[29] A further 200,000 died of hunger as a result of the outcome of the conflict and of the policies pursued by the victorious dictatorship.[30] The number of suicides in the immediate post-war rose considerably.[31] Under conditions of the most barbarous torture, suicide was often both a release and perhaps a final protest against the regime.[32] The violence amounted to a brutal closing down of choices and alternatives: the extermination of memory, of history.

The price paid in the name of order, through physical and economic repression, was enormous, but the fact that the regime was very violent did not mean that time stood still. 'Modernity' could be countenanced by the country's elites if existing cultural hierarchies were reinforced in the process. Society's dominant groups used the voice which they alone possessed in shaping this future.

The violence of the 1940s accompanied a very significant deepening of capital accumulation in the hands of those who would dominate political and social circles in Spain throughout the long Franco era and beyond. In many ways, it was in this period that the foundations of a modern industrialised state were laid.[33] During the war and in the 1940s, the parameters within which social change might take place were established. From the outset Francoism aimed to impose a unity between society and the political system, to reunite people and state 'intimately', so that all Spaniards might 'contribute morally and materially to the resurgence of the Nation'.[34] This process depended on a complex and often contradictory interchange between violence and consent.[35] The meaning of modernisation under Franco was decoupled from the ideas of progress derived from the Enlightenment and associated with the reforms of the Spanish Second Republic of the 1930s. 'Progress' was reduced to a violent purging and 'rechristianisation' of society accompanied by economic development.[36] The taking of this road to development was the principal consequence of the Spanish Civil War.

Defining Francoism

Rationality becomes difficult to describe when the stated objective is the fulfilling of a nebulous idea like 'national destiny'. Franco's Crusade was portrayed as a victory of spirit, of prophecy, and as 'miraculous'.[37] There is a case for applying the Weberian conception of 'charismatic authority' to a dictator who claimed to rule 'by the grace of God' in a quasi-monarchical, sacred state.[38] Certainly, the power of the regime

Figure 2   Painting by Mariano Bertuchi, from an exhibition held at Galerías
Layetanas in March 1939, showing Nationalist troops, decisively reaching the
sea, giving the Falangist salute to the crucified Lord above in dedication.
(Arxiu Fotogràfic Arxiu Històric de la Ciutat, Barcelona.)

was imposed during a time of psychic, ethical, religious and economic
distress and was, moreover, inherently unstable. Extreme nationalism
and Catholicism permeated every sphere and was symbolised in the
person of the Caudillo himself. But beyond this there were relatively few
common objectives among the triumphant elite apart from the, often
irrational, destruction of virtually everything associated with the Republic. 'Charisma', as Weber says, 'knows only inner determination and
inner restraint . . . In general, charisma rejects all rational economic
conduct'.[39] But there are limits to the usefulness of the concept in the
case of the Franco state. Francoism won its legitimacy in a war against
its own people. The regime rested above all on the constant threat of
coercion and the memories of its violent birth. The interest that bound
supporters of the Nationalist war effort to Franco and the new regime
was a 'pact of blood'.

The Civil War destroyed the notion of a progressive state in any
meaningful sense, but it did not destroy the idea of authority or the basis
of the existing administration. War exacerbated Catholic nationalism
and militarism, so that clear continuities in the state institutions were

accompanied by purges and constricting political pressure from above. Judgements about morality carried more weight than the concept of law.[40] The practice of the judiciary shifted violently from due process and a system of guarantees towards the interests of *Patria*, religion and the family.[41] The Francoist 'New State' saw its primary task as destroying all that the Republic had represented. This included a 'purification' of the education system,[42] the judiciary and local administration. The so-called 'Law of Political Responsibilities' (9 February 1939) provided for purges in state institutions, as in society generally. But in some important areas this did not entail a wholesale drafting of new political blood.

Throughout the dictatorship, Franco's ministers were overwhelmingly professional bureaucrats, particularly public attorneys, notaries or solicitors, fiscal experts and inspectors, career diplomats, state engineers or economists, civil administrators, or customs officials. They also had a very high profile in Franco's pseudo-parliament, the *Cortes*, created in 1943.[43]

The social revolution provoked by the military rebellion of July 1936 had unleashed a violent revolutionary justice in the loyalist zone, which was gradually brought under a form of control by the Republican government. Many judges were dismissed under the revolutionary powers demanded by the workers' militias and many more went into hiding. Some were shot, though not as many as Francoist propaganda pretended.[44] As the Nationalists occupied territory during the war, military tribunals provided a structure for repression as judges and lawyers faithful to the 'Glorious National Movement' of Franco were assembled and put in place. In order to take public-entrance exams for the judiciary a party certificate was required, guaranteeing adhesion to 'the Movement'.[45]

Spanish society and the dictatorship changed throughout the regime's duration, but periodisation can lead to undue concentration on change at the expense of continuity. After all, for many people, the dictatorship was experienced as a continuous repetition of loss, entrapment, fear and lack of control.[46]

Juan Linz's famous model of 'limited pluralism', based on the imprecise label of 'authoritarianism',[47] has often been used as a simple taxonomic prop, unsupported by any underlying theory, ignoring economic questions and the complexities of political domination.[48] This empirical sociological model relies on a static periodisation of the dictatorship, arguing that after the end of the Second World War the Franco regime began slowly to 'normalise' itself – a process culminating in 1959 with a concerted strategy of economic liberalisation, heralding a period of relative political pluralism.[49] But this would be to ignore the specific conjuncture of crisis in the 1930s and early 1940s, and the process of the unravelling of the crisis.[50] Francoism was functional because it was not static – it was relatively adaptable, though the essence of its ideology, its reliance on violent methods, and its ultimate social function, remained unaltered.[51]

The Francoist dictatorship evolved in order to adapt to certain conditions. The regime altered, chameleon-like, as society and the international context underwent change.[52] Franco himself was often reluctant to allow change to take place, preferring to retain the 'purity' of the barbaric immediate post-war years. For Franco, there could be 'no redemption without blood'.[53] The repressive apparatus of the dictatorship remained largely in place throughout the almost forty years of the regime's lifetime.[54] The relations between culture, ideology, repression and political economy throughout the Franco years demonstrate that existing forms of power were largely safeguarded while development took place.

In some accounts of the regime a more or less justificatory approach has portrayed the early decades of Francoism as a period during which everything was dictated from outside Spanish borders when the dictatorship was, it is argued, virtually powerless to influence events.[55] However, this image contradicts both the picture painted of the dictator's immense sagacity, attributed to him by these same historians, and, more significantly, the fact that the leaders of the regime, and many of its supporters, from the very outset were ideologically committed to the course taken in the economic, social and political spheres.

Essentially, narrative accounts of the history of the regime outline the relationship among the groups which acted within the constricted arena of 'politics' in this era. The majority of the accounts of this aspect of the dictatorship rely upon analysis of political relations at the highest level of government. Emphasis has been mainly upon the role of Franco himself – his technique of leadership or his conduct of foreign affairs.[56] Attention has also been paid to the basic legislative action of the regime. Not so much has been learnt about the actual implementation and effects of this action within society. The influence of the Falange has been relativised and the perpetuation of monarchist influence stressed, in contrast. The paramount role of the military and the important influence of religion have informed the comparison with other dictatorial regimes, distinctions with Italian Fascism and Nazism in Germany being emphasised.[57] Francoism, it has been claimed, had no ideology, though the relationship between tradition, myth and political control is often not explored. Franco was no fascist, it is claimed, and neither was his dictatorship.[58]

Thus, there is frequently an exculpatory tone to studies of the dictatorship: an apparent desire to liberate Francoism from the charge of fascism. The relationship between extreme nationalist ideology, Catholicism and organised violence in building and maintaining power are not the primary area of attention of these analyses. The social and political functions played by the violence and ideas of the Francoist state, very similar to that played by Fascism in Italy in the 1920s and Nazism in Germany in the 1930s, are given a lowly position in talking about the regime.[59]

Other analyses of the Franco regime, however, have been more critical, viewing the dictatorship as a variant of Bonapartism or 'modern despotism', being underscored by a concentration on the class structure of society and of the class objectives of the regime.[60] Other, in some ways similar, accounts see the regime as coinciding with a particular stage in the development of Spanish society and economy and the country's position in the world economy. Development under Franco is characterised by state protection for key economic sectors and a growing monopolisation of economic power involving the incorporation of in-dustrialists into a power bloc dominated by landowning elites and the financial power of the private banking system. Repressive dictatorship allowed for this process to be finally completed free of any challenge from the restless lower orders of society.[61] The priority was the 'absolute suppression of the class struggle'.[62]

In terms of the economic function of the regime, it has often been concluded by Marxists that Francoism constituted fascism. This analy-sis was, in a way, part of the political struggle responding to claims by the regime that Franco had consciously guided the country to economic prosperity through the application of some kind of personal 'master plan'. Although this criticism was absolutely justified, these accounts left the historical picture somewhat distorted. Inevitably, given the circumstances, the opposition to Franco established its own counter-mythology as part of the struggle. This has tended to determine an unduly economistic tone in these accounts. The origins of Francoism are virtually reduced to a single contradiction – that between monopoly capital and the rest of society.[63] But the assimilation and response to crisis in the dictatorial states of Europe in the 1930s and 1940s involved an extremely dynamic interaction of politics, economics and culture. It is precisely in the interplay of the political economy of the regime, the construction of its myths and ideology, and the experience of what was everyday life for 'the defeated' that the real nature of Francoism is to be found.

The ideology of Francoism

Francoist ideology merged description and prescription according to a 'common sense' of entrenched myths and specific social demands.[64] Sources of power in Spain, as in other societies, were various. For the most part there was a congruence of ideas, beliefs, practices and material interests. Feminism, for example, was seen as a dangerous contagion, in itself, independent of any conscious desire to maintain economic privilege. But women were seen by the regime's ideologues as having specific responsibility for moderating their men folk's propensity to challenge the economic status quo. Similarly, the political exploitation of ideas linked to Darwinist evolutionism was undeniable, and yet, when Francoist psychiatrists examined Republican prisoners it was the '*communist* gene' for which they were searching.[65] Moreover, it was difficult (and remains so) to disentangle the moral impulses behind the public statements of leading Spanish clergy from their interests in the defence of the social system as it existed. In the end, for all the force of symbolism and the cultural or imaginary constructions of reality, elite systems of thought had definable material consequences. Ideology ultimately served practical social purposes.

At the same time, economic interest is insufficient in explaining the Franco regime and cannot effectively show how 'structures of feeling', or 'belief systems', determined actions. Francoist ideology was composed of Catholicism, specifically Spanish myths, exacerbated nationalism and European fascism.[66] 'Spanishness' (*Hispanidad*) was conceptualised through Catholicism, regenerationism, authoritarian monarchism (via *Acción Española* and Carlist *Tradicionalismo*), and the twenty-six-point programme of the fascist Falange.[67] The main ingredients of this nationalism were the eulogising of the Spanish peasantry as the mass embodiment of immortal religious and racial virtues, militarism and martial values, the negation of liberalism, socialism and feminism, and the idea of a national unity and a spiritual and material resurgence based on myths of empire, Reconquest and Counter-Reformation.[68]

An appropriate set of symbols was manufactured. The 'triumph of Franco' was explicitly compared to the exploits of the great warrior heroes and empire-builders of the past, like Philip II and El Cid.[69] The ceremonies of triumph repeatedly re-enacted the victory parades of the heroic figures of the Middle Ages.[70] During the Civil War and the post-war this nationalism was built upon the various meanings of what had become an accepted dichotomy of degeneration and regeneration.[71] This way of conceiving the nation was enunciated in the desire to 'purify' Spain in the course of the Civil War and after. Redemption and regeneration, in individual and national terms, were seen as only achievable through suffering and sacrifice.

The ideology and symbols of the Falange, taken from the imperial era of the Catholic monarchs, from Spanish regenerationism, and from contemporary European fascism, mirrored and reinforced the authoritarian and anti-marxist worldview of the Army[72] and Catholic Church.[73] Purity, an 'exclusive and incontestable claim to the symbolization of immortality', was a concept upon which a natural kinship was founded.[74] The idea of Empire was partly predicated on the belief that the 1930s had ushered in an era which would overturn the supposed rights of smaller nationalities and minority languages. Czechs, Slovaks, Albanians, Poles, Lithuanians, Basques and Catalans had to be forcibly incorporated into the 'historic' empires, heirs to those of Rome, of the Reich, and of the Catholic monarchs. Genocide and eradication played a central role in all these processes.[75]

This did not mean that there were no cultural or ideological contradictions. The Francoist state, from the beginning, was possessed of an industrialising fetishism[76] while Falangism propagated the mythical virtues of Castilian peasant life.[77] Spanish nationalism, as an expression of the ideology of the political right in Spain, was deeply rooted in a specifically *agrarian* understanding of the *Patria*. A similar paradox applied in Nazi Germany and Fascist Italy.[78] Russia suffered communism because the people neither 'knew' nor 'loved' 'the land'.[79] The peasant farmer of central Spain would continue to be eulogised as the embodiment of national virtues, the 'permanent foundation of the Nation's richness', while, in fact, suffering the material effects of the economic strategy pursued by the regime.[80] Moreover, the Spanish Civil War had partly been fought to avoid sacrificing the power of landed wealth. The contradiction with industrialisation had farreaching consequences as the dictatorship attempted to favour both agricultural and industrial elites at the expense of the Castilian peasantry and the defeated working class in its programme of 'national reawakening'.[81]

In spite of this elaboration of 'legitimising' and prescriptive discourse, it has been argued that ideology, as such, was not a central component of Francoism. Rather, a distinction is made with what, it is claimed, was merely a 'mentality', which was not 'rational' but 'emotional'.[82] However, it is not clear how this distinction is made. The notion of rationality is not satisfactorily interrogated in relation to ideology. Thus, a curiously reductionist explanation of 'ideology' is suggested.[83] Moreover, though it is clear that Francoist ideology was formed of a complex of traditions, and that various groups within the reactionary coalition each emphasised particular aspects of doctrine, the 'pluralism' which this implied was always a *unitary* pluralism, in which certain elements, the essence of an 'organicist nationalism', were always agreed upon and determinate.[84] Francoist ideology systematically promoted certain meanings above others, redefining nation and state as a 'purified' body and space. For a substantial part of society these were believable myths, beliefs which were sacrosanct, instrumentalised ideologically in moments of crisis and widely disseminated.[85]

This distinctive unity of ideological discourse was the basis of the Manichean depiction of Spaniards as 'good' or 'evil'. Violence, during the Civil War and in the 1940s, was related to ideas. This same set of ideas, based on national and Catholic purity, continued to be communicated in the press, from the pulpit, and in the schools of the 'New Spain', which had to be 'a continuation of the ideals of the wartime trenches . . . combating more than circumstantial enemies [but also] . . . the permanent and always vigilant powers of Evil itself'.[86]

Ideology helped constitute individuals as subjects, useful to the *Patria*. This was not simply the foundation of the construction of the identity of 'the defeated'. It was an image of difference, which was indispensable for 'the victors' themselves: without 'the defeated', 'the victors' could not be. The actions of the triumphalist regime, and of elite society generally, were, in part at least, defined in opposition to the vanquished as 'plague-carriers', to be bracketed off as 'alien', incapable of assimilation and excluded.[87]

'Spain' was constructed ideologically, first, as a 'natural entity', a 'living organism', composed of a collectivity which shared this understanding of the *Patria*.[88] The land was personalised: she 'lived', 'breathed', 'rested', contracted 'diseases' and was 'violated'.[89] 'Organic determinism' had been a feature of Spanish regenerationist thought at the turn of the century and organicism was to be an important component of the belief-system of Francoist military officers and ministers.[90] According to Franco, 'fascism [was] . . . essentially a reaction of defence of the organism, a manifestation of it wanting to live, of not wanting to die'.[91] The daily implications of organicism for human beings were potentially very significant. The theoretically equal individuals of liberalism, with rights, were formally reincarnated as 'members of a body'.[92] The country's 'organic purity' – moral, religious, biological – had to be guarded.[93]

Second, the notion of unity was central.[94] The *Patria*, according to Franco himself was 'spiritual unity, social unity, historic unity'. Catholicism was to be 'the crucible of nationality'[95] – it unified and purified and those who were not Catholic were not 'true Spaniards'. 'Spiritual imperialism' could be projected outwards as a universalising mission but could not be penetrated from outside.[96] This structure of feeling among elite groups was central to a rationalised strategic set of ideas, well elaborated within Francoist discourse and provided a guide to action. Unity entailed an iron centralism, which denied the validity of regional cultural difference or the applicability of 'foreign ideas' to Spanish society. Moreover, it formed a justification for extirpatory violence, for perpetual 'moral vigilance', and for economic austerity.[97] Its practicality in mystifying realities served well as huge material and psychological sacrifices were called for in the interests of maintaining a strictly hierarchical, repressing and exploitative social structure. The ideological supports of extreme nationalism were reflected daily in economic and social relations.

The social base of Francoism

Spain's long post-imperial social crisis, set within an environment of uneven and dependent economic development, which culminated in the Civil War, might have produced a strictly fascist solution. However, an explicit mass mobilisation concretised in paramilitarism, was not viable as a way of resolving the complex accumulation of contradictions of the pre-war situation. The avowedly fascist Falange's pre-Civil War failure has been attributed to the lack of a sufficiently numerous urban petit-bourgeoisie in Spain except in those regions which had a marked tradition of non-Spanish, anti-Madrid nationalism, and it is true that in the main industrial areas, Barcelona and parts of the Basque Country, the petty-bourgeoisie favoured autonomist solutions which were directly opposed to the totalitarian *españolismo* of the Falange (and of most of the conservative right in Spain).[98] However, in the context of the Republican elections of the early 1930s, the Catholic peasantry and petit-bourgeoisie of central Spain were mobilised by the populist authoritarian-Catholic political groups which became the *Confederación Española de Derechas Autónomas* (CEDA) in 1933.[99] Indeed, the relative failure of the fascist party to take off in Spain had a lot to do with the existence of radical right-wing alternatives, like the CEDA and its youth wing, the *Juventud de Acción Popular* (JAP).[100] The smallholding peasantry provided the austere, self-sacrificing image which was at the heart of the right's ideology and, in addition, became the main cannon-fodder of the Nationalist campaign during the Civil War. In the early stages most of the Falange's numerically insignificant membership was therefore recruited from among the sons of large landowners and within the student ranks of the universities. The non-regionalist provincial petit-bourgeoisie – in Castile and Andalusia – also provided some support[101] and the party was backed financially by large landowners and Basque industrialists.

However, once the legalist tactic of defending the elite hold on state power, through participation in elections, had proved a failure for the right – a failure finally confirmed by the victory of the Popular Front coalition in February 1936 – certain features of this terrain, previously not propitious to fascism, changed. A political space was created for a limited populist mobilisation and the development of a cult of violence 'in defence of Christian civilisation'.[102] Now, after February 1936, the street politics of violence and conspiracy against democracy went hand in hand. But the principal features of the pre-electoral situation determined that civil war rather than a fascist coup d'état would be the outcome of the crisis: the regional petit-bourgeoisie was never dislodged from its support of Republican autonomism, albeit within a strong state structure: the Army remained the most viable and ideologically committed force for carrying out a bid for power through violence: and, finally, the Spanish working class was still powerful, relatively united and maintained a significant grasp on state power.[103]

Thus, on balance, though the right was not led by a typically fascist organisation with a committed mass following, there did exist a relatively broad social base in support of the rebellion, and, subsequently, of Francoism. Substantial sections of society were susceptible to an ideology which constantly sought to criminalise, pathologise or medicalise social conflict. Many doubtless agreed that 'when the rabble governs . . . the death of the state . . . is a biological law'[104] and were grateful to the rebels. This social support was persuaded that it was economically threatened, was culturally at odds with the ethos of the democratic Republic, and dreamed of revenge.[105] In supporting 'Franco's Justice', the strategy of extermination which accompanied the rising against the democratic Republic and the Civil War campaign, the ultimate rationale of the middle classes is plain: 'We lived before without justice, which is the greatest torment that a man [sic] can suffer. But now we have justice, speedy, pure, perfect. It is the bread of the soul . . . Everything is going well. The criminals are falling.'[106] 'Justice' was 'serene and imperturbable . . . day by day, hour by hour removing from society those who by their wicked acts and crimes are a danger and a stain [mancha] on society'.[107]

Moreover, the war itself acted as a catalyst for unity among those that adhered to the cause of the nascent Francoist state. Indeed, the war became an ideological tool in pursuit of this objective. Increasingly, the Nationalist state in embryo came to count upon the support of society's main corporate institutions, and broader sections of society. Spanish society was therefore not 'hi-jacked' by a handful of reactionary generals. The coup d'état against the Republic, and the regime which ultimately followed, were actively supported by a genuine social base.

During the conflict itself, and subsequently, there is plenty of evidence to suggest that there was a degree of consent, if not active support, for the regime from sections of the lower middle classes, ultimately concerned with the protection of property, who might once have been attracted by the populist and unscrupulous demagoguery of the Republican radicals, led by Alejandro Lerroux, or even by regional parties in Catalonia or the Basque Country. By 1937, a prevalent view among Republicans in Barcelona was that had elections been held then the right would have won.[108] War and revolution meant a closing of middle-class and lower-middle-class support, or at least consent, around the Francoist state. This included some pre-war Republicans who had supported the wartime Republican government's repression of anarchist and revolutionary militancy or those who had joined the ranks of the Spanish Communist Party (PCE) during the war – in part as a way of heading-off further revolutionary expropriation by the workers – provided they had no overtly 'anti-Crusade' political background and could now demonstrate their loyalty to the New State.[109] The Francoist repression was occasionally, and openly, viewed positively, since, it was believed, it saved bourgeois Republican groups the trouble of thoroughly purging society themselves in the wake of a possible victory for the government.[110] Political allegiances were occasionally remade in the wake of the war in accordance with the common denominators of state, property and the Catholic nation.[111] Francoism constructed 'Spain' and 'Anti-Spain' largely according to these requirements, as the basis of its legitimacy although it continued to rest upon open violence. Those social groups that supported the Nationalist war effort and a strong state in the aftermath were frequently prey to repression of any claims that deviated from the hermetic political and cultural ideas that the regime allowed.[112]

In sum, the relative lack of a marked, activist social mobilisation in support of the regime had much to do with the reliance by the dictatorship upon a policy of physical repression, of the fear engendered by the war, and the sense of helplessness of a working class already cowed by the conflict and largely fatalistic about the future.[113] In the wake of the war there was no need to mobilise: Franco's victory was omnipresent, replayed daily through an exclusionary culture of physical and economic repression. This was the social and cultural context of economic autarky.

Autarky as social quarantine

Economics during the early decades of the Franco regime can only be understood by analysing this relationship of the embryonic state to society. The depth of the social cleavage which produced the Civil War, deepened by Francoism, recasts our judgement about economic rationality. Changes in the economic structure derived both from the material objectives of particular social groups and the culturally constructed ideology and repression employed in rebuilding state authority. Several areas of human activity were connected by the idea of self-sufficiency as both economic policy *and* repression.

The period 1936–45 saw the thorough purging of society accompanied by a reassertion of the dominance of Spain's elites. Self-sufficiency was the context of both processes. There was never a clear division between the spheres of politics and economics. Isolation was intimately linked to a regression of Spaniards' liberties. The moral imperatives of the regime shaped the course of economic development in Spain.

Autarky was an ideological and cultural construct. It was both coercive and segregating and representational of the 'national solidarity' which the regime sought to foster.[114] At a formal level, Francoism, as we have seen, rejected liberalism. The liberal era of a 'bastard Spain' had coincided with economic, military and moral decline and 'licentiousness'. This 'bastard foetus', with its 'decadent customs and appetites', lacked 'austerity' and had turned the state into a 'rotting corpse' which could only be 'buried' by fascism and strict hierarchical authority. Exchange, of all kinds, meant decaying spirit: the liberal state was like 'an Arab market' in which the exploited *Patria* was 'sold off' to the highest bidder.[115]

The solution to 'degeneration' was 'treatment' through a physical and psychological quarantine. The sense of an attack on 'our world' by 'the forces of darkness', on an 'organic' order by something formless and chaotic, was very powerful. Franco himself warned that 'for the health of society, as for the health of bodies, a quarantine is needed for those who come from the plague-infested ground [*el campo apestado*]'.[116] Indeed, Spain, in this period, could be visualised as a huge mental asylum[117] or isolation ward. Medicine, or, at least, its vocabulary, and the notion of 'the clinic', reinforced isolation, a closing-off from the external world. Once the true Spanish essence had been reconquered it had to be kept pure from any contamination, and so the country's doors had to remain firmly closed.[118]

The exercise of 'pure reason', in organising liberal government, had led to chaos. With liberalism, humankind's most 'automatic' and 'mechanical' elements were permitted free rein without prior 'spiritual purification', thereby 'Russifying Spanish souls'.[119] Spain therefore needed to 'close in upon herself', as she had done at the end of the seventeenth century, to save herself from the 'danger to her very being and substance', represented by 'the sickness of Europe': 'the secularisation of life, laicism, naturalism, positivism, humanism, rationalism, liberalism'. For Spaniards, it was proclaimed, 'humanity' meant 'Christianity': for 'the new mentality, disseminated by rationalism', however, it simply meant the 'ability to trade'.[120] Autarky, or self-sufficiency, the principal manifestation of this rejection, was therefore seen not simply as an economic response but also as political and cultural. Indeed, it was in the economic sphere where state control was, in many ways, weakest. The rejection of liberalism in an economic sense was consistently carried out only inasmuch as it facilitated repression. In terms of the freedom allowed to economic elites, the control of the state was always relative and largely rhetorical.[121]

Autarky was explicitly associated by the regime with a spiritual sense of personal denial and punishment.[122] The 'essence of Spanishness' was to be captured and used to put to labour 'physical bodies' which 'obey[ed] the dictates of the spirit' and not 'greed' and 'lustfulness'. Should they refuse to comply, it would become 'necessary to force them to do so, through violence, penitence, or the punishment of oneself and others'.[123] The material scarcity, which the autarkic dictatorship imposed and which mirrored this relinquishing of the self, was 'Christian' because it 'redeemed' through sacrifice and significantly contributed to national moral and economic resurgence. *Sacrifice* was to be the daily watchword of the regime.[124] The 'Reconquest of Spain' could not be 'total and complete', the 'national personality of the *Patria* [could] not be restored' until 'a true autarky, in the Christian and legitimate sense of the word' was put in place. There were, it was claimed, particular cultural traits peculiar to Spaniards which made self-sufficiency in Spain something unique. Spaniards needed an 'ultimate personal cause which is called God'. While it was to be doubted that a Spaniard would 'happily give his life for the god State, or for the god Nation, or the god Race, or even for the goddess *Patria* . . . for God and for Spain . . . thousands would happily die'.[125]

The other principal idiosyncrasy of Spaniards was that they could only become enthusiastic for material wealth if it was the result of 'working and sacrificing themselves'. Materialism had to be 'conquered in the name of the Cross': it had to be 'Christianised'. The 'realisation of autarky [was] a necessity . . . a sacred right of Christian principles'. 'Religiosity' meant that Spaniards did not live life as something valuable in itself and even less to obtain material goods. It is the salvation of the soul and the eternal glory of God that gives life sense'.[126]

Moreover, it ought to be remembered that the case was argued, for self-sufficiency as a first stage in economic development: autarky was not advocated because it was 'anti-modern'. Rather, it was viewed as an initial stage on the way to the eventual embracing by Spain of modern technology. Fear and closure produced a kind of work ethic, 'stored up' for the future. In economic terms, the 1940s are underscored by an attempt to put in train a process of anti-import development. This strategy was made possible by Franco's victory. Although production levels were far from impressive,[127] Francoism proclaimed the dawning of low labour-cost state-directed industrialisation.

Autarky encapsulated the essence of 'Spanishness' and violations of this incarcerating constructed identity were to be penalised. The discourse arguing for autarky legitimised sacrifice, discipline and national uniqueness, and attempted to silence alternative visions of a future identity.[128] The material reality of this construction was inscribed through the state's physical violence against those 'others' who did not comply, as well as through sacrifice by starvation, devastatingly low wages, and grandiose industrialising schemes which benefited a select elite.

The authority of the Francoist regime was imposed through the manipulation of the supply of the material necessities of the population. This both guaranteed the overriding preoccupation of most of society with personal survival rather than political protest, and ensured that the sacrifices to be made during the long period of economic crisis in Spain during the 1940s would be overwhelmingly made by the working class. 'The defeated' struggled for mere survival and pretended not to hear the firing squads, not to notice the queues outside the prisons, or the systematic destruction of their own identities.[129] The rhythm of daily life, family, work, childhood and old age was dictated by virtual slavery.[130] National material self-sufficiency was mirrored at the level of the individual, ensuring a retreat into the domestic sphere. Social solidarities were thereby broken down and the physical energy necessary for resistance dissipated.

Self-sufficiency, both in theory and in practice, was a form of violent repression. It was not irrational, since it was always more than an economic programme, but was a central part of the repression upon which elite power was rebuilt after 1939. It was the continuation of war fought in the pursuit of a particular social and political project. Autarky originated in political and cultural ideas and practices which came to the fore during the Civil War, as well as economics. Great swathes of social and political life were placed beyond the reach of much of the populace: as the meaning of the *Patria* was reconfigured by the regime, 'Spain' itself became forbidden territory for 'the defeated'. Half of Spain was denied any collective identity beyond the state's own construction of Family and Fatherland. Individual identity was inevitably severely circumscribed in the process.

2 Purifying Spain (I): the elimination of dissent'

> If, in the end, both halves of Spain were partly right . . . then the war was a monstrous caprice, a terrible and useless wrong that led to nothing, a satanic act of anger, infertile and void, and, consequently, those who caused it are . . . guilty of a momentous and unpardonable crime: of having attempted and carried out the elimination of dissent . . .[1]

The Francoist primacy of internalism, self-sufficiency and 'quarantine' in economics and culture in the period 1936–45 cannot be understood without a sense of the environment of violence which pervaded the country. Economic and cultural autarky were, in part, a product of the punishment of the defeated. They were central to the extreme nationalism which gloried in Francoism's version of national identity and 'destiny' and demonised the 'worthless', 'foreign' and 'disease-ridden' Other: Republicans, democrats, liberals, the working class. The material well-being, the identity, conscience and ideals of 'Reds' could be sacrificed in the interests of 'national resurgence'. The repressive social and political function of self-sufficiency, to make Spain 'healthy', therefore, takes us to the heart of the pathological nature of Francoism.

Francoist repression during the Civil War and in its aftermath cannot be explained by the simple resort to justifications based on military requirements or by pleadings about 'the heat of battle'. Nor was it simply a case of 'atrocities perpetrated equally by both sides', the message of some accounts where killing is drained of all motivation beyond 'hate' and victims have no politics or class allegiances and are simply 'the dead'.[2]

There are at least three essential categories of analysis that ought, rather, to be employed: class, ideas and culture, and the fear and vengeance associated with the crisis of the state. Victims were targeted and the perpetrators 'legitimated' according to these overlapping criteria.

The term 'repression' is used here, in talking of Francoism, to refer to state-directed violence and oppression carried out in pursuit of a reactionary political project and moral 'cleansing' justified by a clearly articulated code of ethics and ideas, by an ideology. Although the crisis of Republican authority after July 1936 led to a spiral of horrific and tragic violence in loyalist areas, the Republican government never called for the use of brutality in the sense that the rebels did, and its public ethics were contrary to the use of political terror.[3] There was an understandable lack of popular confidence in a state judicial system that had been uneven, to say the least, in supporting democratic freedoms or even the principle of the Republic itself. A revolutionary consensus emerged that 'popular justice' was, indeed, absolutely *just*.[4] In the exceptional circumstances of a violent assault against the constituted authority, the Republican government justified its judicial activities in the name of the popular sovereignty expressed in democratic elections. The trying and sentencing of rebellious military personnel and members of the forces of public order and of the extremist political organisations of the right, like Renovación Española, Falange Española, and the Comunión Tradicionalista, who had conspired against the government, was carried out, it was believed, under the legitimacy given to the Republican administration by a majority of the Spanish people.[5]

Francoist terror, however, was employed systematically in order to 'purge' society. 'Reds' had to prove their loyalty to the New State and to 'Spain'. As Deputy-Governor Danforth insists in Arthur Miller's *The Crucible*, for a man or woman to live in a Christian country the 'whiteness of their soul' had to be proved.[6] Social relations were determined by a persistent and explicit denial of reconciliation or integration. A 'healing of wounds' went against the logic of the victors' determination to 'purify' Spain.[7] According to the Catholic Church, which blessed the Francoist 'crusade',[8] it was 'impossible to negotiate with evil'. In the aftermath, 'foreign spirit' could not be allowed to 'contaminate the life of the Spanish state' as it had been allowed to do after the spilling of blood in 1808.[9] The words 'forgiveness' and 'amnesty' were to be erased from the Spanish language.[10] The reclaiming of the power of social elites was accompanied by physical, psychological, economic and cultural repression. It was upon these foundations that Spain's future development was based. Violence established the economic and social boundaries of the territories of 'Spain' and 'Anti-Spain'.[11]

Histories of conquest have been the milestones of historiography.[12] The depiction of the Civil War as a religious crusade was a way of avoiding a class analysis of the conflict, although the language of the 'Crusade' doubtless had genuine meaning for many people at the time and subsequently. During and after the Civil War, Falangists, who played a leading role in the repression, considered themselves a 'colonising force'. In early 1940, the British Consul in Madrid reported that the Falange was 'visibly in charge, playing almost the role of a European administration in an African colony'.[13] The scale of the brutality, the way in which it was directed from above, and the ideological discourse which surrounded it suggest that a broader explanatory framework than social class is called for. 'Purification', for example, was a ubiquitous term during and after the war, and was related to the canon of pathological vocabulary which accompanied the purges. According to the collective pronouncements of the Spanish Bishops, the military coup and the consequent war were brought about to re-establish order and to save Christian civilization. There was no differentiation in describing enemies. The Republican *milicianos* were depicted as the 'sons of Cain'.[14] Purity required violence. Falangists, for example, called for 'a new Revolution which could gather together the yearnings of all the revolutions and purify and sanctify them and stamp them with its sacred violence'.[15]

Political repression encompassed more than extermination, physical violence and the deprivation of liberty. Coercion was also applied through work, material deprivation, and within cultural and gender relations. None of these forms of repression was mutually exclusive. They were all based upon a totalitarian conception of power which assumed value and utility in violence and an ideological control imposed against and upon enemies defined according to a particular conception of what (and who) constituted 'the nation'.[16]

The internalisation or evasion of the past, both at a collective and at an individual level makes studying the Francoist repression difficult.[17] Memories of pain, or of shame were internalised and are not easy to recapture, articulate or interpret.[18] The Spanish Civil War and its devastating aftermath represented an overwhelming sense of loss in many ways. Defeat represented more than military failure: it also meant a loss of the past, of identity and ideals, and of visions of the future. Loss was also highly personal: the loss of family members, not only for those who supported the Republic but also for those who found themselves on the other side, either through conviction or through geographic accident. The regime, through the imposition of its totalitarian institutions, attempted coercively to implant its own vision, excluding the Republican voice.[19] Ultimately, Francoism enforced an actual loss of the future itself, a loss of hope, as millions of Spaniards were robbed of a sense of identity and of dignity. 'Progress' was coercively redefined in an individual and social sense as an overwhelming sense of closure was imposed.

Memory, for countless people, was an encounter with a reality they would rather have forgotten. The conditions under which most of the lower classes, were forced to live under Franco determined a necessary obsession with mere survival in the immediate post-war period: a coerced withdrawal into individual consciousness. The politically induced environment of scarcity broke down popular collective solidarities. Franco's victory was replayed in the daily humiliations of the defeated. This enforced retreat into the private domestic sphere in order to survive made resistance all but impossible.[20]

One of the effects of this retreat was a suppression of social consciousness. The hopelessness of the situation dulled the senses. Personal memories of what was a nightmare world for millions were partly shaped by the almost dream-like state into which people entered to get by. The ambiguous compromise between maintaining identity and survival is captured by the Catalan poet Pere Quart:

> Barcelona, look at yourself,
> Barcelona don't sing.
> Listen to your heart trying to beat.
> Don't be entertained.
> Cry a little every day . . .
> Work. Don't talk.
> Don't trust history. Dream about it.
> Reconstruct it . . .'[21]

The official view was doubtless sometimes accepted as a kind of consolation. The novelist Juan Benet suggests that a refuge was sought in forgetting: 'The people of Región [Spain] have opted to forget their own history.'[22] Through forgetting, the horror of the past is assimilated and transformed as a way of healing personal wounds.[23] But for 'power', forgetting a 'factual past' in favour of a higher 'truth' enables a people to be 'healthy' and productive. History was 'un-made' by the regime as it sought a refuge in the past. Spain had been converted into a country 'where the idea of what the future is was lost three-and-a-half centuries ago'.[24] Francoism colluded in a desire to forget by forcing upon Spaniards a static, enclosed, fossilised, triumphant version of the past.[25]

The relationship between pain, fear, memory and evasion is reinforced by personal testimonies. One woman from Seville, for example, recalls the fearfully claustrophobic days following the occupation of her working class *barrio* in the summer of 1936:

We were five days without going out at all . . . There were executions against the wall, right opposite where we lived. But I never saw them. There were those who got up in the morning and went to see who had been shot. They left them there for two or three hours so that the people could see them . . . The lorries loaded with people destined for the cemetery also passed down my street . . . But we didn't want to see them either. When the shots sounded at night we covered up our ears . . .[26]

Several methodological and interpretive problems have to be considered, then, in analysing the Francoist repression during and after the Civil War. In approaching them it is possible to establish a social and ideological context for the concepts of self-sufficiency, interiorism and 'regeneration'. Autarky was born of this brutal environment: 'purification' required isolation and was part of the construction of a Spanishness 'renovated' from inside.

Many accounts of the Francoist repression do not discuss ideological, social and political motivations. The purpose seems not to explore the nature or causes of the Civil War but to reduce historical enquiry to 'body-counting'.[27] Since we know for sure that many officially sanctioned executions took place outside the dictatorial legal framework during the war and in the 1940s and were often not recorded, we will certainly never know the true number of those killed.[28] The serious shortcomings of the philosophy and methodology of this approach have been pointed to elsewhere.[29] However, taking into account both narrowly based quantitative studies and contextualised analyses, more critical of existing records, it seems quite possible that as many as 200,000 men and women were killed in the Nationalist repression following the formal end of the conflict.[30]

Executions did not cease with Franco's declaration of the end of the Civil War at the beginning of April 1939. Thousands of killings took place in Spain during the next five or six years, in particular, although the regime continued to put its enemies to death until the end of the dictatorship in the 1970s. Silence and anonymity shrouded the repression in the years of autarky. In Galicia, as in other regions, an explicit order was given that no death certificates be issued even to those family members brave enough to identify the bodies of the executed.[31] Even publicly to express mourning for the executed was to risk punishment in the immediate post-war. One woman in Córdoba, the sister of a communist, tortured by the authorities, who committed suicide, was arrested for wearing black and forced to ingest castor oil and had her head shaved. Many others suffered similarly.[32]

Sometimes entire families were destroyed. This was not unusual in the Asturian mining districts that had been centres of revolutionary activity during the 1930s. One woman from Asturias tells of how her father, mother, husband and three brothers-in-law were killed. She escaped, but was marked by having her head shaved.[33] In thousands of cases deaths were not registered. Many bodies, to the authorities, counted for little in life and were not counted in death. Civil War fatalities continued to be registered by families even in the period after the death of Franco. In the mining communities of Asturias more than 50 per cent of the victims were recorded in the civil registers *after* 1975, the year of Franco's death.[34]

By any calculations, the magnitude of the repression was enormous. In the argument over 'exact' quantification this reality should not be lost sight of. The scale of repression claimed in even the most conservative accounts would mean that ten individuals, on average, were shot each day throughout the entire period of seven years from 1939–45.[35]

A distinction between the methodical and organised violence in Nationalist areas and the, at first, poorly controlled 'popular justice' of government Spain, is made by writers who spent time in both zones during the Civil War.[36] In spite of its notorious plurality of jurisdictions, with overlapping legislative functions and institutional responsibilities, the Francoist state's repression was motivated by well-defined politico-social objectives. Its methods and structures may have been chaotic, but its ends were perfectly clear.[37]

Francoist violence, in marked contrast to the revolutionary terror of Republican Spain during the early months of the Civil War, performed a similar function to state repression in Nazi Germany and Fascist Italy. It terrorised and liquidated those groups which could not be reconciled with the Nationalist vision of the *Patria*. It destroyed its enemy's political structure, paralysing the reflexes of the Republic and wiping out much of its social support.[38] The elimination of opponents and enemies became a rule of the embryonic Francoist state:[39] 'In all phases of the repression there was one single central intention: the physical destruction of the ranks of the parties of the Popular Front, of the unions and of the masonic organisations . . . one must speak of a perfect operation of extirpation of the political forces that had patronised and sustained the Republic and represented advanced social currents'.[40] The repression was not 'inevitable'. It was only viewed as 'necessary' by the Nationalist military rebels and ideologues because of the social and political possibilities it opened up. By contrast, the terror in the Republican zone was never 'bankable';[41] it was less selective, relatively without direction and performed no particular social function. The wave of anti-clerical violence that swept Republican Spain in 1936 contributed little effectively to the achievement of the objectives of the besieged Republican government. By contrast, the 'social shock' of Nationalist-Francoist terror in this period had a lasting 'value' in terms of social control into the 1950s and 1960s, as Franco's own comments suggests: 'The cruel war sustained today, and the sterile sacrifice made to their regions by the Basque and Catalan leaders, are so hard a lesson that they will never be able to forget it'.[42] The repression was 'intentionally exhaustive, not with a view to present security, but as a way of removing for the future any probable obstacle, any suggestion of opposition, any new outbreak of the condemned forces or ideas' (*significaciones*).[43]

Nationalist (and, subsequently, Francoist) repression was a political activity based on ideological assumptions. The terror was programmed, thought-out and intentional.[44] In the Republican zone revolutionary violence was never planned by state authorities as an all-out assault on 'class enemies'. The attitude of Nationalist political leaders towards violence was quite different from that of Republicans. There was no comparable reaction among the rebel leaders to the moral crisis suffered by the Republic's President Manuel Azaña and its Prime Minister José Giral on hearing of the killings carried out by government supporters in the aftermath of the military rebellion in Madrid.[45] When, at the end of July 1936, in an effort to avoid more bloodshed, Indalecio Prieto, the leading reformist socialist minister of the Republic, suggested to the first director of the rebellion, General Mola, that the two sides might attempt some negotiation, the general responded that 'this war had to end with the extermination of the enemies of Spain'.[46] Republican leaders repeatedly tried to put an end to the terror. The Republican authorities investigated excesses and attempted to put structures in place which would stop the violence.[47] Indeed, on the very day of the shootings at the Prisión Modelo in Madrid, the government decreed the constitution of Tribunales Populares as a way of institutionalising 'popular justice'.[48]

Azaña's public declarations suggest this important distinction with the ethical vision of Nationalist leaders. The President of the Republic made frequent critical reference to the brutality on both sides and demonstrated the constancy of his objective of social reconciliation,[49] an aim which was utterly alien to the mentality of Nationalist leaders, who were interested in a settling of accounts in a social and an economic sense and a moral purge. On 18 July 1937, for example, Azaña's speech given at the University of Valencia addressed the question of the 'moral reconstruction' of Spain and condemned what was a Nationalist policy of 'extermination'. A year later this consistently humanistic understanding was again displayed in his public plea in Barcelona for 'peace, mercy and forgiveness' ('*Paz, piedad y perdón*'). Other Republican leaders, like the socialists Indalecio Prieto, Juan Negrín and the anarchist Joan Peiró, made frequent efforts to limit the revolutionary violence in the Republican zone.[50] Negrín, in the days following the failed military coup in the capital, accompanied militia patrols in an attempt to prevent political assassinations without legal process. This suggests both a degree of humanity and considerable bravery on his part, as well as a sense of outrage at the collapse of the power of the constituted state authority.[51] He agreed that in such a crisis normal procedure had to be suspended in favour of special courts, but a system of evidence had to be upheld: 'You can't arrest an innocent man just because you are positive in your own mind that he is guilty. You prosecute a war, yes: but you also live with your conscience.'[52]

By contrast, there were no protests from Nationalist leaders: only encouragement. On the very day of the rising against the Republic, Franco had himself, in a telegram from Melilla, called for 'exemplary punishment' to be imposed 'without hesitation'.[53] The wholesale 'necessary elimination' of opponents seemed to observers to be a definite policy.[54]

The decision-making process in Nationalist Spain was put in place by what was a coherent state in formation.[55] The Republican government, by contrast, was an incoherent power in a situation of virtual disintegration. A state of war was declared immediately in July 1936 in the Nationalist zone.[56] Ultimate power passed to the military, which guaranteed a rigorous system of authority based on honour, order and discipline. In Republican Spain, however, the state of war was not declared until January 1939, only months prior to Franco's victory. Virtually from the beginning of the conflict the Nationalist system of authority was therefore more secure, solid and stable than that of the government itself. Gerald Brenan, writing in August 1936, suggested that, 'those who point to atrocities . . . on the Government side often forget the provocation and the circumstances. When soldiers and police have to go to the front because other soldiers and police have rebelled, who is left to keep order among an enraged population?'[57] Following the military rebellion, Republican power experienced a profound crisis and was not recaptured from the street until May 1937.[58] In Nationalist Spain, as Pierre Vilar has written, 'contrary to what happened in the Republican camp, democratic forms did not exist – a pluralistic press, parties, open ministerial crises . . . there were no open discussions about methods and ends. The violence of class hatred, when it is exercised from above, is much more coherent and durable than in the other direction'.[59] Reactionary 'purification' was a systematised process in *defence* of existing privilege and the exploitation on which it was based, that employed modern propaganda methods and 'civilised' ideas. The revolutionary purge is a *destruction* of existing symbols based on an informal popular consensus and an appropriation of space and of time itself. Revolution demands more of fantasy and imagination than does its reactionary suppression. While existing elites organise their forces and appeal to 'immortal values', workers shoot at the clocks. This contrast between the unity of purpose in 'Nationalist' (Francoist) Spain and the divisions, or plurality, within areas held by the legal government during the conflict was also to be reflected very clearly in the language used in constructing images of the enemy.

The purges

The rebellion of July 1936 against the democratic government, reflected, in its stated objectives and in its language, a pathological diagnosis of the Spanish 'sickness' as represented by the Second Republic.[60] The violence employed by the Nationalists was justified by both the collective colonial mentality of the *Africanista* generals who led the rebellion,[61] bent on the 'cleansing' of a working class which was considered hardly human, and a totalitarian remaking of the *Patria* through the destruction of all things foreign or alien to the 'national destiny'. The sense of the rising perceived as both a colonial campaign and an action with fascist political and social functions is suggested by a comment of a Captain of the Civil Guard in Pamplona in 1936, a fellow conspirator with General Mola, who described the original aim as 'a march on Rome with more blood'.[62]

The direction, in terms of motivation or justification, was from a colonial 'cleaning-up' operation to a broader, institutionalised repression. This owed something to the changing nature of the conflict itself. Prior to November 1936 there was no genuine confrontation between two more or less homogeneous armies at all, but rather, a series of assaults, street battles, policing operations, purges undertaken by a regular army, supplemented by party militia, against a politicised and hostile people, poorly armed and often little organised. These were violent, despoiling and plundering expeditions that *Africanista* officers, whose battle-cry was 'Long Live Death!', described using the Arabic term *razzia*.[63] But there were also continuities and commonalities with subsequent bureaucratised repression. Both military men and fascists, as well as others in Spain who were strictly neither, spoke and wrote of a process of 'purification' as a necessity in order to purge Spain of the 'sick bodies', of the 'unhealthy organisms', which were a major preoccupation of the authoritarian philosophical and religious ideologues of the Spanish right. Nothing 'inorganic' was wanted. The middle classes had 'healthy bodies' and were 'the nerve texture of the *organismo patrio*' and the absolute 'organic elite' were Falangists and Carlists: 'Spain in nerve, blood and soul.'[64]

The threatening Other, which was the working class, and those 'who put ideas into their heads',[65] were to be the object of a 'barbarous and ancient sport' and, indeed, Franco described the Civil War as essentially a 'frontier war', where the objective was the permanent suppression of the enemy and not simply its surrender. During the Moroccan campaigns there was a fierce pride in brutal violence against the dehumanised villagers, among the Spanish *Africanistas*, which was typified by the decapitation of prisoners and the exhibition of severed heads.[66] In some ways, Franco and his officers applied a similar 'strategy' of liquidation, based on a similar perception of the enemy, during the Civil War. A slow and far from subtle war was fought using what Juan Benet has described as 'butcher's tactics', aiming at maximum loss of life.[67] The 'Red enemy' was 'no regular army' to be confronted in open battle, but 'a pathogenic germ that hides itself even in apparently tranquil homes and must be made to come out to exterminate it'.[68] In 1937 Franco made clear to the Italian Ambassador in Nationalist Spain that victory for him meant the annihilation of large numbers of Republicans and the total humiliation and terrorisation of the surviving population.[69] The Caudillo evidently saw the bloodiest battles of the Civil War as part of a necessary 'cleansing operation'[70] in the process of the national 'expiation of sin'. Mass executions became a central component of the theory and practice of the operation undertaken by the rebels. General Juan Yagüe, one of Franco's leading officers, ideologically close to the Falange, and responsible for ordering the massacre of 2,000 leftists and Republicans in Badajóz in 1936,[71] gave a sense of the priorities and purposes of the Civil War repression: 'the fact that the conquest of Spain by the Army is proceeding at a slow pace has this advantage: that it gives us time to purge the country thoroughly of all Red elements'.[72]

The German Nazi press understood and admired the purposes of the Spanish repression, which was seen as providing an example to be followed: 'The Generals looked for guarantees of victory not primarily in military successes, but in a systematic and thorough cleansing of the hinterland'.[73] 'Fortunately the old attitude of sentimentality has been dissipated among the Nationalists, and every soldier realises that a horrible end is better than endless horrors'.[74] 'The Marxist parties are being destroyed and exterminated down to the very last cell far more drastically even than here in Germany. Every house, every flat, every office is kept under constant observation and supervision . . . Every single citizen, moreover, is drawn into the whirl of political excitement, made to participate in triumphal celebrations and mass demonstrations. The principle of modern Nationalism, "No opponent but shall be destroyed", is thoroughly carried out . . . Just as here in Germany.'[75]

Mola viewed the challenge before the rebels in these terms, although it was increasingly considered inappropriate by the state censor to air such views publicly. His declaration that Madrid, once taken, would have to be 'thoroughly cleansed', was suppressed, for example. Nor were the great many summary executions that were carried out to be written about.[76]

This purgative culture may well have penetrated quite deeply into society during the war. A leading official from Toledo, in central Spain, for instance, wrote complaining ostensibly about 'problems of morality' in the aftermath of the conflict, describing Republicans in the lowest possible terms:

> The first moral problem is to carry out rapid and energetic justice: the families of those killed [in the war], who are the most solid moral mainstay that the province and The Cause possess, become demoralised if they see weakness. The province has approximately 20,000 killers who must urgently disappear: these people have never worked and they never will, they have never been grateful and they never will: assuming that each one costs only 2 pesetas daily, that is still 40,000 peseatas a day: 15 million per year! [W]ith that I could sort out this province economically.[77]

The purge of Spanish society was concentrated both on the urban and rural working class and on the 'carriers' of the 'plague' which was liberalism. Even before the 1936 military rising the conspirators had made clear their commitment to exemplary violence directed against the working class, its organisations, and the leaders of Republican groups in general. Emilio Mola, the general directing the military conspiracy, insisted: 'It is necessary to propagate an atmosphere of terror . . . Anybody who openly or secretly defends the Popular Front must be shot'.[78] Officers were ordered to instil a 'salutary terror into the population . . . Every town along the enemy's line of retreat and all the areas behind the enemy lines are to be considered as battle zones . . . [N]o differentiation must be observed between places harbouring enemy troops and those not doing so.'[79]

The 'reconquest' of *latifundio* Spain was viewed as an opportunity for a definitive settling of accounts between landowners and the landless population which had dared to challenge the social status quo.[80] During the bloody conflict in Córdoba province, for example, legend had it that when land workers were led at gun point to the common grave where they were to be executed they were told by their *señorito* captors that they were about to experience a new kind of 'agrarian reform', a reference to the Republic's attempt at a limited redistribution of land, which had been fiercely resisted, prior to the Civil War.[81] Landowners themselves provided black-lists of so-called 'troublemakers' whose lives they demanded.[82] Workers who had been involved in measures of land collectivisation were particularly singled out for the most severe measures and torture was applied to extract information.[83]

A typical case of those who carried out the repression was the son of the administrator of the estates of a marquis of Jaén in Andalucía who, after the military rising, became a Falangist and was assigned to an execution squad and was responsible for hundreds of deaths.[84] In Cádiz the mayor put in place by the Nationalist forces was the principal *cacique* (local party boss) of the province, who took a leading role in promoting the repression.[85] Following Nationalist occupation, local authority in the towns of Córdoba was again placed in the hands of landowners or their agents. Some of the most brutal perpetrators of executions were the *guarda rurales* (gamekeepers) of the big estates. In this part of Spain gamekeepers were responsible for preventing hungry landless workers from trapping food to feed their families during the many hard weeks without work. They effectively helped maintain the local social structure of dependency. Sometimes, even in normal times, gamekeepers shot those they caught. In the early post-war years some of these *guardas* conducted their own hunt for 'Reds'.[86]

The sense of identity of latifundist landowners was, in some measure, based upon a collective sense of 'their' landless workers, not as people, but as inhuman possessions.[87] The relationship of dependency had been graphically illustrated by the use of the phrase '¡*Que coman República!*' (literally, 'Let them eat the Republic!') by some great landowners when pressured to implement reforms in 1931 to alleviate the starvation conditions of the workers.[88] The so-called 'Pact of Hunger' was also widely employed in industrial areas, employers relying on starvation wages as a way of maintaining a precarious existence and absolute dependency.[89]

In Seville, where plans for the rising against the Republic had been underway for months before July 1936, civilian volunteers, including members of the area's prominent landowning families, co-operated closely with the local military and the Falangist organisation in establishing local power mainly through repression of the working-class population.[90] The parties and unions of the left had already been denied arms by the local Republican authorities.[91]

There were two main phases of terror and repression in Seville.[92] First, the period from July 1936 to January or February 1937 saw a wave of executions in working class *barrios*. Categoric orders were issued to officers that on the occupation of each town, information be obtained from priests and 'other reliable persons' as to the 'attitudes' of the community:[93] 'Insurgent troops kill the ringleaders of the left forces as soon as they capture any town. Then they leave the place in peace for about a week, during which agents investigate. Finally they start rounding up those who supported the Loyalist cause or who are suspected of having done so. These persons are led to cemeteries, where they are shot in groups of about 20 throughout several days and nights.'[94] During this period hundreds, probably thousands, of men and women disappeared. Mass shootings in the streets and in the cemeteries, without any formalised bureaucratic processing, were typical of this era.[95] The authorities devised the tactic of organising motorised squads, or *Brigadas de Depuración*, ('Purification Brigades'), which descended upon 'dubious' villages in order to 'clean up' by exterminating all suspect elements in so-called 'executions of national salvation'.[96] The watchword was *'abreviar trámites'* ('cut short procedures').[97] Only a fraction of these deaths was recorded in the civil register.

This was not violence which was 'necessary' in any military sense: there was no organised armed resistance to speak of. Nor was the repression indiscriminate. It was organised to the extent that both political militias (principally Falangists) and the army used black-lists drawn up by those locals with influence. A second phase began in February 1937. Repression now was principally imposed beneath an appearance of legality: this was the era of the Councils of War. Files were formally called for, but in most cases the 'evidence' was never heard since the judgement had been made beforehand.[98] The secretary of General Queipo de Llano, in effect, the military viceroy of Andalusia during the Civil War and in its aftermath,[99] described the 'parody' of the Councils of War, claiming that in Seville the Delegado de Orden Público, Captain Manuel Díaz Criado, signed some sixty death sentences a day without studying the files. Díaz would refer to his task as 'thoroughly cleansing [*limpiar*] Spain of Marxists'.

Although from this time onward we may suppose that the records of the civil registry begin to reflect the reality a little closer, we know that men and women continued to be killed without their deaths being recorded, since the rough figures of what was known as the Common Grave (*Fosa Común*) of the San Fernando Cemetery are substantially greater than those of the civil register.[100] Common graves became a feature of the landscape throughout Spain as the Nationalist campaign proceeded. Many towns and villages all over Spain had their 'own' ravine, gully or steep bank, a *barranca*, used to bury victims of repression, which many knew of but remained silent about.[101]

The initial 'pacification' of Seville and its environs took a week. In some hamlets, according to the personal secretary of the director of the rising, Mola, the repression was so thorough that virtually the entire worker population was wiped out.[102] While recent 'scientific' study has suggested a figure of around 2,400 executions during the Civil War in

Seville, local estimates at the time suggested that the magnitude of the repression was at least three or four times greater.[103] José María Varela Rendueles, the Republican Civil Governor of Seville in 1936, claimed that it was enough to be found with a membership card of the socialist union, the UGT (Unión General de Trabajadores), to be killed on the spot. He estimated that between July 1936 and February 1937 more than 6,000 were killed in the city of Seville without appearing before any court whatsoever.[104]

Queipo de Llano himself declared his determination to carry through the most fundamental objective of the rebels: 'Eighty per cent of the families of Andalucía are already in mourning. And we shall not hesitate, either, to adopt even more rigorous measures to assure our ultimate victory.' Triumph meant more than forcing the military capitulation of Republican Spain: it signified the annihilation of the *idea* of the Republic and of those who 'transmitted' this ideal: 'We shall go on to the bitter end and continue our good work until not a single Marxist is left in Spain.'[105] This provided an answer to the question posed by Francisco Gonzálbez Ruíz, the Republican former Civil Governor of Murcia, who found himself in rebel territory during the early part of the Civil War: 'Why do they go on shooting after twelve, fourteen months of war, and in Seville, where they were the masters of the situation from the very beginning?'[106] The same question might be asked in relation to Granada or Córdoba or Zaragoza.[107]

While the General Strike called by workers in defence of the city of Seville was maintained, bodies littered the street, left as an example where they had fallen, and had to be piled up against the side of houses so that army trucks could pass. In assembling workers in the factories and railways, 'blind obedience' was demanded and 'the ultimate penalty' threatened to those who did not co-operate.[108] Queipo threatened Seville workers that the conflict could only end with 'the triumph of those who love the *Patria*: of those who, being more decent, have the will of God with us'.[109]

Resistance under such violent conditions was extremely difficult. However, workers in other parts of Spain also attempted to organise in the face of great brutality. In the main population centres of Galicia, for example, the main resistance was manifested by a refusal to work. The first worker shot in response was a striking tram driver. Executions followed as a systematic purge of each section of the local economy in turn was carried out. Engineering works were purged next, then the guns were turned on railway workers. In La Coruña, as in many other cities, workers continued to organise collections of money to help feed strikers. These donations were made illegal but they continued and the strike went on until the authorities took five workers as hostages. In spite of the executions, workers' passive resistance prevented a return to normality.[110]

In Seville, extermination was just one element of the occupation.[111] Physical repression went hand-in-hand with economic measures favouring the dominant social groups of pre-Republican Spain. Queipo de Llano was also responsible for legislation concerning the production and commercialisation of wheat in Andalucía. His Ley de Ordenación Triguera of August 1937 put in place a rigid structure which welded the nascent Francoist state to the interests of the big growers.[112] In a sense, this heralded the resolution of the central conflict of Spanish society in this era, in favour of landed elites. The outcome of the Civil War, as Franco claimed, signified 'the victory of wheat'.[113] The result was the concentration of wealth, economic repression and starvation in the 1940s.[114]

In Granada, much of the brutal repression was carried out by Falangists and by former affiliates of José María Gil Robles' Catholic party of the 1930s, the CEDA, the youth-wing of which, the Juventud de Acción Popular (JAP), had both a fascistic style and street-fighting function.[115] Although the survivng records in Granada give a figure of 2,314 executions, the testimonies of local people suggest that the number of victims was probably as great as 8,000.[116] Indeed, the province was the site of some of the most brutal acts of the war and its aftermath. Local people were anxious to remind an investigating journalist in the late-1970s that it was not only the poet Federico García Lorca who had been shot in Granada, but thousands of other people too. Their memories of the events of 1936 were alive and they wanted to know why these executions were not spoken about.[117]

Málaga also presented a tragic picture during the war and in its aftermath.[118] The city had resisted the initial military revolt but was cut off from the rest of Republican Spain very rapidly. In putting down the rising, the inhabitants of the poor quarter of Málaga had taken possession of the wealthy centre, burning the houses of the rich and influential as they did so. The revolutionary appropriation of space and symbols, like the destruction and throwing into the sea of the famous statue of the Marqués de Larios, located in the centre of the city, appeared as mindless and horrifying vandalism to the middle classes.[119] But it was as the population became subjected to merciless bombing raids by Nationalist warships and German and Italian aircraft that mass shootings of supporters of the rebellion, and members of the middle class more broadly, began in reprisal. The slaughter, for a few dreadful weeks, became uncontrollable. The right made much of the terror: 'The holocaust of the *Patria* and of humanity' was aimed at the ruination of Western civilization. The 'washing away [*limpieza*] of the[se] sins would cost a great deal of blood . . . Málaga has offered her sacrifice for your redemption'. The seven months of Republican control of the city during the war were to be known thereafter as Málaga's 'Calvary'.[120]

The uncontrolled violence of the working class, however, paled in comparison with the wave of violence which followed the final capture of the city by Franco's (mainly Italian) forces in February 1937. In the city of Málaga itself it was estimated that almost 4,000 leftists were shot in the first week alone and the executions continued for months.[121] According to the British Consul, writing in August 1944, and employing 'official records', in the period since the 'liberation' of Málaga, more than 20,000 men and women had been shot there.[122] This extraordinary figure seems hard to believe and the remaining records that have been scrutinised show a much lower figure.[123] Certainly, though, the people living in the *barrios* on the right-hand side of the river were disturbed all night long for months by constant bursts of gunfire. The occupation of Málaga was preceded by a mass fleeing from the city. Thousands took to the road for Almería, like 'an army of ants', seventy miles of people, with feet bound in rags, in silence except when bombed and strafed from the air by Nationalist planes.[124] The British doctor, T.C. Worsley, talked to some of the women *en route* who had been walking for three to six days with no food. Only two had husbands who had not been shot: 'Málaga and the road out had been an inferno. Shelled from the sea, bombed from the air, and then machine-gunned. The terror was alive and blistering in their eyes as they imitated the stutter of machine-guns.'[125]

Repression was also terrible in the north of Spain. In the province of Pontevedra, in Galicia, executions were co-ordinated by the established pre-Republican monarchist parliamentary deputy who accompanied the Falangist squads into the towns and villages in search of leftist agricultural workers. After execution, workers' houses were destroyed. In La Coruña, a civil militia, the Caballeros de La Coruña, operated alongside the Falange in the 'pacification' of the area, although the entire region had fallen in just a couple of days with very little armed resistance.[126] In San Sebastián, on the north coast of the Basque Country, one of the country's most 'European' and 'modern' – though profoundly Catholic – cities, industrialists and financiers, many from Catalonia, mingled with semi-organised groups of local power holders and devised methods for supporting the Nationalist war effort financially.[127] The relative weakness of the Falange in the Basque country did not mean, however, that there was not brutal repression in San Sebastián. Nearly 1,000 executions took place in the first three months of the Nationalist 'Reconquest' of the city in the autumn of 1936, that Mola compared with the expulsion of the Moors in the fifteenth century.[128] By the beginning of 1945 it was estimated that there had been more than 4,500 'mostly illegal killings' of supporters of the Republic.[129] In the city of Bilbao, the industrial heartland of the Basque Country, there were many more killings as a prelude to decades of cultural discrimination and oppression. The city's new mayor, José María de Areilza, rejoiced that Bilbao was now to be 'redeemed for ever from the red scum in the service of Moscow, and the Vizcayan nationalist scum in the service of separatism'.[130] This was in a region where there had been no social revolution and very little violence during the years of the Republic prior to the war.[131] But to support the PNV (Partido Nacional Vasco – Basque Nationalist Party) was, according to the Francoist authorities, to be a 'separatist' and separatism had become, in practice, a capital crime in itself. Areilza wanted to hear nothing of 'pacts' and insisted on application of 'the laws of war, hard, virile, inexorable'.[132] In spite of Franco's pledge that 'those who surrender to our credo have nothing to fear', within a month of the fall of the city in June 1937, nearly a thousand leftists and Basque Nationalists had been executed and a further 16,000 imprisoned. Large numbers of executions were still being carried out six months later.[133] Other regions suffered at the hands of the occupiers with the collaboration of local elites. In Vigo, one of the major port cities of Galicia, the first head of the Falange was a rich manufacturer. He was succeeded by the son of a prominent factory owner. Indeed, all the principal Falangist leaders in the region were from the 'moneyed classes'. Mechanical repression was carried out here under their supervision by docile and disciplined underlings.[134]

The anecdotal evidence, upon which an appreciation of the scale of the repression partly relies, suggests a substantial repressive wave also in the Spanish capital. The Nationalist drive on Madrid, during the conflict, was accompanied by 'a reign of terror'.[135] The shooting in cold blood of innocent men and women shocked the American journalist John Whitaker, who was camped at Talavera de la Reina: 'I never passed a night . . . without being awakened at dawn by the volleys of firing squads in the yard of the Cuartel. There was no end to this purge. They were shooting as many at the end of the second month as in my first days there. They must have averaged thirty killings a day.' The 'quota' that had to be fulfilled consisted of 'simple peasants and workers . . . It was sufficient to have carried a trade union card, to have been a Free Mason or to have voted for the Republic . . . It was called the "regeneration" of Spain.'[136] The British Ambassador reported to the Foreign

Office in mid-June, 1939 that while probably 30,000 were in prison in Madrid, awaiting trial, the number of what the regime labelled 'political assassins and gunmen' tried by court-martial and executed amounted to 1,500. The women's prison at Ventas, in Madrid, constructed to hold 500, had between 6,000 and 11,000 detainees at the beginning of 1940.[137] Women were daily woken by the sound of execution squads in the cemetery close by.[138] Existing records of just one of the many cemeteries of Madrid reveal that 2,663 were shot between May 1939 and February 1944 there. On 24 June 1939, 102 prisoners were shot in this one place. This number of dead does not include those who died in unrecorded executions, either by bullet or strangulation (*garrote vil*), or those who starved in prison.[139] Count Ciano, Mussolini's foreign minister, during his visit to Spain in the summer of 1939, had claimed that 200–250 executions were taking place each day in Madrid.[140]

In Barcelona and Valencia thousands of Republicans, from leading politicians to peasants and workers, had congregated in fleeing the advance of Franco's Axis-backed forces. In Valencia, when the city fell, 'the public' were urged to denounce all supporters of the Republic.[141] The use of the term 'the public' was frequent in Francoist discourse. The intention was to give a sense of a common cause among the people generally. However, the term carried with it a sense of exclusion too. It helped establish a barrier between 'the public', which was necessarily supportive of the 'National Crusade', and 'the others', who were 'criminals'. Through denunciation it was occasionally possible to cross that barrier.

In Valencia, the head of the local *Columna de Orden y Policía de Ocupación*, Colonel Antonio Aymat, described its function as the 'purification of the civil population'.[142] Two hundred death sentences were officially announced for the month of April 1939 and a further 270 for the first fortnight of May. It was generally accepted that the actual number of executions in the city greatly exceeded these figures.[143] Those denounced had been imprisoned up to the highest possible limits of prison capacity. The main prison in Valencia, the Cárcel Modelo, for example, which had 800 cells, housed 8,000 prisoners by June 1939. There were at least fourteen concentration camps in the area.[144] In the province as a whole so many were incarcerated that bull rings, convents and monasteries were converted into prisons.

Franco had boasted in November 1938, as his forces were about to begin their occupation of Catalonia, that the Nationalist government had built up a file with more than two million names of those who were considered enemies, 'with the proof of their crimes and the names of the witnesses'.[145] A massive purge was predicted. The British Foreign

Office received a report warning that 'only a peace which was achieved without unconditional surrender or a fight to a finish can avert such a disaster for Spain. That will not be achieved unless Italy is made to withdraw her planes and troops', which had made Franco's total victory possible. In accordance with the policy of appeasement over Spain, the Foreign Office decided to send a warning to Franco but that the point about Italians 'be ignored'.[146]

Franco's determination to 'purge' Spain was demonstrated by his refusal to consider negotiating a peace and establishing a neutralised zone in the north-east of Spain.[147] As refugees fled towards the French border in January 1939, from Barcelona, the principal industrial city of Catalonia, 'a vital organ of Spain', the Caudillo's aim remained the total annihilation of the Republic and its supporters.[148] The occupation was viewed in pathological terms. According to Franco's Interior Minister, Ramón Serrano Suñer, Catalonia's local nationalism was 'a sickness'. 'Secessionism' had 'lived as a parasite' from what he viewed as an ostentatious and false local patriotism. Now, thankfully, 'criminal separatism' had been 'exterminated': the Catalan Republic had 'died, rotted'.[149] A 'biblical punishment (Sodom, Gomorrah)' was recommended 'to purify the red city, seat of anarchism and separatism . . . as the only remedy to extirpate these two cancers [through an] implacable destructive thermo-cauterization'.[150] The 'secessionist virus' had to be treated: 'Today we have Catalonia on the points of our bayonets. Material domination will take little time. I am sure that the moral incorporation of Catalonia into Spain will be achieved as quickly as its military incorporation.'[151]

Many more contemporary Francoist proclamations suggest an iron determination to extirpate the 'cancer' which had infected the Nation. A Portuguese journalist, on asking about resolution of 'the problem of Catalonia', received a very simple response: the answer was 'to kill Catalans'.[152] Serrano Suñer, who was to be mainly responsible for constructing the formal institutions of the Francoist state, gave his view on the situation in Barcelona after its fall in January 1939 to a German journalist: 'The city is completely bolshevized. The task of decomposition absolute . . . In Barcelona the Reds have stifled the Spanish spirit. The people . . . are morally and politically sick. Barcelona will be treated by us with the care with which one attends to an invalid.'[153] Even if it meant the disappearance of the Puerta del Sol, Madrid also would be cleansed of 'political germs'. Francoism's first Civil Governor in Barcelona, Wenceslao González Oliveros, appointed for his notorious anti-Catalanism in 1939, saw the Civil War as an operation to 'surgically eradicate' the 'putrefaction' in society represented by 'Marxism' and 'separatism'.[154] This eradication was a pre-requisite for establishing power. Barcelona had to be 'a purifying focus of authentically Spanish ideas, clean of French influences'.[155] The state in Spain had remained 'unconstructed' for a century, and no 'regional political concept' could be permitted until central authority had been forcibly imposed.

The official entry into the city of Barcelona, at the end of January, 1939, was led by General Solchaga's Navarra corps. According to the British Assistant Military Attaché in Burgos, the city where Franco's headquarters were situated, 'The Navarrese march first not because they have fought better, but because they hate better. That is to say, when the object of this hate is Catalonia or a Catalan.'[156] Preparations for a post-war purge of the region were put in hand by the organisation of the 'exiled' Catalan Falange,[157] which could boast in 1938 of having built up an archive of 30,000 names of 'Red elements'.[158]

The initial months of military occupation were used to deliver what was called 'Franco's Justice'. The judicial process, such as it was, following the occupation, can be divided into three periods: The initial era was of 'Military Jurisdiction', the application of the '*Código castrense*', or 'military code', from February to the end of June 1939. Second, the period of so-called 'Special Jurisdiction', when the 'Tribunales Especiales', as provided for in the Law of Political Responsibilities, announced on 9 February, 1939, operated, coming into force in Barcelona in June 1939. Those who, even through their 'passivity', had hindered the 'providential victory' of the Crusade, were targets. This tribunal was composed of a high-ranking army officer, a Francoist member of the judiciary, and a member of FET–JONS, dealing with the considerable task of 'hearing' cases. By the end of 1941, in the whole of Spain, some 100,000 cases had been heard specifically under this legislation.[159] Finally, 'Ordinary Jurisdiction' marked a 'return to normality' and the operation of 'ordinary' organs of justice by law of 19 February 1942.[160]

This physical punishment was accompanied by a legislative dismantling of the Republican revolution. The provisions of the military order establishing the Special Regime of Occupation in Barcelona had as a priority the insistence upon a reversion to the pre-1931 situation in the ownership and control of property. All the legislative actions of the Republican government in the city were annulled, the Catalan statute of autonomy, granted by the Republic, having been abolished by a decree of the Nationalist administration on 5 April 1938 as soon as Franco's troops had entered Catalan territory.[161]

The round-up of political enemies began straightaway. Within days of the fall of the city of Barcelona, the new authorities declared that 40,000 Republicans who 'have blood on their hands' had been unable to escape from the city before the arrival of the 'liberating army'.[162] The British Consul did not doubt that they would be unable to escape 'the extreme penalty'. Mass executions without prior opportunity for defence would continue until 1943 when the numbers of 'enemies' disposed of in this way began to decline.[163] According to the US Vice Consul, the new administration organised hundreds of trials and thousands of executions were carried out in just a few months. Firing squads could still be heard regularly in the city as late as 1942.[164] According to a representative of a Catalan exiles' organisation, writing in September 1939, the execution of Republicans and democrats was continuing at the rate of 30 a day.[165]

In contrast to Republican terror, the violence perpetrated by the so-called 'Nationalists' against those social groups which supported the legal government was encouraged by the highest authorities of the nascent Francoist state. 'Purification' was invested with a multiplicity of meanings, unified under the sign of Catholicism, the Francoist state's surrogate nationalism, in a reversal of what was seen as national 'degeneration' to ensure 'Spain's immortality'. The authorities attempted to make propaganda use out of what it described as 'extraordinary cases of conversion'. It was claimed, for example, that 90 per cent of prisoners 'repented' at the end and died 'in a Christian way', receiving the sacrament before execution; although confession was made and communion taken often in exchange for one last sight of or a word with wives and children.[166]

Leading figures of Spain's social elite played a significant part in directing the purges. They drew up the black-lists which were used by the army and the para-military groups in rounding up 'Reds'; they sat on local commissions to decide upon 'responsibilities' for 'Marxist crimes' and helped dish out penalties; they even decided who would eat and who would go hungry according to political criteria; finally, many of them joined the Falange and participated in militia activities. This is not to say that the majority of social elites did these things, but they were disproportionately represented within the higher echelons of local power, as well as influencing the conduct of national policy.[167] Violence both punished and secured a degree of unity among the 'victors', brought together in a 'pact of blood' and counterposed to the image of the defeated as the '*Anti-Patria*'. This purge could only take place within a context of Spain's isolation. Its very purpose was to eradicate, or 'surgically remove' the 'disease' which had afflicted the *Patria* from outside.

3   Purifying Spain (II): degeneration and treatment

The Spanish Civil War was portrayed as a project to pathologically remake the physical stock of the *Patria* and its morality. The 'foreign virus' of liberalism, which bred communism, was an infection which had to be expunged.[1] According to the Falange's handbook of 'political formation' for girls, those who repudiated the destiny of the *Patria* were not Spaniards at all even if they were born in Spain.[2] Politics had been substituted by 'extermination and expulsion'.[3] The 'light of gunfire' had illuminated this reality.[4] It is not therefore surprising that the work of 'purification' was systematically continued after the formal cessation of war on 1 April 1939 and all calls for reconciliation rejected. The repression was seen as a social and political prophylactic on a national scale,[5] as a protective measure to guard physical organisms from a possible future disease: 'We've got to kill and kill and kill, you understand', declared one of Franco's press officers, Gonzalo de Aguilera, absentee landowner, army captain and seventeenth Count of Alba y Yeltes:

In healthier times – I mean healthier times spiritually – plague and pestilence used to slaughter the Spanish masses . . . They are slave stock. They are good for nothing but slaves and only when they are used as slaves are they happy . . . They're like animals, you understand, and you can't expect them not to be infected with the virus of Bolshevism. After all, rats and lice carry the plague. Now I hope you can understand what we mean by the regeneration of Spain . . . It's our programme . . . to exterminate a third of the male population of Spain. That will clean up the country and rid us of the proletariat. It's sound economically too. Never have any more unemployment in Spain, you understand.[6]

Although Aguilera was relatively at the margins of Francoist propaganda, and though no 'programme' of extermination, as such, existed, the perception of the war as a campaign against a sickness at the root of society was an important part of the regime's understanding of the conflict, reflected in its language and actions.

The crisis of the 1930s, culminating in civil war, heightened a sense of panic over the 'health of the race', similar to that experienced in many other countries in this era.[7] Orteguian regenerationism and its panoply of pathological language was recycled to describe the result of Spain's 'defective embryology', and to depict the workers whose 'biological mission . . . to be docile' had been transgressed.[8] Regenerationists, like Joaquín Costa and Lucas Mallada had, some years earlier, compared the Spaniards to the indigenous peoples of Africa, as part of a racial schematization of decline.[9] The agricultural workers and migrants of the south, often referred to as '*africanos*', were particularly viewed as genetically inferior, as a lazy and degenerate caste apart from respectable society that could not compare with the ancient, but endangered, 'stratified' racial and spiritual essences found in the peasants of Castile.

General Mola, the initial director of the military rebellion against the Republican government, was, like Franco, deeply affected by the loss of empire in 1898. He was born the son of a soldier in Cuba, Spain's richest colony, when 'her skies were still Castilian skies' but which were soon to be 'cloaked by storm-clouds of blood'.[10] On his forced return to Spain after the loss of the island in the Spanish-American war, he found 'a country emptied of itself' and 'a degenerated people, an ambience of abdication . . . and a tendency towards suicide . . . sceptical and cowardly young people . . . social putrefaction, hatred of the army . . . rottenness (in need of) military surgery.'[11] The Spanish people considered itself weak and had therefore 'degenerated'. The situation required the resurrection of 'natural law', that is, the 'law of force put into practice by men since the remote times of the ancient tribes', and which had been undermined by decadent parliamentarianism.[12] Regeneration required isolation because 'decadent peoples were the favourite victims of the parasitic way of life of international organisations . . . Pathological germs grow and multiply with maximum virulence within weak nations.'[13]

A psycho-pathological language was employed during the Civil War in an array of revealing synonyms employed in the official discourse to conceptualise the enemy as 'inferior to animals' or 'inhuman':[14] '*turbio*' (restless, disturbed, as well as 'sediment' or 'sludge'); '*escoria*' (scum), '*encenagado*' (depraved); '*inmundo*' (foul); '*hediondo*' (stinking); '*sucio*' (dirty, filthy, vile); '*baba*' (slime); '*cochambre*' (filthy, disgusting): '*detritus*' (detritus, waste), '*tiniebla*' (dark, 'black ignorance').[15] This crude science of character and identity was readily employed in the context of shifting allegiances, demographic movements and threats, violent clashes and death during the 1930s and the derogatory label 'Red', in the post-war, implied not simply a previous leftist political affiliation but a 'dirtiness' or apartness, to be outcast.[16] The prominent Francoist philosopher Manuel García Morente stated baldly the way in which bodies and race were instrumentalised in constructing 'Spain' and 'Anti-Spain', conveniently forgetting how Moors had contributed to Franco's fighting forces:[17] 'The Moor is always the other, in the two inseparable senses of the *other* religion and the *other* nationality'.[18] This contrast helped foster self-awareness through contrast and opposition:[19] 'Spain, which is Christian and Spanish as opposed to the Moor, has to conquer her own body and her own soul . . . at the point of the Christian sword . . . Spain is made of Christian faith and Iberian blood'.[20] This depiction of the enemy as inhuman and un-Spanish was difficult to unravel from the *inhumane* conditions imposed as part of the mechanism of production and domination in the great estates or in urban ghettos.[21]

The response to fear of the degeneration of Spain's 'destiny' was conditioned by ideology: Spanish militarism, the international eugenics movement,[22] the pretended survival of the concept of 'purity of the blood' (*limpieza de sangre*) as cultivated in the sixteenth century by the Spanish aristocracy, and Catholicism's conception of purity and purification were all significant.[23] Although the significance of this strict division to those doing the fighting and the dying is, naturally, difficult to evaluate, the routinised nature of the killing, in what was to be a 'war without quarter', was accompanied by and seemed to require a strict differentiation between the two sides which was reflected in all the subsequent constructions of the *Patria* and the 'Anti-*Patria*' under Franco.

The language of purification was the medium for articulating 'reconstruction' in the post-war. Violence was seen as a means not only to social improvement but to the very life of the Nation: it was 'patriotic impatience', necessary to transcend 'Spain's death'.[24] To witness, during a time dominated by 'frivolity and shallowness', life 'lived as a holocaust' was 'beautiful'; to experience an 'insatiable thirst for immortality'.[25] This kind of 'cleansing' (*limpieza*) was linked to a desire to 'regenerate' Spain which was seen as a decaying entity.[26] The best thing about what was called 'Hitlerism' was its 'task of moral and political cleansing'.[27] Hitler 'is convinced that his people cannot recover while Jews and the parasites of international organisations are enclosed with them inside the nation . . . and for this reason persecutes both without respite and without quarter'.[28] This was a very widespread conviction within the ideological ambience, Catholic, Falangist, militarist, of the regime. One of these ideologues, Vicente Gay y Forner, professor of economics at Valladolid University, and appointed as Franco's Delegate of Press and Propaganda after the July 1936 rebellion, expressed his fervent admiration for Nazi Germany: 'Personal security' was 'completely defended' there, 'order rules all public life' and 'property is guaranteed'. The suppression of political parties, imprisonments and anti-Semitic measures were the logical outcome of a need to 'renovate the state'. Thus, at least one leading intellectual of the Spanish right saw Dachau as 'a truly educating establishment' where prisoners lived as in a kind of 'hygienicised village'.[29] Repressive institutions, Catholicism and psychology were to intersect where Francoist ideology and practice met. The task of the concentration camps which were to be a prominent feature of Francoist society as territory fell to the Nationalists during the Civil War and in the 1940s was 'political and religious disinfection'.[30]

According to Franco, 'the suffering of a nation at a particular point of its history is no caprice: it is spiritual punishment, the punishment which God imposes upon a distorted life, upon an unclean history'.[31] He summarised succinctly the objectives of the repression: Only those 'capable of loving the Fatherland, of working and struggling for it, of adding their grain of sand to the common effort' would be tolerated. The others could not be allowed back into 'social circulation . . . Wicked, deviant, politically and morally poisoned elements . . . those without possible redemption within the human order,'[32] those of 'inferior national and human quality'.[33] Salvation for such people could only come through labour.

Purifying language derived, in part, from the discourse of 'cleansing' articulated via the Catholic Church.[34] Catholic doctrine commended bloodshed in particular circumstances: in ascetic mortification of the flesh, as a voluntary act of self-imposed suffering, or as patriotic self-sacrifice.[35] The latter idea graphically accompanied the suffering of economic self-sufficiency in the aftermath of the war.[36] The 'personification' of Spain, as a living entity, in regime discourse, meant that its [her] 'flesh' suffered. The war, once it became clear that it would not be concluded rapidly, was depicted by the church as a violent form of Lent, during which Spaniards would expiate sins and do penitence, purifying themselves through the spilling of blood. This was seen as preparation for the 'Resurrection' which would come with victory. More important, it was the punishment of 'God's justice' upon a nation, 'so favoured in every way, and yet so ungrateful'.[37]

One model for the 'purity' which was the ideal depicted by the Catholic-Francoist discourse was Saint Teresa of Ávila who was pure because she was believed to be of 'a noble family', an 'old Christian family . . . clean of any strain [raza] or blemish [mácula] of Moors or of Jews.'[38] According to the fifteenth-century Statutes of the Purity of Blood, periodically reinvoked, these other races were to be excluded from public positions.[39] Teresa was constructed as 'immaculate', lit-

Figure 3 Saint Teresa's Day, 15 October 1941. Oath of loyalty, in the
cathedral, of young women (*flechas*) on graduating into the Sección Femenina.
(Arxiu Fotogràfic, Arxiu Històric de la Ciutat, Barcelona.)

erally, 'un-stained', and, as such, became a Francoist symbol as 'the
Saint of the Race' and the exemplification of 'pure Spanish womanhood'. This sanitised image was widely disseminated and, during the
Civil War and in its aftermath, repeated acts of penitence were done in
her name.[40] During periods of 'national cataclysm' a modern version of
certification of 'purity' to denote 'fidelity to a regime' emerged.[41]

The school textbooks used during the dictatorship perpetuated this
idea of purity: 'Another decision made by the Catholic monarchs, to
purify strange elements and to unite the Spanish race spiritually, was to
expel the Jews and the Moors'.[42] This kind of discourse was developed
further in order to suggest that the Spanish *conquistadores* of the period
had 'purified' the blood of indigenous peoples during the conquest of
empire. The argument about the hierarchy of races was employed both
to suggest a Spanish superiority, in the Franco years, and, effectively, to
justify the rape of colonised women during the imperial conquest, a
reflection of Francoist views of women too.[43] In Falangist ideology the
idea of empire, suggesting racial superiority, was as important as the
material reality, which always remained beyond Spain's capability in the
years of the post-war. The *idea* could be used to 'form consciousness'
which would be 'tense', 'obstinate' and 'struggling'.[44] Racism and the

idea of empire were also perceived as a proselytising force in the defence against regional nationalism.[45]

Women, purity, psychiatry

The families of 'the guilty', those punished for political crimes, were stigmatised and made to suffer. In Seville, during the Civil War, prisoners' families had Nationalist soldiers billeted on them[46] and rape became an integral part of the conquest.[47] Under the provisions of the Law of Political Responsibilities, proclaimed in February 1939, those 'convicted' often had their possessions confiscated in a form of political robbery.[48] One woman of thirty-five, whose husband had been executed in the Campo de la Bota, in Barcelona, in April 1939, was interrogated by the authorities to see if she had goods of any kind to confiscate and made to swear that she received no fixed wage. She provided for her two children by doing housework from place to place and working casually at the engineering factory of Hispano Suiza, for which she received 7 pesetas a day.[49] The property or money of individuals who had died in detention were pursued relentlessly by the authorities. A widow of fifty-eight, for example, sentenced to fifteen years for 'a crime of military rebellion', and who had died in prison was later fined 2,000 pesetas, though she had no goods and her family had fled the Francoist advance.[50] In practice, Falangists were given *carte blanche* to go to family dwellings and make off with whatever they pleased. Cruelty was at once institutional and capricious. Often a woman deprived of the principal breadwinner of the household would lose her only means of making a living in this way.[51] A sewing machine, for example, used as a way of making ends meet through taking in piece-work from a local textile factory and improvising rudimentary clothing for the family might be confiscated as a way of 'redeeming' the 'crimes of the family'.[52] This was an element of the day-to-day economic violence which was inflicted upon the defeated in the 1940s.

The Francoist view of women was based on a highly conservative biological determinism, which saw the nature of male and female as absolute and irreducible. Women were seen as essentially passive, born to suffer and sacrifice and to be activists only as guardians of the moral order. The issues of 'moral re-education' and purification were, therefore, focused on the image and behaviour of women. Females were potentially the carriers of purity, but also associated with possible impurity. Their purity was a possible brake on men's moral corruption, but their bodies were the source of dirt and contamination.

Women were seen as being guilty of failing to maintain a 'moral vigilance' over their families and particularly the men.[53] In 1940, there were approximately 30,000 female political prisoners in Spain and it seems very likely that several thousand women were executed in the immediate post-war years.[54] Being the wife of a 'Marxist' could be enough to be shot.[55] Families were subjected to a constant surveillance by state authorities so as to ensure no 'campaign against the state'.[56] The purpose of the Sección Femenina, the women's section of the *Movimiento*, according to Franco's Interior Minister, was to exercise a kind of vigilance over women, to provide a 'moral prophylactic' throughout society.[57] The authorities were indignant when the family-members of Republicans displayed any sense of confidence. In the first years of the Spanish post-war Falangists were ever-watchful of signs of optimism within the working-class population that the Axis powers would be defeated. This optimism, it was claimed, was often manifested in 'an insolent manner', an example of which was when 'families go to take things to the provincial prison to their detained relatives, they do so with ostentation instead of concealing their status as the relatives of prisoners'.[58]

Women also resisted in other ways. Wives and mothers who queued outside the prisons were often informed that their loved ones had been 'given their freedom' (the euphemistic phrase used to refer to the fate of the executed) the night before. In La Coruña, the principal city of Galicia, the women protested by staying day and night at the prison gates, effectively as a guard against Falangist killing expeditions to the cemeteries.[59] It was at the gates of cemeteries and gaols that the under-ground political struggle of women was initiated. To be a '*mujer de preso*' was to acquire a particular kind of political identity.[60] Women also usually led the small-scale and intermittent protests against the black-market activities of state officials which took place in the 1940s.

In areas where some kind of armed anti-regime *guerrilla* movement was achieved, mainly in rural, mountainous, regions, the authorities made the populace in general suffer.[61] The so-called '*pacto del hambre*', ensuring that the wives of *guerrilleros* had no employment and, therefore, no food to live, was widely enforced by the authorities.[62] The tactic of starving out the 'Reds' was used, subjecting entire villages to martial law and curfew regimes.[63] Any shelter given to the *maquis* was punishable by death.[64] Women, for example, were imprisoned as 'bait' for *guerrilla* fighters on the run.[65] They were particular targets for repression against families, reflecting a gender-specific aspect of Francoist violence.

The contradiction between purity and impurity was revealed in discrimination against women. In repressing minds and bodies, the Catholic Church under the Franco regime went to extremes in targeting women particularly.[66] In some girls' schools, children were not permitted to take communion during the days of the menstrual cycle. In 1940, an attempt was made to resurrect the *post-partum* benediction symbolically to purify new mothers, who had to wait on their knees outside the doors of the church to receive a priest's blessing before entering.[67] And yet, women, it was believed, maintained a deep-seated religious belief, even if they did not practise. Isabel la Católica, the various incarnations of the Virgin Mary and St Teresa of Avila were the main examples of rectitude, mystical suffering and forbearance to be followed. Isabel was 'the mother-figure for Spaniards' and held the 'moral maternity of Spain'. The Virgin was the maternal symbol *par excellence*, useful also because, according to the authorities, she lacked power, served and sacrificed, but was also 'unblemished'.[68]

Laws particularly aimed at women, like those for 'the protection of the birth rate' (24 January 1941), against abortion (21 January 1941 – abortion was considered a crime against the state[69]), against adultery, and against infanticide (both 11 May 1942), and against divorce (26 October, 1939), were explicitly shaped by categories of 'crimes against morality', expressed with vague terms like '*escándalo*', or '*faltas a la moral*' and the Patronato de Protección a la Mujer was established in March 1942, by the Ministry of *Justice*, to ensure the 'moral dignification of women' through Catholic instruction.[70] The objective was to impart christian virtues and maintain the family as the bedrock of social stability. This necessarily implied, in the view of the regime, keeping women in the home to 'keep watch' over the morality of the family. Work, in itself, was seen as 'always good, a merit, a laudable fact' but also as 'a punishment for original sin'. And if woman already received 'her own punishment for her first sin, why throw upon her shoulders another additional punishment? Precisely that which seems to be the special punishment of men?'[71] In reality, the dire economic conditions of the post-war decade forced working-class women to work outside the home, where they were exploited hugely, boosting the accumulatory process of business.[72]

The Church's concern for 'the personality of woman' faced with the threats posed by 'fashion, luxury, books, liberalism and freemasonry, theosophy and spiritualism', which caused females to fall into the grip of the devil, was well attested.[73] Women's direct role in Republican popular politics and subsequent involvement in defending the revolution once the war began had shocked 'traditionalist' right-wingers. Women linking arms and marching through the streets in support of revolutionary action were seen as 'the dregs of society', 'dross' (*escoria*), 'whores' (*mujerzuelas*) displaying an 'unbridled lust', and profoundly disturbed those who believed in the maintenance of the existing social order.[74] They were seen as hating their sex, since they went beyond what was natural to it. The 'purity' of society depended on women: the devil, evil and sin were revealed in men when women failed to conform.[75] Women who worked in the textile factories of Málaga who donned blue overalls, the emblem of revolutionary *milicianas* and of a 'new woman', marked themselves out for punishment in the aftermath of the war.[76]

In the Spanish post-war women found out in the streets late at night, or buying or selling on the black market in order to scrape a living together, were often arrested and forced to ingest castor oil or even petrol as a punishment for infringing the moral or political code of the state.[77] The tradition of penitents' caps, worn during the time of the Inquisition, was superseded by ritual shaving. The victim with the shaved head was displayed ritually in order to shame, having sinned against a masculine idea of 'honour'. It also perhaps designated the victim as a bearer of collective guilt.[78] Shaving was certainly seen as a kind of purifying 'treatment' and became a symbol of the early post-war years.[79] A popular song of the time, when small-time trading on the black market was a way of surviving and being relatively independent, warns a woman that if she is caught illegally selling produce she will have her head shaved by the *Guardia*. Another, which became a kind of alternative anthem in the early 1940s, tells of 'Pelona', the woman with a shaved head, whose four remaining hairs she sold on the black market, to get by.[80] The prisoners' song of the women's prison of Ventas in Madrid was also about '*triste pelona mía*' ('my sad hairless one').[81]

Men who were political prisoners, who were sometimes shown in state newsreel films saluting Franco,[82] also had their heads shaved, although the significance was somewhat different, and working-class children were shaved as protection from the diseases which were rife in the social conditions of the 1940s. Other 'purifying treatments', such as the administering of castor oil or the forcing of humiliating acts of labour, like cleaning public places, for example, churches, the victim often adorned with a graphic sign around her neck with her 'crimes' inscribed upon it, were commonplace. Ingesting castor oil, it was said, was a laxative aid to 'purging communism from bodies'.[83]

The hypocrisy and corruption of the victorious culture was demonstrated in the prevalence of prostitution in the Spanish post-war which was not illegal and was a further element of the economic violence of the regime and of the disarticulation of resistance through economic marginalisation.[84] In Francoist 'purification' there was at once an image of 'morality' and a reality of power. Establishments were set up in order to house 'lost women' (*'mujeres extraviadas'*), and bring about their 'moral and physical regeneration through treatment', when the previous system of fortnightly detentions of women proved inefficient.[85] Those who were dedicated to 'the vile trade' might contaminate other women in prison also because of 'Red crimes' but 'honourable in the sexual order'.[86] 'Wine, music and laughter [were] the opium to forget their tragic situation and deceive themselves . . . But when the soul is brought peace through silence, order, the offer of honest shelter and the word of God, deception vanishes'.[87]

The 'health of the race' meant both a concern with the maintenance of population levels *and* the mental or moral condition of the populace. Unless there were more families with many children the country would be 'without producers and consumers, the state without soldiers and the Nation without blood'.[88] Demographic decline was created by the Civil War itself and by the extremely high infant mortality rate in its aftermath.[89] But it was also associated with a modern, twentieth-century dread of bacteria and fears of moral contamination. 'Mental hygiene' was frequently and explicitly equated with 'moral hygiene' by the mass psychopathology of Francoism. The principal aim of the various studies carried out as part of the response to this panic was to analyse the relationship between 'the bio-psychological qualities of the subject and politico-democratic-communist fanaticism'.

The search was for 'the presence of anti-social psychopaths within the Marxist masses', who were motivated by deep 'resentments'. This resentment was explicitly related to the 'secularization of life'.[90] It was no coincidence that, according to the regime's emergent psychiatric orthodoxy, there were 'collectivities' of such men and women in Russia, the site of Marxist revolution.[91] This 'resentment' represented, above all, a 'subversion of values': 'hatred of God, hatred of the *Patria*, hatred of the self'. This thinking was reflected at lower levels within the state. A leading officer of the *Guardia Civil* explained 'Marxist criminality', in part, by a 'subversion of values which brought with it hatred and resentment'.[92]

Perceptions of criminality were determined by the scientific-Catholic discourse of the regime, although some credence was also given to the power of unconscious mental activity. Within all such 'criminals', so full of resentment, there was always 'a real Marxist', even if not organised within the ranks of socialism and, it appeared, even if 'the Marxist' did not know it. The solution lay in reinforcing cultural nationalism, primarily through Catholic thought. Psychiatry thereby contributed to a recasting of socially conditioned political protest into the idiom of a 'mental problem': 'The madman becomes sane through pain, and, in the same way . . . Catalonia will become healthy again'.[93] Marxism was a 'sickness' and its 'treatment' lay with psychiatrists, as well as with firing squads.[94] But Francoist psychiatrists also apparently believed that *Spanish* Marxism was a product of organic matter like Jewish and Moorish blood, and *foreign* Marxism derived from pure Semitic stock. In 'explaining Marxism' the regime's mental doctors drew on an eclectic body of ideas that in the context of civil war had repressive implications.

Among the many state documents which have been destroyed, or disappeared, over the long course of the Franco dictatorship (and subsequently?) is a report (still listed in the archive of the Servicio Histórico Militar), written in 1938, dealing with the creation of an office or laboratory of 'psychological investigations' charged with analysing 'the bio-psychic roots of Marxism'.[95] This was a centre which was established under the auspices of the Psychiatric Services of the Army of Franco, for the purposes of psychological studies of prisoners in Francoist concentration camps.[96] The director of this department was Antonio Vallejo-Nágera (1889–1960), first professor of psychiatry in Madrid[97] and author of numerous works published during the Civil War and subsequently about the 'eugenics of Spanishness' and the 'regeneration of the race', as well as 'madness and war'.[98] Vallejo-Nágera had begun work in the Spanish army's department of health in 1910 and during the First World War was attaché in Berlin. By the time of the Spanish Civil War he was professor of psychiatry in the Military Academy of Health.[99] During the conflict Vallejo-Nágera established fourteen psychiatric clinics in the Nationalist zone.[100]

His eugenic racism was informed by a military training and mind expressed in 'social militarism', an idea of enclosed hierarchy which determined many aspects of Franco's rule, including economic policy, and much of the reality of everyday life under the long dictatorship. General Mola had already, in 1934, argued that 'militarism constitutes in itself a society that creates a civilisation, that is to say, a morality . . . with the objective of the exaltation of the *Patria* by one simple system: war'. This may not have been in accord with 'contemporary philosophical theories' but it would guarantee 'unswerving justice'.[101]

The 'anti-militarism' of the Republic was seen as 'suicidal' for 'a people [which was] eminently military: as much military by its blood and education as it [was] Christian through its deep-rooted faith'.[102] According to Vallejo-Nágera, militarism meant 'order, discipline, personal sacrifice, conscientiousness in service. The military phial contains the pure essences of social virtues, as well as bodily and spiritual vigour'. A 'public and internal [or spiritual] militarization . . . of school, university, family, office, workshop, theatre and of all areas of social activity' was demanded.[103] Students, workers, artists could all become 'perpetual soldiers of the Empire'.[104] Children not 'inculcated' with militarism would not develop a 'love for the *Patria* necessary to defend it with arms when it was in danger': they would be prey to 'defeatists . . . paid agents of foreign organisations'.[105] In 1939, the lesson of 1808 had to be learned again: 'Spanish arms defeated the French, but as they went they left us their grim dissolute ideology'.[106] In order to achieve 'an internal peace and an exaltation of the nationalist ideal', both of which were 'keystones upon which the edifice of the state would be cemented', Spain needed to 'throw off the aggravating dead-weight' of foreign ideas.[107]

Vallejo therefore, was no maverick. His espousal of military traditions placed him firmly within the way of thinking of the Francoist elite: a situation reinforced by his affiliations with political conservatism. Another of the leading psychiatrists of the era, Juan José López Ibor,[108] who would eventually succeed to Vallejo-Nágera's Madrid chair, also made explicit the link between 'genetics' and 'Spanish values': 'Studies of human genes have demonstrated the extent to which we can speak of the hereditary transmission of these qualities'. Modern society could not rob Spain of the 'perennial values of race [*casta*] and of the military 'stock' [*estirpe*]'.[109] Society needed a 'select minority' with the 'aristocratic spirit' of the military profession as an efficient 'organism whose mission is fundamental to the existence of the country'.[110]

Vallejo was, prior to the conflict, a prominent member of the conservative anti-Republican political organisation, Acción Española which he saw as perpetuating the positive virtues of the Spanish Inquisition.[111] The ideologues of Acción Española saw its goal as reconciling Spanish traditions with economic modernisation. In effect, they stood for Catholicism, corporativism and capitalism, although they sometimes were critical of the social effects of the last.[112] As a supporter of this Catholic rightist conspirational organisation, Vallejo was inevitably influenced by the writings of Ramiro de Maeztu (1875–1936), one of its founding intellectual spirits,[113] associated with that generation which had earlier been galvanised by the loss of the colonies in 1898 and for whom Spain had been 'a great oak half-suffocated' by 'poison ivy' from outside.[114] Neither Vallejo-Nágera nor Maeztu were against 'modernity' as such. They simply saw the disciplining of the 'dangerous classes', through Catholic 'morality', and other measures, as an integral part of 'modernisation'. The 'best health of the mind [was] Catholic thought' Those who carried out 'such a transcendent labour as the hygienization of our race' could not 'separate themselves for a moment from the eyes of God'.[115] In forming a 'psychology of the race', the 'inspired conceptions of Spain's mystics', who had created a 'school of psychology', ought to be employed.[116] Unsurprisingly, Maeztu, the author of *Defensa de la Hispanidad*, first published in 1934, was invoked by Vallejo-Nágera in castigating those Spanish 'non-believers' who had no faith in the notion of racial superiority and in the 'collective spirit' that was the *Patria*.[117]

Vallejo-Nágera's extremely conservative 'modernism', with a quite specific, though contradictory, understanding of the concept of progress, was displayed in his attitudes to science. According to him, and in this he was very much part of the Francoist anti-liberal orthodoxy, 'the progressive intellectuals of the eighteenth century . . . brought the ruin of [Spanish] science, the mediocrity of our culture and the disappearance of the sense of moral responsibility in the people'. These intellectual *philosophes* continued their malign influence into the next century, bringing about 'the loss of the colonies', 'political revolts without end' and 'social convulsions' without contributing anything 'stable and organic'. This aggressive anti-liberal tirade was frequently, and not surprisingly, accompanied by the sort of anti-capitalist rhetoric familiar to European fascism. The drift of Britain and America 'towards communism', as the era of Baldwin and Roosevelt was perceived, began 'with the encyclopedists in France' and was then 'picked up with the liberal Manchester school in England . . . the criminals that made capitalism', through Free Trade.[118] Economics jeopardised salvation of the soul and they would be punished by God for propagating carnal desires.[119] These were typical views within military, aristocratic and Catholic intellectual circles. Self-sufficiency would allow for 'internal treatment'. The 'enemy at the door was obsessed by desires for furious revenge [and] the internal enemy had not yet been extirpated, hiding itself within weak souls, deceitfully behind the disguise of vulgar lives incapable of effort or in the frivolous entertainments and immoralities within easy reach'.[120] Communism had culminated in 'the monstrous copulation of Cartesian perfection . . . with the immense, mystical and bestial body of the Russian masses'.[121] Degeneration began with the Enlightenment: 'The Age of Reason indeed! The Rights of Man! The masses aren't fit to reason and to think. Rights? Does a pig have rights?'[122]

'Liberal Doctors' were particularly singled out, for 'speaking ill of tradition and the history of their *Patria*, adopting new foreign developments for the sake of it, putting us in danger of becoming the slaves of oriental barbarism'. The intellectual descendants of these 'progressives' were the '*infrahombres*' (*Untermenschen*) who were resisting Franco's 'Crusade'.[123]

Although publicly critical of the 'coterie of 98', Vallejo, like regenerationist philosophers and political thinkers before him, was primarily
concerned with what he and other doctors called the 'essence of the
race'.[124] This 'essence' could only be protected by shunning foreigness
and had to be perpetuated through patriotism: a race could not exist
without a *Patria*. Patriotism was maintained by the 'racial spirit'. This
inheritance was passed down through the generations and had to be
'promoted' and 'enriched' by each, and not 'destroyed' or 'squandered'
as the liberal politicians threatened to do: 'Race is spirit, Spain is spirit,
Hispanidad is spirit. Those races, nations and peoples which favour
foreign ways, will perish for not knowing how to conserve their spirit'.
This 'racist spirit' had deep historical roots, according to Vallejo-
Nágera, as the tradition of '*limpieza de sangre*' demonstrated.[125]
However, the modern, biological understanding of 'the purity of the
blood' was more difficult to achieve than the old conception based on
aristocratic military codes. Still, 'whiteness' and 'purity' were to be
constructed both in the language of traditional Catholic virtues under
Franco *and* in the 'modern' scientific sense of hygiene under Franco.[126]
Both were part of the 'legitimation' of repression. Moreover, the
language and practice of both suggest a great deal about the nature of
the ideology of the dictatorship and its brutality.

Although not against the mixing of blood as such, Vallejo called for an
'ethnically improved, morally robust, spiritually vigorous, Hispanic
supercaste . . . For this we need to stimulate the fertility of select
groups, for in biology quantity is not opposed to quality'. What was
required was 'racial regeneration'. Races were put in danger by an
increment in the reproduction of 'defective' and 'sick' strains. Medical
doctors could not be 'race hygienists' because they worked to conserve
the life of 'degenerated' individuals. This was a call for 'aristocrats of
body and spirit', demanding 'the collaboration of sociologists, economists, and politicians' ('of doctrine, not parties'). Physical and moral
degeneration accompanied each other. The new 'totalitarian' education
would have a clean and upright style demanding 'exquisite, honest lives
. . . Consciences without faces'.[127]

Although working with dubious raw material, Vallejo-Nágera symbolised his conception of the relationship between the 'physical health' of
an individual and the psychological well-being of that person in the
bodies and personalities of Franco and Manuel Azaña: 'Physical degeneration, bodily deformations, ugliness, are found to be, almost unfai-
lingly, linked to complexes of bitterness and resentment translated into
antisocial conduct, in the widest sense of the term. In comparison, the
attractive bodily figure, physical beauty, harmony of the dimensions of

the body correspond, in the vast majority of cases, to a noble and virtuous soul . . . the comparison of the figures of our unconquerable [*invicto*] Caudillo and of the so-called President of the Second Republic recall and outwardly express the respective psychologies'.[128] The chastely spiritual were 'beautiful', 'sane', while 'materialists' were 'fleshly', 'sick', 'mad'. General Mola brutally attacked Azaña in a similar vein before the Civil War. The President was 'a monster of complex psychological character . . . who must be confined . . . so that selected phrenologists might study what is perhaps the most interesting case of mental degeneration that has appeared since the cavemen'.[129]

Not surprisingly, perhaps, given this thinking and his background, Vallejo-Nágera viewed the rebellion against the Republic in terms of a positive use of violence against degenerative agents: democracy 'liberated psychopathic tendencies in all countries . . . gratifying low [*bajas*] passions . . . bestowing equal rights to the madman, the imbecile, and the degenerate'. Vallejo was in agreement with Mola, the principal advocate of a violent purge of the 'enemies of Spain', that 'universal suffrage [had] corrupted [*desmoralizado*] the masses'. Faced with the 'social levelling' attendant upon the arrival of the masses, where 'that which is most human of humanity' had been 'annulled', he called for an alternative to an Orteguian moral education in an extirpation, or at least, segregation in perpetuity from healthy society.[130] However, the death penalty and 'eternal damnation' would not always be sufficient to compensate for the violation of the pure principles of 'the Empire': it was necessary also for transgressors' off-spring to renounce the family name, in addition, in order not to leave any record of their having existed.[131] With a language, based on a kind of racial anthropology and, at times, redolent of the writings of Unamuno and other regenerationists, or the racist ideologues of their French contemporaries, like Maurice Barrès, Vallejo claimed that, 'A collective movement of the violence of the National Rising [*Alzamiento Nacional*] had to excise thoroughly the slime [*légamo*] of affective complexes sedimented in the race over the course of centuries'.[132]

In a similar essentialist vein, López Ibor insisted that in the 'Red zone' during the Civil War, all had been a 'sterile womb' containing 'everything which was inauthentic'. War represented a process of selection: 'racial hygiene' demanded this kind of sacrifice. The logic was that the war had to continue if the 'infection' was finally to be eradicated.[133] Vallejo-Nágera insisted that ' . . . the regeneration of a race calls for a policy which neutralises the damage which can be caused to its germ plasma by pathogenic agents, both physical and psychological, material and moral. *We share the view of the National Syndicalists* [Falangists] *that every race has a particular cultural significance*,[134] and is endowed with bio-psychological features which must be raised to become its external characteristics.'[135]

Vallejo-Nágera believed that the victors in war would be those who suffered in the course of the conflict a kind of 'paranoid mass psychosis' whose 'mania' would be a 'mixture of grandeur and persecution', rallied in defence of the 'essences' of the *Patria*.[136] Thus, war could play a part in improving the 'health of the race', both spiritually and physically. The 'delirium of imperial grandeur' experienced by those in the Nationalist zone were a positive impulse towards victory.[137] The conflict was understood in a straightforward and brutal manner, simply as an 'action of killing or dying'. The 'spiritual ambience of the Spanish war' was full of value in building a community at the front and in the rearguard of the Nationalist zone upon the 'authentic racial essence'.

This 'psychological essence', or 'national genius', could be found in many of the historic cultural icons appropriated or constructed by the regime: Cervantes, San Ignacio de Loyola, Santa Teresa de Jesús, Philip II, Hernán Cortés, Pizarro, Don Juan, Don Quixote. Those who supported the *Guerra de Liberación*, and fought 'for Spain' were shaped by these same essential psychological qualities. This departure from 'the material' for the 'pure zone of ideals' impeded the 'appearance of (psychological) neurosis'.[138]

Francoist ideology as reflected in the writings of the regime's psychiatrists was clearly and overtly masculinist. The stress on military virtues conveyed by gendered language suggests this of itself. But this also had obvious practical consequences. Females, in particular, given their 'special psychological characteristics', were not to be trusted with books. The middle-class girls of the Real Colegio de la Pureza, in Palma, Majorca, for example, were instructed that it was 'inadvisable to read books, other than religious texts', until the age of twenty-five.[139] Many of these ideas about social control, the Spanish essence and 'isolation' were displayed in a further study carried out into the 'psyche of Marxist fanaticism' through the investigation of 'female Marxist delinquents' incarcerated in the provincial prison of Málaga.[140]

The city, it was believed, had been chosen, before the war, as a site for 'marxist experimentation'. Degeneration and social chaos, explained ethnologically, was due to 'an influx of strains inimical to Spain through the industrial cities of the coast: of this taint in her bloodstream Spain must cleanse herself. She is purifying herself.'[141] Being a port, Málaga had 'imported all kinds of ideas'. Marxism had 'infiltrated the moral senses of everyone and all measures adopted were useless'. 'Citizens'

Figure 4 'A sad memory of Red Madrid', Sección Femenina de FET y de las JONS, *Calendario*, Madrid, 1940. An image of 'the other', complete with 'orientalised' features, against which 'the ideal' was measured (see Figure 5).

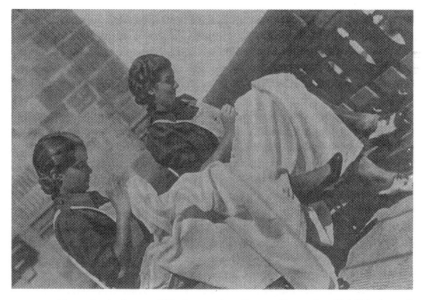

Figure 5 An image of 'ideal womanhood', according to the official ideology of the Sección Femenina. (Calendario, Madrid, 1940.)

were, therefore, 'forced into a holy war which would clean away sins from the *Patria*'.[142]

Through the use of detailed questioning, in studies after the war, it was concluded that 'the Red woman', and women in general, have physical and psychological features which are 'extraordinarily inferior' to men. There were, it was claimed, 'many points of contact' of the psyche of women with those of 'children and animals'. Secondly, it was concluded, through studies of women, that Marxism and the revolution had to be 'treated medically' not politically.

The sexual psychopathology of Francoism, demanding women's psychological and cultural 'closure', was revealed not only in the speeches of its leading figures, like Generals Mola and Queipo de Llano, or Franco himself, or its ideologues, like José María Pemán, but also by its psychiatrists. 'Red women' were 'degenerate', 'ugly', 'short', 'without the treasure of an interior life', filled with savageness and criminal traits and more sexually active than was 'natural'.[143] The devaluing of spirit led to prostitution, free love and a declining birth-rate which had bred on 'the dissolute germs' of a 'deeply rooted evil'.[144] In general, Francoist psychiatrists were convinced that Marxism, although they rarely defined precisely what they meant by the term, was a doctrine of the least intelligent and uncultivated, the 'sufferers' of which could, however, be 'regenerated' by an 'ever-watchful culture' able to draw them away from foreign ideas through the application of 'certain social forms': 'Spirit' could 'resist or direct matter and urges'. Women, in particular, as we have seen, maintained a religious belief, it was thought, which gave hope for the 'spiritual future of the race'. The regeneration of the race was 'necessarily sustained by the regeneration of the institution of the family'.

The 'traditional Spanish family' was seen as an agent of quarantine facilitating the healthy growth of a 'patriotic morality' and acted 'as a type of cell in the social body which forms the race'. The family was a 'sacred repositary of traditions'. The 'exaltation of the spiritual values of the people [required] an incubator . . . so that they might germinate and flower, even in unfavourable atmospheric conditions'. These 'cells', the family, could defend the body (society) 'from becoming infected and poisoned'.[145] Moreover, 'culture and religion' were 'consubstantial with the Christian family, which suffuses the atmosphere with a morally purifying influence that consolidates and preserves racial values. The Greek and Roman civilizations lasted twenty centuries because of the purification effected by Christianity'. The manner in which these isolated ideological constructions of family, of religion, of aesthetics, of politics, all become symbols of each other suggests a high degree of ideological consistency in Francoism. The regime and its supporters shared a common symbolic language that structured lives by including and excluding. All these constructions gave strength to the idea of purification through internalism, a self-sufficient rejection of the Other.

The notion of 'purity' was explicitly propounded through the advocacy of 'chastity' (*castidad*) within the 'military home' (*hogar castrense*).[146] Naturally, the point was not to discourage reproduction, as such: this could hardly be 'healthy' for the race. Rather, the aim was to prevent a 'premature outburst of sexual bestiality. To substitute animality of the appetite by a spiritualization of the genetic instinct necessary for the conservation of the species'. The propagation of 'virtue', by 'pruning defects and vices' and by 'reconquering the home',[147] could isolate women, it was claimed, thereby delaying sexual awakening. Personal 'defects' could be cured by a kind of psychological autarky, cultivating the spirit of a nun's cell, a closed, silent but sacred space within the home.[148] It was society that created impulses towards female sexuality, but, with isolation and concentration on the 'interior manifestations of life', it was 'easy for a woman to remain virgin of body and of spirit for a long time . . . Spaniards must be pure . . . for spiritual cleanliness'.[149] 'Purity' of 'ideals, thoughts and customs'[150] could be ensured by a modern '*Cuerpo General de Inquisidores*', modern-day inheritors of the mantle of the 'purifiers' of earlier centuries.[151]

Analysis of the ideas and work of psychiatrists who supported the Franco dictatorship suggests four things. First, fascism in Spain, as elsewhere, is linked to organicism.[152] The objectives of fascist regimes are to penetrate society in a collective and individual sense by depersonalising, making individuals part of an 'organic' whole, denying their bodily individuality in favour of a collective 'mind'. Second, in the process, social and economic problems are recast as medical (or mental). Third, inwardness and self-sufficiency was a reflection of a collective psychology of the regime in the Civil War era. Finally, there is, potentially, a certain totalitarian kinship between fascism and religion and, particularly, here, Catholicism.

The 'purified spirit of Spain', once precariously achieved and at great cost, had, it was believed by the psychologists of Francoism, to be staunchly defended from 'contamination'. Foreign and decadent ideas, evil spirits from outside, had to be shut out. 'Foreign' ways of thinking had to be silenced: Spain could supply itself with those ideas which were 'organically home-grown'.[153] In the pursuit of this objective, doctors lent their intellectual support to autarky, or self-sufficiency: 'Only an autarky of the intelligence will allow us economic autarky. Without it we will not be internally strong, and we will not gain the external consideration which our historic status imposes'.[154] Only once Spain had been thus strengthened within could her 'universalising mission' begin again. All efforts had to be concentrated upon remaking Spain's true history, her true economic, political, social and cultural forms.[155]

These conclusions were, above all, a dangerous confirmation of the dehumanising imagery which was already apparent in the writings and proclamations of Francoist ideologues and political leaders. Having diagnosed as degenerate those who failed to conform, or who showed themselves rebellious, the cure, in practice, was reduced to the crude application of violence and a dispiriting cultural and material deprivation largely devoid of any more 'subtle' attempts at the kind of socio-psychological practice vaguely promised by the Falangist eugenecists. These doctors gave little practical attention to the mentally ill in the post-war, dedicating themselves to dubious theoretical exegesis, leaving those in need of care to wander the country dependent upon charity.[156] 'Psychotherapy' only existed in official exhortations to 'redemption'[157] and consolation through prayer and moral rectitude. The 'spiritualist' and racist determinism of psychiatric thought under the Franco regime was a reflection of the reactionary ideology of repressive nationalism already prevalent during the Civil War. Francoist psychiatry could never adopt a sociological mode of operating, particularly once the period of the 'marxist terror' of the war was over, since this would have implied a shift from the spiritual world and the myths of race to the real world of the Francoist social structure, its exploitation and violence, which was a silenced intellectual domain, hermetically sealed, at least until the 1960s.[158]

4   The 'verticalisation' of Spain: the state and work

'Verticalism' and sanctified space

Spain's history in the wake of the Civil War can usefully be studied spatially. When reading about Spain in the early 1940s, it is hard not to be struck by a sense of claustrophobia. The most immediately evident of the many closures to which society was subjected in the years of autarky was a closure of *geographical* space, in a national and local sense. Within this, various hierarchies also limited *social* relations, movement and progress.

Social space, under Franco, was organised vertically, as were all the regime's institutions, and the idea of vertical*ism* dominated the organisation of society.[1] As we have seen, time was also 'vertical'; the regime's control of 'history' rejected the extending or progressing of time and its daily imposition of limitations created an everyday sense of static time; 'the morning, that morning eternally repeated' of José Camilo Cela's novel *La colmena*, set in the Madrid of the early 1940s.[2] The threat posed by the left, and particularly, perhaps, the perception of anarchism, during the Second Republic, had been one of horizontalism; an attack on the fundaments of hierarchy and a claim for 'un-directed explorations' in many fields: philosophy, politics, education, work and property, architecture.[3] To traditionalists and much of middle-class society, of course, this seemed like a clamouring for chaos, an uprising from the underworld. José Luis de Arrese, Secretary-General of the *Movimiento* from 1941–45, explicitly recognised the need to control 'all bodies that move within space'. If these movements manage to 'escape authority' then 'society would soon find itself wandering in the realms of the unknown . . . [towards] anarchy'.[4] Franco himself repeatedly called for 'a reinvigoration of the principle of hierarchy', as in Germany and Italy.[5]

Order had been 'bastardised' and it was imperative, at all costs, that it be recovered. Souls needed to be made strong in order to overcome dangerous bodies; martyrs of the 'Crusade' became moral effigies, symbols of eternal truths: the countryside, as the repository of healthy virtues, was supposedly to be given 'new life' to close off and surround 'unhealthy' cities, and the labouring masses were to be regimented in a rigidly hierarchical state-union structure.[6] In the environment of domination created by civil war, the victors' fantasies of 'modernisation' could be reduced to an intensification of repressive power through a mysticism of personal and national regeneration. A violently imposed vertical hierarchy, in morality and in the ordering of recaptured physical space, as well as in economics, extinguishing 'horizontal' or class struggle, was the way in which Francoist military men understood themselves and the world around them.[7] The ordering of enclosed space operated at many levels: in collapsing individual morality into a particular idea of 'Spanishness', Francoists themselves, as has been seen, made no distinction between the psychological and the social. Resistance was only possible in the narrow gap between state institutions and repressed minds.

According to the Francoist psychiatrist Juan López Ibor, the Spaniard was psychologically constructed of two 'vertical poles' which determined his scale of values: one 'spiritual' and the other 'material'. The first was a 'supreme force' directed towards God, with genuine substance, while the latter dictated the instinctive life and was earth-bound, leading to the 'mire [*cieno*] of . . . the lowest passions'. If the 'spiritual' failed then the 'instinctive', in Spain, could lead to nothing but destruction and anarchy. The 'horizontal postures' of man, concerned with the 'superficialities' of philanthropy or democracy, were, fortunately, hardly developed within Spaniards, but when they were falsely imported they led to a resurgence of the 'material', of the basest instincts. In their essence, Spaniards were 'vertical'.[8] This line of thinking is redolent of the notion of a 'cosmic axis', at the centre of a sacred space, significant to christianity: 'Life is not possible without an opening toward the transcendent . . . human beings cannot live in chaos'.[9] The cultural and spritual focus of the Spaniard was the 'diamond-like axis' of which the Roman stoic Seneca spoke and which was glorified by regenerationists like Angel Ganivet.[10] This cultural-religious verticalism constituted a pathological buttress for repression, authoritarian corporativism, economic exploitation and hunger in the immediate aftermath of the Civil War.[11]

Vertical hierarchy was also the only way committed Falangists could make sense of the future society. This is how they constructed the meaning of 'Spain's destiny'.[12] Although the *idea* of empire was important, to Francoist ideologues, it implied less a geographical and more a 'spiritual' expansion as a way of reinforcing the principle of hierarchy and of supplanting Marxist internationalism.[13] The single party FET y de las JONS, which replaced all other political parties in Spain in April

Figure 6   'The Cross of the Fallen' at the symbolically crucial ruins of
El Alcázar, Toledo, 1940. Flowers were presented to mark the anniversary of
the death of the Falangist leader José Antonio Primo de Rivera.

1937, was the 'intermediary between society and state . . . It is the
discipline by which the people, united and ordered, ascends to the state
and by which the state infuses the people with the virtues of Service,
Brotherhood and Hierarchy'. The old liberal state had been unable to
'order' political parties in the 'service of the *Patria*': it believed in
nothing, not even 'the existence of Spain', and least of all in organic
hierarchy. The new 'totalitarian' state would not serve 'the doctrines of
Rousseau', but put itself at the service of 'permanent truths'.[14] Schoolchildren were also to be inculcated with the positive virtues of verticalism: 'We will teach them that in Spain we no longer live with the many
bearing the weight of the few . . . but in a forthright vertical laterality
[*sic*], as in the formations of army units'.[15] In the wake of a devastating
civil war, during which all the values and traditions of Spain had been
questioned, society needed a 'New State', which would, above all else,
be a strong, purifying, well-defined authority, within a well-defined
space, able to orientate society. The war had shown how foreign
influences corroded society, heightening a tendency towards the 'frag-
mentation of experience', weakening the nation's moral code, its economic well-being and its territorial integrity.

Figure 7 Occupying and sanctifying space. Rafael Aburto and Francisco Cabrero, *Monumento a la Contrarreforma*, 1948. (Biblioteca de Catalunya.)

History, divine providence, self-sufficiency and the need to rebuild the state came together in the Francoist notion of 'verticalism'. Spain had been reconquered as sacred space, the Caudillo's great victories during the war, as he pointed out, having coincided, it seemed, with the main festivals of the Catholic Church.[16] Franco described the purpose of the post-war purge as 'cleaning the site ready for our structure'.[17] This was to be the foundation upon which the 'modern state' in Spain would be built. Sacred spaces that had been defiled by the 'Reds' became symbols of moral resurgence born out of sacrifice. The blood sacrificed in a crypt used as a prison, or '*checa*', by the 'Reds' 'fertilised' a humble group of new houses for the poor, with the benediction of the church, over the crypt which now became the district's new chapel.[18]

Figure 8   Flags offered by the Sección Femenina to the Army Corps during the Field Mass at the National Rally of the SF in May 1940 at Medina del Campo, Valladolid, the place where Queen Isabel, 'Mother of the Empire', died.

The 'irrigation' and 'fertilisation' of Spanish soil by the blood of its martyrs, would make the land 'fecund', giving the construction of the 'New State' life and soul.[19]

Time and again, in the post-war years, Franco would relate himself and his regime to the spatial and historic symbols of the new purity, pointing to those places, events, historic figures, and ideas that represented the extent of the country's own 'moral and material reserves'. The dramatic uniting of past, present and future was possible in the consecration of territory, as each region of Spain was 'baptized by the blood of our youth',[20] and in the evocation of the 'pure' medieval guild as a precursor of a harmonious economic and social structure, uncontaminated by 'horizontal' liberal capitalism.[21]

During the war, and afterwards, events and places were systematically sanctified through reference to 'sacred history'. There are countless examples. The Nationalist occupation of the vital mining region of Asturias, for instance, was celebrated as a breakthrough in gaining raw materials but also tied to Castile's reconquest of Spain, ending in the fifteenth century, by allusions to the battle of Covadonga, in Asturias, the holy shrine which was a symbol of the beginning of the expulsion of the Moors.[22] Another example of this sanctifying of place was Franco's homage to the 'martyrs' of the Civil War, evoking their 'purity' by proclaiming it from the symbolically rich Medina del Campo, in Valladolid, heartland of rural Castile, the place where Queen Isabel, 'Mother of the Empire', had died and where St Teresa founded her second convent in 1567.[23] Equally, and more famously, the Alcázar of Toledo, where Nationalist supporters had been beseiged during the Civil War, was turned into a symbol of a heroic, patriotic and Catholic past. One symbolic image, for example, was of the Angel of the Alcázar, a mystical figure who announced the possibility not only of purification through labour but also through the bullet: 'shoot, but shoot without hate'.[24] The very public ceremony of the transferral of the body of José Antonio Primo de Rivera, in November 1939, from Alicante to the monastery of Philip II's palace of El Escorial as its resting place is a further instance of this 'poetic' sanctifying of place and claiming of history.[25] Probably the most famous symbol of the 'Crusade' was Franco's unfortunate re-creation of an ancient pharoah's tomb, the grandiose temple and crypt of El Valle de los Caídos, as a pantheon of the 'Crusade', constructed principally by the forced labour of thousands of Republican prisoners, to house the bodies of the Nationalist dead in the Civil War and, ultimately, the Caudillo's own remains.[26] It was no coincidence either that the grandiose, triumphalist new Air Ministry in Madrid, massive symbol of military power, was constructed upon the ruins of the Model Prison, demonised by Francoism as the site of the execution of supporters of the military rising during the Civil War. Bricks from the ruined prison and from the Montaña barracks, where the rebellion had been put down in July 1936 with the loss of life of many rebels, were used in the construction of Franco's Victory Arch in the University City, again, a place of some of the bloodiest fighting in the war.[27] Another example of this sanctifying of memory was the pompous and ceremonial 'reChristianising of Barcelona' in March 1939, when the tragic and impressive crucifix, El Cristo de Lepanto, was restored to its chapel in Barcelona Cathedral amidst military formations and fascist salutes to the crucified Lord and allusions to Christianity's victory over the Turks in 1571.[28]

The Franco regime was faced with the problem of reconciling a deep suspicion of the city as harbinger of the worst symptoms of liberalism and the need to capture cities where the nerve-centres of state power were located. Thus, an attempt, at an ideological level at any rate, was made to reconceptualise urban spaces: to bind them to a time before the liberal state was established. The physical ruins of the war were turned into purified shrines, 'symbols of life and not of death, of fidelity, not of abandonment', and many of them were 'adopted' by Franco, father of the nation.[29] Ruins, 'stained with blood', were preferred to museums, because they were a living testimony of 'harmonious service . . . Stone upon stone rising up to celestial clarity, as death upon death has arrived there before'.[30] Madrid had to be reconstructed as 'a real symbol of unity, of hierarchy and of the mission of the state'. Before the Civil War, 'urban display was concentrated in the mercantile sectors . . . that constitute, by their materialist exaltation . . . a constant source of social corruption'. The city had to be organised not in the typical 'socialist' way, divided in great zones, 'like class divisions', but as 'an organ of the state'.[31] At a more mundane level, a vertical ordering was applied also to the position of individuals within space. Just as sanctification symbolised the conquering of places, so the state's vertical syndicates, substitutes for free trade unions, symbolised Francoism's conquering of individual and collective freedoms.

Work, Catholicism, fascism

The 'total state', a product of violence throughout Europe, although it remorselessly exploited images of the past, was equated with modernity.[32] Fascism in Italy and Nazism in Germany had created a means of protecting existing traditions while simultaneously adjusting to crisis and new methods of production.[33] Extreme nationalism had reproduced the fundamental values from which a hierarchical social fabric was woven, tackled economic crisis and supplemented 'development' with violence. Under dictatorship the necessary sacrifices seemed to have been safely wrung from particular sectors of society. The 'modern state' ordered society to face the challenges of the future. The basis was the 'harmonious', vertical organization of production and society, accompanied by the constant threat of violence: the coercive organisation of political and cultural space.

This was the doctrine of the economists, academics, lawyers, military officers, medical doctors, priests and businessmen who supported the coup against the Republic and rose to prominence with Franco's victory: men like the economists and bureaucrats Antonio Robert,[34] Higinio París Eguílaz[35] and Manuel Fuentes Irurozqui,[36] or José María de Areilza, the industrial engineer and businessman closely linked to Bilbao industry and a Falangist of the first hour,[37] or the ex-Lliga Regionalista figures, representative of the interests of the Barcelona bourgeoisie, Eduardo Aunós Pérez[38] and Rafael Gay de Montellà,[39] both close colleagues of Francesc Cambó, the political leader of the Catalan business and property-owning class. Military officers such as Luis de Alarcón y de Lastra, Franco's first minister of trade and industry,[40] and Juan Antonio Suanzes who succeeded Alarcón, most closely associated with the establishment of the autarkic trade and industrialisation policy, were also influential.[41] Among them were also Jesuits like Joaquín de Azpiazu,[42] Eloy Montero[43] and José Pérez del Pulgar, the priest and writer on science and industry who published a famous work entitled *El concepto cristiano de la autarquía* in 1939,[44] all of whom contributed to these plans for social engineering.

The 'cure' for Spain's 'sickness' was, first, to bring Spain out of the world economic crisis. The 'modern state', like that in Germany and Italy, was the 'organiser of the national labour', which could 'discipline, awaken, and galvanise the people' and, above all, produce 'sacrifice' based on an 'ideal': 'a faith, always accompanied by a hope'.[45] The appearance of political change belied the fact that the social structure remained essentially unchanged.

Spain's 'decline', the 'weakening of its essence', could be traced back through several decades. In the first twenty years or so of the twentieth century, strong leaders had been frustrated by 'great international forces' with their liberal Spanish social and political allies that conspired to weaken the powers of the state. The dictatorship of General Primo de Rivera put a temporary brake on the chaos: 'Spain had a few years of peace, tranquillity, order, well-being, and positive progress'. But again, 'international elements' did not cease in their labour, 'undermining the fundaments of the Spanish nation'. Primo's profound mistake had been not to rid Spain of the twin foreign 'diseases' of freemasonry and socialism. Indeed, the 'Red revolution' represented by the Republic was directed by masons, socialists, and the Institución Libre de Enseñanza (ILE), the organisation of liberal educationalists and teachers which aimed at modernising (secularising) education in Spain.[46]

The first task, in the wake of the Civil War, was the 'reconstruction of the economic and social order . . . organising the nation socially'[47] and restoring 'the authority of the state'.[48] An exclusivist political power was needed, in the shape of a single party, as in Nazi Germany and Fascist Italy, which would form a purely political elite, largely composed of the middle classes.[49] This organisation would also take control of the security of the state, centralising power and eliminating regional or local autonomies and 'the rights of minorities'.[50]

In Italy, Fascism had not brought down the old structure of the state, as socialism had, but had been able to 'transform and complete' its construction: 'Almost everything of the old state remains standing [in Italy] the King, the administrative and judicial institutions, the schools, the universities . . . The constructions of the new regime have been put in place at the side of the old regime. There is only one thing which is completely different, the spirit and the binding [*vinculación*] of authority, which now comes not from below but from above'.[51] The liberal state in Spain had 'found itself surprised by the progress of industry and by the advances of socialism, which it allowed to organise behind its back. As the country witnessed *economic* development, the state was becoming increasingly weakened *politically*. The 'New State' was now 'obliged to defend itself against two antagonistic forces: on the one hand the working class organised in unions, and on the other the capitalist class organised in trusts and limited companies'.[52]

Corporativism, advocated by Falangists, Catholic ideologues, business and the military, was the obvious system for maintaining property, hierarchy and order. The church would play a role in this authoritarian state: '[we] Catholics must not put ourselves in opposition to that movement known as fascist . . . we must receive it with love and direct it through traditional and Christian channels'. It would be necessary to 'harmonise the modern authoritarian current with our glorious tradition', through a 'spiritual disinfection', so that 'a new state [would] arise, free of the decrepit democratic and liberal traces [*caducas huellas*] which had impregnated our historical institutions'.[53]

Autarky, the state's economic strategy, had also to be political and 'spiritual'. Objectives went 'beyond the mere production and distribution of goods'.[54] Modern economic development, it was argued, had to be reconciled with the historic traditions of Spain.[55] It was not necessary, under an authoritarian government, to see the essence of the country's traditional culture and power diluted while industrialisation took place. Fascism in Italy had been able to bring together modern society's antagonistic forces, 'transforming work not into a *function* of the state as was done in Bolshevik Russia, but into a national *mission* under the direction of the state'. Man becomes producer – this is now his most important function.[56] The 'directed economy' incorporates all 'producers', while, at the same time, the state only intervenes where the power of private initiative is insufficient for achieving 'national' objectives.[57]

Stalinist Russia was also grudgingly admired, though. The tasks of economic development carried out by Stalin, through the sacrifices of the working class, were seen as similar to those which Spain faced. The country did not want '*socialism* in one country' but the notion of internalised authoritarian development seemed perfectly appropriate. In Russia, the regime had forgotten about God and allowed communism to breed hatred and despair. This collective 'thirst for sacrifice', without religious belief, represented a 'fleeing from the self'.[58] But in Spain, the 'moral force' represented by the Catholic Church was seen by the regime as offering a way of disciplining the workforce by granting the possibility of 'redemption' through total obedience to authority. The totalising concepts of the Falangist ideology severely circumscribed the meaning of civil society. Individual consciousness would be forcibly channelled towards a recognition of the hierarchies of Family and Fatherland above any claim to class loyalty.[59]

The institutionalisation of repression and the protection of existing elites was rapidly formalised in a bewildering array of totalitarian measures. In April 1938 a Press Law was announced to control the dissemination of information and freedom of expression.[60] Further reconstructive legislation followed, such as the Law for the Suppression of Recreational Associations (July 1939), the ordering of purges within schools and the education system (July and August),[61] and the annulling of all laws passed by the Republican Catalan Parliament, the *Generalitat* (September), aimed at making concrete the state's domination of civil society. In Barcelona, the first edicts of the military regime, installed at the end of January 1939, related, above all, to repression and measures returning factories and land to their pre-revolutionary owners.[62]

As part of the exercise to discredit the popularly elected Republic, and to justify the military rising against it as Francoism's legitimate moment of creation, a commission was established in December 1938 with the task of proving the 'illegitimacy of the current authorities of Republican Spain'. In the construction of a pseudo-constitutional framework for the 'New State' history was rewritten. A group of pro-Nationalist ex-ministers, professors and lawyers were assembled to provide the military rising with a spurious legal justification proclaiming the actions of the elected government unlawful. The Popular Front was accused of having come to power through electoral falsification, of having planned the assassination of the right-wing deputy José Calvo Sotelo, and of having provided the example for the killing of what the commission claimed ludicrously to have been 400,000 supporters of the military rebellion.[63]

Having attempted to delegitimise the Republican government, a task with which it was aided by foreign right-wingers in Europe and America,[64] the Francoist authorities rapidly put in place an alternative legislative structure, which, in practice, allowed an extremely high level of discretion and prerogative power to ministers, local military authorities, civil governors and more lowly party bureaucrats, while still claiming adherence to the dictatorship's broad principles.[65] This lack of guarantees, wrapped in a falsifying terminology, typical of totalitarian states, created a generalised sense of fear as well as an enormous scope for corruption. Class hatred was consciously stirred up and the denigration of difference institutionalised. The spatial pattern associated with the war was memorised and served to identify and limit.[66] Basic civic needs, like education, food, freedom of movement, were purposely neglected. Effectively, Spaniards became unequal before the law according to the battle lines drawn during the Civil War and to the constructed categories of gender, faith and nation.[67]

With no apparent sense of irony, the long series of dictatorial edicts issued by the Franco regime was initiated by a law against 'military rebellion', proclaimed just ten days after the illegal rebellion of July 1936 which, itself, was the first act of the embryonic Francoist state. According to the military rebels, the defence of the previous legal constitutional and democratic order became the true rebellion.[68] Under this law, which was not rescinded until 1969, a series of ill-defined acts became illegal and perpetrators subjected to trial by military court. This law, originally devised to control the civil population behind Nationalist lines, effectively became the hallmark of a regime which saw itself permanently at war with society and gave a semblance of legality to the thousands of summary executions carried out as the Francoist state was made.

'Crimes' were considered 'political' for the purposes of allowing a military tribunal to be held in each case, but became 'non-political' at the point of imposing the sanction. Political prisoners were denied the right to any specific consideration, as such, except in as much as they were treated more harshly than were 'common criminals'.[69] One woman recalled that 'what the directors of Franco's prisons wanted to show was that there *were* no political prisoners, and we had to take a great deal of punishment for insisting that this wasn't so. When a visitor came along and declared "There are no political prisoners here" we would take a step forward and respond that "Yes, *we* are political prisoners"'. The punishment was complete *incomunicación*, without food or contact of any kind.[70]

Political representation was formally restricted to the victors. Anyone who did not integrate themselves into the new single party – FET y de las JONS, created by Franco in April 1937 – was denied political participation in the 'New Spain'.[71] Imposed political unity was complemented by enforced national unity and, as Franco's troops approached Catalonia in April 1938, the statute of regional autonomy granted by the Republic was, according to the authorities of the Nationalist state, 'abolished'. 'Separatism' was seen as having provided the breeding ground for proletarian unrest in Catalonia.[72] Popular resentment at the perceived wealth of Barcelona in the rest of Spain was fomented to claim legitimacy for a policy of blanket cultural repression as Catalonia had returned to her 'the honour' of being ruled from Madrid.[73]

One of the foundation-stones of the repressive apparatus was the so-called 'Law of Political Responsibilities', proclaimed in the wake of the occupation of Barcelona by Nationalist forces in February 1939, but applicable to the entire state.[74] This law was directed against those 'who by their actions or omissions' had supported the 'Red subversion' or 'hindered' or opposed the victory of the National Movement. 'Evidence' about the background and political activities of the accused was taken from the local parish priest, the mayor, the police and the investigation department of FET–JONS. The juridical basis for the purging or purifying of Spain's economy and society was thereby reinforced. Those found guilty, often in their absence, since they had been forced into exile, were often formally 'banished for life (*'extrañamiento perpetuo'*) from national territory'.[75]

It should be remembered that this law was retroactive, treating as crimes legal political or trade-union activity going back to October 1934.[76] In practice, the state and employers frequently persecuted individuals for political activities dating back to 1917 or even 1909.[77] The state redrew the boundaries of 'criminality' so widely as to make imprecise that which actually constituted a crime. 'Justice' thereby became a very broad purge of morality, ideologically defined as party officials reported on individuals' 'public and private life'. Accusations amounted to such claims as 'subject to criminal instincts'. Mercy was recommended on such bases as a claim by a regime figure that the accused was *'católico'*. Franco, in April 1939, explained: 'Of course, given the fantastic amount of criminality some mistakes are inevitable . . . But nobody could demand that in so vast a work of just redress everything would be perfect as if we were carrying out a task of arch-angels.'[78] One individual who had been a member of the moderate nationalist Esquerra Catalana (Catalan Left) before July 1936, who joined the PSUC (Partit Socialista Unificat de Catalunya) during the Civil War, was accused by the Guardia Civil of infringing against the New State in having always 'flown the Catalan flag from his balcony on holidays and during demonstrations'. The report of the Jefatura Superior de Policía, however, considered the same man 'directly responsible for the spilling of blood in our beloved Spain', although no further evidence was supplied.[79] So-called 'mistakes' were built into the mechanism of repression, they were inevitable and desirable, since they helped produce an all-enveloping sense of fear from which it was difficult to escape.[80]

This repressive framework was completed by the so-called 'Law for the Repression of Masonry and Communism' (March 1940).[81] The preamble made explicit a perceived connection between these 'pernicious' social forces. Communism and freemasonry, apparently, were constantly present in times of disorder or at key moments of 'national humiliation' and decline: the loss of the remnants of empire in 1898, the civil wars of the nineteenth century, the fall of the monarchy, and, finally, the Civil War of 1936–9. The definition of a crime was again sufficiently vague to allow for wide discretion in delivering punishment. The disemination of ideas against 'Religion, Fatherland and its fundamental institutions', or simply against 'social harmony' were punishable by imprisonment.[82]

Work was also a forum for the imposition of power. In October 1938, in the midst of the conflict, the Nationalist authorities had issued an order for prisoners to 'redeem' themselves through labour, and companies were authorised to apply for work detachments to be used as labour in factories.[83] Food was desperately lacking and epidemics within the penal establishments in the 1940s were commonplace. In April 1940, the government ordered that prisoners not be sent to hospitals for treatment, since the uncontrollable spread of disease was feared.[84]

Through legislation, at the height of Spain's 'labour pains', the so-called Patronato Central de Redención de Penas por el Trabajo (The Central Association for the Redemption of Punishment through Labour) was created to organise the forced labour of prisoners.[85] Its founder was a convinced advocate of autarky.[86] Its task, according to the propaganda, was not only to impose 'a strict juridical order' but also to express 'Spain's mercy'. The idea of the 'missionary empire', developed in the writings of Ramiro de Maeztu, was turned inwards on to Spaniards themselves. The 'Christian missionary state', led by Franco, 'redeemer of prisoners', could grant this mercy once 'spiritual atonement and repentance' had been demonstrated through the 'physical effort of labour'.[87] 'Moral redemption' would come through work as the offender recognised 'the damage caused to society and to his own family'.

In theory, for each day worked two days were to be deducted from a prisoner's sentence. In fact, according to prison sources, by 1942 only thirty-eight prisoners released from the teeming Barcelona provincial gaol owed their liberty to 'redemption through labour'.[88] This was a grindingly slow way of addressing the overcrowding of the regime's prisons, but was, at least, a way of securing cheap labour for certain industries and the state.[89]

Prisoners were rewarded with payment of 2 pesetas per day, paid directly to their spouse, and an extra peseta for each child under fifteen years old. In the conditions of the immediate post-war, prisoners were anxious to help feed family members outside and, although the authorities often had to punish 'passive resistance' to prison work, in the work batallions outside prison gates, or in penal colonies established in state projects or private industry, 'active resistance' was rare.[90]

Attendance at mass was rigidly enforced as was the singing of patriotic songs each day and the ritual learning of the Falangist ideology enshrined in the twenty-six points and the regime's 'Labour Charter', the *Fuero del Trabajo*. When the motif cry of the regime, '*España Una, Grande y Libre*', was called for, the last word ('free') was shouted by prisoners with all their force.[91] It was a condition of release that the rudiments of Christian doctrine be shown to have been learnt.[92] The official newspaper of the Francoist prison system, *Redención*, took pride in claiming that the number of illiterates in Málaga prison had been reduced through instruction: 'Blessed is the Cross of Teaching that penetrates souls which live in darkest ignorance'.[93]

In Asturias new stone prisons were erected around coal mines so that use could be made of captive labour.[94] Parts of the region had been centres of revolutionary worker activity, particularly during the years of the Republic. In the aftermath of the Civil War, therefore, the mines were 'purged' and thousands of miners were executed or incarcerated.[95] Although coal was a central part of the regime's industrialisng strategy, a significant shortage of 'free' labour was created. The authorities of the *Patronato* argued in 1941 that 'at the current time the necessity of augmenting the production of coal and of various metals is grievous . . . from the point of view of obtaining foreign exchange with which to sustain the value of our currency and the industrial life of our country'.[96] Cheap forced labour was one way of extracting greater sacrifices from workers in the pursuit of higher productivity. Indeed, workers were brought daily, in this period, from the mines, fainting because 'they [were] starving – not in ones and twos, but in scores'.[97] In spite of such conditions, a constant simmering protest was maintained even in these most repressive years. In December 1941 troops had to be dispatched from Madrid to quell unrest, and in May 1943 the local authorities cabled the Secretary-General of the *Movimiento* in an attempt to put a stop to the sending of workers expelled from other industries as punishment to Asturias, since they stirred up trouble.[98] However, gradually, as a strategic sector of the economy, food provision in the coal mines was improved and company canteens legislated for. So much so that by 1945 the mines were attracting more and more workers drawn in search of enough food to survive.[99]

The British-owned pyrite mines of Tharsis, in the southern province of Huelva, had also witnessed violent class conflict prior to the Civil War. In July 1936, when the rebellious generals rose against the

Republic, the workers at Tharsis had formed themselves into committees in support of the defence of the government. Although the men could handle arms, since most had been conscripted at one time or another, there was a good deal of confusion. But 'every intrusion upon the company was carefully explained by the committees' and, although the leading figures of the right in Tharsis were arrested, this action was 'infused with legality and mercy'. There were no summary trials or executions. This was in stark contrast to the treatment of workers and villagers when the area fell to the Nationalists at the end of July. In Tharsis, four men, including the mayor, were immediately shot. This was the prelude to a cacophony of firing squads in the area as the appeals made to the manager of the mines to intercede proved useless. Though hundreds of men were able to flee to join up with Republican army detachments, the wave of summary executions and terror effectively cowed the workforce, and the mines were able to recommence work on August 24. The 'cleaning up operations' continued.

Probably about 1,000 men and women were executed in Huelva, in spite of the fact that there had been no outburst of popular violence there against the right in the short time that the province remained in Republican hands. In the aftermath of the Nationalist occupation the widows and families of those executed were expelled from the villages. A very thorough purge had taken place, leaving no hope of resistance. All fit men of military age were conscripted into Franco's army and workers were compelled to donate a day's wages each month to army funds. The company, not surprisingly, welcomed the return of order. The Popular Front government had obliged it to take on extra men and these, on the authority of the Nationalists, could now be dispensed with: 'The company was thus able to bring its employment into line with the needs of the economy and efficiency. Industrial peace returned. Wages, raised by the Republican government, reverted to the former level, just as war inflation began to accelerate.'[100]

A similar situation prevailed in the British-owned pyrite mines of Rio Tinto. When the mine fell to the insurgents in August 1936, hundreds of Republicans were executed and a decisive end was put to the labour problems which had previously dogged the company. When work began again in September, the company was rapidly able to increase production beyond the 1935 level with 2,500 fewer workers. Wages were eroded and workers now had often to support widowed relatives. As at Tharsis, one day's earnings each month was taken to support the dependants of men away on Nationalist military service. Tremendous hardship was experienced by the local population, although the company was able to declare, at the end of the war, that it had come through 'with its property undamaged'. Subsequently, at Rio Tinto, hundreds of men, women and children died during the winter of 1940–1, having lived for months on only about 6 ounces of bread and thirty or forty chick peas a day.[101]

In the coal mines of Arboleda in the Basque Country each prisoner was said to be forced to load 15 tons of coal per day. For this the official rate of pay was 25 centimos or 2 pesetas for men with families to support. Conditions in the mercury mines of Almadén were so bad that, even before the war, for reasons of safety, men had worked only three hours a day for two days a week. In 1941, they were forced to work for four and a half hours on three days a week. These prisoner-miners of Almadén were housed in the town's damp and filthy eighteenth-century prison: many died from the physical strain and the effects of the unhealthy working conditions. Men who were put on to work of 'national reconstruction' were forbidden to talk to the populace,[102] and contact with 'free workers' was strictly regulated.[103] Moreover, in Almadén the workforce had already been 'purged' of the most unreliable elements.[104]

Other coal mines, in León, for example, and another for tin mining in Galicia, also used prison labour. But even nominally 'free' miners were strictly regimented in the 'militarised' mines and factories, having to assemble for inspection each morning, sing the Falangist anthem and give appropriate responses to patriotic shouts. Absence from work was considered resistance and, therefore, punishable by the military.[105] Other prison labour was used in engineering factories like Trefilera in Gijón and Babcock-Wilcox in Bilbao, which was working 23 per cent overtime hours in 1940.[106]

At the end of 1939, according to regime figures, there were more than 270,000 held in the regime's prisons.[107] Thousands of others were forced to accept the humiliation of imprisonment in France, having been coerced into exile to avoid the likelihood of summary execution by the triumphalist 'New State'.[108] Substantial numbers fought in the French Resistance and many were returned to face a firing squad as Germany occupied France in 1940, or were interned in Nazi concentration camps as 'stateless' enemies. Between six and seven thousand Republicans from Spain were to die in the extermination camp of Mauthausen.[109]

Although at several moments the regime was forced to consider the reduction of the unmanageable numbers it had condemned to imprisonment,[110] the thought of granting a very far-reaching amnesty of any sort was considered impossible to contemplate. Prisoners were liable to be conscripted for the Francoist cause, though, while the Civil War continued. In the summer of 1938, for example, 1,500 internees were sent to the front from concentration camps in Murcia, chosen with the assistance of the local organisation of FET–JONS and local employers. A further 1,000 were deemed '*desafectos*' (hostile) and their fate is not recorded in the archives.[111] The Nationalist authorities were at pains to ensure the political reliability of conscripts. The recruiting commissions had orders to reject all suspected persons: 'industrial workers, unemployed, persons with spectacles, etc.'.[112]

Despite occasional and well-publicised 'amnesties', the rhetoric of 'mercy' consistently failed to reflect the reality. In January 1940, the government issued an order 'restricting imprisonment without trial'. While this order contained a series of startling admissions of the chaotic state of arrest and detention procedures it had little provision for humanising the system. It left wide scope for the continued detention of prisoners by the 'confirmation' of their imprisonment at regular intervals.[113] It was anyway difficult to calculate the figures, since prisoners were frequently moved from place to place to avoid the formation of internee solidarity. This was the popularly called 'imperial tourism', a term ironically invented to comment on the grandiose, comic, expansionist rhetoric of the regime.[114]

Beyond the prisons, directors of companies had to show that they would 'attend to the civic-patriotic moral formation' of workers in line with the dictatorship's idea of hierarchy. Many of the bigger companies built chapels for the workers.[115] This did not alter the fact that the vertical unions savagely drove down wages. The state's own statistics for 1948 suggest that real wages for men were only 50 per cent or 60 per cent of those in 1936. This was based upon official indices for cost of living and wages, which were notoriously unreliable. In a society dominated by the black market, then, actual real wages were quite staggeringly low.[116]

The Sindicatos Verticales

Self-sufficiency was an element of all of the modes of repression by which the 'New State' cemented its authority. The regimentation of labour, through state corporativism, and autarky itself were two interrelated aspects of this totalitarian oppression.[117] A hierarchical 'organic structure', according to the state's quasi-biological nationalism, was gradually established.[118] The 'organicity and the semi-automatism of the autarkic tendency' required 'social and economic collaboration in benefit of the nation' through corporativism.[119]

Employers and rightist political leaders had been calling for the imposition of an authoritarian corporativist labour structure through the

1920s and 1930s.[120] Under Francoist verticalism, 'producers', officially both employers and workers, were forcibly united in the national effort. José Calvo Sotelo, the highly influential leader of the political right in the 1930s, had summed up authoritarian corporativism as it was understood on the eve of the Civil War, calling for an end to strikes, lock-outs, demanding an end to the 'criminal destruction' of production, claiming that 'national production' was above all 'classes, parties or interests'.[121] A 'totalitarian state', a 'directed economy' and a 'disciplining' of the workforce were demanded. Uncontrolled workers were 'stirred up by the virus of Marxism': 'Each worker, considered as a citizen, thinks whatever he wants. But as a *producer* he submits to the national expediency, interpreted by a totalitarian state without class prejudices'.[122] The middle classes would not resign themselves to being 'proletarianised' as the 'inhabitants of Russia had been'. This call for an authoritarian state was accompanied by Calvo Sotelo's declaration of himself as a 'fascist'.[123]

In September 1936, all organisations which had supported the Popular Front government were expressly made illegal and the first state-union structures put in place.[124] This was only to formalise a *de facto* repression of trade unionists from the outset, as has been seen. In April 1937, the state's new Centrales Nacional Sindicalistas (CNS) were created as the state party itself was formed from above, integrating workers and employers in each company into a vertical union structure.[125] Chapter 7 of the party statutes made clear that the state syndicates would be run solely by Falangists themselves and that 'their internal order would have a vertical and hierarchical ranking in the manner of a creative, just and ordered army'.[126]

The reality was somewhat different from the rhetoric. Employers were permitted to maintain some level of organisation through professional guilds (*agremiaciones profesionales*), although, in fact, they came to rely heavily on less formal mechanisms of economic power, as we will see. There was no democratic provision in the functioning of the new state syndicates in each industry. This structure, in closing off any opportunity for representation or the articulation of dissent, provided an essential framework for ensuring that the main burden of the economic crisis fell squarely upon the shoulders of the economically most humble in society.

The panoply of state intervention in the labour process was completed by the declaration of the nationalistic 'Labour Charter' (*Fuero del Trabajo*), in March 1938, based on the Italian *Carta del Lavoro*.[127] The nature of this pseudo-constitution, a 'pathology and therapeutics of the economy', was implicitly recognised by the fact that the principles of private property and private enterprise were expressly maintained as the basis of production.[128] Property was seen as 'completing the human personality', and as 'the economic foundation of the family without whose basis it is useless to even think of autarkic productivity in such sectors as agricultural labour, or small and artisanal industry'.[129]

Through the promulgation of the *Fuero*, Spain became 'a National-Syndicalist State': 'National' because 'it is an instrument at the service of the integrity of the *Patria*' and 'Syndicalist' because 'it is a reaction against liberal capitalism and Marxist materialism'.[130] But no single group within the regime had dominance in devising the *Fuero*, or any other legislative proposal. While the reification of the state reveals Falangist influence, monarchists could also express satisfaction that specifically Spanish characteristics – Catholicism, traditionalist values, the family as social institution – were also given prominence.[131] In fact, the *Fuero* was closely related to self-sufficiency in its stress upon extreme nationalism and discipline, making strikes crimes against the state. Work constituted 'one of the most noble attributes of hierarchy and honour' and the right to work was 'a consequence of the duty imposed on man by God, for the compliance of his individual objectives and the prosperity and grandeur of the *Patria* . . . Work, as a social duty, will be required of all Spaniards without excuse . . . because it is esteemed as an obligatory tribute to the national patrimony.'[132]

As Franco proclaimed, 'freedoms opposed to the *Patria* could not be'.[133] The nationalist 'mysticism' represented by autarky allowed the regime to claim that in the pursuit of this patriotic economic crusade, all threats to production were acts of treason and strikers, therefore, were to be executed as traitors. As the new mayor of the conquered Bilbao, José María de Areilza, exclaimed, 'victorious Spain will submit classes to the strictest service of the national interest: No more strikes!'[134] Franco demanded that the war could not be finished 'in a liberal manner with monstrous and fatal amnesties'.[135] The main organisers of the first strike in Barcelona under Francoism were shot without trial.[136]

The concepts of work, nationalism, sacrifice, discipline, austerity and purification were blended together in an effort consciously to create a kind of 'mysticism' in the interests of a closed, hierarchical society and a 'modern state'.[137] FET y de las JONS, the state party, was explicitly charged with disseminating autarky as a 'watchword' through the press and through its various off-shoot organisations.[138] Autarky and state corporativism were indivisible, according to the Falange:

The reality of Spain at this moment requires a strong organisation that will safeguard her from all foreign interference . . . [T]he anarchic forms of liberal economies are totally ineffectual: what is required are Vertical Unions that will be a firm barrier to the competition of foreign economies. Bear in mind that their assault will be ferocious and that Spain requires that its *Sindicatos Verticales* have the agility and power of an army on the field of battle.[139]

This amalgam of ideas about strengthening the state and welding society to it were articulated in everyday relations and in the legislative action of the regime. The aim was to impose this construction by redefining economic, political and moral space, vertically.

The Falange, operating through this structure, saw its priority as easing social tensions by 'reincorporating the working class into the state', particularly the anarchist masses of Barcelona, through the application of the party's twenty-six-point programme. Party *militantes* were charged with proselytising among the working class, with disseminating a workerist message, but one based upon an archaic doctrine of 'the essence' of Spain. This was hardly a promising foundation: 'To believe that the old slogans, without any favourable climate among the masses, can achieve such a reincorporation, is a mistake.'[140] A 'combative spirit, capable of winning over the people of common aspirations' was required. The precedent of Bilbao, which fell to the Nationalists in June 1937, did not present a propitious example. Here, power had been handed over to the established social elite which looked upon the 'National-Syndicalist Revolution' with 'indifference'.[141] There was also disquiet in the Party elsewhere: in Granada, for example, a party militant articulated the lack of real content in the 'revolution':

What alarms me isn't that injustices are committed, they are inherent in the human condition since men are not angels . . . What alarms me is that with an old liberal and masonic style we are constantly mouthing empty, banal and pompous words like 'Justice' etc., and invoking wonderful-sounding slogans which lose all their noble meaning when they are not translated, in practice, into realities.[142]

This sense of doubt presaged the hopeless battle that party radicals would half-heartedly engage in with the real wielders of power in Franco's Spain during the 1940s, especially after the defeat of the Axis in 1945. The Falange was partly emasculated during the Civil War itself, having only recently found itself in a position of bidding for power.[143]

The so-called 'spiritual' elements of autarky, 'the will and discipline of producers and consumers', as well as the 'patriotic consciousness' of employers, were bound up with the practical requirements of the state. But this mystification was relatively ineffective in concealing the fact that autarky did not simply require the lower classes to *display* 'discipline', but was used as a way of *imposing* discipline. 'Patriotism' was a form of cover for the perpetuation and coercive enforcement of many of the pre-existing features of economic and social relations in Spain.

Spatial confinement was an essential defining quality of Spain under the dictatorship.[144] This was a psychological, physical, geographic and political internment in the early 1940s. It was made very difficult for workers in the factories or the fields to show any signs of dissent, and perpetrators were dealt with very severely. People were individualised as social groups were forcibly split apart. Indeed, as some Spanish novelists have suggested, for most people in Francoist 'vertical' society in the immediate post-war years, there were but two avenues of escape: upwards or downwards. Redemption, through sacrifice, labour and suffering, meant 'eternal life', according to the regime, in place of contentment and personal fulfilment in the material world. Alternatively, resistance in this period could mean a hole in the ground, or, at least, 'eternal damnation', according to the Catholicised official docrine. Only gradually, after 1945, were new spaces carved out by people, though the psychological weight of closure remained until Franco's death.

Part II

The practice of self-sufficiency

5   The politics and economics of autarky

'The limits of autarky always depend on the habits and customs of a country.'[1]

The political and cultural origins of autarky

The guiding principle of the Franco dictatorship's economic policy during the years 1939–59 was self-sufficiency or autarky. The factors that influenced this particular strategy were numerous, although historians continue to argue over the relative significance of each. The regime itself, and historians who have been relatively favourable towards Franco, have stressed the fact that the country was engulfed by world war within months of the formal end of the Spanish Civil War and was then 'ostracised' by the international powers.[2] The world conflict certainly made trade difficult, and the Allies, reluctant to provide Spain with food and other material when Franco's sympathy for Nazi Germany was so manifest, fought an 'economic war of movement and manoeuvre', using a little of both bribery and restriction, to draw the regime closer to their point of view. Britain's ambassador during the world conflict insisted in 1943 that Britain had to continue with a strategy which was essentially positive for Spain, and that,

economic sanctions, though in the last resort it may be necessary to use them, are in Spain more effective *in posse* than *in esse*. The threat to apply them . . . is much more likely to succeed than an actual withdrawal of supplies that turns Spaniards into half mules, half martyrs. The threat, however, to be effective, presupposes economic exchanges that are benefitting Spain.'[3]

Although the 'International Blockade' was used by the regime as a way to explain all of its own problems, it amounted, in fact, to a useful myth, magnified and employed ideologically to arouse suspicion of 'outsiders'. 'Ostracism' was never total: Spain continued to trade with both the Axis powers and the Allies. Indeed, Britain had always traded with the rebel generals: a commercial agreement was signed with the insurgents as early as December, 1936.[4] After the formal end of the Civil War, financial aid was offered by the US government, but this was rejected by Franco because he refused to accept the political conditions attached.[5] Although exports to Britain and France declined from 1939, in comparison with pre-1936 levels, trade with Germany and Italy rose spectacularly.[6] In fact, when news filtered down to people, through the firmly controlled state newspapers, that food was being exported to Hitler's Germany in return for technical equipment in the interests of Spanish industrialisation, justifiable resentment was expressed, although this was quickly repressed.[7]

More recent research on the early decades of the Franco dictatorship has drawn attention to the ideological commitment of the dictator and his advisers to autarky as an expression of extreme nationalism, a rejection of liberalism, a desire for national industrialisation, a sympathy for fascist ideas, and as a way of preparing for a desired role in the world conflict on the side of the fascist powers. Moreover, autarky fitted very well with a broader belief in the need to seal Spain off from the outside world politically and culturally. The physical and psychological suffering that this largely self-imposed isolation created was seen as being a punishment for the 'sins' of those Spaniards who had questioned the social system of pre-Republican Spain.

Economic self-sufficiency was certainly a disaster for the Spanish people. The value of total Spanish imports was reduced from 876,140 pesetas in 1935 to 342,754 in 1939. Exports were also drastically down, although they recovered more quickly.[8] Throughout the 1940s and 1950s, foreign trade reduced by 50 per cent on the 1935 level.[9] The Director General of the Ministry of Industry in 1939, José María de Areilza, was explicit in outlining the strategy: first, certain essential materials upon which Spain relied very heavily and had previously imported, had now to be nationally produced. These included fertilisers, essential for food production, motor cars and synthetic rubber. Second, imports of other items important to industry had to be reduced: cotton, machinery, electrical material, pharmaceutical products. Finally, efforts would be made to prevent the importation of a range of foodstuffs, some of the staple dietary necessities of the population.[10] The attempt to achieve complete autarky in the unreformed wheat-production sector was disastrous and, ironically, the country became dependent upon imports from the sympathetic Perón regime in Argentina from 1946 until the early 1950s. Amid the already bleak landscape of mass executions in the immediate aftermath of the Spanish conflict, as many as 200,000 people died of hunger during the first few years of Francoism.

The regime finally discarded autarky in 1959 when a programme of economic liberalisation – the so-called 'Stabilisation Plan' – was agreed. However, this did not signal a complete change of faith. Franco remained reluctant and was persuaded only by the manifest failure of autarky rapidly to industrialise the country.

The nature of the Franco regime and the way of life of those who lived under its shadow were intimately linked to its political economy. Ideology, culture and material reality intersected in a dynamic manner in the reimposition of pre-revolutionary economic and social relations.[11] It was to property owners and those who felt 'saved' by the Francoist remaking of the state that a Falange informant referred when he reported that:

[t]he public in general responds ever more in the direction of the current government, judging it irreplaceable since it has created an environment of peace, tranquility and respect for Spain . . . One of the main factors of our dignified and immoveable position is without doubt the posture of the Spanish government on not agreeing to any foreign loan. This allows for an enviable independence, economically, which is the best proof of the fact that Spain continues in her reconstructive labour . . . and that she possesses a great vitality, undoubtedly owing to wise government.[12]

The military and political groups that had organised the Nationalist war effort were in a strong position to influence the organisation of the economy.[13] Often, in practice, this influence coincided with the desires of economic elites. However, a return to pre-war 'normality' was neither necessary nor possible. Indeed, analysis of the social effects of autarky reveals what happens to political economy when, in the wake of complete social polarisation, a whole section of society is physically defeated and its aspirations swept away. There was an overwhelming desire to reverse all the legislation of the Republic, since it was representative of the 'Anti-Spain'.[14] 'Economic policy' becomes a way of confirming defeat and uniting those who could consider themselves 'victors'. In effect, the burden of Spain's catastrophic political and economic crisis was carried by the working classes and the peasants of central and northern Spain.[15] But those who suffered most, in general, were the defeated in the war, as if they now had to pay for their political ideology.

Autarky has been usually understood as referring to economics. Most straightforwardly, it signifies an attempt to achieve national economic self-sufficiency. In a general sense, it can be interpreted as an extreme manifestation of economic nationalism, characterised in the first instance by strong trade protectionism initiated by the state. Autarky has been associated with attempts by 'backward' or developing states to industrialise through import substitution,[16] or with strategies adopted by states preparing for war.[17] All these ways of rationalising self-sufficiency are relevant to Spain in this period.[18] Self-sufficiency in post-Civil War Spain can only be explained by reference to several factors.[19] Autarky was seen as 'technical', 'practical' and 'spiritual'. From the outset it was central to a totalising programme to organise society from above.[20] Only through an analysis of social relations in the aftermath of the Civil War can the Francoist 'economic strategy' be understood.

The etymology of the word 'autarky' suggests this overlapping of various kinds of power. *The Oxford English Dictionary* records that, historically, the words 'autarky' and *autarchy* have been used inter-changeably. The first normally refers to economic self-sufficiency, the second to autocratic rule or despotism. However, it should be noted that 'autarkic' states have tended to be 'autarchic' also.[21] Protectionist trends in the trade policy of some states in the 1930s and 1940s were, in part, founded upon a desire to create an authoritarian system of government, or, at least, were facilitated by authoritarian rule.

The *Diccionario de la Lengua Española* of the Real Academia, published in 1947, defines the autarkic condition as the 'quality of a being which needs no other for its own subsistence or development',[22] while another, complementary, definition suggests that autarky is simply 'well-being' and 'tranquility'.[23] Milton was among the first to introduce 'autarchy' into modern English usage in the late seventeenth century in referring to a form of government of which he made God the only judge: '. . . That absolute and imaginary Right of Sovereignty, that Autarchy'.[24] Francoism represented a similar kind of absolutism. In founding Spain's autarky (or autarchy) as a response to the political and social crisis of the 1930s, it was proclaimed in the statutes of the Falange, the guiding principles of the regime's system of authority composed in 1937, that the Caudillo would be responsible only 'before God and before History': if sovereignty resided in society it could not reside in heaven and, therefore, popular sovereignty was 'atheism'.[25] The attempt at economic self-sufficiency in the Spanish post-war can be seen as a mark of the modern despotism which was in the process of being installed.

Perceptions of the economy and society under autarky are, naturally, influenced by recognition of its many irrationalities.[26] The drive for self-sufficiency in Spain during the 1940s has been explained by most historians in one of two ways. First, as a strategy forced upon the regime by the circumstances created by the Second World War. Notably, the highly influential Falangist economists Juan Velarde Fuertes and Higinio París Eguílaz argued that the regime was obliged to opt for a policy of economic self-sufficiency against its will because of the exigencies of the world conflict when international trade was interrupted. París Eguílaz, indeed, in spite of having frequently recommended a policy of autarky, publicly, in print, and in private, at the highest level, attempted, decades later, to deny that the Francoist political economy of the 1940s was ever devised in accordance with autarkic principles. Claims that Spain had been autarkic were, according to him, simply an attempt to label Francoism as 'fascist' or 'Nazi'.[27] But the reality was quite different. In fact, the statements of Franco, his ministers, and leading figures of the regime prove a dogged determination to employ autarkic ideas in a variety of ways. Autarky was a freely chosen option selected primarily for ideological reasons. This is the second and more persuasive manner in which autarky has been viewed in recent years.[28] 'Political doors . . . were firmly closed' from inside, and the only window of opportunity which gradually opened was in the Ministry of Trade and Industry.[29] Indeed, British diplomats, who wanted a more liberal economic policy, sensed, at times, that there were elements within the regime who 'wanted to open up a little . . . to modify economic self-sufficiency . . . [and] . . . to increase trade with Britain and France',[30] but who were hemmed in by political 'closure'.

The idea of autarky, as extreme economic nationalism, had a long and respectable history in Spain.[31] An ideological preference, developed during the Civil War, reinforced this strong cultural tradition related to sacrifice and internalisation. Self-sufficiency thus found a ready reception among elite groups. More specifically, we might group 'explanations' into four broad categories: First, particular Francoist myths, usually a vulgarisation of identifiable strands of thought associated with regenerationism and Catholicism, were evident in autarkic thinking.[32] Second, the context of political and economic crisis of the 1930s heightened the importance of ideology, pushing 'solutions' to extremes.[33] The ideological input of the fascist Falange established links between violence, 'modernisation' and the protection of Castilian traditions.[34] The history of the nation was reduced by Falangists to that of Castile. 'Modernisation' had to begin with the protection of 2,000 years of Spanish existence.[35] Although in matters economic Falangist ideologues were poorly prepared,[36] this solidifying of myths of identity and violence – a brutal sacrificing nationalism – was instrumentalised during war and was seen as a way out of the crisis. In December 1938, Franco announced that 'the experience of our war will have to influence seriously all the economic theories which have been defended until recently as if they were dogmas'.[37]

Finally, although the crisis was far from purely economic, the protection and development of the interests of specific economic elites gave an impetus to autarky.[38] Self-sufficiency, then, in its totality, was to do with the reconstruction of power. In view of the strongly nationalistic nature of the insurrectionary coalition which rose up against the Republic and of the strongly protectionist instincts of economic elites, it should not seem surprising that autarkic ideas began to take form from the first months of the Civil War.[39] What is perhaps more surprising is how autarky in Spain in the post-war period represented such a qualitative change from the past. Franco's victory gave a degree of autonomy to self-sufficiency as an idea which was previously unknown, as it became the agglutinate of the state in reconstruction, affecting the totality of political and social relations. Friedrich List was invoked to emphasize the importance of the nation in economics: '[B]etween the individual and humanity exists the nation . . . Just as the individual acquires spiritual culture, productive force, security and prosperity by virtue of the nation . . . so the civilization of mankind cannot be imagined . . . except . . . through the development of the respective nations.' Economics was indeclinably to be dedicated to the growth of national *political* power.[40]

Complete economic autarky was never the goal: what mattered was that autarky was 'aspiration itself', it was 'force', 'spiritual, economic and social mobilization'.[41] Self-sufficiency suggested faith in homegrown solutions to problems of dissent, a unifying idea for society as nation, and a confidence in the 'power' of Spain to rebuild on its own: a fantasy of resurgence in isolation. This idea of 'purifying space' worked at several levels within a hierarchical structure. Wartime plans for rebuilding Madrid, for instance, relied heavily on three concepts: industrialisation, segregation and isolation.[42]

There is no doubt that at one level Francoism was a highly personal dictatorship in which there were no formal limits imposed upon the will of the Caudillo. Franco's enthusiasm for autarkic principles had much to do with a limited set of immovable ideas, to which he clung for decades.[43] These ideas, were political as well as economic. The dictator made no distinction between such categories: 'Political fortitude [*fortaleza*], economic fortitude, and military fortitude. The collapse of any of these would ruin the other two. Economic power cannot be conceived of without political fortitude and stability, and military power nowadays has to be backed by industrial and economic power.'[44]

Franco's priority was to maintain power by prosecuting his victory to the full in the aftermath of the war.[45] The most dangerous threat to the regime, as he saw it, was from outside.[46] Spanish national unity, which was seen as the responsibility of the army itself,[47] could only be defended by shunning all things foreign. Heretical ideas, like socialist revolution, were always implanted from abroad and the Civil War was conceived of in these terms. 'Foreign', liberal ideas were impossible to incorporate into a hierarchical, militarised society. Spain was, indeed, according to the military rebels, threatened by the 'Asiatic hordes of Moscow' and had to be united within itself to defend the *Patria*.[48]

But autarky did not simply originate with Franco. Political and social elites and individuals associated with the dictatorship grasped autarky for their own purposes. Self-sufficiency crystallised in the idea of a 'strong nation': the myth of an in-bred common will, a deeply entrenched shared 'national interest', and in a need for a 'treatment' of Spain. Ramiro de Maeztu, the evangelist of *Hispanidad*, had written in 1934 how the 'evils' of liberalism could not be compensated by material wealth: 'Today the hope that the world had placed in the ideal of free trade has been dispelled. The principal countries are fixing their gaze upon regimes of autarky.'[49] Autarky was 'collective benefit', 'the supreme interest of the nation', the 'progress of the state itself'.[50]

Autarky was not just economic but also political and social. As the Minister of Trade and Industry, Demetrio Carceller, announced publicly in August, 1944, 'to give free reign to economic laws, whose defects could not be cured by the moral force of society, led to anarchy'. In Spain, the end of her era of historic splendour coincided with the adoption of the ideas of the nineteenth century, a time which saw not only the emigration of kings sent into exile, but also of ordinary men, who apparently had the right to vote but not to eat and went abroad to escape economic slavery. While workers were forced to flee, foreign adventurers took control of the country's mines, railways and factories.[51] The irony was that this description of the country during the nineteenth century better fitted the reality of Francoist Spain.

According to José María de Areilza, the Falangist representative of Bilbao industry, to isolate Spain was to put in tension 'all the nation's resources . . . promoting the inventive nature of the race, the manufacturing skill of the workers, the productive capacity of businessmen and of technicians'. These general concepts were linked 'indeclinably to the ideology which forms the state itself. What I mean is that whoever situates himself against them, disagreeing or [going into] opposition, puts himself at the same time against what is the essential part of what the rising of the 18th of July meant and which brought us military victory on April the 1st, 1939.' To go against 'the policies of restriction and self-sufficiency, or the proposal of achieving an organic and syndical structure [for] the Spanish economy (was) equivalent to being an enemy of the independence and liberty of Spain and opting for perpetual social anarchy and class struggle among us'.[52] Autarky provided ideological symbols for the regime and it could be used as a unifying principle. Critics of the regime, it was claimed, failed to understand that there existed 'as many political shades [in Spain] as there are individuals in our territory, but that all of that range of shades is united into a single hue when it comes to defending the independence of our country'.[53]

Moreover, according to the panegyrists of the regime, the 'organic' concept of autarky had a 'moral' dimension. Poverty was elevated to the status of positive virtue, as it had frequently been in the past, signifying the noble characteristics of 'Spanishness'.[54] The symbols were weak (particularly since the Party was heavily implicated in the operation of a black market partly created by autarky) but, combined with the role of the Catholic Church in preaching a need for expiation through sacrifice, autarky defined a way of life before which attitudes and opportunities were highly complex and always culturally mediated.

Self-sufficiency both required and allowed for drastic measures of state intervention in virtually every aspect of life. Coercion became all-encompassing. Autarky and the defeat of the working class were complementary, the one facilitating the other. It signified 'the economic independence of a state in relation to foreign parts. That is, when the country, because of its position, because of the wealth of its soil and sub-soil, *because of the labour capacity of its inhabitants*, etc., is capable of producing everything it needs'. Spain, *'with some effort and, if necessary, sacrifice*, could achieve independence', at least as far as articles of prime necessity were concerned, once the agrarian policy of the *Fuero del Trabajo* and the state's complementary legislation were put into practice.[55] Spain was critically short of foreign exchange generally. Sterling and dollars were particularly scarce, a factor which threatened the grandiose industrialising plans of the Franco regime, which required machinery from abroad. The priority of obtaining foreign exchange was placed ahead of the need to feed the people and agricultural produce was exported to buy industrial machinery.[56] State intervention in the economy in Spain, as in Nazi Germany and Fascist Italy, put private consumption in jeopardy in favour of grandiose public schemes that might heighten national prestige. Autarkists throughout Europe in the 1930s and 1940s were not primarily concerned with improving standards of living. Economic autarky meant imposing sacrifices throughout society, and by violent means if necessary, 'justified' by an ill-defined but better and far-off future prosperity.[57] Resources had to be channelled towards the industrial productive base rather than towards private consumption. The principal beneficiary of this drastic contraction was the public sector. Private consumption as a percentage of national expenditure fell from 78.7 per cent in 1935 to 70.2 per cent in

1940 to 64 per cent in 1943. In 1935, public consumption reached an historic high, at that time, of 14.4 per cent. By the years 1940–5 the average figure had risen to 19.4 per cent. Much of this reordering of consumption was dedicated to military expenditure. In 1935, defence spending represented 22.4 per cent of public expenditure, from 1940–5 it was usually above 50 per cent.[58] Leading elite figures, like the director of the Spanish Central Banking Committee, Luis Olariaga, advocated a diversion of consumption from the private to the public, 'sacrificing' the former to the latter.[59] The political exile of the defeated was united with a kind of internal economic exile.[60]

Autarky and civil war

While the Civil War was still being fought the possible benefits of an autarkic strategy were under discussion among leading figures of the nascent Francoist state. A favourable attitude towards self-sufficiency existed within the regime well before the formal end of the war in April 1939. More policy formulations were forthcoming in the period between the end of the Spanish conflict and Hitler's invasion of Poland in September and the declaration of war by the British government. Autarky in Spain was not simply a pragmatic response to the fact of European war. As early as 1936 the leading economist of the era, Román Perpiña Grau, observed that 'the politico-economic system of Spain is clearly moving towards a complete autarky' wherein the protection of wheatgrowers and industry was paramount. According to Perpiña, the era was to be dominated by the 'constant influence of particular interest groups in the sphere of politics'.[61]

Among industrialists there was general acceptance during the post-Civil War years that the intervention of the state in the economy was a necessity;[62] indeed, the interests of the Francoist military and of Spanish industry coincided in many respects. Demetrio Carceller, who was to become Minister of Trade and Industry in October 1940 and who was closely associated with Catalan industry, declared in February 1940 that, 'the formula to consolidate our internal peace and our external independence, is, at present, and in the near future, an economic policy of a military kind, oriented towards satisfying the important requirements of a military order which the world situation imposes upon Spain, around which . . . the national economy develops, and which must, if only for this reason, be nationalist and autarkic.'[63] While the Generals, in particular, saw in autarky the possibility of augmenting the nation's military potential through the industrialisation already begun during the Civil War,[64] Spanish industry had proved unreliable in providing the capacity of military hardware necessary for modern warfare. An added impetus was given to the notion of industrialisation by the recognition during the conflict and in the aftermath that military operations had actually suffered because of the uneven development of the Spanish economy. In 1944, Carceller stressed that twice in twenty-five years Spain had suffered at the hands of two groups of belligerents and he thought it only right to make some attempt to produce in the country some of the essential goods which they were now importing from abroad.[65]

The most important ideological concept driving the insurgent war effort was nationalism.[66] At the same time, from virtually the first moment, the generals who led the rising resorted to foreign assistance in fighting the war. On 21 July, Franco requested military aid from Nazi Germany through a German intermediary, while at the same time a Spanish representative was dispatched to ascertain the possibilities of acquiring assistance from Mussolini.[67] This reliance was to have several, sometimes contradictory, results.

The military and financial power of Germany and the equipment and manpower sent by Mussolini, as well as Axis recognition of Franco's 'state' in November 1937, were to be of vital practical importance, undermining and, ultimately, destroying the Republic. Inevitably, Nationalist Spain gradually aligned itself more closely with the Axis powers, relying on advice and training from the Nazi Gestapo in organising public order forces and learning a great deal about the use of propaganda.[68] Moreover, the instinctive sympathy of the rebel generals for the hierarchical societies and economies of the European dictators confirmed this commitment.[69] Franco also remained eager to join the war on the side of the Axis powers until the fortunes of Germany and Italy declined. In August 1942, the Caudillo was still speaking of making Spain ready 'for the supreme test', which required 'moral preparation, military preparation, political preparation and industrial preparation'.[70]

The motives for setting up the authoritarian political and labour structures of Nationalist Spain were the same as those which prevailed in Italy in the 1920s and Germany in the 1930s.[71] As the Francoist state drew up the legal instruments which would shape its authority the precedents provided by the dictatorial regimes installed in Berlin and Rome were leant upon heavily. 'Order . . . [would] allow the country to increase her wealth a hundredfold and develop her constant and exploitable resources, so abundant in Spain.'[72]

However, reliance on military aid could only reinforce the sense felt by the insurgents of a weak and dependent Spain which lagged behind the industrial states of Europe. This sense of dependence was exacerbated by the fact that the rebels were immediately successful only in rural areas of Spain, where they could count on the support of Spain's traditional classes. Industrial Spain, meanwhile, centred in the cities of Madrid, Barcelona and Bilbao, with a growing working class, remained under the control of the democratically elected Republic. The Nationalists could count only on a few industrial 'islands' within a sea of agricultural land, like the British-owned Rio Tinto mines, occupied in August, 1936, to provide militarily useful raw materials, until the northern campaign succeeded in taking Bilbao in June 1937, almost a year into the war.

The potential economic benefits which Germany, in particular, might derive from intervention in the Spanish conflict were quickly made evident. Trade between Nationalist Spain and Nazi Germany was facilitated by the setting up of trading companies for the purpose.[73] On 31 October 1936 a contract was signed by which the Nazi regime agreed to take 840,000 tons of ore from the Spanish mines in Morocco. By February 1937, Göring was able to emphasise the increased German investment in Spain, particularly in mining, as one of the main effects of Nazi participation in the conflict.[74] In July 1937 the economic ties which partially bound the future of the Nationalist wartime economy and military effort to Nazi Germany were formalised by the signing, in Burgos, of an economic treaty which included a series of secret protocols which agreed to maximise trade between Burgos and Berlin. Significantly, Spain granted Germany first option on contracts in assisting in the reconstruction of the Spanish economy, whereas previously Britain, France and the United States had been particularly favoured in trade with Spain.[75] In November 1938, as Franco became more dependent upon Nazi military assistance, Spanish mining concessions were granted to Germany as a way of paying off part of the debt.[76] Germans had already received land concessions from General Queipo de Llano, Franco's military ruler in Andalusia, as well as the ownership of real estate in Bilbao, confiscated from alleged Republican sympathisers in an effort to liquidate part of what was owing to Hitler.[77] Later, after the Civil War, the debt would be partly repaid by sending Spanish workers to labour in Nazi Germany. In 1942, for example, 490 workers were sent from the poverty-stricken agricultural region of Murcia. In an era of political executions and starvation, Spanish workers wasted no time in telling their hosts they had gone in order to save their lives, not because they had any love for Nazi Germany.[78] Prior to their dispatch they were treated to a meal – a rare thing at the time in this part of the country.

Better food was also available in Germany; some of it had been imported from Franco's Spain.[79]

The British government, internally at any rate, had always partly justified its policy of inactivity in the face of Nazi and Fascist intervention in Spain by arguing that a post-war Francoist government in Madrid would not be 'fascist' but would constitute instead a somehow less repugnant military dictatorship, which was seen as being more acceptable. The future seemed to offer a 'liberal military dictatorship . . . capable of giving the country what it has needed for years: firm leadership, progressive ideals, education (not purely on clerical lines) and perhaps even equal justice'.[80] In particular, it was felt that Spain would continue to look towards London for economic assistance and trade. However, faced with the growing realisation of increasing penetration by Germans into the Spanish economy, particularly after the fall of Bilbao, which had historically been a bastion for British commerce, the British government dispatched a diplomatic 'agent', Robert Hodgson, on 22 October 1937, in an attempt to protect British interests and secure harmonious relations with the Francoists.[81] Despite attempts to play down the significance of this contact with the Nationalists, Hodgson was accorded full diplomatic privileges.[82]

In reality, economic autarky in Spain was always relative. Trade, particularly with the US and Britain in commodities that were of specific value to the Francoist industrialising project, continued.[83] The Anglo–Spanish trade agreement of March 1940, though not mentioned in the Spanish press, was of some considerable value to the regime in this sense.[84]

It was partly the reliance upon Nazi and Fascist assistance which, within a couple of months, made imperative some degree of rationalisation of the Nationalist administrative structure. Contacts with the Axis powers required a unified command structure within the nascent state of rebel Spain. Since Franco had been instrumental from the beginning in acquiring the necessary aid, his case for leadership of such an authority was considerably reinforced. Accordingly, on 29 September Franco was named head of state.[85] A few days later the Junta Técnica del Estado was established as the new directing body within the rebel zone.[86]

German and Italian involvement, however, was viewed ambiguously. Admiration for the Axis powers was always tinged with resentment and even jealousy.[87] There was certainly some resentment at the state of dependency which Spain suffered in relation to the industrialised world generally.[88] Franco himself pretended that the Nationalists were 'self-sufficient' and able to win the war with 'their own resources' and those captured from the enemy, avoiding talk of outside help whenever possible.[89] Calls for a nationalist policy were inevitable and were epitomised in the article by the Minister of Trade and Industry, Juan Antonio Suanzes, published to celebrate the third anniversary of the 1936 rising against the Republic,[90] calling for Spain to cease 'speaking in a modest and timid tone in the world (turning her) into a colonised land'. To speak 'with a new language': 'Spirit, unity and discipline, cultivated in battle and stained with blood', these were necessary elements for an economic resurgence. 'Spirituality' was the key: 'We have to be stubborn [cerrados] enemies of materialism, which is bringing about the ruin of the world'. Even those who had erred in the past, 'having paid their debts with human justice' could, 'with sufficient sacrifice, contribute to Spain's exaltation'.

Autarkic plans were already being drawn up.[91] As Franco declared in December 1937, 'we have no need to import anything, we produce with abundance and the standard of living is identical to that of 17 July 1936'.[92] The so-called 'technical' component of autarky referred to public-works programmes and the intensive exploitation of national raw materials. One of the useful results of such organisation, based as it was on the 'protection of territorial integrity', would be the development of the country's military defence capabilities.[93] As far as trade was concerned, 'financial technicians' would be required to devise a method which would allow for the breaking away of Spain's monetary system from the uneven relations imposed by the operation of the Gold Standard.

Franco displayed a constant obsession with Spain's historically negative trade balance, which was seen as the most serious problem for the country, stunting economic progress and 'development of Spain's personality'.[94] The 'directing principle' of economic policy, he declared, before the end of the Civil War, was the 'cancelling out' *(anulación)* of the deficit in trade. Any other course would allow 'the national wealth to continue being exhausted in this draining away of hundreds of millions which annually strengthen the economy of the exporting countries'.[95] 'Servitude [to] foreign economies, alien to our destiny', had to be resisted and reversed.[96]

As an agrarian economy, Spain was seen as condemned to become ever poorer while the industrialised world used her as a source of cheap food, at the same time depriving the country of her raw materials.[97] World-wide uneven economic development had condemned some states to a perpetual poverty, which exacerbated social tensions, provoking repeated political conflicts and civil wars. Spain was trapped within a world economic system from which she could only break free by isolating herself in order to develop her national resources.[98] The dawning of the 'New Spain' would herald the development of the country's economy. The population seemed to have burgeoned without a commensurable growth of the economy, while the chronic trade deficit continued to drain resources. Thus, unemployment and the low standard of living of the people created constant social conflict for which there seemed to be no easy remedy.[99]

The Second Republic had sought to resolve this dilemma through agrarian reform. But under Franco the notion of state-imposed rural reform was detested, accursed, or 'against-God'.[100] Agriculture would have to be protected while a native industry could, at last, be created, as the rest of western Europe had managed.[101] Agriculture was seen as the base of the country's welfare and Spain's peasantry, which had given proof of its 'great Christian and patriotic fervour', deserved the support of the state. Simultaneously, with the erection of protective trade barriers, the country would be able to develop a modern industrial base, including even the production of motor cars. In the process, Spain would 'stop paying out' to foreigners.[102]

Industrialisation, which, according to social Darwinist regenerationism, as reformulated in the Spanish post-war, was necessary for survival, required the breaking of uneven trade relations. Although states would vary in the extent and manner in which they operated an autarkic strategy, the unevenness of the international trade system was a common aggravating factor motivating self-sufficient tendencies. This economic activity would necessarily be carried out by 'totalitarian' states, first, because control of the economy required a strong state and second, because liberal democracy as a system was seen as discredited.[103]

Industrialisation was seen as a way of 'modernising' society generally and, for Francoists of the first post-war years, modernity began with defining the terms of the unity of the nation. Industrial development was viewed as the only solution to Spain's decline. Industrialisation had a 'strong ethical sense'. Just as men needed 'upright standards' (*rectas normas*) which 'incorporate them into society, so nations require equality of opportunities . . . and justice'. Spain needed such a 'reactivation': 'the creation of industries, which only at the cost of a protectionism which – and why not say it? – for the moment can partially sacrifice the comforts of a generation, is indispensable'.[104]

This obsession was ideologically determined. The idea and reality of Spain could not be traded with: those who toyed with the 'secession' or 'sale' of her territory were 'masons' and the dupes of the 'Internationals' and could not be considered 'legitimate sons of the *Patria*'. 'Spain [was] self-sufficient enough to defend her territory', Franco declared in October 1937.[105] The objective would be to continue with economic self-sufficiency, and efforts to obtain foreign credits were explicitly renounced.[106] There was no need, it seemed, for foreign reconstruction loans: all the necessary work could be done with Spanish labour and materials and at the Madrid victory parade in April 1939 Franco proclaimed that 'there could be no question in any way of infringing our sovereignty and our political and economic liberty'.[107] In August 1938 he had already boasted to a French journalist that: 'Spain is a privileged country which can be self-sufficient. We possess all that we need to live, and our production is sufficiently abundant to assure our survival. We have no necessity to import anything'.[108] Months later he announced again that Spain was on the verge of self-sufficiency in armaments and was in the process of resolving its housing, education and health problems. The 'miracle' of self-sufficiency in war industries would take place, according to Franco, within a very short space of time, and 100,000 or 200,000 houses for the 'lower classes' would be quickly constructed: 'Spain has more than enough resources to resolve autarki-cally the fundamental problem of housing for the middle classes and the proletariat'.[109] He remained certain that an autarkic Spain, 'an eco-nomic policy based on patriotism', could achieve complete economic well-being,[110] and in October 1939 he put his name to a plan for economic resurgence, which, once again, placed emphasis on self-sufficiency.[111]

Self-sufficiency, state and finance

In spite of the neglect of agriculture, capital accumulation was one of the most noteworthy features of internal colonisation under Franco.[112] During the early decades of Francoism, Spanish agriculture performed one of the functions necessary to give impetus to economic develop-ment. Capital was accumulated for financing industrial growth.[113] Industrialisation was funded through the channelling of national re-sources by the state,[114] the 'privatisation of public funds'.[115] Wealth was not increased by the creation of a growth in demand but by a redistribu-tion through forced savings.[116] The 'atmosphere of peace and tranquil-lity' created a resurgence of investment: 'Thousands of millions of pesetas' were raised in subscriptions for shares in companies, such flotations constituting 'a sure sign of prosperity . . . The accumulation of savings is a mark of the elevation of the national income. The decision of money to invest is an evident symptom of the existence of possibilities of profits.'[117]

The requirement of people to save was part of the everyday discourse of the dictatorship: 'austerity' implied a 'closing' of society around the national wealth in the interests of 'resurgence'.[118] The Minister of Industry, Demetrio Carceller, in proclaiming the 'industrial reconstruction' of Spain, declared in early 1944 that 'almost all of Spanish savings have been directed to the growth and improvement of existing industries'.[119] Pablo Garnica, President of the Banco Español de Crédito, in his report to shareholders in 1943, gave a good sense of this mechanism: '[the Banks] have, in fact, converted themselves into entities of public law, whose functions are placed above all interests and private profits, they have come to situate themselves in the highest position, given the irreplaceability of their labour in the job of gathering savings and channelling them through investment in the benefit of the work of the nation through lending and credit'.[120] In fact, the profits of the five major banks multiplied by a factor of seven in the hungry decade of the 1940s.[121] Luis Olarriaga, the director of the banks' Consejo Superior, admitted that 'the Spanish bank has substituted foreign capital in the creation of national industry'.[122] Autarky meant that the door to competitive foreign investment was closed.[123] Investments by the Banco de Bilbao, for example, doubled in the period 1941–1945 and the amount deposited also grew by more than 100 per cent. By 1950 this figure had again increased by more than twice.[124] Grand new branches sprung up on the proceeds of inflation: they were to the Franco regime what the great cathedrals were to the Middle Ages, symbolising the ruling passion.[125]

The agrarian elite was able to participate on favourable terms in the financing of industrialisation: *latifundismo* was not a brake on development, as such,[126] although its continued protection by the state determined the style of development. Industrialisation did not necessarily require an agrarian reform, since it is evident that industrialisation eventually took place without it.[127] Instead of an agricultural reform which raised incomes and production in the countryside, Francoism instituted a mass fleecing of the workforce through devastatingly low wages combined with increasing prices and the regimentation of production.[128] The process in the 1940s meant that the landed oligarchy became more closely fused with the industrial elite. Increasingly, throughout the first half of the twentieth century, banking power had become concentrated in fewer and bigger institutions, founded upon landed, colonial and industrial wealth.[129] In the 1940s, the financing of industrial projects became even more dominated by these institutions. Indeed, it was on the boards of directors of the six main banks where agricultural and industrial interests came together in the Franco years.[130]

From the very first, financial interests linked themselves closely to the cause of the military rebellion against the Republic. As early as November 1936 a decree-law was announced, in conjunction with the Bank of Spain, establishing the validity of a Nationalist currency within the expanding rebel zone, in the process denying validity to money issued after 18 July in the Republican zone. This agreement made possible the flow of capital towards the rebel section of the Bank, now split in two. While in July 1936 the Bank of Spain showed a total figure in current accounts for the whole country of 1,128 million pesetas, by 31 December 1937 the Bank in the Francoist zone alone possessed assets in current accounts of 1,714 million pesetas. Franco was in little doubt where financial confidence lay.[131] These funds helped in financing the war. The Bank's report in 1942 declared that since 1936 it 'had lent to the treasury the amount of resources it has needed to attend to the demands of national defence and to the supreme service of the national interest'.[132] A British businessman, enquiring into Franco's internal finances in late 1938, commented 'it is really astounding: no increase in taxes, no loans, the Treasury and banks full. A most interesting experiment in a totally enclosed economy.' The financial state of the rebels was, indeed, healthy: first, much of the military aid supplied by Germany and Italy was granted on credit terms:[133] second, there were a large number of substantial voluntary contributions. According to British diplomats in Spain, much of the cost of the war was met by 'vast sums from patriotic Spaniards' both inside the rebel zone and from abroad. It was believed that wealthy individuals like Juan March and the Duke of Alba had 'handed over whole fortunes'. Joaquín Bau, the Catalan financier and politician who was briefly head of the Commission of Industry, Trade and Supplies of Franco's Junta Técnica during the conflict, owed his position to his ability to arrange finance through Catalan contacts who had fled abroad.[134] Finally, wealth was confiscated from supporters of the Republic as the Nationalists occupied territory.[135]

This financial support to the Nationalist cause during the Civil War was rewarded in the post-war.[136] In May 1940 the Finance Minister announced a 'banking status quo' which prevented the establishment of new institutions.[137] In August 1936, a National Committee of Private Banks had been set up with the support of many of the most influential individuals and groups.[138] It became ever more difficult to distinguish any clear dividing line between the leaders of private banking and the Francoist Ministry of Finance.[139] Economic policy was thereby coordinated well away from the more mundane political concerns of the Movement's syndicates.

The 1940s also saw a drastic reduction in labour costs.[140] An enormous degree of freedom of action was, in practice, given to employers. Actual unemployment rapidly reached levels which exceeded those of the 1930s, since industrialisation was extremely slow and uneven. Though official figures are unreliable, they show that there were some 500,000 unemployed in 1940. But regime statistics only related to workers who were in touch in some way with official organisations. These were often, in effect, the cyphers of repression and therefore discouraged contact. The head of the state unemployment board admitted in April 1950 that the figure was still 287,084−43,484 of these were in Madrid alone. This was almost certainly a gross underestimation.[141] Probably more significant was the fact that *under-employment* and starvation wages were the norm in much of the country and particularly the rural south. In poorly developed rural areas like Murcia unemployment was, according to the Falange Investigation Bureau, causing a 'profound social malaise'.[142] Newspaper reports on unemployment levels were frequently censored. However, it was known, by 1950, that a considerable amount of 'clandestine emigration' was already underway.[143]

In agriculture, especially, unemployment continued to be used as a weapon to drive down wages and safeguard profits. In latifundio Spain, labourers worked for a maximum of 180 days a year. Defeat in the Civil War meant a return of working from sun-up to sun-down for an official wage of only 4 pesetas, although in some places it was only 3. Women were paid 1.25 ptas. Landowners controlled the agricultural syndicates, which workers refused to join unless threatened with dismissal.[144]

The price system was enormously favourable to the biggest producers. The black market dominated economic relations. In 1950 it was estimated that 'legal' supplies, food at state prices, still covered only 25 per cent of the bare necessities of the working class.[145] The prices of bread and oil in the 1940s, the daily staples upon which the Spanish working class relied, reached levels which were not to be repeated until 1975.[146]

An informant of the local party organisation in Córdoba in 1942, concerned with the increased power of what he called '*tradicionalista*' elements, complained that, although landowners moaned about increased red tape, they had succeeded in increasing their capital by two or three times since the end of the war.[147] This was in a region of the country suffering enormous poverty and widespread starvation, where Gerald Brenan, when he travelled there in 1949, was reminded of Belsen.[148]

The priorities of the regime were also revealed in the lack of fiscal reform under the 'New State'.[149] A tentative plan for taxation of 'extraordinary profits' accumulated during the Civil War[150] was finally shelved,[151] a series of tax moratoria having been granted, giving impunity to massive fraud.[152] An informant of the *Delegación Nacional de Seguridad* reported that the law had been 'received by the neighbourhood with real jubilation, although the difficulty of carrying it out in practice in the majority of cases was not concealed'.[153] There was considerable resistance to the registration for tax purposes of industrial and landed wealth.[154] Only 14.76 per cent of national income in 1948 was collected in state revenue, according to official statistics, whereas the level in France and Italy was 21 per cent and in Britain 33 per cent.[155] The only genuine increase in state fiscal pressure was indirect taxes, which, naturally, were spread throughout society and, therefore, were in no sense progressive. In fact, the black market, which dominated the economy, effectively constituted a kind of punitive taxation upon the private consumption of basic necessities.

When Antonio Robert, head of the Dirección General of the Ministry of Trade and Industry in post-Civil War Spain, claimed that the 1940s were 'foundational', since they witnessed the accumulation of 'painfully achieved investments which allowed for the breaking of certain bottlenecks which limited economic development', he was, in essence, reflecting the stark reality. Under dictatorship there existed no necessity to placate a society undergoing 'directed' economic development with the material rewards of growth. Economists sympathetic to the regime were precisely those who had encouraged the regime along this painful road, ignoring the social costs and rarely specifying who were to make the 'sacrifices' demanded.[156] Individuals within the regime and in industry attempted to paint a picture of a collective 'national' sacrifice, shared equally among all social groups. It was claimed that the sacrifice of the Spanish people of their economic well-being was 'more than compensated for by the achievement of the peace and security that our regime provides'.[157]

To the regime, 'progress' meant industrialisation and social control. Alternative images of a resurgent *Patria* were silenced. In these early years the basis was laid by the creation of a cowed workforce, a financial bonanza, and a mysticism of national rebirth.[158] Even in the relatively restrictive atmosphere of the 1940s, then, there is little evidence to support the contention, still current today, that the years 1936–1975 were marked by little room for manoeuvre in politics and in the economic and social fields by elites because of the intervention of the state.[159] Autarky originated in the historic social structure of Spain and, primarily, in the triumphalism of Francoism during the Civil War itself. It cemented the victorious coalition together and confirmed the subjugation of 'the defeated'.

6   The wages of autarky (I): self-sufficiency and industry

Our crusade is the only struggle in which those who were rich before the war came out of it richer still. This is because that wealth and those riches which were devalued and at the point of being lost when we raised our flag . . . have been revalued now the war is over. We have saved Spain and we have saved that wealth.[1]

Although the Franco regime saw one of its motives as protection of the ownership of land as an inviolable prerogative, the ultimate cumulative effect of its actions was to set a course towards greater industrialisation.[2] Under the dictatorship the two were not mutually exclusive. A strike-free, low-cost production increased profits and smoothed the tensions of state intervention. The state aimed to oversee the channelling of national resources towards priority sectors – public funds towards the private sector – selected for their potential in lessening Spain's economic dependency. This did not mean that autarky was always accepted uncritically by individual elite figures, but, for many reasons, it was of relative utility in the 1940s.[3]

In general, economic elites were supportive of the Francoist 'Crusade'. The dominant private banks had seen the Republic as bringing nothing but 'postponements, delays, low worker productivity'. Spain suffered 'an economic crisis (and) an industrial slump'. The Republic and the Depression, which were inseparable in the eyes of industry, had encouraged 'disorder of the spirits, decline in productivity, crisis in public confidence, mistrust of money'[4] and elites gratefully accepted the opportunities provided to overturn the reforming project which the Republic had represented. In 1951, Alfonso de Churruca, the President of the Centro Industrial de Vizcaya, the main organisation of Bilbao heavy industry, wrote that 'the economic boom which has marked the recent period is founded upon the social peace maintained by the Franco government, just as by its decided protection in favour of mining and national industries'.[5] This broadly summed up the relationship of state and industry during the 1940s.

Even prominent individuals who officially became *personae non grata* in Franco's Spain because of their support for regional nationalism, like the Catalan Francesc Cambó and the Basque Ramón de la Sota, had always been suspicious of the Republic and essentially supportive of the monarchy.[6] In the aftermath of the Civil War many of the regionalist middle class who had sponsored local nationalist politics would trade these political claims for a guarantee of the continued protection of existing property relations.

Basque industry was historically linked closely with the central state in Madrid. Industrialists had done splendidly in the post-First World War era, and benefited hugely from the industrial policy of Primo de Rivera's dictatorship in the 1920s.[7] The majority of Basque industrialists supported centralist political formations, owing much of their success to policy formulated by central government. Shipping and shipbuilding, Ramón de la Sota's main interests, for example, were among the leading sectors of the economy and his support for the Basque nationalist political party, the Partido Nacionalista Vasco (PNV), remains something of a mystery and was a taboo subject during the dictatorship. However, after the war his financial assets were seized by the regime, because of his political allegiances, and his shares in major companies sold by the state at a knock-down price to some of his former business rivals who could show themselves as much more unequivocally *'españolista'*. However, few members of the high Spanish bourgeoisie were thus treated[8] and Basque industry and banking experienced a real boom in the 1940s.[9] The biggest national institutions swallowed dozens of smaller banks, in the process tightening their hold on hundreds of industrial concerns across the country.[10]

The Nationalist authorities had become accustomed, during the Civil War, to dealing directly with industry, militarising those sectors which could directly aid the war effort. They were assisted in developing organs for economic control by 'exiled' economic elites within Nationalist-held territory.[11] The co-operation of heavy industry in Bilbao was particularly valuable. Industrial production in the Basque Country was rapidly transformed from virtual stagnation under the Republican Basque government to buoyant vitality under the military authorities. In return, the political influence of local industrialists and bankers was rapidly reasserted following the fall of the city.[12]

Basque elite society was quick to show its adhesion to the Francoist 'Movement'.[13] By the time of the first anniversary of the fall of Bilbao, in June 1938, the barons of Basque heavy industry were able to declare themselves satisfied with the progress made under the authority of the Francoist state: 'Bilbao, like the whole of Vizcaya, demonstrates her fervent patriotism with her spirit, with the offering of the lives and blood of her sons, with her money, with her labour, with her best sentiments'. The province was proud to proclaim the sacrifices made by *vizcaínos* at the front line and to declare that some 12,000 of its inhabitants had joined up to serve in the militias of the rearguard to act as police or prison guards, for example, or in censorship offices. More than 20 million pesetas had been publicly donated in the province, by private individuals, companies and organisations.[14]

The economy, which, according to businessmen, had been 'taken to pieces' by 'the Marxist-separatist rabble', was on the way to reconstruction, a remarkable achievement in just a year.[15] The mining industry had returned to activity. While the average monthly production of iron ore had been 110,543 tonnes in 1935, in April 1938 production had reached 168,690 tonnes. Iron-ore exports from Bilbao, which had declined to 69,507 tonnes, rose to 152,973 tonnes. Coastal trade in ore, around the peninsula, increased from 633 tons in 1935 to 14,044 in 1938. Other industries of the region, like cement and chemicals, were also experiencing a resurgence. Many had been able to substitute their own products for those which had previously been imported from abroad, thereby conforming to the autarkic direction of the state which was actively being developed.

Iron and steel production had also seen impressive improvements. The biggest producer in Spain, Altos Hornos de Vizcaya (AHV) proclaimed that the recuperation of activities had permitted significant quantities of cast steel to be exported to Italy and Germany as a contribution to the fulfilling of Spain's debt obligations to those countries. In 1938, Italy would receive 60,000 tons and Germany 40,000. Unsurprisingly, production in the Basque Country continued to be extremely labour intensive: in mining, for example, being militarised, the rhythm of work increased so as to boost exports and earn vital foreign exchange. Mining companies were able to make up some of the losses of specialised labour, as miners fled to help establish a Republican front to defend Santander, by using the forced labour of prisoners of war.[16] In 1945, 35 per cent more workers than in 1940 produced 100 per cent more iron.[17] AHV expected that its contribution to the war effort in providing material would allow Nationalist Spain to become completely self-sufficient in military supplies. This, it was proclaimed, was what had prompted Franco himself to declare that 'the war was won with the liberation of the North'.[18]

The profits declared by AHV were over 10 million pesetas in 1939. By 1946, profits were up to over 23 million and by 1950 totalled almost 35 million. The company's reserves more than quadrupled over the decade. However, production and profits may have been greater still than this. While industrial prices and the prioritisation of orders were supposedly 'controlled' by the state, a parallel, and technically illegal, market flourished in particular sectors.[19] Industrial legislation was one of the bases of the black market.[20]

AHV was able to absorb other firms and create new companies during this period. In 1940 it took over the iron and steel company Siderúrgica del Mediterráneo, for example. It also bought up the mining preserve of the old English iron-mining company Orconera, as well as the hydro-electric facility of Aguas y Saltos del Zadorra. By the beginning of the 1950s, the firm had consolidated its virtual monopoly status, controlling or participating in a majority capacity in no fewer than thirty companies.[21]

Private and state capital were central to the regime's programme to develop the national production of nitrogenous chemicals for fertilisers and explosives. Production was through the use of the gases emitted from the furnaces of the Basque iron and steel industry, particularly AHV. The Ministry approached the company in 1938, making clear what was considered to be the good business sense behind the project. The state offered the company a virtual monopoly of production and trade as well as the bonuses of land expropriation for construction of a new plant and significant tax breaks. The state undertook to provide foreign exchange to buy machinery from Germany and Italy. A new company, Sefanitro (Sociedad Espanola de Fabricaciones Nitrogenadas), controlled by AHV, was established and declared an 'industry of national interest' in October 1941. The majority of the necessary capital was provided by the company, most of the rest was supplied by three of the dominant industrial banks – the Banco de Bilbao, the Banco de Vizcaya, and the Banco Urquijo.[22]

Another company, Sociedad Ibérica del Nitrogeno (SIN), was granted a concession in April 1941 to use the by-products of the Asturian mining and metallurgy company Duro-Felguera and was made an 'industry of national interest'. In 1938, the company had reported that it expected demand to be high because of 'the great development that Spanish industrial production must experience in the present circumstances,' and added that the coal industry 'will be able to offer to the public authorities all that the nation requires'. It had always been the company's wish to see industries in Spain for producing nitrogenous fertilisers and synthetic gasoline, using Spanish coal, thereby reducing national dependency on foreigners.[23] Protection of the Spanish coal industry increased further than ever under Franco. The *Plan de Hidrocarburos*, announced in January 1942, introduced a tariff which enforced the use of nationally produced coal in industry.[24]

The protection of 'national industry' was the main legislative preoccupation of the regime in the economy during 1939. Two major legislative enactments enshrined this principle: the Law for Protection and Development of National Industry (October), and the Law for the Regulation and Defence of National Industry (November). The aim was to apportion resources in accordance with the priorities of the regime. The installation of new industry requiring materials or machinery could only be authorised by the Ministry of Trade and Industry. In theory, the Ministry controlled imports of material as well as national economic activity. The following year saw a further elaboration of this system. Those industries which could claim the benefits accompanying the application of the epithet 'industry of national interest' were formally defined according to strict criteria.

This legislation, designed to 'free' industrial development from 'foreign dependency', would supposedly 'revalue' Spain's natural assets. The forced expropriation of land was given state sanction in certain situations. Tax reductions or exemptions of up to 50 per cent were provided for. A guaranteed minimum profit margin of 4 per cent of invested capital was assured. Finally, a reduction of duties on necessary imports was available. The Law for the Regulation and Defence of National Industry, proclaimed in November, instituted a greater degree of autarky. This addressed directly the participation of foreigners in industrial operations in Spain. Only those industries in which at least a 75 per cent holding was owned by Spanish nationals (100 per cent in the case of industries of national defence) would be favoured by the benefits outlined in the legislation. It was also stipulated that such industries should have no more than 25 per cent foreign technicians.[25] Foreign capital invested in companies in Spain was limited to 25 per cent of the total.[26] Companies were compelled to use domestic resources, if available, whatever the cost.

Finally, the role of the state in the development of Spanish industry was crowned by the creation of a state holding company, the Institute of National Industry (Instituto Nacional de Industria, INI), in September 1941, originally to be called the *Instituto Nacional de Autarquía*.[27]

The moving force behind the regime's industrial plans was Juan Antonio Suanzes, Minister of Industry for two spells in the early years of the dictatorship, as well as head of the INI from its inception until 1963.[28] It hardly needs to be said that Suanzes was politically staunchly anti-Republican, a factor which had some influence upon his ideas about economics. He had been imprisoned by the Republican authorities in 1936 in the Model Prison of Madrid for his intervention during a strike at the company, where he was one of the directors, in an attempt to avoid implementing the measures laid down by the Republican state labour council in resolving the dispute.[29] His policy and personality were encapsulated by his belief in industrial regenerationism, Catholic corporatism, and 'the traditional mentality of the engineer'.[30] According to Ramón Garriga, a contemporary observer of Franco's cabinet, Suanzes believed in two things above all else: Hitler's Germany and the directed economy.[31] He was to insist that 'conscious and hindering resistance [to industrialisation] must be swept away'.[32]

More specifically, he was concerned with the development of Spain's Navy. At least one historian has claimed that the INI was set up in 1941 precisely 'to cut through the difficulties which the expansion of Spanish shipbuilding was facing'.[33] In 1938, when the dominant shipbuilding firm La Sociedad Española de Construcción Naval came to put forward its case to the Ministry of Industry to be considered an industry of national importance, a claim which hardly needed reinforcing, the company made much of the fact that its annual production capacity was 'very much higher' than the country's present demands, thereby presenting the argument for augmenting the state's requirements.[34] Suanzes had previously been employed by the company as an engineer and clearly resented the domination of the firm by its British parent company Vickers.[35] The merchant naval programme outlined in a law of May 1942 defined the extent and conditions of the state's activity. Again, the aim was 'to focus, frame, and compliment the actions of private initiative, overcoming common obstacles which impede the achievement of the anticipated rhythm'. Nowhere was there any sign of a will to tackle the defects caused by an excessive concentration of capital.[36]

The establishment of INI, modelled upon Fascist Italy's state holding company, the Istituto per la Ricostruzione Industriale (IRI), crowned this process. It was argued that the imperatives of national defence required the creation of new industries. The preamble to the founding law of INI proclaimed that Spain's 'racial values' would be strengthened through 'the indispensable support of a powerful industry'. National resurgence would have to be accelerated if Spain was to realise its 'historic destiny'.[37] The sums required were so large and the potential profit margins so small that the intervention of the state was demanded. However, it is also claimed that though private investment was normally attracted to more productive areas, INI enterprises will offer an attractive prospect for investors (Article 1).[38]

Ultimately, the INI served the interests of economic elites in Francoist Spain as well as those of the state.[39] Nationalism was used as the justification of a policy to boost the confidence of private initiative. The state had failed to act strongly enough in the past to fill the investment vacuum, it was claimed.[40] Those state companies constituted with the participation of the INI would automatically receive the benefits outlined in previous legislation to industries deemed 'of national interest'.[41] In short, Francoism proposed a form of state capitalism as the logical alternative to the state socialism threatened by the Republic.[42]

In early 1940, a strategy of import-substitution industrialisation (ISI) to develop artificial fibres based on Spanish natural resources was announced, which was to be carried forward via the INI. The urgency of the project was underlined by the fact that the importation of the raw material of textile production was a drain on the national reserves to the tune of over 500 million pesetas annually. With some justification, the Ministry claimed that private initiative, by itself, had failed to develop a nationally based supply of raw materials. The new plan[43] proposed, with the aid of technological assistance from Italy, Germany and Japan, to translate agricultural products into production of fibres.[44] Tax and duty reductions were offered to reduce the cost of production. Approximately one-fifth of investment in new industrial development in the first three years of the regime was directed towards textiles.[45] The Dirección General de Industria authorised a total of 28 million pesetas' worth of production of artificial fibres in the years 1941 and 1942.

Production of artificial textiles revolved around the INI and two new companies, FEFASA (Fabricación Española de Fibras, SA) and SNIACE (Sociedad Nacional de Industrias Aplicaciones Celulosa Española).[46] The initial capital of FEFASA was 75 million pesetas, more than doubling in 1944, with a majority injection of funds via INI, and reaching 280.50 million by 1951. However, the difficulties in developing the productive process of cellulose manufacture requiring German machinery during the world war made progress relatively slow.[47] Production rose rapidly after 1944, when the first Spanish manufacture took place. In 1946, more than 6,000 tons of viscose was produced. By the 1950s, average annual production was 30,000 tons. By 1950, national production covered entirely the requirement of the home market and Spain was able to begin to export artificial fibres in 1947. By 1950, SNIACE declared a profit of over 80 million pesetas.[48]

The INI constituted, even into the 1960s, a bunker for the ideologues of interventionism within the regime. This bulwark against economic liberalism, with Suanzes as figurehead, claimed the egalitarian high ground, utilising the Falangist-inspired rhetoric of the *revolución pendiente*. A myth was constructed that 'economic liberalism has been definitively surpassed . . . the ideals of personal profit, of economic dominion, of uncompromising technicality, have been overtaken by new, more noble [*generosas*] ideas'.[49] 'Faith can move mountains, and that same faith and enthusiasm which gave us victory will enable us to triumph in the cruel battles of peace'.[50] Demetrio Carceller, Minister in the early 1940s, defined the role of INI: 'to help private initiative to serve the general interests of the nation'.[51] In practice, this meant a deepening of the socialisation of industrial costs, which is a feature of the modern state.[52]

Under dictatorship there existed no public control of the distribution of these massive resources.[53] The INI would be run along the lines of a massive private corporation, military in style, as befitted an organisation propelled by a mission to modernise Spain's national defence, but never seriously challenging the interests of the country's big firms. In a sense, the grandiosity of such plans had an ideological role. The prospective manufacture of cars, for example, amounted to a possible 'display industry', which existed in propaganda images of regeneration but not in reality.[54] This was the perpetuation of a tradition of state intervention carried to new extremes in the context of political and social repression.

Particular attention was to be paid to the geographic distribution of industrial centres. When it could be avoided, investment by the state would not increase the concentration of industry in already industrialised zones. This had something to do with a fear of the growth of the working class in established areas like Barcelona.[55] Of the 2,180 textile factories in Spain registered in 1942, 1,391 were in the province of Barcelona.[56] The province had 116,829 textile workers officially, while Alicante, for example, had 4,895.[57] But development away from such centres, it was thought, would mean a more equitable sharing-out of the national wealth and development. It was for these reasons that industrial development was to be given priority by the regime in agricultural areas like Valladolid, the heartland of peasant support for the Falange.[58] In the vital area of fertilisers, for example, financial concessions were granted to new companies like Nitratos de Castilla, SA, declared an industry of national interest in July 1940, located in Valladolid, although most of the private finance came from the Basque banks.[59]

Basque capitalists generally saw no need to complain. The Bank of Bilbao professed only a sense of gratitude: 'The state would endow it [INI] with the adequate financial means applying to its plans and programmes a good part of forced savings: . . . the Institute would never aspire to be more than a developing organisation for enterprises, whose ownership would pass into the hands of private capital insofar as the possibilities for the pacing of the national interest advise it'. The INI may have had its detractors, but, according to the bank's report, the future of the Spanish economy was rosier than at any time in the previous hundred years.[60]

The president of the electricity-generating companies' interest group, UNESA, for example, was the Bilbao banker and Francoist politician José María Oriol. In December 1944, the government accepted a plan for development put forward by UNESA. The Bank of Bilbao paid tribute to the subsequent collaboration of UNESA with the government 'during the difficult years of disequilibrium between production and demand'. The INI was to finance the development of a national network of power generation and supply.[61] In the same year, in September, the two dominant Basque-financed generating companies, Hidroelectrica Iberica and Saltos del Duero, fused to create Iberduero, a new company with the potential to dominate this sector whose founding 'coincided with the moment in which the exploitation of the Spanish electrical system achieved a national status'. The share capital of Iberduero in 1944 was 458 million pesetas; by 1956 it had risen sharply to 2,617 million in shares and 746 million in bonds. Declared profits in 1945 were more than 30 million pesetas; by 1950 they had increased by more than three-fold. An examination of the names represented on the board of Iberduero from its inception shows how the main banks played a leading role.[62] Concentration of the industry was justified, according to UNESA, because of the need to exploit new sources of energy, to produce sufficient funds for modernisation (by pressuring the state), to avoid duplication and waste of resources, and more easily to prevent 'fraud', which apparently flourished in an atmosphere of 'open competition'. However, it was claimed that this should not be interpreted as the establishment of a monopoly, since the industry would be rigidly controlled in its capacity as a public service[63] and prices would be regulated by the state. Turn-over in sales of electricity rose from 68.6 million pesetas in 1945 to 423.3 million in 1953.[64] By 1948, though the costs had been high, national production of electricity was twice as high as it had been in 1935.[65]

The fall of Barcelona to the rebels, in January 1939, was at least as significant as that of Bilbao.[66] On the day following the occupation of the city the executive of the Bilbao Chamber of Commerce sent Franco a message of congratulation for having 'rescued Catalonia and Barcelona for Mother Spain'.[67] The significance of the fall of Barcelona was underlined by the fact that, within a month, while Republican resistance continued in Madrid, Britain and France officially recognised the Franco government. The determination of the Western democracies to maintain cordial relations did not, however, prevent either Franco's adhesion to the Anti-Comintern Pact on 27 March, or the considerable

Figure 9 Franco's visit to the Barcelona industrial suburb of Sabadell, January 1942. The fascist salute of textile workers in a factory adorned with Falangist symbols. (Arxiu Forogràfic, Arxiu Històric de la Ciutat, Barcelona.)

presence of German and Italian military, political and business personnel in the Catalan capital. Finally, on 1 April, Franco announced the Civil War at an end as the disintegration of the Republican state became inexorable. Again, the interest organisations of Spanish business were keen to express their gratitude and adhesion.[68]

In spite of the propaganda claims of the regime that 'the Reds' had done incalculable damage, when Barcelona industrialists returned to their factories in 1939 they frequently discovered that all was in order, warehouses full and, indeed, some functioning more efficiently than before the conflict.[69] Although significant political rivalries remained,[70] the public renunciation of 'Catalanism' by many leading figures of the industrial middle class, including prominent individuals associated with the Lliga Regionalista, paved the way for a relative normalisation of economic and political power in the region as some of the most important representatives of the local elite underwent a voluntary process of 'españolization'.[71] Besides, the Catalan bourgeoisie was itself traumatised by the experience of war and, in some ways, welcomed intervention by the state in economic affairs. Industry had little in the way of a coherent alternative to state intervention, but was fearful of 'revolutionary' fascist ideology.[72] To some Catalan industrialists, it seemed that the only thing that distinguished the Falange from Marxism was the salute with the hand open rather than with the clenched fist.[73] Leadership of a modern liberal Spanish state, the prior objective of bourgeois Catalan nationalism, was sacrificed. The slide into civil war condemned such an outcome to failure as the leaders and followers of the Lliga ceased to be a national *Catalan* bourgeoisie. The growth of industry in the region in the post-Civil War era perpetuated development *a la Catalana*: economic growth without state power.[74]

Sectors of the economy more closely linked to the central state could easily display *españolista* credentials. Individuals of the heavy manufacturing industries were quickest to secure positions in the state party and local administration. It was not coincidental that men like Miguel Mateu, Francisco Luis Rivière, Felipe Batlló i Godó or Wilfredo Ricart, the leading figures in car, aircraft, railway equipment, and heavy engineering and electrical manufacture, were among the leading figures of Barcelona political administration from the very first.[75] Indeed, employment figures in these sectors suggest a relative dynamism. The number of workers employed in Catalan metallurgic industries rose from 59,367 in 1940 to 85,149 in 1950, and the number of licences issued by the state for the establishing of industries in Catalonia in this sector increased from 5,357 in 1944 to 6,769 six years later.[76]

The owners of companies in more traditional sectors, like textiles, also participated in the diversification. The proprietors of the biggest textile companies became involved in other areas, like chemicals and electronics. A similar pattern characterised the 'decline' of the Catalan banking sector.[77] Spanish banks were able to acquire millions of pesetas' worth of government bonds, which they could sell on immediately at a profit.[78] It was calculated that the 'census of millionaires' in Barcelona increased during the 1940s by fifteen or twenty times over the number in 1936.[79] Monopolisation, as it affected the Catalan banking sector, culminated in the absorption of Barcelona's Banco Hispano-Colonial by the Banco Central of Madrid in 1950.[80] The Catalan bank had been the sixth-biggest private bank in Spain in terms of total deposits while the Central was the third. At the same time, some of the leading figures in Catalan banking were able to locate themselves in prominent positions within the new enlarged 'national', that is, Spanish, banks.[81]

These developments took place in a political context of fascistic rhetoric. The 'unruly element' within the Catalan bourgeoisie had to understand that,

the National Syndicalist Revolution is not only an extremely violent reaction which imposes the unity of Spain against local separatists . . . but also a determined social movement which blocks the way [of] the despotic capitalist, of those few gentlemen who have always managed the Catalan economy to their own advantage . . . not only to the detriment of other social classes and against the other regions of Spain, but also through morally unacceptable institutions . . . like the stock market, security accounts, and the dividends of the big companies . . .[82]

The state-union structure was, in theory, to be the main agent of the Falangist 'revolution'. In reality, its level of control was always relative.[83] The Chambers of Commerce, the traditional mouth-pieces of industry, and other patronal pressure organisations, were never effectively done away with, despite calls for such action to be taken.[84] Local employers had not even been inclined to join the CNS. Many saw little point, given that they had safely taken back their land and factories from workers who were totally defeated and 'in a state of complete despair'.[85] By May none of the syndicates in Barcelona had yet even managed the elemental task of compiling a census of companies and workers. None of the leaders of the state unions, if asked, would have been able to give a report of the work carried out thus far.[86] The syndicates were 'nothing more than agencies for the collection of dues'. Moreover, the work of the union delegates in the workshops and factories was completely negative: 'The great majority of them tolerate all the arbitrary acts of unscrupulous bosses, which are only discovered because of the actions of other comrades who lend their services in the same companies.'[87] Local industry wanted 'to establish a standard of social conduct contrary to the National Syndicalist Revolution'. They had not comprehended, according to Falangists, that this 'blindness' could only bring with it a resurgence of the class struggle, with 'fatal consequences'.[88] In May 1945, the National Syndical Delegate complained to the Minister of the Movement that the syndicate was struggling in the face of the 'selfish resistance of the patronal classes'.[89] Mediation between the syndicates and private organisations was more often facilitated in behind-the-scenes deals.[90]

In the city's port, within a year of the end of the Civil War, the so-called 'Servicio Sindical' was simply operated by employers who were freely employing and dismissing workers with no control by the local branch of the CNS. This had allowed wages to be sharply driven down. Neither was enough bread provided for workers in the company kitchens, another area which party leaders saw as one in which the union should be ensuring efficiency.[91] Falangists insisted that their reports on the political reliability of workers and prisoners have precedence over information supplied by employers, although they were often thwarted in the attempt.[92]

However, employers gradually co-operated as it became clearer that their fears of Falange radicalism were unfounded: 'resolutions which affected the interests of the workers had not been resolved as they had feared'. But still, by the middle of 1940, it was lamented by Falangists that the local CNS had resolved none of the problems of the working class. Very few workers voluntarily joined the union, and by the middle of 1940 thousands of those who, for whatever reasons, had joined – and usually it was out of a sense of fear – were resistant to the idea of renewing their union cards. Moreover, the workers boycotted all the meetings.[93]

In reality, though, many leading Falangists took a pragmatic approach to capitalism in Catalonia and in Spain.[94] While the perceived historical 'policy of privileges' toward Catalan society could not continue, neither could the problem of reconstituting local power be tackled from the point of view of an 'anti-Catalan phobia', according to Party pragmatists.[95] The industrial economy could not simply be destroyed: the contribution of Catalonia to the nation in 'setting about emotional problems in a relentless and brutal way . . . [had been to] perform an unmistakably Spanish duty'.[96] Indeed, some party bureaucrats in Barcelona saw part of their task as *explaining* Catalonia to Madrid. Those charged with directing Catalan society had to realise that, in social terms, the region was ahead of other parts of Spain. The cultural and social advances which had been made could not now be destroyed simply because they might have been achieved through the actions of 'separatists or regionalists'.[97] Giving a party membership card to such people would amount to 'handing them a certificate of political purity that they were far from deserving', it was true, but, to an extent, suspicions about the political loyalty of Catalan Falangists were partly assuaged by the experience of fighting the war: 'Those that had a blemished past . . . were cleansed at the front.'[98] Once any dangerous enemies had been eliminated, 'politically pure' Catalans could be useful in the work of 'social renovation' throughout the country, coalescing with the National Syndicalist ethos of the Falange.[99]

Regionalism was played down and renovation or resurgence emphasised. The 'renaissance' of Spain could be built with Catalan support. The old-style Spanish decadence of the Restoration era was attacked. There was a 'yearning for a stronger and more just *Patria* than the decadent Spain of the liberal systems', which had only constructed 'an empty Spanishness, content to mourn past glories'. Conservatives and Liberals had taken turns in 'bleeding our Spain white', and Francesc Cambó, the figurehead of the Lliga, was attacked as a 'political juggler' and a 'corrupt grafter', but he had at least realised how the 'monstrosity' of Spain's 'imperial disaster' of 1898 had turned Catalonia upside-down.[100]

The business and industrial communities of the region continued, in the post-war, 'blindly' to associate with the circle of high finance linked to the old Lliga leader Francesc Cambó. But the local head of FET–JONS argued that the regime had to realise that, since old Lliga affiliates represented a powerful 'conglomeration of politico-economic interests', it would be 'infantile' to ignore it or to claim that it had melted away as a result of the Civil War. This was no insignificant social force, peripheral to elite society. The financial middle classes hankered after prosperous past times associated with the era of the political influence of bourgeois Catalan nationalism. Care had to be taken in incorporating such elements into the regime because, collectively, 'they feel an irrepressible inclination towards mutual protection'. But, individually, they were useful.

During the Civil War links between the political and social organisations of Spanish economic elites had been reinforced. Both Juan Ventosa and Cambó himself spent most of the period of the Civil War abroad, mainly in Switzerland and Belgium engaged principally in 'business affairs', including the aiding of Nationalist Spain. Indeed, Cambó recalled that he and Ventosa 'worked from the first moment to assist the triumph of the Army'.[101] Contacts between the exiled Falange of Barcelona and members or sympathisers remaining clandestinely in Catalonia were maintained throughout the Civil War. The party leadership claimed in 1937 to have 20,000 supporters behind the lines, described by officials as the 'Fifth Column', including members of the business community who remained at liberty in the region.[102]

According to Juan Claudio Güell Churruca, the Conde de Ruisenada:

The fifth column was everywhere and faithfully carried out its task. Slowly and inexorably all the economic and industrial organisation of irredentist Catalonia was extinguished. The factories had their work paralysed by the lack of raw materials and for other reasons. The sending of goods abroad was boycotted so as to prevent the Reds obtaining exchange. The warehouses were seen to have their shelves empty, businesses closed their doors so as not to attract transactions. This is how the strangulation of the Red rearguard was brought about, creating a climate of protest and despair which was shared by everyone. This was the valuable help which Catalonia could offer to the Caudillo.

Such support was rewarded in the aftermath of the conflict. Once Barcelona was occupied by the Nationalist forces, Ruisenada was named vice-president of the City Council (*Diputación*).[103] During the war, the representatives of big business also carried out 'acts of espionage . . . for the triumph of the National Cause'. The agent of the

Banco Hispano Colonial, who had founded the Lérida branch of the Falange in 1934, was a co-ordinating member of the section of the sabotaging fifth column known as the 'Grupo Concepción'.[104]

During the conflict exiled Carlist sympathisers from Catalonia also lent a hand in co-ordinating 'Investigation and Information'. This meant, first, channelling resources for the war effort and organising sabotage behind enemy lines. The wartime Carlist Commission claimed that several Requetés (members of the Carlist militia) had succeeded in infiltrating anarchist groups in Barcelona, disrupting vital services to the Republican front and rearguard. Indeed, many of the directors of groups of fifth columnists were Carlists. Catalan industrialists reorganised the traditional regional militia, the Somatén, as a direct contribution to maintaining public order and property.[105]

Second, it involved participating in repression. Carlists, who were usually individuals of high social standing in Catalan society, participated in the so-called 'Red-Separatist Committees', judicial bodies which operated in semi-obscurity giving a veneer of legality to the imprisonment and execution of political enemies. Positions were set up on the roads entering Nationalist territory for the collecting of information and an archive was built up as the basis of systematising punishment. These records, although often amounting to little more than anecdotes, were later used as 'evidence' in Political Responsibilities 'trials'. One 34-year-old married woman from Barcelona, who had lived a precarious existence from casual work since the occupation of the city, and later had been sentenced to thirty years by a military tribunal for 'a crime of military rebellion', was already incarcerated when her 'Responsibilities' case was heard. Evidence consisted of a claim by the local Guardia Civil that she was 'of bad conduct and antecedents'. The FET–JONS 'card index' (fichero) revealed that she was 'affiliated to the Popular Front prior to the Glorious National Movement . . . [and was] characterised by [sic] extremist propaganda . . . was considered as the 'Pasionaria' of Sabadell [and] took an active part in the collectivizations', regularly attending union meetings.[106]

By early 1938, virtually a year before the fall of Barcelona to the insurgents, a front in defence of elite interests began to cohere, based, first in Burgos and then in San Sebastián.[107] At first, there were so many ex-civil servants from Barcelona in Burgos that the seat of government, the Palacio del Cordón, was known as 'La Lliga'.[108] Attempts were made to resurrect pre-war associations like the landowners' Instituto Agrícola Catalan de San Isidro, historically a part of the Lliga, for example, as an alternative agrarian economic body to a projected state 'agrarian syndicate' sponsored by FET.[109] These groups were in contact in San

Sebastián with Carlists, whose Traditionalist Communion had been reformed in Zaragoza after the failure of the coup in Barcelona by some of the old leaders of the Party and the *Sindicatos Libres* of the 1920s. Generally, leading Carlists, representing one traditional wing of the Catalan middle class, were, like the 'Lliguistas', concerned for the financial future of a Spain in Falangist hands.[110] 'Radicals' in the state party in Barcelona were, in turn, concerned that the number of 'Traditionalists' incorporated, 'whose political origins [had not] been taken into account', had grown considerably, so that '. . . all those *caciques* and old Catalan politicians who were rejected by the Falange or who did not dare to seek admission to it, have become members of the Catalan *Requeté*'.[111] Elements within the party feared that the growing organisation of big business 'would make derisory all political activity of a national-syndicalist or simply national type'. In a highly prophetic passage, one party informant warned that, 'The industry [and] business of Catalonia would be controlled by them and only the road of agitation campaigns would remain open to the Falange.'[112]

Control of economic relations by the state was, as predicted, difficult to make effective. On countless occasions, businessmen declined to comply with the decrees of the regime.[113] Leading representatives of industry openly criticised intervention and flaunted their continued dominance of the local economy.[114] The priority was the protection of existing property relations and business. Barcelona's biggest chemical company, the Sociedad Anónima Cros, was an example of a private company which saw considerable success during the early Franco years, doubling its invested capital in 1942 from 100 million to 200 million pesetas. Annual profits, already impressive in 1940, rose from nearly 19 million to almost 35 million in just six years.[115] Some of this success was undoubtedly due to its ability to avoid state control. The transactions of the major chemical companies like Cros, or the Unión Española de Explosivos, were already beyond the control of the syndicate by 1942, if not before. The boards of directors 'systematically disobeyed' the directives of the state union in preferring to supply those clients which provided the biggest profits rather than the small farming co-operatives, which were the pride of die-hard Falangists. The policy of autarky, in practice, applied to fertilisers, allowed a few large companies to monopolise production and commercialisation.[116] This was only confirmed, in the minds of Falangist militants, at least, by the forming of a new company, the S.A. Auxiliar de la Industria Química, with capital of Cros and Explosivos together, directed by members of both boards.[117] Members of the board of Cros were accused of being part of 'a Judaeo-Masonic conspiracy' and of having 'separatist' backgrounds, as well as having escaped the purge which was carried out after the end of the Civil War.[118] In fact, the directors included individuals who had explicitly and publicly criticised Catalan nationalism as a movement, a process of self-denunciation which was undergone in order to maintain a position at the pinnacle of the local social structure.[119]

One of the many Catalans who moved in these circles during the Republic and the Civil War was Miguel Mateu Pla, Franco's first mayor of the city of Barcelona.[120] Local power was exercised by the mayor, the Civil Governor, and the military authorities of the region, assisted by the most important of the city's Falangists, and the party man most associated with industry and finance, José Ribas Seva who had helped co-ordinate the efforts of exiled Catalan businessmen in San Sebastián, from whom he obtained finance.[121] Mateu Pla exerted considerable influence in business circles from his position on the board of directors of seventeen major companies, including some of the principal national banks and engineering firms.[122]

It seems plain that, in spite of periodic squabbles with the state party, industrialists and bankers, both in the Basque Country and in Catalonia, placed themselves securely in support of the Francoist 'New State'. There was a firm consensus that the working class had to be isolated from all autonomous political activity. Moreover, although formally distanced from political power, the industrial class continued to wield considerable influence, and, while some Falangists professed to be guided by a radical, or even revolutionary, doctrine, their activism was always expressed within what were, in fact, extremely conservative boundaries.

The paramount concerns of some military men and of many committed Falangists seem to have been genuinely associated with the nebulous ideas of national resurgence or 'the destiny of the *Patria*'. If economic elites and party bureaucrats did not share such faith in abstract ideals, they were at least sure, for the most part, that their own concerns coincided more often than not with this vision of the nation and that Franco's state was infinitely preferable to the proletarian revolution that they associated with the Republic. Indeed, in many ways, autarky represented an extreme form of economic protectionism, which had always been the basis of elite demands upon the state.

7   The wages of autarky (II): the myth and reality of rural life

'If there is not bread to eat in Spain, we are strong in the hope of producing it at once, and in the immense pride of being Spaniards who have reclaimed [the] *Patria* . . . We would happily say: we have no bread, but we have the *Patria*, which is something that is worth much more than anything else, and a *Patria* in which our children will have bread and justice, and power, and pride in its strength and in its glory. We would never want to eat bread which was not of our *Patria*, bread which would be eaten at a price insulting to the *Patria*.'[1]

The first decade of Francoism saw a deep crisis in the Spanish country-side. Rural communities were put in jeopardy, production was precarious and uneven, agricultural labourers suffered starvation, and small-holding peasants and tenant farmers lived the effects of the huge gulf separating regime rhetoric from harsh reality. As the state deserted small farmers, 'spiritually' and materially, peasants were forced to migrate to industrial areas or, ultimately, to face the uncertainties of emigration.[2] This decadence of rural Spain was accompanied by a growing mono-polisation of economic and political power by elites. The Spanish peasant was accorded a high-ranking position in theory but no real interest was shown in materially creating a 'peasant status', a real standing in society, and 'rural well-being was made cancerous by absenteeism'.[3] The rural idea was instrumentalised to legitimise the actual dominance of big landowners. As before, in the 1930s, the political right in Spain insisted on grouping together all wheatgrowers as *labradores* (peasants/poor farmers), regardless of their relative wealth and power.[4] In fact, 'producers' often had very different interests, but a return to the pre-Republican agricultural order was indispensable to the Francoist 'New Order'.[5]

Autarky required the intervention of the state, primarily in the foreign trade market, but also in the domestic market to control shortages. The task of 'disciplining consumers' was recognised as being more difficult than regimenting Spaniards as 'producers', since they could not be located 'safely' within 'organic structures'. Here was a potential threat which had to be faced: 'The consumer remains, as a general rule, free to wander in the arena of liberty'.[6] It was in the process of distribution and rationing that this 'freedom' was confronted by the manipulation of scarcity.[7]

One of the principal features of social conflicts in Spain, particularly after the turn of the century, was the tension between rural and urban society.[8] Often bitter relations between industrialists and landowners, in the face of social protest from below, have marked the contemporary history of Spain.[9] The path to modernity was full of contradictions, with faltering steps towards industrialisation checked by Spain's lack of resources.[10] Politics were mainly shaped by landed interests' dependency on an ideology framed by Catholicism, insisting on the maintenance of the 'national essence' residing in the Spanish soil and the Castilian peasant.[11]

This tension was displayed in the different reactions of Spanish society to the military rising in July 1936. The director of the military conspiracy, General Mola, dreamed of a 'reagrarianisation of Spain', claiming that the solution to the 'social question' was the elimination of the industrial proletariat through the physical destruction of heavy industry.[12] Indeed the simultaneity of distinct urban and rural ways of life and ways of understanding the world perhaps made mobilisation for violence easier than otherwise.[13] The social life of much of the countryside, that had been supported by the local priest, doctor and schoolteacher, was threatened by the 'perverse politics' of the Republic. In the wake of the war, calls for the punishment of the defeated were predictably impregnated with lamentations for lost values 'forgotten by liberalism': 'An enormous popular culture has been despised . . . Legends, sayings, singing, habits, weaving, embroidery, costume, housing styles, household industries. Such a varied richness, just in one province!' But more than this, the 'foreignism' of 'scientific progress' threatened to destroy 'essence' itself.[14]

Apart from most workers in *latifundio* areas, who were committed to left-wing trade unions, rural Spain, in the main, supported the military rebels: four-fifths of the 'National Army' during the war was said to be made up of peasants.[15] Meanwhile the population of the cities, especially the working class, but also considerable numbers of the provincial lower middle class, had voted for the Popular Front in February and supported the Republic.[16] This situation was reflected after Franco's victory, when society had forced upon it the maintenance of pre-Republican agricultural systems. The regime formalised the violent reclaiming of collectivised land by estate owners in a decree of November 1939, and legislation in February 1940 officially overturned the

reforms of the Republic's Institute of Agrarian Reform.[17] While small-
holders and tenant farmers migrated because they increasingly could
not make their land work for them, the landless labourers of *latifundio*
Spain did so because they had lost the hope they had before 1939 of
owning the land upon which they worked.

The contradictions of the countryside–city relationship did not simply
disappear. In a sense they were heightened as the glorification of rural
values played a proselytising function, helping to establish the identities
of 'us' and 'them' in Francoist discourse.[18] But the political and military
forces that had won the Civil War, while eulogising the intrinsic merit of
the smallholding peasantry and the mystique of the Spanish soil, were
also concerned with the 'decline' of Spain, as revealed in the decay of
the political system as well as its reliance upon the resources of
foreigners in fighting the war itself.[19]

Franco's own pronouncements revealed this contradiction. Frequently, Spain would be referred to with evident pride as being 'eminently rural' (*campesino*), while the system of *latifundismo* was staunchly
defended. At other moments the word *campesino* became equated with
poverty: rural Spain was 'the Spain that never receives'.[20] According to
Franco, foreign industrial interests prevented Spain from becoming
industrialised and 'wanted her to remain rural which is the equivalent of
her becoming every day poorer'.[21]

Urbanisation, with its inevitable accompaniment of a growing industrial working class, had always carried with it a huge threat to the
established order. The 'leprosy of liberalism' rested on two insidious
sources of power: '*el capital*' and '*la capital*' (capitalism and Madrid).[22]
Spain's cities 'swallowed energies, preoccupations and enormous quantities of money, without creating permanent values', whereas rural and
'austere' Castile, though it was 'the leaven of nationality', hardly existed
to liberals.[23] Francoist natalist policy was supposed to show that the
'neoMalthusians' were wrong and 'regenerate the race' in those 'pau-
perised' rural provinces of the country which were the 'trunk and root of
our people' and 'had generously given their sons' during the war.[24] The
fear of urbanisation was used as support in arguing for a 'permanent
rooting of the producer on the land [as] a political guarantee of the state
itself'.[25] But the dictatorship proved itself better at controlling the threat
of the burgeoning urban sector with violence and coercion than at
caring for the needs of 'obedient, quiet' Spain.[26] Ultimately, Francoism
acquiesced in the withering away of rural society and the slow death of
'the old' hegemony while supervising the long and difficult birth of 'the
new'.[27]

A party official from the rural Castilian province of Toledo wrote in late-1939, giving a sense of the enormous resevoir of resentment in the countryside at the perpetuation of this perceived exploitation by 'the city': 'The state [did] nothing but extract money from the poor farmers [*labradores*], putting it into foreign exchange [and] employing a good deal of it in Madrid, Barcelona and Bilbao, the worst enemies of Spain: and how they use it! Cars, foreign machinery for the Catalans'. This Falangist claimed to have seen the Civil War coming for ten years because of this disequilibrium and prophetically feared he would now pass another ten seeing the peasantry giving up and moving to the cities, 'causing another economic catastrophe, similar to the one we have just suffered'.[28]

Far from winning a rural paradise, the conservative, Catholic small-holders of Spain, on the whole, experienced a profound crisis as they were gradually divested of any influence on policy-making or the social orientation of the regime:[29] 'The circumstantial renovation of strength that [the] Glorious Crusade injected into the mass of people who until then had been without belief [would] degenerate, perpetuating us as a weak nation, unworthy of esteem, poor, and grieving.'[30] Radical Falangists went as far as attacking the intransigence of *latifundistas* and suggested land confiscations in order to control the sources of production. But their pleas fell on deaf ears.[31]

Trapped between the power of large landowners and the industrialising objectives of the dictatorship that they had suffered to create, peasants had no place to go politically: 'Entire sectors of the Nation [would be] sacrificed' if some sense of equilibrium was not introduced.[32] However, to the regime, the future resided in Spain's urban centres, those places where control of the state had been wrenched from the Republic, even though burgeoning cities were fraught with danger.

Agricultural policy was a product of the experience of civil war itself, in many ways. Blanket repression carried out as the Nationalist forces proceeded north through the *latifundio* regions of Andalusia and Estremadura toward Madrid, in the summer and early autumn of 1936, was a harsh disciplining of a workforce whose aspirations had in some part been met by the reforms of the Republic.[33] On many of the farms and estates of central and southern Spain in the aftermath of the Civil War the workforce was seriously depleted by the number of executions and imprisonments and the enforced exile of workers from home communities.[34] Landowners, or their estate managers, were often responsible for the identification of the guilty. Agricultural workers who survived the Civil War purges in Seville, for example, were rounded up and sent to their own villages to be detained in purpose-built camps to be 'examined'.[35] In central Spain, during 1940, it was not unusual for a farm which had employed around 500 workers prior to the war to be employing only 25[36] and for much of the first post-war decade imprisonment and conscription into the army adversely affected agricultural production levels.

In rural Catalonia, where political conflict had revolved around relations between tenant farmers and landlords, family farms went into rapid decline as the fear of leases ending provided little incentive to work efficiently. At the same time, many farmers' sons had been killed at the front, while others had escaped to France and dared not return. Others had been conscripted, while hundreds were rounded up and sent into work battalions as punishment for past misdeeds.[37] The feeding of the working population of industrial Barcelona was severely affected by the repression of small agrarian producers in the Catalan countryside. Farm labourers were unable to work the traditional twelve-hour day because they were so under-nourished and theft of vegetables and cereals from the fields was habitual as workers attempted to feed themselves and their families.[38] In some areas, labourers refused to work for money, which was useless if bread could not be bought.[39] A programme of help from army conscripts promised by the state never materialised.[40]

Rural production was painfully slow in reaching pre-Civil War levels. It probably did not reach 1936 levels in most sectors of the economy until 1951.[41] The 'new order' in fact meant the return of an old inefficient, dependent and parasitic system of production. Official figures show that agricultural production remained depressed throughout the 1940s. It has been estimated that total wheat production in 1949 was less than that of 1939–40.[42] The total area cultivated for the production of wheat did not apparently rise appreciably until the early 1950s. In 1941, wheat production, at least according to official figures, was probably a million tons short of the amount needed to feed the population.[43]

In terms of material damage, though, *latifundio* Spain had been hardly affected by the conflict.[44] The impression of Robert Hodgson, Britain's 'diplomatic agent' in Nationalist Spain, writing in 1938, was that damage had been on the whole extraordinarily small, and 'reconstruction' was 'taken in hand at once as territory was 'liberated' using Spanish resources'.[45] In some instances, as old landowners were handed back their land, they stood to benefit from the improvements in production or investment introduced under the reforms of the Republican Institute of Agrarian Reform.[46]

The agricultural regions appear to have fed Nationalist Spain relatively well, during the conflict itself, there being sufficient supplies for

Franco's planes to bombard Republican Madrid and Barcelona with loaves of bread as an exercise in propaganda.[47] Moreover, the loss of livestock may have been overestimated. According to a bureaucrat of the Falangist national agricultural syndicate, there had been 14 million head of sheep in 1936, a figure which had risen to 17 million by 1944.[48] The only lasting material effect in *latifundio* Spain, it seemed, resulted from the political purges which continued for several years after the formal cessation of the war, though labour shortages have also been over-estimated.[49]

The production and trade of wheat determined much of economic development and everyday life in Spain. In the 1940s, both were regulated, first, according to ideological considerations, and, second, according to a desire to discipline and punish the politically suspect. Both were also traditionally characterised by speculation and exploita-tion.[50] The state's intervention in production and distribution of wheat and other crops was to be effected by the National Wheat Service (Servicio Nacional del Trigo – SNT), established in August 1937.[51] The project adopted for its operation was principally the work of the prominent Falangist landowner and keen advocate of the economic 'theories' of Mussolini, Dionisio Martín Sanz.[52]

Two basic features determined the ethos of the SNT. First, it was believed that the miserable standard of living of agricultural labourers and peasants in Spain was due to the poverty which 'capitalism' and 'the city' imposed upon rural society. Martín Sanz warned that the country-side had almost been 'killed' by 'the viruses' of industrial capitalism.[53] The social problems of the countryside were caused by an unjust distribution of resources and, principally, by a lack of profits generated in rural society.[54] The ideology of the Falange was almost wholly based upon eulogies to rural society and hardly touched upon urban Spain or industry.[55] The party's twenty-six-point political programme included a lengthy section dedicated to the land question (points 17 to 22). Point 18, for instance, stressed a need to '[guarantee] the farmer an adequate minimum price for all his produce . . . By seeing to it that much of what is nowadays absorbed by the cities in payment for their intellectual and comercial services is returned to the land, in order to endow rural areas sufficiently'.[56]

A more coherent explanation, and that identified by the reformers of the Republic, although only effected by them in a half-hearted manner, lay in the structure of ownership of the land, to be left fully intact under Franco.[57] The artificial protection of agricultural prices in defiance of the needs of 'the city' was a reflection of the outcome of the Civil War itself. But agricultural protection was only systematic in playing into the hands of big producers at the expense of the small. Accumulation of capital was founded on the sacrifices of both urban and rural workers and the smallholding peasants of central and northern Spain.

From the first pronouncements of the Franco authorities it was clear that the maintenance of the price of wheat, in particular, was more important than guaranteed supplies to the population.[58] When *graffiti* appeared on Madrid walls calling on women to protest against the constant rise in the price of bread, this was an opportunity to accuse 'the city' of being greedy and selfish, typically careless of the needs of the peasant farmer.[59]

Although the Republican governments of the 1930s stood accused of being reckless in failing to protect farmers, they had, none the less, hardly been free-marketeers either. But the democratic reforming government of the first years of the decade had been unlucky when, in the early 1930s, it put the priority of feeding the population above agricultural profits and imported wheat only to be faced subsequently with a bumper Spanish wheat harvest and plummeting prices. The effect upon rural Spain's attitude to the democratic regime was enormously damaging.[60] Past mistakes, in the wake of civil war, would have to be rectified by 'just measures' in the 'search for the desired economic autarky'.[61]

The experience during the early years of the Republic reinforced the claim that, since 1932, Spain had entered a phase of over-production of wheat. This interpretation, or myth, perhaps, was strengthened by the fact that several harvests prior to the Civil War had been exceptionally good, and that the Nationalist side during the war had suffered no food shortage. Repression seemed to guarantee Spain's abundant production: 'The harvests this year [1937] are magnificent, because the farmers have been able to work in peace . . . and prices have not risen . . . [S]ufficient so that we will not be obliged to look abroad for two years.'[62]

This view was fortified ideologically. According to Martín Sanz, state policy on wheat could lead the way towards a 'closed economy', 'autarkic' except perhaps for possible links with nations pursuing a similarly planned economy. All that was required was a recognition of the capacity of the Spanish countryside to produce all the wheat necessary for internal consumption. There was no need to look beyond Spain's frontiers. Explicit in the plans of the SNT, as early as 1937, was a freely chosen strategy of self-sufficiency.[63] At the same time, the free market would be 'purified of its imperfections'.[64]

In reality, under repressive dictatorship, Spanish agriculture was incapable of feeding the population though this did not preclude substantial capital accumulation. By the second half of the 1940s, the government would be forced to look beyond the country's frontiers for food as the only salvation from total collapse.[65] Estimates for the 1940s demonstrate how consumption of wheat decreased from over 33 million quintales (100kg) in 1931–5 to under 24 million in the period 1941–5 and again decreased in the period 1946–50. Consumption of other food followed a similar pattern. Doubtless a part of this contraction owed something to the operation of the black market, far from the prying eyes of statisticians.[66]

Consumption was inevitably shaped, not only by social class, but by political considerations. The black market was the economic counter-point of Francoism's triumphal cheers and repression,[67] supplying that part of the population which was least provided for by the state rationing system.[68] Autarky and rationing was no simple 'emergency measure'. Intervention was seen as permanent, where self-sufficiency explicitly repudiated the contagion which was liberalism and the Republic. The exploitation created by intervention was preferable to the 'real black market', which was economic liberalism.[69] Indeed, the black market could legitimately be viewed as the central government's method of levying tribute in favour of a parasitical hierarchy, 'the food-control-lers'.[70] Franco's own attitude is suggested in an often-told anecdote related by the leading Falangist bureaucrat Dionisio Ridruejo, who, when he complained to Franco, in April 1942, about the corruption and the extent of the black market, was told by the Caudillo:

'Look Dionisio, in the middle ages, and also later, there was a custom of sharing out titles, lands, goods and even the hand of some maiden among the combatants who had excelled in battle. Isabella and Ferdinand had to comply with these norms following the conquest of Granada. However, in our days there is no way of rewarding properly those who we think have efficiently contributed to the triumph of the Movement. Some are resigned to accepting this fact: but others listen to people who suggest earning some easy money through some commercial operation and fall into temptation.'[71]

While calorific intake per inhabitant appeared to have plummeted by 21 per cent, the reality for the lower classes was almost certainly much worse.[72] The writer Francisco Umbral commented how disease in the 1940s and 1950s was treated, for 'the rich', with 'the best ham', while the poor were 'cured with the saying of mass and the cemetery'.[73]

The wheat 'programme' of the Franco regime was from the beginning characterised by confusion, inefficiency, and corruption. The state intervened at all levels of production, harvesting, manufacture, sale and distribution. A series of contradictory objectives led to the setting of a relatively low *official* price by the SNT from the outset so as to discourage over-production.[74] When combined with scarcity, this meant that, very quickly, large growers began to disregard the official price and to deal in higher prices with the collusion of state officials. In practice, neither prices nor quantities were fixed according to any definite plan or co-ordinated study.

The official price, of wheat, for example, was set separately in each province regardless of distinctions in production costs. The authorities controlling the local supply of foodstuffs (this department was known simply as *Abastos*) would set a price according to the requirements of local political or economic interests and to the extremes that devastatingly low wages would allow. Neither was there an effective control of distribution. At first, if the official price of a certain product was higher in one place than in another, that product would soon disappear from the shelves where it sold cheaper even if it was locally produced. Very quickly, as the collusion of state authorities became entrenched, official prices became virtually meaningless. An illicit market developed, which dwarfed 'official' transactions.[75] Scarcity was used to control the population. At least twice the quantity of essential food was sold on the black market as was issued officially.[76] Significantly, this black market, or *estraperlo*,[77] as it was known, was popularly considered as a central part of the Francoist terror.[78]

Control over 'the defeated' was, thereby, implemented in the distribution of food. In May 1940, the Comisaria General de Abastecimientos y Transportes (CGAT), the state body charged with the supply and distribution of basic foodstuffs to the population,[79] declared that the provision of supplementary rations of bread would be controlled by a local board, comprising the mayor, the parish priest and the head of the local party.[80] The barest necessities in post-Civil War Spain depended on acceptable social and political behaviour.[81]

Not all of the produce had to be sold to the state. In a conveniently vague manner, it was stated that only that amount necessary 'to attend to the needs of national consumption' was to be put at the disposal of the state. Succesive new regulations, introduced in 1941 and 1943, stipulated that not even this vague directive had to be complied with. Gradually, the state's insistence upon controlling supplies became, even at a formal level, more elastic. Effectively, 'free'-market activity was given official sanction.[82]

The benefits of this informal 'system' were spread very unevenly. While *latifundistas* had the storage capacity to hold wheat back and direct it to the most lucrative market at the right moment, small producers were forced to rely on whatever prices they could obtain. Often this meant the very low state-set price virtually ignored by big producers. This process facilitated a concentration of landholding as landowners able to benefit utilised the capital they were amassing.[83]

A considerable proportion of the harvest in all crops, including wheat, was 'disappeared' by producers for a variety of reasons. Wheat production was almost certainly greater than official figures suggested.[84] Precise quantification remains impossible, since records of transactions, particularly between state agencies, the banks and the military, have been destroyed and access to official documents is still very restricted.[85] However, examination of what we know of the process of commercialisation suggests the enormity of scope for profiteering.

Farmers, both large- and small-scale producers, began by reserving, 'for their own consumption', a proportion of the harvest which was not included in the sworn declaration to the regional office of the SNT. False declarations were the norm: 'It is always inexplicably a bad year'.[86] This was in accordance with the government's ineptly formulated regulations. In fact, in the case of wheat, much of this reserved amount was milled into flour and sold on or used as an alternative article of exchange.[87] But such operations were considerably easier and more lucrative for some producers than for others. Before the production of flour could take place an official warrant (*guía*) was required. A contact within the local state authorities was therefore necessary as well as the financial wherewithal to capitalise on such a relationship before indulging in a highly profitable disposal of supplies.

The remainder of the 'controlled' produce, that which was actually sent to the SNT for distribution, was divided in the following way: first, a percentage was explicitly reserved for the local authorities, ministers and high government officials, 'for banquets and state occasions'. It is difficult to be precise about how this produce was actually disposed of, but a great deal of hoarding took place.[88] Second, a further amount was put aside for the seed requirements of the following season. If prices were favourable, there was a temptation to sell part or even all of this immediately, thereby jeopardising future production. Third, an amount was immediately earmarked for the use of the services: army, navy, air and police.[89] In practice, this meant the feeding of officers and their families: although, again, a great deal was sold. Conscripts were cared for in a very haphazard way and often were fed little better than prisoners. The good folk of Vizcaya received a very poor impression in 1942, for example, when men in uniform attached to a labour battalion were seen to be asking for charity in the streets.[90]

While it was claimed that the Ministry of War had been accumulating stocks of wheat since the end of the Civil War in preparation for any further conflict, it was also well known that a large amount of food was sold by the military on the black market.[91] One of the masterminds of the military rebellion in Barcelona, Colonel Ricardo Rada, who was to

become Captain-General of Andalusia in 1948, caused uproar in a
Madrid hotel in 1942 when he publicly denounced the Civil Governor
of Barcelona, Antonio Correa Veglison, who had taken a tough line in a
case of financial corruption in which Rada was accused of receiving
profits of 50,000 pesetas a year.[92] Correa was something of a hero figure
in certain quarters, making propaganda from a very public prohibition
of the exportation of a consignment of foodstuffs from a hungry
Barcelona.[93] Others have been less positive, seeing him as a corrupt
populist.[94] He was certainly convinced of the basic function of the
regime: 'We defend private property and we cannot forget the rights
thereby acquired . . . [A] difference in culture prevents the transforming
of landworkers into agricultural businessmen'.[95] However, he was
clearly not beyond reproach, ending up in the prison of Carabanchel for
'shady business dealings'.[96]

Another cause of popular indignation was the regular shipping of food
abroad, particularly to Germany and Italy.[97] A proportion of the SNT
wheat quota and other food was regularly sent in this way.[98] Large
quantities of olive oil were sent to Germany and, as a result, although
the olive harvest in 1941 showed a marked improvement on the previous
year, olive oil, a staple of the Spanish working-class diet, could hardly be
found at official prices.[99] A British trade delegation was offered hundreds of tons of olive oil by the Spanish government in early 1940,[100]
and oil continued to be exported very lucratively throughout the hungry
decade of the 1940s. A Falangist report, written in 1950, reviewing the
years since the Civil War and signed '*varios amigos del campo*', exposed
the situation and made a spirited protest at government plans to award
the coveted *Cruz del Mérito Agrícola* to the head of the syndicate of the
olive-oil industry. His only contribution, it was claimed, was to have
'enrich[ed] those who lived from the sweat of the Andalusian peasant
who was dying of hunger'. The Caudillo had been deceived, since the
state union was simply a 'business house' and was in need of 'purification'.[101]

In 1948, popular unrest was created in Valencia when the authorities
tried publicly to deny that rice, the traditional staple diet of the local
working population, was being exported. There was widespread
shortage and a great deal of hunger, despite the good harvest, though it
was reported that rice growers themselves were 'not dissatisfied'.[102]

Campaigns in the regime's press to deny that food was being exported
proved to be increasingly counter-productive, especially when some of
these exports were recorded in the Ministry of Labour's own review.[103]
The motivation was partly to pay off the debt for Axis military aid
accrued by Franco during the Civil War. In effect, the population was

forced to go hungry in the 1940s to pay for the war material which had been used to bomb Spain's cities and crush democracy.

In the south, while it was common knowledge that the harvest in 1940 had been surprisingly good in the circumstances of the post-war, bread was difficult to acquire.[104] The working-class population of Seville and the surrounding countryside had to live on potatoes. In other localities the situation was even more desperate. In late 1941 the headquarters of the state union, the CNS, in Seville, was burned down, a target of popular frustration.[105] An English sailor aboard a cargo ship docked in Cádiz wrote home: 'A couple of Spaniards have been making a shout about the potatoes going to England in this ship. The whole crop is going to England for that matter. Franco has sold us the whole damn lot. The Spanish people have not even seen a potato here for three months.'[106]

The dispatching of food to Germany and Italy aroused open protests, in spite of the dangers. In Cádiz, women seized sacks of beans which were being loaded on to a ship for Nazi Germany, and in Chantada, Lugo, others surrounded the carts which were carrying away the produce and demanded that they should first be given the supplies. A delegation was formed which demanded to see the Civil Governor, successfully obtaining authority for a free market.[107]

Although progress reports on the 'great achievements' of the dairy industry and the sugar industry and of olive-oil production were shown in Spanish cinemas, the people often responded negatively, hissing and booing, since they saw very little of this 'progress' in material terms.[108]

It was popularly believed that rationing was unnecessary and only maintained so that the authorities could enjoy the benefits. This 'artificially contrived shortage' *was* the economy.[109] Within the state syndical organisation (CNS) itself, the 'black-market sector', at least in Barcelona, was powerful and resisted any attempts to curb illicit activities.[110] The party investigation bureau in Madrid reported in 1942 that although 'in the last few days supplies of food had been more regular', the distributing body was 'not in favour' of such efficiency. Supplies were therefore stopped for a week so as to strengthen the link 'between each family and its particular illegal provider'.[111] The identities of the main operators were common knowledge, yet they usually functioned with impunity. Reporting them inevitably entailed an investigation into the 'political background' of the denouncer. State authorities thereby colluded in the strengthening of an economic dependency which was part of social control in the 1940s.

In the industrial province of Vizcaya the black market in food was run by the head of the Civil Guard. In Málaga, one of the most populous cities of the south, the Civil Governor was transferred to Pontevedra (Galicia) in August 1939 on account of his 'shady transactions with foodstuffs'. His successor resigned just a few months later, because he was unable to obtain any satisfaction when he went to Madrid to see how the deplorable food situation could be improved and because he was 'too energetic in his efforts to stamp out abuses among local tradesmen known to be supporters of the Movement'.[112] The Civil Governor of Córdoba, who had managed to quadruple the size of the paltry bread ration by seizing the stores hitherto disposed of by the Falangist syndicates on the black market, was 'got rid of' as a result of this attempt to break out of the grip which the party had over the starving population.[113] The Civil Governor in Gerona, where food prices were three times the official level by 1940, was also implicated in the black market and spent more time in meetings with the proprietors of the city's principal commercial enterprises than with state authorities.[114]

'Rationed' goods, like sugar and butter, were so expensive that the poorer classes sold their right to these items to buy bread.[115] But all manner of obstructions were put in the way of people obtaining ration cards by the authorities, thereby forcing the populace into what were illegal relations with 'unofficial' suppliers. Indeed, in order to receive a ration card (or employment) it was necessary to have an identity card, having gone through a rigorous 'purging' process often involving queuing for days. A black market in these identity cards was soon flourishing, run by officials of the local Party.[116] The need of an individualised ration card to get food at state prices, though in tiny proportions, meant that Republicans in hiding could not feed themselves 'officially'. Rationing became an added layer of repression. Small-scale production of food and the 'illegal' selling of such produce was a defensive measure in the struggle. This was not a question of exploiting the situation to make money but became a political act.[117] Many women, in particular, the wives, daughters or mothers of 'Reds', executed, imprisoned, or in hiding, who recieved no pension from the state and were often not permitted to work, sought a living by selling a little produce illicitly.[118] Detentions in women's prisons rose dramatically during the height of food shortages in the summer of 1941 as a result of a clamp-down on small-scale black-market trading.[119]

In many towns in the province of Barcelona in the winter of late 1940 there had been no supplies of flour for three weeks and therefore there was no bread to be had.[120] There was a simple and quite evident discrepancy between the size of the harvest of various crops, particularly wheat, and the quantities actually shared out at the state's fixed price, according even to Party officials. How could it be that the people were without bread at the beginning of harvest time and without oil in a country which produced more oil than practically any other?[121]

The non-application of the sanctions announced by the state was notorious and created an enormous sense of popular scepticism.[122] Small-time black marketeers were often sanctioned but the authorities repeatedly failed to act on reports of major illegal dealings.[123] Action against offenders who were simply attempting to make ends meet, or helping feed and provision family-members in prison, were generally unpopular.[124]

One member of the opposition movement summed up the situation in 1942: 'When they catch a reactionary [facha] black marketeer nothing happens to him, but if its a 'Red' they stick him in a labour batallion. They only shoot regime people as black marketeers when there is an enormous scandal and they have to shut people up.'[125] Franco continued periodically to lambast the 'speculators': it was a way of deflecting criticism on to shadowy, almost mythical figures who could be depicted as holding back progress, but, at the same time, implied no necessary concrete commitment.[126]

The only noticeable effect the announcement of tougher sanctions against 'clandestine selling' was that prices increased still further as 'offenders' feared, for a while, at least, that they might be running a greater risk.[127] Indeed, there was a real risk for the small operator, producing a tiny quantity of produce on a small plot of land as a way of supplementing miserly wages, that he or she may be arrested and imprisoned. However, as the Party itself admitted in May 1942, no case had yet been seen of the serious punishment of any black marketeer of importance.[128]

Occasionally, however, reports of black market 'abuses' were used as a pretext for 'weeding-out' incipient political opposition within the regime at various levels. In 1942, for example, a member of the dissident Falangist breakaway group Falange Española Auténtica,[129] which operated clandestinely and was considered a real threat by some ministers, was executed, having been accused of illegal wheat sales. Another case was that of the pro-monarchist, and therefore suspect, General Heli de Tella, who was dismissed from the army on the pretext that he was producing black-market flour in his mills.[130]

The state failed to provide peasant farmers with facilities to augment output: 'nobody cares about providing farmers with seeds, fertilisers, animals, animal feed . . . , the farmer has to be procure all this himself, on his own account and at much higher prices than those prevailing before the 18th of July [1936]'. Most of this material continued to be

supplied by major landowners and farmers who could afford to manip-
ulate prices.[131]

Authorities in urban provinces called upon the central administration
to take action to obtain produce[132] and in rural areas local authorities
were pressured to procure supplies and despatch them to the cities.[133]
Peasants were reminded of their 'duty' to repay the state for the creation
of the SNT, 'born in the hard years of our war', to end 'the isolation of
the landworker', by declaring their whole harvest.[134] Peasant producers
were thus prey to state officials (*fiscales*), who forcibly requisitioned
produce that small growers tried to hold on to and had the power to
impose sanctions without any legal process.[135] Peasants at a local inn at
San Martín de Valdeiglesias, near Madrid, declaimed bitterly against the
regime which had sent two Falangist officials to the village, accompanied
by Civil Guards, who ransacked it and removed every vestige of wheat
and flour they could find, paying the fixed government price. The
villagers firmly believed that these officials would later sell a substantial
part of their haul at '*estraperlo*' prices.[136] It hardly needs to be said that
large landowners were not vulnerable to this kind of coercion.[137]

Resistance to the authorities was mounted by peasant communities.
Tenant farmers, the social group which had formed the nucleus, conscripted or otherwise, of Franco's army in the Civil War, were forced
now to organise protests against evictions for non-payment of rents.[138]
An order by the local authorities that the harvest of 1940 be coman-
deered by the state was the occasion of a riot in a village in the province
of Logroño. In La Rioja, smallholders set insects on to the wheat and
the sugar beet, saying that if their children could get neither bread nor
sugar then the locusts should have them instead.[139] In Navarre, local
mayors reacted to an attempt to requisition produce and held a meeting
at which it was decided to resist.[140] Towns in Majorca were also
bordering on famine in 1941. In the town of La Puebla there was a riot
resulting from the sending of inspectors to fine farmers for feeding
maize to their horses and for retaining for their own use too high a
percentage of the flour produced. The National Syndical Delegate
warned that communities which were 'healthy and loyal' were rebelling
against the state's activities.[141] Those who resisted were imprisoned.[142]

The effects of the much-vaunted 'colonisation' programme, an
attempt to create 'family farms' by reclaiming land, were meagre
indeed. Not a great deal could be expected of a system that had begun
by violently clearing the land even of those peasants who had supported
Franco's war effort.[143] Between 1939 and 1954 only 37,000 'colonists'
were settled.[144] The Institute of Colonisation, which decided upon
applications, could hardly be seen as democratic. Speculators were able

to collude with those who sat in judgement over applicants to push up land prices: 'Fancy prices were being paid for inferior land, several intermediaries sharing a rake-off.'[145] Furthermore, the colonised farms were effectively just a recreation of the *minifundio* – the small, fragmented and economically non-viable farm, traditionally found in Galicia but also in other parts of the peninsula. In the 1940s, they became dependent 'islands' adrift in a vast sea of great estates which continued to employ the cheap labour of colonists unable to survive on their own. It was also the big landowners who benefited from state-financed irrigation schemes.[146]

The very worst conditions were suffered by the landless labourers of *latifundio* Spain. In Huelva, for example, workers were to live worse than during the poorest pre-Republican years, relying upon the consumption of acorns and chestnuts, though these were scarce and expensive. A major crisis broke in the winter of 1939–40, when the local authorities were forced to make desperate efforts to obtain wheat from other provinces, like Valladolid, Badajóz and Salamanca, at high expense. Occasionally, there was no alternative but openly to admit that the blame lay with the intervention of the state.[147] Although the wheat harvest in central Spain in the autumn of 1939 was reported as good, the food situation in wheat-growing areas was dire.[148] Circumstances were little better in Badajóz, where children were sent to school across the border in Portugal, where they were better fed.[149] Large sections of the population were starving or on the verge of starvation. In their desperation people resorted to eating dogs and cats caught in the street. Defeat in the Civil War meant the denial of even the most basic vestiges of dignity to much of the population.[150] In the Falangist heartland of Valladolid, one of the prime wheat-producing areas of the country, the food situation was determined by both economic and political considerations. A student at the English Catholic seminary wrote: 'If you say, "*is there plenty of food in Spain?*", the answer is "yes". If you say, "*Is there plenty of food for Spaniards?*", the answer is "No". If you ask where it goes, well you must not ask questions.'

Landowners displayed no sympathy for the plight of rural labourers.[151] Whole areas of the south of Spain, in particular, were riven by disease. Some Falangists debated the possibility of applying some kind of sanctions against absentee landlords who were responsible.[152] Large estates were administered in an extremely unhealthy manner: irrigation channels which provided water to landless labourers and their families were often infected. Many parts of the biggest *latifundia*, like that of the Duque de Huete in Murcia, were malarial. While the number of recorded deaths from malaria in Spain, on average, in the years

1933–5 was 263, in the period 1941–2 it was 1,544. These were epidemic proportions.[153] In the *pueblo* of Fortuna (Murcia) of the 100 townsfolk who had died between the 'liberation' and December 1939, about 50 had died through starvation.[154]

In Madrid, class divisions in the consumption of basic necessities were evident. The condition of the lower classes was rapidly deteriorating by the end of 1939. There was an abundance of bread, cakes and buns, at a price, for the middle classes, but the virtually inedible bread was difficult to obtain at official prices.[155] Flour sold officially at 1.25 pesetas but was actually traded at 12 pesetas per kilo. Black-market bread normally also sold at 12 pesetas the kilo. Potatoes were officially priced at 0.65 pesetas, while the real black-market rate was 2.5. Beans were supposed to be sold at 2.25 per kilo but could not be found for less than 8.5. Meat was rare, except in the best hotels and restaurants. Officially, it ranged in price from 7–12 pesetas the kilo but sold at anything up to 30 pesetas. The lower orders did not partake of this, or much of any kind of protein.

Official wage levels were often not complied with by employers. A casual labourer, in an urban centre, was due 9.4 pesetas per day, but there was no effective mechanism for enforcing the regulations. In the countryside wages were much lower. Rural Spain benefited industrialisation not by feeding the workforce but through the supply of cheap labour. The labour-intensive agricultural system which has been described, paying devastatingly low wages, provided a cowed and harshly disciplined workforce with extremely low expectations.[156] Industrialists, moreover, were as adept at avoiding paying official wages as were landowners.

The US Red Cross found 'appalling conditions of starvation and need of every kind' in the capital. In the summer of 1941 this organisation was 'feeding more than 20,000 starving people in Madrid [and] 30–40,000 [were] living in ruins without a roof over their heads'.[157] Much of the country was in a state of famine, which the press would not mention and to which the possessing classes closed their eyes.[158] Anyone living in the city with money could get enough to eat, and yet, people were fainting from hunger outside well-stocked shops.[159] Comments collected in British government censorship reports suggest something of the scale of the hunger: 'Food has eclipsed politics as the universal topic of conversation'; 'The present state of things is not only tragic but shameful . . . it is the poor who are starving while the rich eat their fill'; 'Madrid is a place of misery, the poor people are starving and the Grandees taking no notice of it'. To one native observer Spain seemed like a 'country of cannibals, in which one half of the population eats the other half . . . As I am an eater, . . . I belong to the Right'.[160] Vegetables were the mainstay of the poor, but a cabbage at 6 pesetas costs a worker's daily wage.[161] Children were 'dying like flies . . . In the streets of Madrid you see figures just like those we can remember from pictures of the great Russian famine'.[162]

There were famine conditions also in the province of Seville. In the village of the mines of the Esperanza Copper and Sulphur Company people were dying of starvation at the rate of five or six per day in a village of some 4–5,000 inhabitants. The urban working class in the city itself was no better off than those in country districts,[163] where the mortality rate from starvation was on an even larger scale.[164] In parts of the province of Cáceres, in central Spain, it was reported that for months on end there were people who had been forced to live off only grass cooked with salt. In August 1941, the regime's own medical commissioners, appointed by the Spanish Director General of Health, warned that in the coming winter some 1,700,000–2,000,000 deaths would occur through hunger and diseases related to malnutrition.[165]

The state strategy of import substitution, since it could never have succeeded rapidly, implied that the regime was prepared to risk food production in the interests of making Spain independent.[166] The production of chemical fertilisers in Spain was justified by the government because of the drain which importation had previously on national finances rather than as an attempt to increase food cultivation. Fertiliser production was granted all the benefits laid down in legislation to protect 'national industry' proclaimed in October 1939.[167] The autarkic pretensions of the regime thereby threatened agricultural production. The Provincial Secretary of FET–JONS in Zaragoza, an agricultural engineer, wrote to the provincial party chief, in 1940, complaining that, however much more chemical fertiliser was being manufactured in Spain, the lack of sufficient supplies made agricultural production very difficult.[168]

This issue became a cause for resistance. A protest leaflet of June 1942, printed in Catalan and distributed in Barcelona by the underground remnant organisation of the Catalan Communist Party (PSUC), pointed to the fact that chemicals for fertilisers, which were so badly needed for agricultural production, were also being exported and used in German armaments factories.[169] While the Axis was supplied, Francoism failed to provide bread for the masses and simply ordered them 'to keep silent and be happy'.[170]

Hunger and the search for food meant that the extent of population change varied from place to place. A combination of the direct control of demographic movement and the parlous material conditions under which the population lived meant that during the 1940s, internal

migration was limited.[171] To relocate required a 'safe-conduct' issued
by the political authorities. But migration was often a question of life
and death. In some industrial areas workers returned to familiar rural
communities in an attempt to grow their own food to survive. A report
issued by the Bilbao Chamber of Commerce complained that, 'many
unmarried miners, from other provinces, who lived in shelters where the
board and lodging absorbed almost their entire daily wage, prefer to
return to their home provinces and dedicate themselves to work on the
land, generally with a guarantee, besides, of more abundant nourishment'.[172] But population movement was complex. It was often determined by local factors. In the Catalan province of Lérida, for example,
the 1940s saw a substantial influx of immigrants from other parts of
Spain attracted by the up-turn in mining and by the construction of
hydro-electric plants.[173] Overall, in the 1940s, there was a shift towards
slow urbanisation as workers from unproductive rural areas fled hunger
and moved to industrial zones looking for work.[174] The Civil War itself
was also an impulse towards urbanisation as the population fled the
repression. In the ten-year period from 1935–1945 the population of
some Spanish cities had grown considerably: Las Palmas by 25%,
Valencia and La Coruña by 40%, Salamanca by 44%, Burgos by 50%
and Albacete by 56%.[175]

The regime treated agriculture with the benevolent disregard required
by elites who were satisfied simply by guaranteed protection and guaranteed prices. Industry, on the other hand, was subject to rather more
activism. While the Ministry of Agriculture was run by inefficient and
uninterested figures on the margins of the government,[176] industrial
policy was largely controlled by Franco's long-time close acquaintance
Juan Antonio Suanzes. Budget estimates for 1949 showed 32.74 per
cent of total expenditure dedicated to the army, navy and air ministries,
while 0.85 per cent was proposed for the Ministry of Agriculture.[177]
However, above all, the regime's activities revealed its propensity to use
corruption as a way of mediating between sectional interests, united in a
kind of 'pact of blood', determined to enjoy their victory, rather than
invest directly in the economy.

By the 1950s, the chaotic state of agriculture could no longer be
'explained' by reference to the Civil War. The social situation in the
olive-producing *latifundio* region of Jaén, in Andalucía, for example, was
disastrous still in 1951. The provincial head of the Movement reported
to the National Syndical Delegate that unemployment was rife, and
permanent for many labourers: 20,000 families lived an 'utterly
wretched' existence in the constant hope of 'getting a scrap of bread and
oil regularly throughout the year in order to live: clothing, shoes,

housing no longer worry them since they are something quite out of reach: they are dressed in rags, the majority barefoot, many live in caves . . . in many cases in such a rudimentary fashion that was surpassed even by palaeolithic man'. For the rest, close to 60,000 families, for five or six months of the year they lived in a similar condition on the edge of starvation, 'dependent on a little bread and oil in order not to perish'. This Falangist was at a loss to understand how such a province, with 32 million olive trees, producing a third of all Spain's olive oil, could suffer so.[178] Although the people 'knew nothing of statistics', they 'intuitively' sensed that a catastrophic epidemic threatened because they understood better than anyone how their lives depended upon a particular minimal amount of bread and oil. In 1946, almost a quarter of all those who died in the province had suffered a deficiency disease.[179]

The defeat of agrarian reform in the 1930s was consummated in the aftermath of the Civil War, through autarky, by a sacrificing of the landworkers of the south in the interests of national industrialisation and the concentration of wealth. Paltry industrial development could not absorb excess rural labour despite the resumption of the urbanisation process in the 1940s. Ultimately, Francoism would export Spain's unemployment problem in the massive emigration of the 1960s. By this time, Falangist calls for land redistribution were somewhat beside the point: the future of Spanish agriculture resided with the owners of mechanised large-scale operations carrying on commercialised farming who had benefited from the huge forced sacrifices of the working population in the 1940s.[180]

It was through the inculcation of this daily sense of sacrifice that economic modernisation took place in Spain in the decades after the Civil War. According to the leading Falangist, José Luis de Arrese, '[t]he Spaniard lives more on pride than on bread and knows better how to die of hunger than to humiliate himself'.[181] A kind of 'work ethic' was produced in the immediate post-war years when masses of people had to labour at several jobs at once in order simply to survive. The Spanish worker was turned into a worker of the 'double-day': '[S]he would leave one job to go straightaway to another. For many years, in order to obtain a remunerative wage [s]he would duplicate the hours worked, expending an incalculable amount of energy'. In the process of forced accumulation, 'repression did not begin with prison but in th(is) labour . . . to obtain the reproductive wage'.[182] The violently imposed sacrifices wrung from the defeated in the 1940s, driving down popular expectations, formed the psychological foundation of Spain's post-war industrial growth and determined who the beneficiaries of this subsequent development would be.

8   Austerity and resistance

'*Populorum progressio*: thanks to the cleverness and the competence of your brilliant technocrats, the zealous male nurses of a patient who had been ill for decades, who despite a provident bloodletting was under strict orders to remain in bed around the clock and not move a muscle, to take a sleep cure, to stick to a diet of plain water: but who is now on the way to recovery thanks to the ubiquitous power of a certain barrel-shaped gentleman.'

(Juan Goytisolo, *Reivindicación del conde don Julián*)

Silence and austerity

In September 1939, the Rome correspondent of the principal Barcelona daily newspaper, *La Vanguardia Española*, in recommending Italian society under Mussolini to Spaniards, suggested the possible function of self-sufficiency: 'that vague concept of autarky was translated into a graphic image which was inserted into the senses of the people . . . sublimating it, converting it even into a catechism, a true guide to politico-social perfection: in a word; into a mysticism'. This was a succinct explanation of how self-sufficiency was supposed to function ideologically and socially in Franco's Spain, contributing to the silencing of resistance.[1]

The notion of silence is not an unproblematic one applied to any society, however totalitarian. Resistance, very often, is mounted and symbolised at a distance from public politics. Under Franco, education, religion, press, radio and the censorship of literature were all aimed at the depoliticisation of social consciousness. And, inevitably, resistance was shaped by the extent of this authoritarian rule. But, however strident and unremitting the pronouncements of the regime, rejection was expressed in a kind of popular cynicism, which was articulated in the spaces between the official rhetoric promising the fulfilment of 'destiny' or the 'transcendence of the nation'. The 1940s saw what Vázquez Montalbán has dubbed 'the reign of the ellipsis' in order 'to express that which could not be expressed'. Popular songs, for example, served as a way for people 'to express their right not to understand at all things as they were and to turn this professing of the absurdity of things into a declaration of the utmost lucidity'.[2] Indeed, perhaps *silences*, in the plural, would better capture the multiplicity of ways in which repression and resistance ought to be understood.

'Exchange' itself, particularly of ideas, was considered dangerous,[3] and the significant exchanges, close to real power, were beyond reach. It may now be a little clichéd to say it, but post-war Spain can be visualised through the analogy of the beehive.[4] The aim of the dictatorship was to prevent an erratic dispersal of images and to repulse foreign ideas: 'order' was everything. The symbol of the regimented beehive could theoretically have been used as an example to aid the 'casting out of fleeting images that invade the spirit like a disorderly swarm of flies'.[5]

The idea of an all-enveloping silence is misleading: thousands of daily social exchanges were obviously taking place. There existed a dialectical relationship between silence, on the one hand, and absorption in a seemingly constant febrile activity of production and reproduction, on the other. In a negative sense, the beehive analogy can be taken further. Much of this activity, in the end, seems almost useless because it was comparatively without meaning. It was in the interest merely of survival. But the image can also be too restrictive and excessively discounts people's capacity to make their own meaningful 'movements' in defiance of patterns described from on high; with neither a real nor a metaphorical 'safe-conduct' issued to the politically and morally reliable.[6] Viewed through the Marxist lens of social reproduction, ordinary people 'reproduced themselves', in some ways, better than did the regime itself, which rested on the contradictions of self-sufficiency and the threat of violence.

In the wake of the Civil War the regime tried to turn back the clock to a more 'secure', less uncertain, time. In order to transport society towards this image a utopian vision of Spain was constructed. But, traumatised though Spanish society undoubtedly was, this vision of the nation could never 'mystify' sufficiently people's experience to be persuasive. The gulf between the ideology and the reality was huge. People experienced the harmful effects of dictatorship and self-sufficiency daily and were hardly likely to be convinced of the 'merits' of Francoist social quarantine.

Although seemingly abstract, the concepts of hierarchical unity, purity and redemption all directly affected people's daily lives as the regime justified its oppression and sought ideas around which the dictatorship's component parts could cohere. Those forced to flee and

Figure 10   Regimentation and 'modesty' of dress of young women at the
Escuela Mayor in Málaga, 1940.

fight for sheer survival in the *guerrilla* resistance (or, at least, actively to
support it), liberal teachers, people who did not attend mass, women
who infringed the Francoist moral code, those with a 'Red' or 'separatist' past, and many other groups, were likely to suffer physical and
mental torture and humiliation, internal exile or banishment, denial of
work, starvation wages, the confiscation of goods and property, even
execution. All of this was part of the regime's 'purifying mission'.
Preying on 'the defeated' was legitimated by ideas and bound elites to
each other. But, in practice, most people led far from 'pure' or 'austere'
lives in the way that the ideology pretended. Nor could it be argued, as
we have already seen, that regime functionaries or ministers themselves
lived according to the official moral dogma, given the corruption that
was intrinsic to Francoist authority.

Most people suffered enormous material hardship and the psychological pressure of living restricted, partially closed lives, culturally, spiritually and materially. But it is to be doubted that most ordinary people
accepted either the 'diagnosis' of Spain's 'sickness' or the 'cure' offered
by the regime. If people sought consolation in religion, or appeared to
accept the dictatorship's version of the 'New Spain', even mouthing the
slogans, or joined associational organisations founded by the state, it
was not necessarily because Francoist socialisation had 'succeeded'.[7] In

leading 'impure' lives, individuals both expressed rejection and also experienced repression as they were forced into a multitude of 'small prostitutions' in order to get by.[8] Most people concentrated on assimilating defeat, the sense of horror and loss that had befallen the country and their lives. This meant a complicated interplay between acceptance and defiance.[9]

In small ways, the significance of regime institutions and ideas was subverted and people, anyway, sought discreet, alternative 'off-stage' spaces within which to articulate and express their differences with the dictatorship's normality.[10] For the majority, most time and space was occupied in surviving materially and most thinking was absorbed in grieving or forgetting. Everything, especially buying and selling food, was done urgently, but, apparently, 'in silence', without 'talking politics'.[11] 'Legitimacy' meant very little in a post-Civil War society, where simply to be alive seemed 'tremendously surprising'.[12] And yet, it is possible to talk about resistance even in these harsh years of the early 1940s.

It is pointless to attempt analysis of society in Spain in the early 1940s without referring, above all else, to the Civil War. The regime sought legitimation largely on the basis of its military triumph. As the Civil War drew to a close, Franco proclaimed his determination to complete the task which the military rising against the Republic had initiated. Those who desired some form of mediation or intercession only,

served the Reds and the hidden enemies of Spain. Her war is not an artificial thing: it is the coronation of an historic process in the struggle of the *Patria* against the *anti-Patria*. He who thinks of mediation proposes a broken, materialist, divided, wretched and subdued Spain . . . A peace for today and another war for tomorrow . . . National Spain has conquered and it will not allow its victory to be snatched away or impaired, not for anything or anybody.[13]

Autarky, or self-sufficiency, was an expression of the will to pursue a 'pruning' of 'Spain's enemies', of the utopian and grandiose Francoist image of 'the triumphant Nation', and of the instability of the 'New State'. Power was both violent *and* ill defined, at once 'traditional', 'charismatic' and 'rational' in unpredictably varying degrees. It was Spain's turning inwards and meditating on the victory, implicit in autarky, that welded the victors together. The fiction of 'the Crusade', and its mentality, developed during the war, was enlarged as a kind of passion play occupying the national stage, and played out before an unenthusiastic audience for the gratification of a parasitic elite.

On New Year's Eve 1939, Franco broadcast to the nation. He insisted that no amnesty could be granted until the 'murders' of the Civil War

had been 'expiated' and promised that henceforward, nine months after
the formal cessation of hostilities, measures would ensure that 'justice'
would be carried out in a 'calm' manner, in contrast to the way in which
repression had been carried out hitherto.[14] Guaranteed security, at least
for the politically reliable, seemed like salvation to those who had felt
their ways of life threatened by the Republic and seen themselves as
virtually 'stateless' under its government. In fact, thousands of others
who identified in one way or another with the ideals of the Republic or
exposed their differences with the 'Glorious National Movement' were
still to fall victim to Francoism's violence.

Self-sufficiency fed the appetite of Francoist nationalism for administering difference. It reinforced the daily social segregation of 'defeated'
from 'victors' through economic coercion, continually re-presenting the
boundaries of 'the Nation' in official discourse, while economic details
were glossed over. Just as Spain's 'liberal capitalism without roots' was
'finished', so too would the 'filthy [sucio], subjugating workerism of the
rope-sandal and the gangster' be finished.[15] The 'eradication of error',
with no consideration of reconciliation, ultimately determined the social
reality of the 1940s.[16] The enforced estrangement of two broad sections
of society in a country to be 'purged', while sealed off from the outside,
was the environment for the exercise of power.

British diplomats were convinced that only when this job of purging
was done would the authorities return to formal politics.[17] Spain had
'turned inwards, living in an artificially created vacuum'.[18] From the
first moment, the task of 'disciplining' the population was associated
with a 'quarantine' of the 'New Spain'.[19] The head of the forces of
occupation in Barcelona, General Eliseo Álvarez Arenas, promised that
the economy of the city – so important to the economic future of Spain –
would be swiftly reconstructed, but only after a 'period of transition' in
which a 'strong principle of authority' backed by an 'iron discipline' had
created the conditions for a return to 'normality'. The 'New Spain'
would be 'autarkic and independent': 'from the Pyrenees to the dividing
line of Gibraltar, Spain was to be Spain and Spain only'. Isolation would
enforce a national and social unity imposed at the point of a gun.[20]

The notion of a collective purging through sacrifice permeates the
Francoist proclamations concerning social relations in post-war Spain.
It was believed that industrialisation could take place on the backs of the
population because the Spaniards were historically accustomed to
making sacrifices: this was the supreme quality of the Spanish race.[21]
The ability to improvise with food (and with hunger) was an 'essential
condition of the Spanish woman'.[22]

Self-denial was not merely imposed in a material sense, but was central to the regime's ideology. The military virtues of 'abnegation, discipline, obedience, submission to hierarchy, restraint, and an elevated sense of honour' were to be propagated.[23] Although poverty inevitably caused dirtiness and illness, it was also linked to *limpieza*, cleanliness or purity, because it implied a lack of 'contamination' by worldly goods.[24] *Austeridad* was taken to mean both austerity, in a material sense, and severity, implying domination, and the constant reference to self-abnegation, meaning either, was full of ambiguity. Franco was depicted as possessing this quality as the personification of military virtues and Spanishness itself. Austerity 'elevated and purified' according to Falangist doctrine.[25] According to the myth, the Spanish peasantry, in particular, was able to survive on only the barest necessities. This ascetic construction of small-holders and tenant farmers, principally in northern and central Spain, as submissive, long-suffering and peaceful, had been reinforced by their providing the backbone of the Nationalist fighting forces.[26]

A deeply entrenched sense of austerity legitimised the action of the regime, at least in the eyes of the victors themselves. Asceticism was an important public and private part of the economy of Catholicism employed to justify the formal economic policy of self-sufficiency. The relationship between 'denial' or restraint and 'government of the body', between asceticism and 'regimen' is evident. The etymological relationship is relevant: '*Régimen*', from *regere* or rule, which also refers medically to therapy, especially a regulated diet. But the term also carries the archaic meaning of 'a system of government'. 'Asceticism' comes from the Greek term for monk and from exercise, but is also associated with the notion of work or disciplined practice.[27] In the aftermath of war and revolution in Spain there was security in encouraging the 'training' of minds and bodies.[28] Asceticism in Franco's Spain served as a basis of self-discipline drawn from both Catholic and Falangist doctrine. It implied a form of penitence and sacrifice to atone for 'national' transgressions and the 'ascetic repression of natural impulses'.[29] The notion of a kind of enforced material abstinence was seen as the economic counterpart of cultural self-sufficiency, and shunning contact with the outside reflected Spain's denial of decadent democratic political systems. Seclusion, isolation, poverty, the infliction of pain, sexual continence, even fasting, these were all a part of the ideological picture painted by the post-war dictatorship. Austerity rested on restraining cultural reference points as, for instance, in the image of the manly ideal of the 'warrior-monk' reconstructed during and after the Civil War.[30]

The formulation of the 'warrior-monk' drew upon the past as a continuous crusade beginning with the Reconquest, embodied in the

Spanish combatant, 'soldiers of the faith', who carried with them the ideals of the nation: religion and war. These conferred a willingness to display the 'austere and virile discipline' of 'Franciscans',[31] renouncing material and bodily pleasures and submitting to military obedience. In the language of Francoism, matter and the body disappear except in talking of evil and punishment. The 'taut ascetecism of peace' offered no material comforts but, rather, produced 'ever-watchful angels with swords' imbued with 'discipline, soldiering, hierarchy, mission, brotherhood: virtues rejuvenated by torrents of blood and tears, by horrendous sacrifices and immortal deeds'.[32]

'Military asceticism' or 'militant Catholicism', which amounted to virtually the same, signified a mystical historical continuity: 'From Captain Iñigo de Loyola, who called his Holy Institution "the Company" [of Jesus], to the cry "Long Live Death" of our Legionnaires, an elevated mysticism burns in the Spanish military soul',[33] and the Caudillo's lieutenants would be fortified by 'austerity, morality and labour . . . as monastic orders'.[34]

The well-known manual of asceticism, the *Ejercicios espirituales*, of San Ignacio de Loyola (1491–1556), frequently invoked by Francoists, was a prescription of isolation, shunning the external world, which aimed to control all activities and direct everything in life toward 'profitable' endeavour.[35] Its asceticism was at the heart of a Catholic religion that, in the orthodox view, constituted Spanish identity.[36]

Two features are particularly relevant to discussion of early Francosim. First, what sets the mysticism of Ignatian austerity off from the histories of other Spanish mystics, is the extent of the institutionalism of the *Ejercicios* within the Church.[37] But, second, since the relationship between the hierarchy of the Catholic Church and the Franco regime in the aftermath of the Civil War was such an intimate one, the early 1940s saw encouragement from both church and regime for institutionalised collective acts of penance in the name of the Ignatian tradition and to the glorification of the 'Crusade'.[38]

In Barcelona, centre of 'dissolute doctrines', according to the review *Ecclesia*, an 'immense throng' attended a mission in March 1941, which culminated in a procession of the sacred crucifix, the *Cristo de Lepanto*, symbol of a previous victory against 'Godless hordes', accompanied by church dignitaries and leaders of the local Falange. Some 50,000 people attended a similar occasion in Seville at the same time, where 'not a single detainee in the teeming city prison failed to take communion'.[39] This activity on the part of Acción Católica dwarfed most of the *Movimiento*'s own public displays of support. *Ecclesia* also claimed that, by April 1941, 100,000 youngsters had participated in 'spiritual

Figure 11   Prayer to 'The Fallen' in the austere 'shelter of rest' (*albergue de reposo*) of the Sección Femenina. An Ignatian retreat to meditate on the losses of the war, August 1942.
(Arxiu Fotogràfic, Arxiu Històric de la Ciutat, Barcelona.)

exercises' arranged by Acción Católica.[40] The first congress of Ignatian *Ejercicios Espirituales* in Barcelona, in May 1941, was presided over by Cardinal Pedro Segura y Sáenz, Archbishop of Seville, the Captain-General, Luis Orgaz y Yoldi, and the Civil Governor of the province Correa Veglison, and was ceremoniously concluded by the Minister of Justice, Esteban Bilbao.[41] Those who voluntarily underwent courses of 'closed' spiritual training in this way were overwhelmingly middle-class believers. By the early 1950s the 'Golden Age' of mass exercises was drawing to a close, criticised for being excessively propagandistic and psychologically damaging to young *ejercitantes*, since concentration was inevitably upon the 'first week' of the Ignatian prescription, dealing with sins, hell and purgation. While it is true that 'open' sessions *en masse* were arranged for workers in factories, as part of this propaganda and purification, they generally seem to have been taken up as a way of enjoying a paid break from the work routine.[42] 'Wholly unpopular' collective papal homages, to give an opportunity for displays of political rhetoric before the workers, were organised 'without taking into account the reaction which they produce in the minds of the working mass, as if it consisted of schoolchildren or Sisters of Charity'.[43]

Figure 12   Confirmation Day, July 1939, Plaça de San Jaume, Barcelona.
Symbolising the victory of Catholic–fascist giganticism.
(Arxiu Fotogràfic, Arxiu Històric de la Ciutat, Barcelona.)

Ignatian thought was never far from the political discourse of early Francoism. For Spaniards, according to one of the dictatorship's prominent psychiatrists and ideologues, 'the most sublime in life, its sanctification, consists in restraint', in 'stripping away' that which is extraneous to 'the most profound and most unadorned': '*Hispanidad* [Spanishness] supposes an ascetic posture in life . . . *Hispanidad* is asceticism of the person . . . hastening as soon as possible in this life the pure immateriality and intemporality of eternal glory.'[44]

The three pathways of the mystical tradition, purgative, illuminative and unitive, had obvious attractions in re-establishing social order in a Catholic society such as Spain in this period. But, wrenched from the private, contemplative context envisioned by San Ignacio and many Jesuit followers, they became a more violent tool of social repression. To Roland Barthes, the *Ejercicios* represent, anyway, a totalitarian economy where time itself is strictly organised from waking to sleep, creating a linguistic vacuum in the exercitant, necessary for 'the triumph of a new language'.[45] Under Francoism, they were employed to accentuate isolation and the political division of pure and impure that has already been described. This division was strengthened by comparison with 'less

Spanish' groups, particularly in children's books: 'Castile, faithful to her destiny, satiated with austerities, wretched in her wastelands and in her self-denying people, did not waver a moment and put herself at the side of tradition, which spoke of sacrifice but also of grandeur. Catalonia, rich, proud of its prosperity, wanted nothing of sacrifices . . . [and] . . . rose with the Anti-Spain.'[46]

Austerity was not only revealed by *displaying* purity but, necessarily, also by *imposing* it. Spanish soldiers, Francoist militias and the Catholic church all had a 'purifying mission' which tended to sanctify violence and repression. Blood became redemptive, spilt in order to 'renew' as part of a 'regenerating purification'.[47]

Autarky and resistance

Repression and resistance in the aftermath of the Civil War were effected in the overlapping rural and urban contexts of backward-looking ideas, emphasising a style of living prescribed by Catholicism and soldierly hierarchy, on the one hand, and more 'modern' class domination, on the other. 'Tradition' and 'modernity', morality and economics, the payment of tribute and the accumulation of capital, all inevitably intertwined in a situation of violence and enormous hardship.

Hunger, the black market, unemployment and organised discrimination and terror formed an unfavourable context for the articulation of working-class protest. Collective worker dissent was, indeed, relatively rare in the early 1940s. However, the concentration by historians on the political organisations of the left, which had organised the war effort but were mostly functioning in exile after 1939 and therefore distanced from the workers themselves, has, apart from the armed *guerrilla* campaign,[48] left an overwhelming image of passivity and submission, which is not borne out by the details of Falangist intelligence reports, which make constant reference to rejection of the dictatorship by the populace.[49]

A semi-underground spirit of defiance and cynicism displayed in popular stories, refrains, rumour-mongering and complaints existed side-by-side with more organised dissent and the brutality of the forces of order. Manifestations of protest, either by workers or by other groups, were harshly dealt with. The organisers of the first strike in Barcelona under Franco, at the major industrial factory of La Maquinista, in March 1941, were executed without trial.[50] In the immediate aftermath of the Civil War collective protest was almost impossible to mount. But leaflets calling attention to the iniquities of the black market, the corruption of the *sindicatos* and of Francoist rule in general and making comparisons with the atmosphere of hope associated with the Second Republic were regularly in circulation.[51] Full-blooded strikes, however, were rare and of short duration. The wonder, perhaps, is that protests took place at all.

In the traditionally militant railway workshops of Valladolid, during these early years, workers and their families suffered a serious lack of rations and were paid a paltry 8.5 pesetas for a day's exhausting and hazardous work. Faced with this situation, employees began by following officially prescribed channels and approached the state union to call for a wage increase that would cover the barest necessities. But this plea was ignored, as was quite normal, by the officials of the *sindicato*. Despite the bloody purge that had accompanied the military rising in Valladolid in July 1936, directed principally at the railway workers, a 'Marxist cell' had become active by early 1942, organising protests and collecting funds as part of a network stretching to Miranda de Ebro and León, incorporating mineworkers as well. The movement, however, like most during this period, was rooted out by the local forces of public order and suppressed.[52]

In the face of similar intransigence by the local state syndicate, Madrid metro workers, finding it impossible to afford sufficient food even as company profits grew, also voiced their harsh criticisms of the system that 'only favoured capitalism' and sabotaged the system.[53] Factories in Seville too were plagued by worker sabotage.[54] Asturian miners, called upon to work extra hours as an 'obligatory service to the state' in the militarised coalmines, where dissent could lead to execution, vented their anger by leaving work early or not turning up at all. Even in these difficult, hungry years strikes were organised for increased rations and regular go-slows were mounted with the objective of decreasing production.[55] Old traditions, like the abandonment of work by the labour force whenever a miner was killed in a mine accident, a regular occurrence in these years, were upheld against explicit orders from the authorities.[56]

Resistance, or at least, defiance of authority, was also carried on in the perpetuation of certain rituals. To the consternation of Falangists, symbolic occasions, like 14 April, anniversary of the proclamation of the Republic in 1931, were, in many places, always marked in some manner by leftists and a strong vigilance by the forces of party and state was mounted on these occasions.[57] May Day, the traditional 'holiday of the proletariat', continued to be celebrated by bands of Republicans absenting themselves from work. Indeed, a 'great mass' of people, in the Basque province of Guipúzcoa, during the early 1940s, for example, continued to be 'in opposition to the cause', and chose particular significant days to express their dissent, sometimes in spite of the fact that there was no immediate food shortage.[58]

Popular rejection of the dictatorship was articulated daily in people's attitudes developed far from the machinations of exiled political organisations. The people were 'defeated but not convinced'. 'Marxist ideology' had not been 'replaced by another'.[59] But it was the Allied victory in 1945 that brought the first real *wave* of worker protest, although, once again, action was, on the whole, spontaneous.[60] The transport and metal workers of Barcelona, for instance, celebrated Nazi Germany's capitulation in May, by laying down their tools, signifying their defiance of what was seen as a moribund authority and in expectation of the consequent downfall of the Franco regime that had been installed with the substantial assistance of Hitler and Mussolini. Strikes were declared again in August to mark the end of the war in Asia.[61]

These actions began to tarnish the regime's image of invincibility. Soon after, protest actions were called in one of the industrial heartlands of the country, the textile sector of Barcelona. Throughout the latter 1940s, there was maintained a relatively constant pressure from below pushing for improved conditions, culminating in the Barcelona general strike of March 1951.[62] In particular, the factories of the industrial area of Manresa became a centre for protest. It was here in January 1946 that the first general strike of the Franco era took place, called in protest at the docking of a day's pay for a compulsory feast day to mark the fall of the town to Franco's troops in 1939.[63] The workers, mainly women, succeeded not only in their initial objective but also forced a wage rise from employers. Within months, leaflets were seen to be distributed at the factory gates of the biggest textile works in Barcelona and a constant 'go-slow' had been instituted in support of a change of government.[64] This pressure was heightened considerably by the May Day strikes in the Basque Country in 1947, when between 25,000 and 50,000 industrial workers stayed away for several days in spite of the risk of losing their jobs and suffering the repression of the state.[65]

Workers also resisted joining state syndicates, to which they had to pay a fee for obligatory membership. Indeed, in spite of the threat of detention and imprisonment, workers frequently maintained their own illegal organisations within the workplace, directly rejecting state institutions and resisted paying the union 'quota'.[66] More usually, though, and increasingly through the 1940s, activists used the state unions for their own purposes, infiltrating the official organisation in order to call for improvements in wages and conditions.[67]

Popular rejection of the regime was manifested in various ways. In Ripollet, in 1940, the Falange was investigating the putting-up of posters in the market place demanding 'bread and potatoes at state prices' and protests in food queues were common.[68] In Vivero, after a week without bread, women broke open a baker's shop and in Aboleda, Bilbao, several women were imprisoned for wearing red carnations, a Republican symbol, at a local *fiesta*. In the capital, customers in cafés left slips of paper under glasses inscribed with the words, 'More food and less Empire.'

In Valencia, street disturbances – the chalking up of slogans or lampoons on the walls, for example – threatened to provoke the immediate execution of prisoners in the gaol who had been awaiting sentence for months.[69] This was a way of controlling the already suffering working class 'on the outside'. In this response was a recognition, though, that one of the major successes of resistance to the regime, necessarily limited though its activities were, was to cross the boundary artificially set up by the 'victors' between those defeated still 'in liberty' and 'criminals' who were incarcerated.[70]

The most direct instrument of this solidarity between prisoners and their families and supporters was the so-called Socorro Rojo, or 'Red Aid', the mutual assistance organisation that collected money and food and thereby saved many lives.[71] Collections for the thousands imprisoned as areas succumbed to the Nationalist onslaught began during the Civil War itself, as part of the defence effort. Falangist intelligence reports show how these activities were considered as defiance of the state or even as resistance.[72] In May 1939 thirteen young women, aged from 18–21, members of the PCE-affiliated socialist youth wing Juventudes Socialistas Unificadas (JSU) were detained by the authorities for aiding the resistance, as thousands of others had done before and been punished. The 'thirteen roses', as they became known, had organised contributions of money, food and clothing for the families of prisoners left destitute and discriminated against as dependants of 'Reds'. The women also helped care for children abandoned in the course of the conflict and the repression. Officially, they were 'charged' with plotting an attack upon Franco. A military tribunal was held, and they were executed at the Cementerio del Este in Madrid on the 5 August 1939. Forty-three other prisoners died at the same time.[73]

Political protests cannot be disentangled from economic protests in the aftermath of the Civil War. The extent of the material exploitation of the defeated shocked even party die-hards. Some argued that the significance of the victory had been misunderstood by powerful social groups that were contributing to the social malaise: 'Anyone who believes, after a civil war, that, from an economic point of view, there is a victor, is deluding himself, since what really triumphs is a conception of the *Patria* and a way of life – the Nation, economically speaking, is the defeated'.[74] In reality, this victory for a particular 'way of life' could not be separated from its economic and social implications. It was precisely the effects of what was obviously, in part, an economic victory that were experienced by the population in the first decades following the Civil War.

It was impossible to deny that particular social groups were benefiting economically from the outcome of the conflict. Not surprisingly, the situation of the 'masses' was 'truly disagreeable'. The attitude of hostility on the part of the people was 'almost manifest', although, thanks to the constant presence of the forces of order, this was not often outwardly expressed. Indispensable items were so hard to come by that it was difficult to 'live and produce'. It was 'utterly impossible to live on the average wage'. As winter approached it would be vital to attend very carefully to the state's duty of vigilance and the upholding of public order, 'since one cannot rule out, because of this terrible situation, an attempt at some sort of street riot or personal attack'. According to a British censorship report on communications leaving Spain in spring 1940, machine-gun posts and troops were being kept in readiness all over the city in order to 'quell the rioting' should it take place and in other areas troops were wholly occupied in keeping order in the towns and villages where discontent was rife. Unrest was also mounting within the army among thousands of conscripts forced to live under canvas, since 70 per cent of barracks were being employed as prisons.[75]

Party officials were understandably sensitive to rumours of planned resistance. In November 1940, there was talk in the markets of the city of a movement of 'rebellion against public order', in which women were being 'advised to follow the methods used in Madrid and Valencia . . . [where] . . . food shops and government warehouses had been stormed' and nothing had been done to the perpetrators.

While party militants themselves feared the consequences of such plans, other elite figures could be reasonably confident that officials of the Movement, at a local level, would absorb most of the criticism if voiced. While elites were benefiting most from socio-economic conditions, the Falange was at the 'frontline' in the economic civil war which followed upon the military struggle. Economic repression further discredited a Movement which economic elites had always looked upon in an ambiguous, often hostile, way.[76]

The working class was seen, in Party circles, as formed by two main groups – one that had 'faith in National Syndicalism' and another which remained in 'a defeatist attitude' as far as the Falangist revolution was concerned, characterised by their 'complete idleness' (*desidia*), which was seen as the product of doctrines that had very deep roots, which had 'made sick the moral vitality of the worker'. Without party membership records it remains impossible to say which group of workers were considered by the party ideologues to be sympathetic. What is beyond doubt, however, is that the majority of the working class remained indifferent to the blandishments of the party, 'in a convinced state of withdrawal or seclusion'. Of Prat de Llobregat it was said that only 3 per cent were sympathetic to the Falange, while 40 per cent were 'indifferent' and 'the rest' were 'Red'. In the industrial town of Sabadell on the outskirts of the city of Barcelona, where of the 60,00 inhabitants in 1940, more than 15,000 were textile workers, the majority 'poisoned by Marxist theories', it was not unusual for six or seven weeks to pass without rations of rice or oil being distributed. Party activists complained in early 1940 that 60 per cent of the populace 'continues to be Red'. 'Defeatism' was rife in factories, workshops, cafés and in the many queues at the food market. Republican flags regularly appeared in some doorways and inscriptions of the CNT, FAI and POUM were to be seen on many walls. Industrial production in the town was in a state of considerable chaos, since raw materials were in short supply and 'Reds' had burned down six factories.[77] In Sant Quirze del Vallés the people '[were] especially Red . . . with the same criminal ideals as before the 18th of July'. The 'evil seed' of 'leftism' was seen to be reviving.[78]

But the effect of the state's policy of physical and economic repression was to impose a forced isolation of workers, which mitigated against a genuinely widespread mobilisation either in favour of the state or against it.[79] It was virtually pointless for Falangists to complain that these 'obdurate' masses were unaware of the championing of their cause by the state – the everyday experience of workers proved the reverse. Although the powerful ideas that motivated the workers were seen as the product of 'unhealthy agents' carried within 'governmental and spiritual decadence', which had defined the Spanish state for decades before 1936, the truth was that the workers' consciousness of class was reinforced by their own experience.

While Falangists complained that there was no 'constructive force' motivating the actions of the working class – that all was 'negative and destructive' – they were able to convince themselves that only the correct ideology was required to fill this vacuum. But the discourse of the Falange, which was designed to draw favourable comparisons between life under Franco and life under the Republic, inevitably failed to become popularised in quite the manner intended. The phrase *'los tiempos de los rojos'* ('the time of the Reds', meaning 'of the Republic') was designed as the Spanish post-war equivalent of Nazi Germany's 'fourteen years of humiliation used to refer to the era of the Weimar Republic as a disaster of democratic experimentation. However, although it was transmitted by being read in every newspaper and heard in virtually every propaganda speech as an era of national disgrace, it was popularly appropriated in a wholly unintended way. In day-to-day conversation one would hear: 'Can one buy this or that here? No, in *"los tiempos de los Rojos"* there was some, but not today. In *"los tiempos de los Rojos"* this cost 3 pesetas, today it costs 18.'[80]

In the city of Barcelona, in mid-1940, the bread situation was very serious. For the working population, bread was a staple of the daily diet. Despite the declarations of the Civil Governor of the city that each person would receive a ration of 500 grams every two days, only half that amount was normally distributed. Occasionally, on good days, people would receive 375 grams.[81] The population declined to believe that, as a consequence of world war, they had to suffer a shortage of flour while so much of it was being used to produce pastries and confectionery, of which only the well-heeled of the city could afford to partake. Flour producers, unchecked by the state authorities, could get a much better price from bakers able to sell such items to the middle classes.[82]

In January 1942, Franco made his first visit to Barcelona since the victory. The party in the city tried to raise spirits by pretending that his speech delivered on 26 January[83] would somehow cause 'the hopes of the producers [of the city] to be reborn'. Some Falangists obviously maintained the faith that the Caudillo was above the corruption and inefficiency of the authorities and that he would find a solution to all problems.

The leader's visit seemed to cheer local party militants. There was particular satisfaction on hearing that the course of the world conflict was continuing to favour the Axis powers. It was also rumoured that, as a result of the visit of the dictator, the industrial towns of Sabadell and Tarrasa would soon be receiving considerable quantities of wool, enabling the textile industry to normalise production. Indeed, it was normal for provinces to be materially favoured by the state in such a way so that the image of the dictator might be seen in a favourable light.[84] Party officials in Cartegena were put into a state of some excitement the same year, when news broke that the Caudillo would be visiting to review the state of the port in preparation for Spain's prospective 'armed intervention' in the world war. The local populace was to receive an extra share of provisions so that it would 'present a positive prospect' on his arrival.[85] But Franco failed to draw a large and enthusiastic crowd as the newspapers pretended. His first public appearance in Barcelona, after the occupation of the city, had been on the 21 February 1939, when he reviewed a parade of forty military divisions, and that occasion was marked by what the US Vice-Consul described as a 'characteristic Catalan lack of enthusiasm – with the exception of organised cheering'.[86] When Franco toured the South in 1943, shops, cafés and industries were closed and crowds were forcibly marshalled by the Falange. In Almería, farm labourers were brought in from the country-side and given a suit of clothes and a pair of boots for the occasion which were taken away from them when they were dismissed.[87]

Party officials, recognised that 'with however much good will the facts are viewed, with however much understanding foreign circumstances, which influence in a decisive manner the development of our internal life, are studied, there is no satisfactory explanation for the rapid and inordinate appearance of "*nuevos ricos*" born out of suffering, depriva-tion, and [at the cost of] the general welfare'.[88] The working masses, it was admitted, were 'crying out' against this situation, as they realised 'that before as now and . . . even in the future, they will be the only ones to suffer the consequences of all our misfortunes'. The result, for the party, could only be that the working class would increasingly separate itself off from the policy of National Syndicalism.[89]

Poverty also contributed to crime. As well as organised robberies, designed to secure funds for underground opposition groups, there was also a great deal of crime on a smaller scale, often thefts committed by women and children.[90] While claiming that 'the public' were pleased with the work of the police in rounding up various bands of 'gangsters', the party authorities had to admit that the general understanding was that much crime was the result of 'the current misery which reigns in the homes of the most humble'. At the same time, a section of the public, doubtless the well-to-do middle class which continued to support the regime as the best defender of its property, complained that in the press some robberies were reported as simple 'news items' with no sense of condemnation, as if the perpetrators had 'strayed from the straight and narrow by chance and still [were] morally good at heart', so that the public had begun to 'sympathise' with the 'delinquent' and 'forget the victim', suggesting that the crime was due to a necessity and not to 'wickedness'.[91]

Neither was the regime able to provide work by maintaining industrial production, principally because of raw material shortages. In Barcelona, by the middle of 1940, the effect was to reduce working in factories to three days a week. In manufacturing and textiles the conditions of the workforce was 'critical'. The wages of industrial workers, cut first by the reduced week, were at the same level as 1936, while prices had leaped several hundred per cent. The barest essentials were beyond reach.[92] To the North of the city of Barcelona itself, in the textile town of Granollers, a region with a strong tradition of worker radicalism, there were some 700 workers, men and women, unemployed, and this according to official statements. The state party's social welfare service, the Auxilio Social, such as it was, helped to feed around 400 of them.[93] But this corrupt Falange-inspired charity was a very poor substitute for real state provision. In rural Murcia, during the late spring of 1942, Auxilio's supplies were virtually exhausted and there was a general resistance on the part of the middle classes to contribute, though workers themselves were forced to do so. This was in an area where the well-to-do frequently celebrated local festivals with a lavish display of consumption.[94] Such Falangist activity as the Auxilio Social provided an opportunity for political speech-making in favour of Franco's 'revolution', and for the distribution too of clothing made by the middle-class women of the Falange's Sección Femenina.[95] But elites who were suspicious of the activities of the Falange, particularly in urban areas, like industrialists and army officers, were less willing to contribute, preferring to support the charitable endeavours of Acción Católica.[96]

Workers also attended religous festivals in the hope of obtaining something to eat. Ecclesiastical and party authorities were a constant presence. This humiliation was a part of the day-to-day living out of the defeat. Food was incredibly scarce, a situation not aided by the fact that the families of prisoners and 'those condemned for Marxist crimes' also congregated at Auxilio's feeding stations in search of something to eat. Falangist officials were clearly indignant at this situation. There was certainly no guarantee that food would be distributed to 'unreliable elements', those without 'a certificate of good conduct'. Auxilio Social could also be a way of 'keeping tabs' on the families of 'Reds'. The wife of a building worker sentenced to death in April 1939 was said to have no goods to be appropriated by the state Political Responsibilities Tribunal, since, according to the Guardia Civil, she 'ate every day in Auxilio Social'. Even so, the final sentence of the court was 'total loss of all goods'.[97]

Despite the rhetoric of 'social justice' the provision of decent housing for the working class of urban centres like Barcelona was not a priority of the 'New State'. By the beginning of 1940, there had been little in the way of new construction in the city. The priority had been to repair the city's churches, enabling a return to religious observance. Such work was symbolic of the lack of power of the working class, forced to assist in the reconstruction of religious buildings which had been the main targets of the anti-clerical anger unleashed during the revolution.[98]

Housing, though, was a low priority. By February 1940, hundreds of families were living in sea-front shacks.[99] By the end of the decade the housing situation in the city was as catastrophic as in Madrid.[100] The problem was accentuated by urbanisation. Worker migration to Greater Barcelona, for example, began in the 1940s. While the percentage population growth in the city of the expansionary period 1920–30 had been 7.5, in the first post-war decade, from 1940–50, it was 21.7. The urban population of 1,081,175 in 1940 had swelled to 1,280,179 by 1950, an increase of almost 200,000. Moreover, it was the most heavily industrial areas which grew most rapidly of all.[101] Industrialising projects also brought workers to Madrid. During the 1940s, 225,000 more workers arrived in the capital than left, a similar figure to the 1920s.[102]

Urban overcrowding, particularly in working-class districts, the 'natural incubator of Marxism and all kinds of regressive hatreds', was a bigger problem than ever before, giving way to a periodic siege mentality and bringing the threat of 'declining Christian values and dangerous diseases'.[103] The local authorities in the capital were themselves forced to admit to a press conference, via the city's mayor, that there were still 138 groups of *barracas*, the notorious shanty towns which were a true symbol of the Franco regime even until the 1970s, housing some 60,000 people.[104] The truth may well have been worse still. The total housing deficit in Spain in January 1943 was officially 500,185. By the end of the year it stood at more than 600,000 and almost 800,000 by 1945. In 1948, the country lacked more than a million dwellings.[105] The city council in Barcelona declared itself determined to reduce the number of huts to 7,000 as quickly as possible, although no plan for carrying out such a programme was detailed.[106] The dire housing situation was also reflected in the large number of families forced to live in caves, close to the centre of the city, while 'protected' housing built with syndical funds was distributed amongst civil functionaries and the military.[107]

The black market became a whole way of conceiving of the world, 'a way of being' which affected all social relations.[108] The smallest details of small-scale illegal trading were a function of the instability of the post-war situation. Much of this trade was carried on aboard trains as people moved from town to town, looking for places of safety, returning to families or home *pueblos* from which they had become estranged or been forcibly exiled, or simply feeding the desperate need of urban areas for the products of the countryside. Individuals who moved from place to place, who did not 'fit', were already marked out as suspect: their 'guilt' was assumed. Ingenious ways were found to make ends meet. Food for sale was secreted in bags and cases with hidden pockets or compartments. Hunger and disease themselves, both rife in this period, facilitated the subterfuge. Items were hidden in the layers of children's clothing worn apparently to keep the sick warm, or inside false bandages wrapped around imaginary wounds or scars.[109]

The political nature of the struggle for food was recognised popularly and by the authorities. The daily search of baskets taken by visitors to prisoners confirmed that those who, because of 'political crimes', ought to have been deprived of food were being supplied by political organisations.[110] The target of robberies by groups of Republican *guerrilla* fighters were political symbols, like the Civil Governor's house in Santander, or wealthy flour producers and merchants who were seen to be making fortunes at the expense of the population. In the province of Granada, for example, in early 1942, a group were detained by the Civil Guard after setting fire to the flour factory of a producer from whom they had demanded 100,000 pesetas.[111] Bakers' shops became the target of young protesters with incendiary devices, labelled as 'communists' by the authorities. In Madrid, some members of the state bakers' syndicate were proceeded against by a military court after demonstrations by students, although they were expected to escape with only fines.[112]

Spaniards made hunger 'a work of art' through the black market, or *estraperlo*.[113] In 'recovering their reason', in the immediate post-war years, personal mythologies inherited from revolution and war were substituted by a mythology of simple things: wheat, bread, olive oil, soap.[114] When popular cultural forms made reference to the way of life which was the black market it was looked upon seriously by the authorities. The hero of the post-war 'Song of Villagarcía', for example, sings of wooing his sweetheart with a luxury, coffee, that he alone could get his hands on. To sing it was subversive, since coffee was scarce, substituted usually by evil-tasting ground lentils, and overwhelmingly traded 'clandestinely', more often than not by party officials themselves. The regime preferred to pretend that such scarcities simply did not exist.[115] But in some localities verbal protests in markets became too numerous to punish individually.[116]

The 'enormous' unemployment of workers in some areas aroused concern by the authorities at the growing groups of children begging in the streets of many localities. This created 'a deplorable impression' and it was suggested that a 'Special Brigade' be established for the 'rounding up and questioning of child beggars' in the interests of 'material and spiritual health'. Among 'the female section' of the population, there were 'lamentable cases . . . a legacy which the Red Government left to us . . . [of] little girls who launch themselves into "loose-living", in some cases without respecting their parents, and, in others, with their toleration . . . who don't work and have to live somehow'.[117]

The Guardia Civil and Falangists were ordered to ensure 'the highest morality in customs' and to threaten 'the most severe sanctions'. But the economic and political situation weakened any claims the regime made regarding the strengthening of morality. One of the primary concerns of Falangists was that the grinding poverty of the 1940s destroyed what party adherents believed to be the foundations of stable society. In order, for example, to supplement the wages which a family had to live on or to compensate for the imprisonment of a main breadwinner, women and children were forced to resort to drastic and demeaning extremes. Prostitution, despite the veneer of 'respectability' which the regime attempted to portray, boomed in the 1940s.

Part of the task of local authorities, and particularly the party, was to seek out and punish those who lacked 'discipline in customs and habits'. The Civil Governor of each province had the discretionary power to impose heavy sanctions. These were particularly cruel in rural Spain. In 1942, two women in the town of Torreaguera, in Murcia, for example, were condemned to thirty days' imprisonment and expulsion from their town, for carrying on 'clandestine prostitution' and 'provoking a scandal'.[118] It seemed that party officials looked upon such occurrences as indicating some kind of personal failure on their part. And yet, it was well known that in the 1940s it was state officials who used their discretionary powers – over the distribution of food and work as much as anything – to obtain 'sexual favours'.[119]

Nourishment to feed and keep children healthy was far from abundant in these years, as we have seen, and women, partly because of this situation, resisted complying with the crude pro-natalist policies of the regime.[120] In much of Spain in 1942 there was widespread starvation. People were naturally drawn to take all possible measures in order to attempt to survive and to feed families. The Party's Investigation Service ordered the detention of women 'dedicated to quackery', and involving themselves in what officials described as 'spiritualism', and the carrying out of abortions.[121] Women who transgressed attempts to control behaviour, ideas, markets, were considered a threat. Females had to be 'attached', within the family or to the church: 'free movement', individual endeavour, like dealing on the black market, having and expressing political ideas, possessing access to knowledge or mysteries that were not understood, being potentially unrepressed sexually, all this threatened the social order.

It was a cause of some frustration that party officials found themselves spending all their efforts safeguarding 'public morality' against the 'evil' caused by revolution and war's 'corruption of customs', rather than carrying out political campaigns.[122] Ultimately, the solution was always perceived through an 'intervening state', a 'Christian authoritarian state', responsible for 'moulding the nation', distinct from the state known by previous generations where juridical considerations ruled. As far as education was concerned, 'what we long for now is a structured national body . . . [T]he child is not naturally good: it is born with persistent passionate inclinations, the loss of human purity through original sin'.[123] 'Tolerance' could not be a 'sedative for lustfulness'. The old liberal attitude had to be replaced by intervention in 'life, morals, religion, science, economics'.[124]

In political and material terms, the working class in particular had been pushed into a kind of clandestine existence by the force of repression. In this situation individuals were increasingly liable to fall foul of the state authorities. Most people found themselves at some time infringing some decree or other or the regime's strict moral code. Life in Barcelona, for example, seemed at times to be lived in the realms of unreality. A party official in January 1946 observed that although it seemed strange in an industrialised city, the traditional ways of dressing of the industrial worker were rarely seen. The canvas sandal and blue overall which had been ubiquitous in the city during the Civil War, becoming a sign of worker identity, and which George Orwell commented had displaced 'bourgeois dress', was now, in the post-war, somewhat outmoded.[125]

Expressions of working-class identity in the city and in much of Spain were not safe. Though it sat in uncomfortable contradiction to Francoism's grandiose claims to favour industrialisation, this had been the aim of the regime from the outset. Stoppages due to shortages in industry contributed to a generalised feeling of disaffection among workers. There was a profound lack of enthusiasm for work itself. Part of what was destroyed in the Civil War and in the 1940s was pride in a consciousness of being a class with collective aspirations. Pride was atomised just as the working class itself was physically dispersed. The assault on identity was so pronounced that one hardly saw on the streets any longer a 'typical worker . . . Everyone has become a young lady or gentleman'. This certainly was not a case of mass upward social mobility. Rather, people were living a 'fictitious' existence, according to one party official. The 'glad rags' which people wore with such pride, hid the physical emaciation which the post-war years had created. Doubtless there was also an element of escapism (and resistance) in such displays. Other 'typical workers', to be sure, did not venture out very much.[126] If they went to the cinema, an industry that boomed in these years, it was because the stark comparison of Hollywood images, or the stars of the Spanish screen, with most people's daily existence focussed a common resentment that could not be openly voiced individually: 'the cinema gave us the measure of our misery. It gave us the measure of our lives, of everything that we were not.'127 Víctor Alba, in 1948, commented upon this same phenomenon, 'In display there is everything. There have never been so many cinemas, electric signs, cabarets . . . And they are all full . . . For even the workers wish to enjoy themselves. . . . Then, if one fine day they have a share in a good black market deal, or happen to purloin a good tool from the workshop, they spend the money to make up in one evening the frozen monotony of long months of privation.'128

The substantial contradictions that formed the shaky foundations of Francoism – between populism and élitism, Catholic charity and cruelty, 'purity' and 'impurity', austerity and greed, legitimacy and coercion – were heightened by the activities of ordinary Spaniards. They were, to a large degree, an almost inevitable consequence of the crisis that reached its height in the Civil War and continued in its aftermath. Autarky itself was a product of this crisis. The defiance and resistance of the population, though it could never defeat the dictatorship without help from foreign democracies, which was not forthcoming, eventually forced a significant measure of economic liberalisation during the 1950s.

Conclusion

Any account of the Franco years in Spain has to be concerned, in some measure, with the issues of memory, war, violence, Catholicism and economy. The memories of those who suffered defeat and repression in the Spanish post-war years are shrouded in darkness and silence. A sense of fear, absence and insecurity cast an oppressive shadow over lives in the early 1940s: 'After the Civil War, events, people, living together, everything became terribly ambiguous: lack of information, disappeared people.'[1]

The history of countless individuals and the story of families was of entrapment, hunger, blood: the fearful mysteries of parents' and grand-parents' tears: 'Nobody seemed to be aware that we [children] were there, that we existed, that we also . . . had suffered that evil war. It was written on our skin, in our eyes, in the trembling of our hands.'[2] A wall of silence was constructed in Spain in 1939, the year of Franco's triumph, which remained a barrier to the past for decades:

Every time you asked about something that happened before that year the adults would put a finger to their lips and look from side to side. We were a people without a past, without memories. Neither did the present of those days . . . offer much attraction. It was necessary to look to the future. A future that, in the end, never arrived, however much they concealed our past.[3]

Existence was shaped by an often indefinable sensation of loss and isolation. When many Spanish people talk of 'the years of autarky' this is what they mean.

The dictatorship was founded upon victory in the Spanish Civil War: Francoism cannot be understood without reference to the war. However much society and economy changed throughout the almost forty years of the regime, the essential fact of bloody military conflict and the devastating repression was always present and constantly alluded to by the government itself. To poverty and fantasy, the turn-of-the-century regenerationist Lucas Mallada's indispensable categories in judging recent Spanish history, can be added the aggravating factor of total victory and defeat.[4] The dictator's 'legitimacy' was established over-whelmingly through violence and the continual threat of violence. Many things followed from this; Francoism's conception of nation, state and economy rested on militarism, war and blood.

In Nazi Germany and Fascist Italy a similar trilogy of ideas structured dictatorial authority. There are numerous apposite similarities to point to in comparing what were, in some ways, regimes with analogous aims and methods. But, however much German and Italian societies were conflictual and divided on the eve of the Nazi and Fascist take-overs of power, no full-scale bloody civil war was fought out in these countries. For many reasons, mass political mobilization with paramilitary poten-tial was not likely in Spain. Political nationalism in Spain was a complex, many-sided phenomenon. Catholicism dominated elite ideas and struc-tured many ordinary people's lives. Opposition to rightist extremism was strong and progressive parties had secured a foothold within the state whereas conservative parties were relatively ill prepared. Spain, though displaying many similar contemporary social and cultural fea-tures to Germany and Italy in the first half of the twentieth century, was developed in an extremely uneven way. Rationalisation of an industrial economy was not blocked by the intransigence of the working class and their political representatives, as much as by the grip of a protected agriculture on the economy and the lowly position of the country within the international trading system. There was no large enough unifiable social mass, centred on the middling classes, capable of articulating Spanish nationalism and of capturing state power by resorting only to the relatively mild violence of intimidation and demagoguery. The several deep fissures that ran through society were politically unbridge-able, it seemed, without war.

The Civil War did, however, create a kind of unity: one based on depicting everything and everybody associated with the Republic as a threat to society – as 'degenerate', 'diseased', 'sick', representative of the antithesis of Spain. The depth of social divisions in Spain, heightened by the war itself, left a profoundly traumatised society. Autarky and the isolation of Spanish society was the result of this extreme polarisation. While Nazi and Fascist violence was principally projected outwards, towards eastern Europe or Africa, Franco, his ministers and elite supporters were particularly concerned with internal enemies, as the Spanish army had historically been, and obsessive about the 'contagion' within because of the Civil War itself.

Though it had complex social roots, Franco's war was constructed, virtually from the outset in 1936, as a religious 'Crusade'. Catholic teaching, and particularly the attitudes of the leading figures of the church hierarchy in Spain, helped justify the military rebellion and the war that followed. Religion also provided consolation for human losses, but, at the same time, made the social and military divide of the war even more rigid. That Catholicism would be employed in this way by Francoists is in no way surprising given its centrality in Spanish life and culture. But its effects, when blended with fascism, the other primary ideological support of the war and violence, were usually repressive.

The similar totalitarian potential of fascism and of Catholicism as understood by the Spanish church hierarchy in the 1930s and 1940s are evident: ideological exclusivity, purity, interiorism, asceticism, punishment, the subordination of women, a preference for mysticism, or spiritualism, above materialism. Castilian nationalism was intimately linked to Catholicism. In Spain during the Civil War they became firmly allied as the ideas they represented overlapped, employed as justification for the suppression of the democratic Republic, of liberalism, and of minds and bodies. Only gradually, in the aftermath, did the church reveal its differences with Falangists, over relations with Nazi Germany, for example, or because of the apparent social radicalism of some fascist 'revolutionaries', or the evident contradiction between Christian charity and the unending repression and domination. By this time, church, party and military were enmeshed, not only in a network of common ideas, but in a 'pact of blood' entered into during the war itself. The fall of Mussolini, moreover, and the social conflict in Italy that followed, made elite groups and much of society generally adhere desperately to the dictatorship in one way or another for fear of a return to civil war.

Franco's 'Crusade', the Civil War, was at the heart of the ideology of the regime, central to the relative unity of the component parts of the state, and to the repression that was employed against much of society. There was a concerted attempt to sanctify physical and mental space. Franco's triumph, it was proclaimed, was the fulfilment not only of Spain's destiny but of the Caudillo's personal mandate from God. Providence and triumphalism produced a heightened sense of fantasy in the victors and divine sanction for violent repression.

Fantasy, poverty, triumph and defeat also came together in economic autarky. The 1940s saw an extraordinary regression in economic terms in Spain. One of the most striking features of an already bleak landscape is the gulf that opened up between the comfortable middle-class minority and ordinary people, particularly industrial workers and peasants. The coercive regimentation of labour nullified dissent from below, while, in practice, preserving employers' right to influence policy. Internal colonisation meant capital accumulation and concentration of economic power of unprecedented levels, accompanied by unheard of

...iumphalist economics persecuted the masses, making them pay for grandiose and fantastical industrial projects designed to display the resurgence of the *Patria*.

Studies of the 1940s in Spain, however, have tended to look at the economy in isolation. This makes it difficult to set autarky within this context of the social, ideological and political crisis of which the Civil War is the most dramatic part. The pursuit of self-sufficiency was a response to a partial loss of rational state authority, a devaluing of existing status and a questioning of the meaning of 'the Nation', all associated with the Second Republic, as well as a need for economic protectionism. The regime consciously developed autarky as a guiding principle. Interiorism, at a national, social and individual level, became the reflexive response to all threats to authority. A constant and silent reflection on sin (particularly of revolution and war), purity, and the 'health' of the nation was prescribed.

In some respects, the uni-dimensional view of autarky as catastrophic is absolutely justified. There can be little doubt about the damage done to individuals, society and sections of the economy in the 1940s. The priority of any study of the Civil War and the 1940s is to show this sense of wholesale destruction and the magnitude of the sacrifice made under the early Franco regime. The struggle for physical survival prevented the organisation of resistance, beyond the largely unsuccessful *guerrilla* warfare maintained as a constant irritant to the regime during the 1940s. People spoke less and less of 'politics' as a consequence of the preoccupation with finding enough to eat.[5] The collective identity of social groups identified as 'the defeated' was broken apart, denied expression, as Franco's victory was recreated day-by-day. The protests of the working class, when they could be articulated, were often reduced to a despairing plea for a return of the monarchy, ensuring a free market in bread.[6] There was an orchestrated depoliticisation of social consciousness, formally delegitimising and denigrating other views of the world, fomenting ignorance, particularly by explicitly denying a modern education to women, through a lack of information, a disorientation that was painfully rectified by some in reconstructing episodes from the past years later and exchanging them with others.[7] As Spain retreated within, in order to 'purify' itself and search for 'redemption', people were forced to retreat into the domestic sphere in an attempt to get by. Even here, though, the regime intervened to shape the politics and economics of the family.

The repressive experience of Francoism is illuminated by exploring the realities behind the loud pronouncements of the colonisers and the silences of the colonised. It is only through an understanding of the meanings to the autarkic regime of such ideas as purification, expulsion or redemption that the scale and nature of the violence can be comprehended. It is only when it is recognised that ordinary people viewed autarky as everyday 'terror' that we can understand how economic policy was inextricably linked to the desire ruthlessly to confirm Franco's victory.[8] The dawning of industrial society in Spain was both desired, for reasons of national prestige, and, at the same time, dreaded by the country's social and political elite, because of the potential threat to social order and to cultural 'normality'. It is only when the absolute priority of 'neutralising' social dissent during urbanisation is highlighted that we can see how the practice of economics was itself both violent *and* rational in the 1940s.

Autarky, sealing the country off from the outside world, facilitated treatment of a 'sick' Spain under conditions of 'quarantine'. It is only through a recognition of the pathological nature of elites' understanding of the 'problem of Spain' that we can obtain a fuller idea of the significance of autarky as a whole culture which ordered power. Self-sufficiency, in the sense of a denial of any political, cultural or economic dialogue about the future, was an essential part of Francoist reconstruction.

INTRODUCTION

1 For a recent major deconstruction of myths about Franco, see Paul Preston, *Franco: A Biography* (London, 1993). Also Alberto Reig Tapia, *Franco 'Caudillo'; Mito y realidad* (Madrid, 1995).

2 *Corriere della Sera*, 4 December 1938; *Palabras del Caudillo* (19 abril 1937–31 diciembre 1938) (Barcelona, 1938), p. 287.

3 Gabriel Tortella, 'Sobre el significado histórico del franquismo', *Revista de Occidente*, 59 (1986), 104–14; J.A. González Casanova, 'El franquismo a diez años vista', *Historia 16*, 10 (November 1985), 35–40.

4 The principal works on autarky are Angel Viñas, *Guerra, dinero, dictadura: ayuda fascista y autarquía en la España de Franco* (Barcelona, 1984); Carlos Velasco Murviedro, 'Sobre una posible caracterización de la autarquía española (1939–1945)', in Manuel Tuñón de Lara (ed.), *Estudios sobre la historia de España*, vol. II (Madrid, 1981) pp. 391–406; 'Sucedáneos de posguerra', *Historia 16*, 131 (March 1987), 11–20; 'Las pintorescas ideas económicas de Franco', *Historia 16*, 85 (May 1983), 19–28; 'El ingenierismo como directriz básica de la política económica durante la autarquía', *ICE*, 606 (1984).

5 For example, Josep Ballester, *Temps de quarantena (1939–1959)* (Valencia, 1992). One prominent socialist philosopher saw society as living 'a culture of hibernation'. Enrique Tierno Galván, cited in Thomas Mermall, *The Rhetoric of Humanism* (New York, 1976), p. 9.

6 The relation between economics and culture is explored in Marxist terms by writers associated with the Centre for Contemporary Cultural Studies at the University of Birmingham. See, for instance, Richard Johnson, George McLennon and Bill Schwarz, *Economy, Culture, Concept* (Birmingham, 1978); and in post-industrial economies by Scott Lash and John Urry, *Economies of Signs and Space* (London, 1994). For an anthropological guide, see Michael Taussig, *The Devil and Commodity Fetishism in Latin America* (Chapel Hill, NC, 1980); W. Roseberry, 'Political Economy', *Annual Review of Anthropology*, 17 (1984), 161–85; Stephen Gudeman, *Economics as Culture: Models and Metaphors of Livelihood* (London, 1986); Terence Turner, 'Production, Exploitation and Social Consciousness in the "Peripheral Situation"', *Social Analysis*, 19, pp. 91 115.

7 'España y Franco', *Fe y Acción*, 1 (1938), 8–9. On the 'sickness' of the Republic, see also, among countless works, José María Albiñana Sanz,

España bajo la dictadura Republicana: crónica de un período putrefacto (Madrid, 1933)

8   Ernest Menze (ed.), *Totalitarianism Reconsidered* (New York, 1981).
9   See, for example, Vicente Gay y Forner, *Constitución y vida del pueblo español:
    análisis sobre la estagnación y decadencia de las razas de la higiene contemporánea*
    (Madrid, 1905). By the 1930s Gay y Forner was praising the 'hygienicising'
    merits of Nazi concentration camps.
10 Angel Ganivet, *Idearium español* (Madrid, 1897). A great deal of writing by
    Ganivet, or about him and his ideas, appeared in the aftermath of the Civil
    War, and an anthology appeared in 1943, to coincide with the very public
    transfer of the author's mortal remains to Spain from abroad. See *Antología*
    (Madrid 1943); *Obras completas* (Madrid, 1943). Juan José López Ibor sees
    Ganivet as an 'immense figure', *El español y su complejo de inferioridad*
    (Madrid, 1951), p. 44. Luis Furones Ferrero, 'Influencias de Angel Ganivet
    en el pensamiento de José Antonio, *Seminario*, 6, 85.
11 On the influence of regenerationism in Falangist and Francoist thought, see,
    for example, Pedro Laín Entralgo, *La generación del noventa y ocho* (Madrid,
    1945); Thomas Mermall, 'La ideología del '98 bajo el franquismo', in John
    P. Gabriele (ed.), *Divergencias y unidad: perspectivas sobre la generación del '98
    y Antonio Machado* (Madrid, 1990), pp. 49–60; 'E. Giménez Caballero:
    Una cultura hacista: revolución y tradición en la regeneración de España',
    Anthropos, 84 (1988); Sebastian Balfour, *The End of The Spanish Empire,
    1898–1923* (Oxford, 1997), pp. 230–4. Regenerationism has been seen as
    Spain's own 'pre-fascism', Enrique Tierno Galván, 'Costa y el regeneracio-
    nismo', in *Escritos (1950–1960)* (Madrid, 1971).
12 José Félix Lequerica, cited in Carlos Fernández, *Antología de 40 años,
    1936–1975* (La Coruña, 1983), p. 488.
13 Franco, 4 December 1938, *Palabras* (1938), p. 287.
14 Officially known after April 1937 as *Falange Española Tradicionalista y de las
    Juntas de Ofensiva Nacional-Sindicalista*, or FET y de las JONS, Franco's
    single-state party.
15 Rafael del Aguila Tejerina, *Ideología y fascismo* (Madrid, 1982), pp. 216–31.
16 The concept of silence is not used here to imply complete acceptance and
    resignation on the part of the population. There were undoubtedly a multi-
    tude of alternative visions expressed in one way or another. But the
    'vocabulary' of silence has frequently been used to describe the regime's
    monopoly of public discourse in these years.
17 See Eduardo Pons Prades, *Los derrotados y el exilio* (Barcelona, 1977); Antonio
    Soriano, *Exodos: Historia oral del exilio Republicano en Francia, 1939–1945*
    (Barcelona, 1989); Antonio Vilanova, *Los olvidados: los exiliados españoles en la
    segunda guerra mundial* (Paris, 1969); A. Fernández, *Emigración Republicana
    española, 1939–1945* (Madrid, 1972); Vicente Fillol, *Los perdedores* (Caracas,
    1971); Avellí Artís-Gener, *La diáspora Republicana* (Barcelona, 1975).
18 Some perspectives of political theorists are offered in Joseph A. Camilleri,
    A.P. Jaravis and A. Paolini, *The State in Transition: Reimagining Political
    Space* (Boulder, CO, 1995), particularly parts 1 and 2. See also Mary
    Douglas, *Purity and Danger: An Analysis of the Concepts of Pollution and Taboo*
    (London, 1991).

1 López Ibor, *El español y su complejo de inferioridad.*
2 Franco, *Palabras* (1938), p. 137. Franco talked of making 'a pact of the future with the past', p. 32. See also Paloma Aguilar Fernández, *Memoria y olvido de la guerra civil española* (Madrid, 1996).
3 On the 'paralysing of time' under Franco, see, for example, Carmen Martín Gaite, *El cuarto de atrás* (Barcelona, 1978).
4 Daniel Sueiro, *La verdadera historia del valle de los caídos* (Madrid, 1976), p. 16. More generally, on the rejection of 'profane', continuous time, in preference for 'pure', mythical time, see Mircea Eliade, *The Myth of the Eternal Return* (New York, 1954), pp. ix, 49–54.
5 See Jonathon Morse, *Word by Word: The Language of Memory* (Ithaca, NY, 1990), p. 3.
6 Paul Preston, 'War of Words: the Spanish Civil War and the Historians', in Preston (ed.), *Revolution and War in Spain, 1931–1939* (London, 1984), p. 2.
7 See Herbert Southworth, *El mito de la cruzada de Franco* (Paris, 1963). In his acceptance speech as Head of State in October 1936, Franco declared that 'the Spanish flag carried within it the echo of western civilization, and of a race that did not want to die out'. On the Civil War as a replaying of the medieval *Reconquista*, see, for example, Enrique Espérabe de Arteaga, *La guerra de reconquista española que ha salvado a Europa y el criminal comunismo* (Madrid, 1940); Fernando Herce Vales and Manuel Sanz Nogués, *Franco, el reconquistador* (Madrid, 1939); Manuel Sánchez del Arco, *El sur de España en la reconquista de Madrid* (Seville, 1937).
8 Anti-liberal Spanish tradition, couched in terms of orthodoxy and heterodoxy, has a long heritage reaching back to the eighteenth century; writers in the 1930s and 1940s habitually referred to Marcelino Menéndez Pelayo, the 'spiritual father of Spain's renaissance', in particular. See especially his monumental *Historia de los heterodoxos españoles* (Madrid, 1880–2).
9 Juan Goytisolo, 'Remedios de la concupiscencia según Fray Tierno', in *Libertad, Libertad, Libertad* (Barcelona, 1978), pp. 95–6. See also 'El lenguaje del cuerpo', in *Disidencias* (Barcelona, 1977); Jordi Roca i Girona, *De la pureza a la maternidad: la construcción del género femenino en la postguerra española* (Madrid, 1996), particularly pp. 43–63; Mary Winkler and Letha Cole (eds.), *The Good Body: Asceticism in Contemporary Culture* (New Haven, CT, 1994), pp. 234–5.
10 Franco, *Palabras* (1930), p. 070.
11 José Antonio Pérez Bowie, *El léxico de la muerte durante la guerra civil española* (Salamanca, 1982).

12 According to Franco, 'The strength of communism is not to be reckoned in numbers, but in its power to contaminate ...', Fuller, *The Conquest of Red Spain* (London, 1937), p. 3. See also Manuel García Morente, *Ideas para una filosofía de la historia de España* (Madrid, 1943), p. 60. Ross, *La pureza*, p. 25.

13 Radio Sevilla, 3 August, 1936, in Fernández, *Antología*.

14 José Antonio Pérez del Pulgar, 'El concepto cristiano de la autarquía' in *Anales de mecánica y electricidad de los ingenieros del ICAI* (Madrid, 1941), p. 93.

15 Enrique López Galua, *Futura grandeza de España según notables profecías* (La Coruña, 1941), p. 15. The Orteguian notion of Spanish collective destiny was taken up by García Morente, justifying Franco as an instrument of divine providence. *Ideas para una filosofía*, pp. 36–9. See also José María Bover, *Los soldados: primicias de la gentilidad cristiana* (Barcelona, 1941), p. 44.

16 María Escudero, 'The Image of Latin America Disseminated in Spain by the Franco Regime: Repercussions in the Configuration of a National Identity', PhD thesis, University of California, San Diego (1994); Manuel de Burgos y Mazo, *¿Quién es España?* (Seville, 1940).

17 Cristóbal de Castro, *Mujeres del imperio* (Madrid, 1941), p. 5. The Civil War was 'a new expulsion of the *moriscos*'. See, for example, José María Peman, radio broadcast, Seville, 15 August 1936. Virulently ant-semitic public statements were commonplace. See Carlos Fernández, *Antología*. Jews were not numerous in Spain by the 1930s, but the *idea* of expulsion served as an important symbol.

18 Between 400,000 and 500,000 Spaniards were exiled in 1939. See Vicente Llorens, *El exilio espanol de 1939; la emigración Republicana de 1939* (Madrid, 1976), p. 16, which also traces the historical precedents of expulsion from Spain, pp. 25–93. On the repressive effects of the dictatorship's control of public (and private) discourse – the 'occupation of language' and the construction of 'mental prisons' – see, for example, the literary works of Juan Goytisolo, especially *El furgón de cola* (Barcelona, 1976, originally written in the 1960s); and *Disidencias*.

19 *Arriba Espana*, 1 August 1936. One symbolic Falangist book burning was held in Madrid on 2 May 1939, the anniversary of the rising of the people of Madrid against the French invaders in 1808. A particular target were 'liberal' and 'cowardly pseudo-scientific' publications. See *La vida cotidiana en la España de los 40* (Madrid, 1990), p. 16.

20 José Luis de la Granja Sainz, 'La historiografía española reciente: un balance', in Carlos Barros (ed.), *Historia a debate*, vol. I (Santiago de Compostela, 1995), pp. 299–307; Pasamar Alzuria and Peiró Martín, *Historiografía y práctica social en España* (Zaragoza, 1987).

21 Manuel Vázquez Montalbán, *Crónica sentimental de España* (Madrid, 1986), p. 33; Robert Jay Lifton, *History as Human Survival* (New York, 1970), p. 153.

22 Aguilar Fernández, *Memoria y olvido*.

23 See the article by Antonio Elorza, *El País*, 4 January 1990; Francisco Umbral, *La derechona* (Barcelona, 1997).

24 Manuel Vázquez Montalbán: *Barcelonas* (Barcelona, 1987), p. 164. See also Aguilar Fernández, *Memoria y olvido*, especially pp. 21, 26, 43–8.

25 See Javier Terrón Montero, *La prensa en España durante el régimen de Franco. Un intento de análisis político* (Madrid, 1981), particularly pp. 15–79; Justino Sinova, *La censura de prensa durante el franquismo* (Madrid, 1989); Miguel Delibes, *La censura de prensa en los años 40* (Valladolid, 1985).

26 Alberto Reig Tapia, *Ideología e historia: sobre la represión franquista y la guerra civil* (Madrid, 1984), especially pp. 91–122; Granja Sainz, 'Historiografía española', pp. 299–300.

27 See, for example, Vizconde de Eza, *El progreso social en suspenso* (Madrid, 1934); Rafael Gay de Montellá, *El Fuero del Trabajo y sistema del estado sindical-corporativo* (Valladolid, 1939); Román Perpiñá Grau, *Destino hispano. El movimiento. La lucha. La nueva vida* (Valencia, 1939); Olegario Fernández Baños, *Trabajo y capital* (Barcelona, 1940); José Larráz, *La meta de dos revoluciones* (Madrid, 1946).

28 See Juan Goytisolo, *Señas de identidad* ([originally 1966] Barcelona, 1980), p. 154.

29 The debate about methodology in determining the scale of the repression is summarised in chapter 2 of this study. The state's own *Anuario oficial de estadística* shows a figure of 192,684 persons 'executed or died in prison' for the period 1939–44. Matilde Eiroa San Francisco, *Viva Franco: hambre, racionamiento, Falangismo, 1939–1942* (Málaga, 1995), p. 214.

30 Stanley Payne, *The Franco Regime, 1936–1975* (Madison, WI, 1987), p. 252. It has been calculated by one demographer that during the period 1936–9 there were 344,000 deaths in excess of the level that might have been expected had the Civil War not occurred. An additional 214,000 are calculated for the period 1940–2, as a result of hunger, disease or political repression related to the conflict. Juan Díez Nicolás, 'La mortalidad en la guerra civil española', *Boletín de demografía histórica*, 3, 1 (March 1985), pp. 52–3. Death from starvation in prison was recorded as caused by 'cardiac arrest', 'bronchitis', 'tuberculosis', etc. See Eiroa, *Viva Franco*, pp. 238–44, for example.

31 The number of suicides and attempted suicides in official statistics are: 1936 – 1,816; 1937 – 1,671; 1938 – 1,605; 1939 – 2,527; 1940 – 2,458; 1941 – 2,540; 1942 – 2,226. *Anuario estadístico* (Madrid, 1943); I. López Sainz, 'Algunos datos y sugerencias sobre el suicidio en España', in *IV Congreso nacional de neuropsiquiatría* (Madrid, 1954). One of the explanations offered in this last work is 'profound economic change'.

32 See Francisco Moreno Gómez, *Córdoba en la posguerra* (Córdoba, 1987), p. 63. The authorities felt cheated by suicides and sometimes, as a reprisal, executed a relative of their 'escaped' prisoner, pp. 64–5.

33 The point has been made, and shown in varying degrees of detail, by many writers. For example, Payne, *The Franco Regime*, pp. 623–8, 635–6; José Luis Leal, et al., *La agricultura en el desarrollo capitalista español (1940–1970)* (Madrid, 1975), especially pp. 17, 91–2; José María López de Letona et al., *La empresa pública industrial en España* (Madrid, 1973); Charles W. Anderson, *The Political Economy of Modern Spain: Policy-making in an Authoritarian System* (Madison, WI, 1970), pp. 30–2; Miguel Buesa Blanco,

'El estado en el proceso de industrialización: contribución al estudio de la
política industrial española en el período 1939–1963', PhD thesis, Madrid
(1982); José María Lorenzo Espinosa, *Dictadura y dividendo: el discreto
negocio de la burguesía vasca (1937–1950)* (Bilbao, 1989), pp. 16, 72;
Amando de Miguel, *España cíclica: ciclos económicos y generaciones demográficas en la sociedad española contemporánea* (Madrid, 1986), pp. 173–6.

34 Franco to the *Leipziger Illustrierte Zeitung,* July, 1937, *Palabras,* p. 163. There
was to be no distinction between state and civil society.

35 See José Javier Moreno Luzón, 'El estudio de los apoyos sociales del
franquismo: una propuesta metodológica', in Santiago Castillo ed., *La
historia social en España: actualidad y perspectivas* (Madrid, 1991); Miguel
Jérez Mir, *Elites políticas y centros de extracción en España, 1938–1957*
(Madrid, 1982).

36 *La recristianización de la cultura española* (Madrid, 1949).

37 For instance, López Galua, *Futura grandeza de España según notables profecías*; Giuliana di Febo, *La santa de la raza: un culto barroco en la España
franquista* (Barcelona, 1988), pp. 63–71; Ernesto Giménez Caballero, *Genio
de España* (Madrid, 1932). *Genio,* here, can be taken to mean 'permeation
by the 'spirit', the original sense of the word 'genius'. 'Franco is like the
miracle-worker of old: like the mysterious wise man who, in the heart of his
inaccessible abode, conjures up the spirits of science and combines
unknown substances, until the secret of life and death is obtained. From
these hours of hermetic solitude and concentrated labour miracles appear.
Because General Franco is, principally, a maker of miracles', *El Ideal
Gallego,* 15 December 1936, cited in Fernández, *Antología,* pp. 30,487.

38 On the instrumentalisation of a monarchical fiction, whereby Franco ruled
for life, able to name a successor as *king,* see Glicerio Sánchez Recio, 'En
torno al régimen franquista: revisión de una antigua polémica,' in Anales de
la Universidad de Alicante, *Historia contemporánea,* 8/9 (1991–2),
pp. 18–19; Max Weber, *Economy and Society* (New York, 1968),
pp. 212–16, 241–55. Weber's 'ideal types' do not exist in pure form, and
Francoism was never without a bureaucracy, which became gradually more
rational in the 1950s and 1960s. It could be argued that the Caudillo's
'charismatic authority' became routinised. The economic Stabilization Plan
of 1959 might be seen as a symbol of this process. On *'Caudillaje',* 'a system
of authority founded on the prestige of its chief', see Martín Alonso,
Enciclopedia del idioma (Madrid, 1958), p. 998; José Pemartín, *¿Qué es lo
nuevo? Consideraciones sobre el momento español presente* (Santander, 1938),
pp. 9, 404, 415. On Franco's 'divine Caudillaje, divine origin of the power
of the state', see the speech of Minister of Education, José Ibáñez Martín,
Arriba, 266, 285, May and October, 1940. Also Francisco Javier Conde,
Contribución a la teoría del Caudillaje (Madrid, 1942); *Representación política y
régimen español* (Madrid, 1945); Pascal Marín Pérez, *El caudillaje español:
ensayo de construcción históricojurídica* (Madrid, 1960); Juan Ferrando Badía,
El régimen de Franco: un enfoque político-jurídico (Madrid, 1984), pp. 47–65;
Alfonso Botti, *Cielo y dinero: el nacionalcatolicismo en España, 1881–1975*
(Madrid, 1992), pp. 119–121. Also S.N. Eisenstadt, *Max Weber on Char-
isma and Institution Building* (Chicago, 1968), pp. 48–66.

39 *Wirtschaft und Gesellschaft*, part III, chapter 9, pp. 753–7, in H.H. Gerth and C. Wright Mills, *From Max Weber: Essays in Sociology* (London, 1964), pp. 246–7; Eisenstadt, *Max Weber*, p. xix.

40 As Miguel Primo de Rivera had said, justifying his own dictatorial rule in 1928, 'A dictatorship ought never be accountable for breaches of the law: this would contradict its very essence. It should be accountable, however, for breaches of moral norms.' Shlomo Ben-Ami, *Fascism From Above: the Dictatorship of Primo de Rivera in Spain, 1923–1930* (Oxford, 1983).

41 Membership of the state single party, FET–JONS became virtually obligatory. Juan Cano Bueso, *La política judicial del régimen de Franco* (Madrid, 1985); Francisco Bastida, *Jueces y franquismo: el pensamiento político del Tribunal Supremo en la dictadura* (Barcelona, 1986).

42 Gonzalo Pasamar Alzuria, *Historiografia e ideologia en la postguerra espanola: la ruptura de la tradicion liberal* (Zaragoza, 1991), pp. 19–87. The Ministry of Education was overwhelmingly run by university professors. Julián Alvarez Alvarez, *Burocracia y poder político en el régimen franquista: el papel de los cuerpos de funcionarios entre 1938 y 1975* (Madrid, 1984), p. 32.

43 Alvarez, *Burocracia*, especially pp. 25–51, 90.

44 Glicerio Sánchez Recio, 'Los tribunales populares y su actuación durante la guerra civil en el País Valenciano', in *Historia y memoria de la guerra civil* (Salamanca, 1986), pp. 156–8, for example.

45 Miguel Fenech, *La posición del juez en el Nuevo Estado* (Madrid, 1941), p. 115.

46 Recent contributions to the debate on 'defining' Francoism include Sánchez Recio, 'En torno al régimen franquista'; Alfonso Botti, 'Los fantasmas de Clio: a propósito de franquismo y fascismo en la perspectiva de la historia comparada', both in Anales de la Universidad de Alicante, *Historia contemporánea*, 8/9 (1991–2), pp. 9–34; Gregorio Cámara Villar, 'Analizar el franquismo: interpretaciones sobre su naturaleza', in J. Aróstegui, *Historia y memoria de la guerra civil* (Castilla y León, 1988), pp. 645–72; Enzo Collotti, 'Cinc formes de feixisme europeu: Àustria, Alemanya, Itàlia, Espanya i Portugal', *Afers*, 25 (1996), pp. 511–24. They all point to a relative lack of theory in analysing Francoism since the late-1970s, which, in the 1980s, was displaced by empirical accounts as archives started to become more accessible.

47 Juan J. Linz, 'An authoritarian regime: Spain', in Stanley Payne (ed.), *Politics and Society in Twentieth-century Spain* ([originally 1964] New York, 1976), pp. 160–207. For criticism, Manuel-Jesús González, *La economia política del franquismo (1940–1970) – Dirigismo, mercado, y planificación* (Madrid, 1979), pp. 21–3, 34.

48 See José Maravall, *Dictatorship and Political Dissent: Workers and Students in Franco's Spain* (New York, 1978), p. 3; Salvador Giner, "Comentario" al libro de A. de Miguel, *Sociología del franquismo'*, *Papers*, 6 (1976), 152–3; Juan Martínez Alier, 'Notas sobre el franquismo', *Papers*, 8 (1978), 35–6. Francoism could be seen as totalitarian, during its early years, if the concept is used to imply rule by institutionalised coercion, fear and 'ideological totalism'. See Menze, *Totalitarianism Reconsidered*.

49 The thesis of Linz was recycled in the mid-1970s as the regime was drawing to a close: 'Una teoría del régimen autoritario: el caso de España', in Manuel Fraga et al., *La España de los años setenta*. vol. III: *El estado y la política* (Madrid, 1974), pp. 1467–531.

50 Josep Fontana, 'Reflexiones sobre la naturaleza y las consecuencias del franquismo', in Fontana (ed.), *España bajo el franquismo* (Barcelona, 1986), p. 9. See also Ismael Saz Campos, 'El franquismo: ¿Régimen autoritario o dictadura fascista?', in Javier Tusell et al. (eds.), *El régimen de Franco (1936–1975)* (Madrid, 1993), pp. 189–202. Saz asserts the relative importance of fascist ideas and institutions under Franco. He mediates between the 'fascist' and 'non-fascist' positions on Francoism by employing the notion of 'fascistisation', arguing that, in certain conditions of crisis, sectors of the political right and of society's elites adopt a series of instruments 'whose novelty and functionality is clearly attributable to fascism'. The result may not be fascism 'in the strict sense', but neither is it traditional authoritarianism. See 'El franquismo', in Tusell, *El régimen*, particularly p. 194.

51 Javier Tusell, *Franco en la guerra civil: una biografía política* (Barcelona, 1992), p. 9.

52 José Felix Tezanos, 'Notas para una interpretación sociológica del franquismo', *Sistema*, 111 (1978).

53 Speech to Asturian coal miners, May 21 1946, in *Franco ha dicho* (Madrid, 1947), p. 21.

54 See *Cuadernos para el diálogo*, XVII Extraordinario, 'Justicia y política' (December 1969); Julio Aróstegui, 'La violencia política en España', *Ayer*, 13 (1994); 'La oposición al franquismo: represión y violencia política', in Tusell et al. (eds.), *La oposición al régimen de Franco*, vol. II (Madrid, 1991), pp. 235–56; A. Fernández Asperilla, 'Justicia y sociedad bajo el franquismo: de la ley de vagos y maleantes a la ley de peligrosidad y rehabilitación social', in Tusell et al. (eds.), *El régimen de Franco*, vol. II (Madrid, 1993), pp. 87–96.

55 See, for example, Luis Suárez Fernández, *Francisco Franco y su tiempo* (8 vols.) (Madrid, 1984); Torcuato Luca de Tena, *Franco, sí, pero . . . Confesiones profanas* (Barcelona, 1993); Manuel Fraga, Juan Velarde Fuertes and Salustiano del Campo, *La España de los años setenta* (Madrid, 1975); Ricardo de la Cierva, *Franco: un siglo de España* (Madrid, 1973); *Los años mentidos: falsificaciones y mentiras sobre la historia de España en el siglo XX* (Boadilla del Monte, 1993); Ángel Palomino, *Caudillo* (Barcelona, 1992); L. López Rodó, *La planificación del desarrollo* (Madrid, 1970).

56 See, for example, Edouard de Blaye, *Franco and the Politics of Spain* (Harmondsworth, 1976); Max Gallo, *Spain under Franco* (London, 1973); Brian Crozier, *Franco* (London, 1967). These studies have been and continue to be valuable within the terms of the approach adopted.

57 For example, Stanley Payne, 'Spanish Fascism in Comparative Perspective', in H.A. Turner (ed.), *Reappraisals of Fascism* (New York, 1975), pp. 142–69; Stanley Payne, *Politics and the Military in Modern Spain* (Stanford, CA, 1967). By contrast, the cultural and historical roots of fascism are explored in Roger Griffin, *The Nature of Fascism* (London, 1991); Herman Glaser, *The Cultural Roots of National Socialism* (London, 1978), for example.

58 According to some hagiographers, nor even was Franco a dictator. See Gonzalo Fernández de la Mora, '¿Franco, dictador?', in Fundación Nacional Francisco Franco, *El legado de Franco* (Madrid, 1993).

59 A recent corrective to this limited approach is provided by Martin Blinkhorn, 'Conservatism, Traditionalism and Fascism in Spain, 1898–1937', in Blinkhorn (ed.), *Fascists and Conservatives* (London, 1990), pp. 118–37.

60 Eduardo Sevilla Guzmán, Salvador Giner and M. Pérez Yruela, 'Despotismo moderno y dominación de clase; para una sociología del régimen franquista', *Papers, Revista de Sociología*, 8 (Barcelona, 1978), pp. 103–41; Benjamín Oltra and Amando de Miguel, 'Bonapartismo y catolicismo: una hipótesis sobre los orígenes ideológicos del franquismo', in the same volume, pp. 53–102.

61 Guy Hermet, *Los católicos en la España franquista: (i) los actores del juego político* (Madrid, 1985); Sergio Vilar, *La naturaleza del franquismo* (Barcelona, 1977); Carlos Moya, *Señas de Leviatán: estado nacional y sociedad industrial: España 1936–1980* (Madrid, 1984); and *El poder económico en España (1939–1970); un análisis sociológico* (Madrid, 1975).

62 Franco, 19 July 1937. *Palabras*, p. 168.

63 These studies rarely ventured as far as the still Marxian terrain of 'social reproduction'. See, for corrective examples, the edited collection, *Franquisme: sobre resistència i consens a Catalunya (1939–1959)* (Barcelona, 1990); Botti, *Cielo y dinero*, pp. 101–40.

64 See A. Saez Alba, *La otra 'cosa nostra'; la Asociación Católica Nacional de Propagandistas* (Paris, 1974); José R. Montero, *La CEDA: el catolicismo social y político en la II República* (Madrid, 1977); Manuel Ramírez Jiménez et al., *Las fuentes ideológicas de un régimen: España, 1939–1945* (Zaragoza, 1978); Juan Carlos Losada Malvárez, *Ideología del ejército franquista, 1939–1959* (Madrid, 1990), pp. 35–44; Aguila Tejerina, *Ideología y fascismo.*

65 There was an evident contradiction between evolutionism and creationism in Catholic Spain that was prone to surface in debates in the immediate post-war period. On Darwinism in Spain, see Diego Núñez, *El darwinismo en España* (Madrid, 1969).

66 On Catholicism and Francoism, see Alfonso Botti, *El nacionalcatolicismo en España (1888–1975)* (Madrid, 1992); C. Martí, 'Iglesia y franquismo', in J.L. García Delgado (ed.), *El primer franquismo: Españe durante la Segunda Guerra Mundial* (Madrid, 1989) pp. 295–308; *Iglesia y sociedad en España, 1939–1975* (Madrid, 1977); José Angel Tello Lázaro, *Ideología y política: la iglesia católica española, 1936–1959* (Zaragoza, 1984); Frances Lannon, *Privilege, Persecution and Prophecy. The Catholic Church in Spain, 1875–1975* (Oxford, 1987), pp. 198–256; Feliciano Blázquez, *La traición de los clérigos en la España de Franco: crónica de una intolerancia, 1936–1975* (Madrid, 1991); Alfonso Alvarez Bolado, *El experimento del nacional-catolicismo, 1939–1975* (Madrid, 1976); Santiago Petschen, *La iglesia en la España de Franco* (Madrid, 1977); Juan José Ruiz Rico, *El papel político de la iglesia católica en la España de Franco, 1936–1971* (Madrid, 1977).

67 Alfonso de Ascanio, *España imperio: el nuevo humanismo y la hispanidad* (Ávila, 1939); Feliciano Cereceda, *Historia del imperio español y de la hispanidad* (Madrid, 1940); Manuel García Morente, *Idea de la hispanidad. I.*

España como estilo. II. El caballero cristiano (Madrid, 1938); Guillermo Lohmann Villena, *Menéndez Pelayo y la hispanidad* (Madrid, 1957); Eduardo González Calleja and Fredes Limón Nevado, *La hispanidad como instrumento de combate: raza e imperio en la prensa franquista durante la guerra civil española* (Madrid, 1988); Ángela Cenarro Lagunas, 'Poder polític i discurs espanyolista a Aragó (1936–1949)', *L'Avenç*, 197 (November 1995), pp. 28–32.

68 The sense of a harmonious blending of these ideas is very strong in the influential review *Acción Española*. See Raúl Morodo, *Acción Española: origenes ideológicas del franquismo* (Madrid, 1980). A foretaste of Francoist ideas is clearly given in the editorial, 'Reconquista de España', 8, 43 (16 December 1933) pp. 640–2. To prevent the Republic 'burying our glorious historic tradition like a putrefying corpse', Fascist Italy's 'modern concept of the corporative state' was pointed to. The wartime anthology issue published in 1937 carried Franco's dedication.

69 For example, Eduardo de Santiago, *Cuando España renace* (Burgos, 1939). Franco was also variously seen as, among others, the reincarnation of Juan de Austria, victor at Lepanto, Cardinal Cisneros, Santiago the Apostle, Charles V or the Catholic Kings. See Di Febo, *La santa de la raza*, pp. 23–59; Demetrio Carceller and Carrero Blanco cited in Fernández, *Antología*, for instances. On the teaching of history to secondary school children in the 1940s, see Esther Martinez Tórtola, *La enseñanza de la historia en el primer bachillerato franquista, 1938–1953* (Madrid, 1996).

70 Preston, *Franco*, pp. 329–30, 582–3.

71 Regenerationism revolved around essentialist ideas. The 'problem of Spain' could be resolved, it was thought, by defining and perpetuating the Spanish 'essence', as opposed to 'foreignness'. See, for example, Angel Ganivet, *Idearium Español*; Miguel de Unamuno, *En torno al casticismo* ([originally 1895] Madrid, 1986). From here, and from Catholic doctrine, would come the idea of the 'Anti-Spain' during the Civil War.

72 Losada Malvárez, *Ideología del ejército franquista*.

73 José María de Areilza and Fernando María Castiella, *Reivindicaciones de España* (Madrid, 1941); Antonio Tovar, *El imperio de España* (Madrid, 1941); Ricardo Arco y Garay, *La idea de imperio en la política y literatura españolas* (Madrid, 1944); Eleuterio Elorduy, *La idea del imperio en el pensamiento español y de otros pueblos* (Madrid, 1944); Servicio de prensa y propaganda de la FE de las JONS, *El imperio de España* (Valladolid, n.d); Herbert Southworth, 'La Falange: un análisis de la herencia fascista española', in Paul Preston (ed.), *España en crisis: la evolución y decadencia del régimen de Franco* (Madrid, 1977), pp. 29–60.

74 Robert Jay Lifton, 'Death and History: Ideological Totalism, Victimization, and Violence', in Menze, *Totalitarianism Reconsidered* (New York, 1981), p. 214; Mary Matossian, 'Ideologies of Delayed Industrialization: Some Tensions and Ambiguities', in *Economic Development and Cultural Change* (April 1958), pp. 217–28. This 'essence of being', society's 'centre', in the realm of values and beliefs, and threats to it, are linked to 'charismatic authority' by Weber. See Eisenstadt, *Max Weber*, pp. xix–xxx. Also, Clifford Geertz, 'Centers, Kings and Charisma: Reflections on the

Symbolics of Power', in Geertz, *Local Knowledge* (London, 1993), pp. 121–146.

75 See Josep Benet, *L'intent franquista de genocidi cultural contra Catalunya* (Barcelona, 1995), esp. pp. 329–35.

76 The phrase was coined by Manuel-Jesús González, *La economía política*, p. 46.

77 See Joan Clavera et al., *Capitalismo español: de la autarquía a la estabilización* (1939–1959) (Madrid, 1978), pp. 134–5.

78 See Gustavo Corni, *Hitler and the Peasants: Agrarian Policy of the Third Reich, 1930–1939* (Oxford, 1990), pp. 18–38, 116–42, 220–44; J.E. Farquharson, *The Plough and the Swastika: The NSDAP and Agriculture in Germany, 1928–45* (London, 1976), pp. 141–60, 203–20; Karen Pinkus, *Bodily Regimes: Advertising Under Italian Fascism* (Minnesota, 1994).

79 José Luis de Arrese, *La revolución social del nacional-sindicalismo* (Madrid, 1940), p. 169.

80 Franco, radio message, 1 October 1937, *Palabras*, p. 124. Also Eduardo Sevilla Guzmán and Manuel González de Molina, 'Política social agraria del primer franquismo', in J.L. García Delgado (ed.), *El primer franquismo: España durante la Segunda Guerra Mundial* (Madrid, 1989), pp. 135–87; Cristóbal Gómez Benito, *Políticos, burócratas y expertos: un estudio de la política agraria y la sociología rural en España (1936–1959)* (Madrid, 1996).

81 On francoism, industrialisation and regenerationism, see Manuel-Jesus González and Pedro Schwartz, *Una historia del Instituto Nacional de Industria (1941–1976)* (Madrid, 1978), pp. 22–5.

82 Linz, 'An Authoritarian Regime'. The argument is based on the theory of Theodor Geiger, which claims that an 'ideology' is extensively elaborated and disseminated throughout society, where 'mentality' refers rather to unspoken assumptions. 'Mentality' tends towards a rather consensual approach to ideas, whereas ideology could be said to suggest a conflictive context. However, these 'rival' concepts do not seem necessarily to be mutually exclusive.

83 The suggestion that Francoism relied upon a 'traditional' discourse, or set of beliefs, rather than a 'modern' one, must be open to question. Laclau's distinctions, relating myth, reproduced 'automatically', to periods of stability and ideology, using a 'system of narration' counterposed to other ideologies in a period of 'crisis', is useful but is also unnecessarily rigid. Ernesto Laclau, *Politics and Ideology in Marxist Theory* (London, 1977), pp. 102–3. See also Gregorio Cámara Villar, *Nacional-catolicismo y escuela: la socialización política del franquismo (1936–1951)* (Jaén, 1984), pp. 17–53.

84 See Carles Viver Pi-Sunyer, 'Aproximació a la ideología del franquisme en l'etapa fundacional del règim', in *Papers*, 14 (1980), 19–20. See also Manuel Ramírez, *España 1939–1975; régimen político e ideológico* (Barcelona, 1978). The exemplary figure of the Caudillo was symbolic of a rejection of pluralism in favour of a 'new community of values' based on the 'Cross and the Sword'. 'Organicism' meant that nation and state had 'living' properties: they were irreducibly superior to 'inanimate', or 'inorganic species', and could 'reproduce' themselves.

85 An anthropological perspective on nationalism as not simply *an* ideology, but as belonging with 'kinship' or 'religion' is provided by Benedict Anderson, *Imagined Communities: Reflections on the Origin and Spread of Nationalism* (London, 1983), esp. here, p. 15.

86 *Boletín del estado*, 21 September 1937. On Francoist schools and education, see Cámara Villar, *Nacional-catolicismo y escuela*; Antonio Molero Pintado, *La educación durante la segunda república y la guerra civil (1931–1939)* (Madrid, 1991); Alejandro Mayordomo Pérez, *Nacional-catolicismo y educación en la España de posguerra* (Madrid, 1990); Martínez Tórtola, *La enseñanza de la historia*; Ramón Navarro Sandalinas, *La enseñanza primaria durante el franquismo (1936–1975)* (Barcelona, 1990); Andrés Sopeña Monsalve, *El flórido pensil: memoria de la escuela nacional-católica* (Barcelona, 1994); María Immaculada Pastor i Homs, *La educación femenina en la postguerra (1939–45); el caso de Mallorca* (Mallorca, 1984).

87 J. Goytisolo, 'Remedios de la concupiscencia', pp. 95–6. The sharing of the common standards of the Catholic Church was the basis of the cohesion of the ruling group of Francoism, locally and nationally.

88 López Ibor, *El español*, p. 180, for example.

89 'Spain' was normally feminine. Franco was 'the legendary Caballero defending the honour of his maiden – taking the field of life and death, for the honour of our women, for the purity of our brides, for the holiness of our mothers', José Pemartín, 'La Cruz Laureada del Generalísimo Franco', in *Laureados de España* (Madrid, 1940), p. 52.

90 Losada Malvárez, *Ideología del ejército franquista*, pp. 28–30. The most famous example of organicist language and Darwinist metaphor is José Ortega y Gasset, *España invertebrada: bosquejo de algunos pensamientos historicos* (Madrid, 1921). See also Giménez Caballero, *Genio de España*, especially pp. 111–12 where *España invertebrada* is hailed as a seminal work in the development of Spanish fascism. Organicism and degeneration had been part of liberal and leftist discourse since the nineteenth century. See, for example, Fernando Alvarez-Uría, *Miserables y locos: medicina mental y orden social en la España del siglo XIX* (Barcelona, 1983).

91 Declarations to Henri Massis, 18 August 1938. *Palabras*, p. 261.

92 Franco wanted 'to wipe from our history' the liberal nineteenth century. Speech, Baracaldo, 21 June 1950. See also point seven of the Falange's twenty-six: 'The only truly free man is he who forms part of a strong and free nation'.

93 Guillermo García Pérez, *La economía y los reaccionarios: la Inquisición y los economistas al surgir la España contemporánea* (Madrid, 1974), p. 370; Franco, *Palabras*, pp. 10–12.

94 The annulment of press freedom in April 1938 was to prevent 'propaganda . . . against unity' and the decree against freedom of association (2 March 1938) charged the Minister of Interior to give 'unity and discipline to public demonstrations of thought'. See Fenech, *La posicion del juez en el Nuevo Estado*, p. 92. Bastida, *Jueces y franquismo*. See also Ramiro de Maeztu, *Defensa de la hispanidad* (Madrid, 1934), p. 201; José Pemartín, *¿Qué es lo nuevo?*, p. 74.

95 Franco's speech, 24 June 1938, *Palabras*, p. 60. See also *Palabras*, pp. 197–266, for example: 'In Spain, you are Catholic or you are nothing', p. 261.

96 López Ibor, *El español*, pp. 43–4; José María Sánchez, *The Spanish Civil War as a Religious Tragedy* (Notre Dame, IN, 1987), p. 2.

97 Asceticism, severe abstinence or strict self-denial, was central to Falangist doctrine. The ascetic austerity of Falangist militants was, according to the party's founder, José Antonio Primo de Rivera, displayed in their activities as 'half-soldiers half-monks', and in their praise of the 'austere' countryside and poetry of Castile. Also Franco, *Palabras*, pp. 13, 99, 140–1. See also chapter 8.

98 Franz Borkenau, *The Spanish Cockpit* ([originally, 1937] Ann Arbor, MI, 1963), p. 178.

99 Mary Vincent, *Catholicism in the Second Spanish Republic: Religion and Politics in Salamanca, 1930–1936* (Oxford, 1996).

100 See Martin Blinkhorn, 'The Iberian States', in Detlef Muhlberger, *The Social Basis of European Fascist Movements* (London, 1987), pp. 320–48. The nature of the Catholic corporativist mass party, the CEDA, is still debated. However, the evident sympathy of both its leadership and many of its rank and file seems beyond question. Thousands of militants of the party's youth wing, the JAP, defected to the Falange in the wake of the election defeat of February 1936. This did not necesitate any drastic change in political views.

101 The evolution of party membership prior to the Civil War is difficult to trace, since the records have not survived. Estimates suggest that at the beginning of 1936 the national membership was, at the most, 25,000, although half of these would have been 'unofficial' student affiliates. However, some writers suggest the figure was not likely to have been more than 6,000, although it grew significantly between February and July 1936. See Ricardo Chueca, *El fascismo en los comienzos del régimen de Franco: un estudio sobre FET-JONS* (Madrid, 1983), pp. 130–2. During the Civil War the party grew, attracting thousands of new members anxious to ingratiate themselves with the new power, but, at the same time, lost many pre-war affiliates in battle. Guy Hermet suggests that there were 36,000 members by July 1936, rising to 240,000 in 1937 and 650,000 by 1939. By early 1940 there were, according to Hermet, 725,000, although British diplomats estimated that the state party had around 3 million members by this time. Dispatch, 2 January 1940, PRO/FO371/24507/C380/40/41. Hermet, *Los católicos en la españa franquista* (I), p. 373.

102 See Paul Preston, *The Coming of the Spanish Civil War* (London, 1978), pp. 177–201.

103 See Ronald Fraser, 'The Spanish Civil War', in Raphael Samuel (ed.), *People's History and Socialist Theory* (London, 1981), pp. 196–9; Antonio Elorza, 'Caballeros y fascistas', *Historia 16*, 91 (1983), pp. 33–41. The dominant political input at state level of progressive political forces was in marked contrast to the dominance of political conservatives prior to Hitler's and Mussolini's seizing of power.

104 Antonio Vallejo-Nágera, *Divagaciones intranscendentes* (Valladolid, 1938), p. 66.

105 Pierre Vilar, *La guerra civil española* (Barcelona, 1986), p. 16.

106 *ABC*, Seville, 1 June 1939, cited by Moreno Gómez, *Córdoba*, p. 31.

107 *Levante*, 10 May 1939, Ballester, *Quarantena*, p. 18.

108 Exp. 5 Joan Lluhía Vallesca, ATRP, for example. For the similar situation in France, see Robert Soucy, 'The Nature of Fascism in France', in *Journal of Contemporary History*, 1, 1 (1966), pp. 27–55.

109 Víctor Alba, *Sisifo y su tiempo: memorias de un cabreado, 1916–1996* (Barcelona, 1996), pp. 203, 223.

110 Rafael Abella, *Finales de enero de 1939; Barcelona cambia del piel* (Barcelona, 1991), p. 50.

111 Some individuals who joined the Republican forces of order, like the Guardia de Asalto, during the conflict, were later exonerated by FET-JONS as being people 'of order and inclined towards the Glorious National Movement'. Exp. 445, ATRP, for example.

112 Several monarchist bankers who had supported the Nationalist side were fined in 1950 for arranging political meetings, for example. PRO/FO371/WS1015/19, 17 May 1950. The Republican millionaire head of the Appeal Court of Catalonia who left his post and Barcelona soon after the military rebellion and rendered services to the Nationalists during the war, narrowly escaped imprisonment or worse in the aftermath of the conflict. The political responsiblities court was satisfied that he was a Catholic whose family spoke Castilian at home. See ATRP, expediente 408.

113 Martínez Alier, 'Notas sobre el franquismo'.

114 Rafael Gay de Montellá, *Autarquía: nuevas orientaciones de la economía* (Barcelona, 1940), p. 96; Antonio de Miguel, 'Autarquía', *Información Comercial Española* (ICE), 33 (10 November 1941), p. 9.

115 Franco, *Palabras* (1938), pp. 11, 14–15, 35, 48, 137–40, 219, 243; Arrese, *La revolución social*, pp. 205–8.

116 Published message, 18 July 1938. *Palabras*, p. 137.

117 The suggestion is made by the professor of medical history, Luis Granjel. See 'La medicina en la guerra', *Historia 16, La guerra civil*, 14 (Madrid, 1987), p. 100.

118 Enrique González Duro, *Historia de la locura en España: del reformismo del siglo XIX al franquismo* (Madrid, 1996), vol. III, pp. 312–13.

119 *Palabras*, p. 275.

120 García Morente, *Ideas para una filosofía*, pp. 8–12, 82–7; López Ibor, *El español*, pp. 52–60.

121 Dionisio Ridruejo, *Escrito en Espana* (Buenos Aires, 1962), p. 98; Angel Viñas et al., *Política comercial exterior en España (1931–1975)* (Madrid, 1979), pp. 290–452.

122 See, for example, Angel Carbonell, *Cartas de combate: en defensa de la fe dirigidas a las juventudes cristianas* (Barcelona, 1940); Juan José de Pablo Romero, *Teología ascética y mística* (Soria, 1940).

123 García Morente, *Ideas para una filosofía*, p. 63; Franco, *Palabras* (1938), pp. 78/138.

124 Ramón Serrano Suñer, speech, July 1939, *De la victoria y la postguerra:*

discursos (Madrid, 1941), p. 50; Franco, *Palabras* (1938), pp. 51, 140, 263. See also Roca, *De la pureza*, p. 22.

125 See Pérez del Pulgar, 'El concepto cristiano', pp. 89–94. The author was the founder of the Francoist state's system of prison labour, the so-called 'Redemption of Punishment Through Labour'. See also Arrese, *La revolución social*, pp. 169–75.

126 López Ibor, *El español*, p. 181; Perez del Pulgar, 'El concepto cristiano', pp. 92–3; Arrese, *La revolución social*, p. 170.

127 For studies of the Francoist economy, as such, which deal with this period, see Albert Carreras, 'Depresión económica y cambio estructural durante el decenio bélico (1936–1945)' and Jordi Catalan, 'Autarquia y desarrollo de la industria de fabrica durante la segunda guerra mundial: un enfoque comparativo', both in J.L. García Delgado (ed.), *El primer franquismo* (Madrid, 1989); Clavera et al., *Capitalismo español*; Manuel-Jesus González, *La economía política*.

128 Alternative visions were articulated under the most difficult circumstances. See the last defence and testimony of the young Republican medical doctor, Luis Campos Osaba, movingly describing a progressive, democratic and popular patriotism. Campos was a member of the PCE, a captain in the Republican military health department, who was imprisoned in 1939, conditionally released in 1944, when he fled to France to fight in the Resistance, later returning clandestinely to fight against the Spanish dictatorship. He was captured and executed in 1949. Encarnación Barranquero Texeira and Matilde Eiroa San Francisco, 'Hacia la recuperación de la memoria perdida: notas sobre la vida y la muerte en la prisión provincial de Sevilla en 1949', in *Actas del IV congreso sobre el andalucismo histórico* (Seville, 1989), pp. 635–47.

129 Vázquez Montalbán, *Barcelonas*, p. 168; *Crónica sentimental*, p. 34.

130 Pilar Folguera, 'La construcción de lo cotidiano durante los primeros años del franquismo', *Ayer*, 19 (1995), 165–87; R. Sánchez López, *Mujer española: una sombra de destino en lo universal* (Murcia, 1990); Juan Marsé, *Si te dicen que caí* (Mexico City, 1973); Ana María Matute, *Libro de juegos para los niños de los otros* (Barcelona, 1961).

2   PURIFYING SPAIN (I): THE ELIMINATION OF DISSENT

1 Luciano de la Calzada, 'El espíritu del 18 de julio como realidad histórica y proyección hacia el futuro', in *La guerra de liberación nacional* (Zaragoza, 1961), pp. 605–6.

2 For example, Fernando Díaz-Plaja in *La vida cotidiana en la España de la guerra civil* (Madrid, 1994), pp. 113–24.

3 Republican violence is in urgent need of analysis. Any such study would centre upon anti-clericalism. To an extent, our view of terror in the Republican zone has been distorted by Francoist propaganda. An analysis that explores the distance between the virtual exoneration of Republicans for anti-Catholicism, on the one hand, and the vague label of 'Jacobinism', on the other, would be welcome. For the former, see Hilari Raguer, 'La "cuestión religiosa"', in Santos Juliá (ed.), *Política en la segunda república*,

Ayer, 20 (Madrid, 1995), pp. 228–40; for the latter, Stanley Payne, 'Political Violence During the Spanish Second Republic', *Journal of Contemporary History*, 25 (1990), p. 272. A typology of repression would set Republican violence within a context of living conditions, political participation and manipulation and popular ideas and culture. *Organised* political violence was used in Republican Spain as part of the state's reconstruction of authority after May 1937. This violence was against anarchists and supporters of the dissident Marxist parties, not against Francoist supporters. Republican labour camps seem to have interned in them more dissident leftists than Francoists. Alba, 'De los Tribunales', p. 229.

4 Alba, 'De los Tribunales', pp. 223–5; Bermejo et al., 'Cartagena', p. 109, both in Ministerio de Cultura, *Justicia en guerra: jornadas sobre la administración de justicia durante la guerra civil española: instituciones y fuentes documentales* (Madrid, 1990). The pre-war years of the Republic saw a great deal of violence, much of it from the government. But it was overwhelmingly used in putting down worker unrest and rarely employed against the right. See Manuel Ballbé, *Orden público y militarismo en la España constitucional, 1812–1983* (Madrid, 1985), pp. 317–96.

5 Republican decree, 25 August 1936, *Gaceta de la República*, 26 August. 'Popular Justice' meant the participation of 'the people'; those same people who had saved the Republic by their actions on 18/19 July and who would be called upon again to defend the government in armed combat.

6 Arthur Miller, *The Crucible* (Harmondsworth, 1973), p. 122. See also p. 85. On 'clean souls', see Franco's speeches 1/12/22, October 1937, *Palabras*, pp. 34, 37, 125.

7 Although the refusal of reconciliation contradicted the Christian belief in community. 'La unidad entre los hombres de Espana', in *Revista Internacional de Sociologia* 2/3 (1943), pp. 346–7.

8 Antonio Bahamonde y Sánchez de Castro, *Un año con Queipo: memorias de un nacionalista* (Barcelona, 1938), p. 71; F. Stampa Irueste, *El delito de rebelión* (Madrid, 1945), for example. See also, *Iglesia y sociedad en España*; Tello Lázaro, *Ideología y política*; Lannon, *Privilege, Persecution and Prophecy*; Feliciano Blázquez, *La traición de los clérigos*; Alvarez Bolado, *El experimento del nacional-catolicismo*; Petschen, *La iglesia*; Ruiz Rico, *El papel político de la iglesia*.

9 The Primate of Spain, Cardinal Isidro Gomá, *Pastorales de la guerra de España* (Madrid, 1955), p. 69, Pamplona, 23 November 1936. Gomá insisted on the censorship of a pastoral letter in August 1939 for use of the word 'reconciliation' instead of the officially prescribed 'recuperation'. Lannon, *Privilege, Persecution, and Prophecy*, p. 215. Also *Boletín del Obispado de Santiago de Compostela*, 31 August 1936. The crusade image was formalised in the pastoral letter of the Bishop of Salamanca, Enrique Pla y Deniel, issued on 30 September 1936. It was here too that the notion of the 'two Spains' entered into the justificatory theory of the Civil War.

10 *ABC*, 1 November 1936.

11 On the theme of the marking of boundaries among social groups, see G. Olsson, 'Towards a Sermon of Modernity', in M. Billinge, D. Gregory and R. Martin, *Recollections of a Revolution: Geography as Spatial Science*

(London, 1984), pp. 73–85; 'to define is to distinguish what is inside a boundary from what is outside it: to split open a natural whole: to sift friend from foe like wheat from chaff'. Also Derek Gregory and John Urry (eds.), *Social Relations and Spatial Structures* (London, 1985).

12 Stephen Yeo, 'The More It Changes, the More It Stays the Same?', *History Workshop Journal*, 30 (Autumn, 1990), p. 123. See, also Eric Wolf, *Europe and the People Without History* (Berkeley, CA, 1982). On Spain, see Herbert Southworth, *El mito de la cruzada*; *Guernica! Guernica! A Study of Journalism, Diplomacy, Propaganda and History* (Berkeley, CA, 1977); Paul Preston, 'The Politics of Revenge: Francoism, the Civil War and Collective Memory', in *The Politics of Revenge* (London, 1990); Pasamar, *Historiografía e ideología*.

13 Report on Ciudad Real, PRO/FO371/24507/C758/40/41, 10 January 1940.

14 See Di Febo, *La santa de la raza*, p. 25.

15 *Arriba España*, 17 January 1937. See also José Antonio Primo de Rivera, interview, *La Voz*, 14 February 1936; Sancho Dávila and Julián Pemartín, *Hacia la historia de la Falange*, vol. I (Jeréz, 1938), p. 24; Pemartín, *¿Qué es lo nuevo?*, p. 16; Ramiro Ledesma Ramos, *Discurso a las juventudes de España* (Madrid, 1954); 'La legitimidad y la fecundidad de la violencia', *La Conquista del Estado*, 23 May 1931; 'La violencia, primera misión', 'La vitalidad nacional', 27 June 1931; Onésimo Redondo, *El estado nacional* (Madrid, 1939), pp. 27–9; Marqués de Eliseda, *Fascismo, catolicismo, monarquía* (San Sebastián, 1935), p. 103. On Falangist involvement in executions, see Dionisio Ridruejo, *Escrito en España* (Buenos Aires, 1962), pp. 91–8; the interview with Raimundo Fernández Cuesta, 'Los Falangistas realizamos el trabajo sucio: fusilar', *Diario 16, Historia del Franquismo*, I (1984–5), p. 23; Juan Antonio Ansaldo, *¿Para qué . . . ? (De Alfonso XIII a Juan III)* (Buenos Aires, 1951), pp. 71–87.

16 Pedro Castellanos, *Policía integral o policía nacional-sindicalista* (Valladolid, 1939), for example.

17 For comparison see Henry Rousso, *The Vichy Syndrome: History and Memory in France since 1944* (Cambridge, MA, 1991). See also Anton Pelinka, 'The Great Austrian Taboo: The Repression of the Civil War', in K. Harms et al. (eds.), *Coping With the Past: Germany and Austria after 1945* (Madison, 1990), pp. 56–65. In both places, and in Spain too, the trauma, in terms of memory, is not only of pain but also of guilt. See Paul Preston's comment about comparison of the Spanish and German situations for an alternative view. 'The Politics of Revenge', p. 33.

18 See, for example, Paul Thompson (ed.), *Our Common History* (London, 1982), p. 16; Luisa Passerini, Introduction to Passerini (ed.), *Memory and Totalitarianism* (Oxford, 1992). Also Marsé, *Si te dicen*, especially pp. 27–8, 185, 247–8, 253–5; Teresa Cuevas Gutiérrez, *Cárcel de mujeres (1939–1945)* (Barcelona, 1985), pp. 178–9.

19 Although the effects of this kind of institutional indoctrination were impossible to predict or control. For some women, in particular, Francoist organisation offered greater possibilities for social interaction outside of church and home. See, for example, María Teresa Gallego Méndez, *Mujer, Falange y franquismo* (Madrid, 1983). On Spanish youth under Franco, see J. Saiz Marín, *El Frente de Juventudes: política de juventud en la España de la*

postguerra (1937–1960) (Madrid, 1988); G. Germani, 'La socialización política de la juventud en los regímenes fascistas: Italia y España', in *Revista Latinoamericana de Sociología*, 5 (November 1969).

20 It was partly this enforced retreat which explains the prominence of women in the sporadic expression of resistance which occurred in the 1940s.

21 Cited in Vázquez Montalbán, *Barcelonas*, pp. 167–8.

22 Benet (trans. Gregory Rabassa), *Return to Región* (New York, 1985), p. 5. (Original Spanish version, 1967.)

23 Olsson, 'Toward a Sermon', p. 76; 'remembering is a sanctioned technique for purifying one's individual and collective conscience.' See also Alba, *Sísifo y su tiempo*, p. 205; Aguilar, *Memoria*, pp. 43–8.

24 Luis Martín-Santos, *Tiempo de silencio* (Barcelona, 1962), p. 236. The relationship between silence and evasion, of various kinds, is one of the main themes of the novel. The future was replaced by the Orteguian concept of 'destiny', something quite different, which was also used to compensate for a lack of freedom. See the excellent analysis of Jo Labanyi, *Ironía e historia en Tiempo de Silencio* (Madrid, 1985).

25 See David Herzberger, *Narrating the Past: Fiction and Historiography in Postwar Spain* (Durham, NC, 1995), especially pp. 37, 82, 106.

26 Cited in A. Braojos Garrido, L. Alvarez Rey and F. Espinosa Maestre, *Sevilla '36; sublevación fascista y represión* (Seville, 1990), pp. 218–19.

27 See, particularly, Ramón Salas Larrazábal, *Pérdidas de la guerra* (Barcelona, 1977); Ricardo de la Cierva, *La historia se confiesa* (Barcelona, 1976); *Historia ilustrada de la guerra civil española*, 2 vols. (Barcelona, 1990), particularly vol. II, pp. 215–16; *Francisco Franco: un siglo de España*, 2 vols. (Madrid, 1973), vol. II, p. 172. The methodological approach is suggested in the title of such volumes as Salas Larrazábal's *Los datos exactos de la guerra civil* (Madrid, 1980).

28 Gabriel Jackson, *The Spanish Republic and the Civil War, 1931–1939* (Princeton, NJ, 1965), p. 526; see also the Spanish edition, *La República Española y la Guerra Civil 1931–1939* (Barcelona, 1976), p. 13; Tamámes, *La República*, pp. 348–56.

29 See particularly Reig Tapia, *Violencia y terror: estudios sobre la guerra civil española* (Madrid, 1990); Fontana, 'Naturaleza y consecuencias', especially pp. 20–4. For a summary in English, see Michael Richards, 'Civil War, Violence and the Construction of Francoism', in Paul Preston (ed.), *The Republic Beseiged: Civil War in Spain, 1936–1939* (Edinburgh, 1996).

30 The state's own *Anuario Oficial Estadístico* gives a figure of 192,684 dying in prisons between 1 April 1939 and 30 June 1944 which is identical to that given to the American journalist Charles Foltz by an un-named official of the Spanish Ministry of Justice. See Eiroa San Francisco, *Viva Franco*, p. 214; Charles Foltz Jr, *The Masquerade in Spain* (Boston, MA, 1948), p. 97. Foltz also points out that the Ministry of Justice had nothing to do with the recording of executions of prisoners held by the Falange, the Ministry of the Interior or the army, implying that this figure did not include many other 'judicial' killings. This seems to be supported by the British Foreign Office communication of 3 January 1945: 'it must be borne in mind that the number of prisoners detained under the charge of the

Ministry of Justice is small compared with those described as "Detenidos Gubernativos" . . . held under the authority of the Dirección General de Seguridad or central police headquarters'. Bowker to Eden, PRO/FO371/ 49575/Z89/89/41. Gabriel Jackson calculated that a minimum of 150,000 and a maximum of 200,000 were killed in reprisals and formal executions in the Nationalist zone from 1936–44. See his *La República Española y la Guerra Civil*, p. 14. The figure of 500,000 'murdered behind the lines' by Falangists, suggested by the war correspondent John Whitaker, who witnessed a great many executions, seems inflated. John T. Whitaker, 'Prelude to World War: A Witness From Spain', *Foreign Affairs*, 21, 1 (October 1942), p. 109.

31 See *Lo que han hecho en Galicia: episodios del terror blanco en las provincias gallegas contados por quienes los han vivido* (Paris, 1938), p. 46; Thomas, *The Spanish Civil War*, p. 261.

32 Moreno Gómez, *Córdoba*, p. 63–4. Also Pilar Fidalgo, *A Young Mother in Franco's Spain* (London, 1939), p. 31. Wearing black may well have been a kind of protest. See Carmela Gonzalez, *The Bitter Fruit of a Broken Tree* (London, 1992).

33 Giuliana di Febo, *Resisténcia y movimiento de mujeres en España, 1936–1976* (Barcelona, 1979), p. 107.

34 Ramón García Piñeiro, *Los mineros asturianos bajo el franquismo, 1937–1962* (Madrid, 1990), p. 175.

35 See Juan Pablo Fusi, *Franco: autoritarismo y poder personal* (Madrid, 1985), p. 79.

36 See, for example, Bahamonde, *Un año con Queipo*, pp. 90, 100, 102. Bahamonde, a devout Catholic, was the Propaganda Delegate of Nationalist General Queipo de Llano. He had been in the Falange militia and was involved in guard duties in prisons and cemeteries, but did all he could to escape because of the horror he witnessed there. His book was seen as treachery and was withdrawn, subsequently being published in Mexico. See also *Lo que han hecho*, pp. 31–2. Ridruejo, *Escrito*, p. 92; Herbert Matthews, *The Yoke and the Arrows* (London, 1958), pp. 15–16; Whitaker, 'Prelude', p. 117. Recent detailed local historical studies support this basic distinction. See, for example, Manuel Ortiz Heras, *Violencia política en la II República y el primer franquismo: Albacete, 1936–1950* (Madrid, 1996), pp. xiv–xvi, 71–2.

37 Cano Bueso, *La politica judicial*, pp. 89–92. Plurality of jurisdictions are a marked feature of totalitarian states. For example, Jerzy Gliksman, 'Social Prophylaxis as a Form of Soviet Terror', in Carl Friedrich (ed.), *Totalitarianism* (New York, 1953), pp. 61–3.

38 Fontana, 'Naturaleza y consecuencias', pp. 17–24.

39 Moreno Gómez, *Córdoba en la posguerra*, p. 18; Arthur Koestler, *Spanish Testament* (London, 1937), p. 82; Alfred Mendizábal, *The Martyrdom of Spain* (London, 1938), p. 236.

40 Ridruejo, *Escrito en España*, pp. 93–4. Dionisio was regime insider, co-author of the Falangist anthem 'Cara al Sol', and head of Franco's Department of Press and Propaganda in the early 1940s, who fell out with the regime because of its social conservatism.

41 Tuñón de Lara, prologue, Reig, *Ideología*, p. 9.

42 *Palabras*, p. 202.
43 Ridruejo, *Escrito en España*, p. 92.
44 Pierre Vilar, *Spain: A Brief History* (2nd edition, London, 1977), p. 113.
45 Manuel Azaña, *Obras completas* (Mexico, 1968), vol. IV, pp. 850–1. About seventy rightists, including many Falangists, were shot in Madrid's Model Prison on 23 August 1936 'in revenge' for the massacre of about 2,000 leftists following the capture of the city of Badajóz by Franco's forces a few days before. See Blaye, *Franco and the Politics of Spain*, p. 456. Of course no foreign state had any sympathy with 'revolutionary violence', but the position of Republican leaders from the beginning was a moral as well as a calculated one.
46 José María Iribarren, *Con el General Mola* (Zaragoza, 1937), p. 169.
47 Josep María Solé i Sabaté and Joan Villarroya, in *La repressió a la reraguarda de Catalunya (1936–1939)* (Barcelona, 1989); Francesc Bonamusa, 'L'administració de justicia a Catalunya, setembre-desembre 1936' *Recerques*, 4 (1974), pp. 191–222; C.Bermejo Merino et al., 'El Tribunal Popular de Cartagena', in Ministerio de Cultura, *Justicia en guerra*, pp. 109–126. So-called 'uncontrollables' became 'controlled' by incorporating them into new state institutions. Alba, 'De los Tribunales Populares'. In Málaga, all the political organisations of the Republic, even the anarchists, 'condemned and deplored the killings'. Gamel Woolsey, *Death's Other Kingdom* (London, 1939), pp. 114–15.
48 Francisco Cobo Romero, 'La justicia Republicana en la provincia de Jaén durante la guerra civil: la actuación de los Tribunales especiales populares (1936–1939)', in *Justicia en guerra*, p. 127. The re-establishment of 'judicial normality' was a priority of the Republican government. See the decrees of 6 August 1937 and 24 March 1938, *Gaceta de la República*, 7 August 1937 and 26 March 1938. Republican lawyers were a moderating force supporting the correct functioning of popular justice. Glicerio Sánchez Recio, 'Justicia ordinaria y justicia popular durante la guerra civil', in Ministerio de Cultura, *Justicia en guerra*, pp. 96–7.
49 Manuel Aragón, 'La velada en Benicarló o la agonía Republicana', in *Ínsula* (Barcelona, 1990).
50 Joan Peiró, *Perill a la reraguarda* (Mataró, 1936). Also Ramón Serrano Suñer, *Política de España, 1936–1975* (Madrid, 1995), p. 75.
51 Juan Marichal, *El intelectual y la política* (Madrid, 1990), p. 100; Santiago Alvarez, *Negrín, personalidad histórica* (Madrid, 1994), pp. 43–280. See also Negrín's government decree calling for 'tolerance and civility . . . in the work of national reconstruction . . . as the basis of living together . . . (convivencia)', *Gaceta de la República*, 25 December 1938. I am grateful to Helen Graham for several insights into the character and objectives of Negrín.
52 Quoted by Whitaker, 'Prelude to World War', p. 118. Even in relatively moderate Vizcaya, where there was no social revolution following the attempted coup, it was recognised that 'traditionalist' judges would inevitably have to be replaced by those who actually supported the Republic. Germán Rueda Hernanz, 'Suspensión de jueces y fiscales municipales por

ideología política, Vizcaya, 1936', in Ministerio de Cultura, *Justicia en guerra*, pp. 167–9.

53 *Partes Oficiales de Guerra, 1936–1939*, vol. I, Servicio Histórico Militar (Madrid, 1977), p. 1.

54 Charles A. Thomson, 'Spain: A Civil War', *Foreign Policy Reports* 12, 21 (15 January 1937); *New York Herald Tribune*, 31 July 1936.

55 Ramón Serrano Suñer, *Entre Hendaya y Gibraltar* (6th edn, Madrid, 1963), especially pp. 33–70; Stanley Payne, *Franco's Spain* (London, 1968), p. 23.

56 In Seville the state of war was declared in article 1 of a decree of 18 July 1936. The priorities were quite clear: article 2 decreed that strikers would be shot. Julio de Ramón-Laca, *Bajo la férula de Queipo: como fue gobernada Andalucía* (Seville, 1939), p. 16.

57 *Manchester Guardian*, 31 August 1936. The cases of Bilbao, Málaga and Cartagena, to cite only a few, show how uncontrolled mob killings were often a response to Nationalist bombing raids on cities.

58 Burnett Bolloten, *The Spanish Civil War: Revolution and Counterrevolution* (Chapel Hill, NC, 1991); Pelai Pagés i Blanchi, 'La administración de Justicia en Catalunya durante la guerra civil española (1936–1939)'; Alba, 'De los Tribunales Populares', both in Ministerio de Cultura, *Justicia en guerra*, pp. 47–63; Sánchez Recio, 'Justicia ordinaria y Justicia popular', pp. 87–108; Ortiz Heras, *Violencia política*, pp. 5–66.

59 Pierre Broué, Ronald Fraser and Pierre Vilar, *Metodología historica de la guerra y revolución españolas* (Barcelona, 1980), p. 90.

60 Santos Juliá, David Ringrose and Cristina Segura et al., *Madrid: Historia de una capital* (Madrid, 1995), p. 547.

61 Tuñón de Lara, in Reig, *Ideología*, p. 9.

62 Vicente Cacho Viu, 'Los escritos de José María Iribarren, secretario de Mola en 1936', *Cuadernos de Historia Moderna y Contemporánea*, 5 (1984), pp. 241–50.

63 Queipo de Llano, for example, talks of one operation as a 'dreadful [*espantosa*] razzia'. *La Unión*, 24 July 1936, cited in Gibson, *Queipo*, p. 170.

64 Franco, *Palabras* (1938), pp. 56, 201.

65 Southworth, *Guernica*, p. 51.

66 The only kind of war known by Franco, Mola and other *Africanistas* was a brutal one without mercy. See Preston, *Franco*, pp. 29–30; Southworth, *AntiFalange*, p. xxii, 112–13. Since the end of the previous century 'Moor hunting' had been a sport enjoyed by 'Death Squads' like Captain Ariza's *Partida de la Muerte*. On Mola's own harsh treatment of the Moors, see Madariaga, 'The Intervention', pp. 78, 79, 89. Franco was a product of this '*Africa Hispana*', 'passage of invasions'. He had 'saved the world from the abyss' just as Atlas 'sustained the Firmament' standing in Africa, the 'keystone of the world'. Pemartín, 'La Cruz Laureada', p. 45.

67 Juan Benet, 'Military Strategy in the Spanish Civil War', in Frieda Brown et al. (eds.), *Rewriting the Good Fight: Critical Essays on the Literature of the Spanish Civil War* (East Lansing, MI, 1989), especially pp. 18–22. See Franco's comments on the Battle of the Ebro, 'a combat of punishment', 31 December 1938, *Palabras*, pp. 296–7.

68 Vicente Gay y Forner, *Estampas rojas y caballeros blancos:* (Burgos, 1937), p. 303.
69 Preston, *Franco*, pp. 276–83.
70 He boasted that his Spanish forces had provided a great service in killing '50,000 men of the International Brigades', for example. 4 November, 1938, *Palabras*, p. 281.
71 Jay Allen, *Chicago Tribune*, 30 August 1936; *Times*, 17 August 1936.
72 *Franco's Rule*, p. 154.
73 Kurt Kranzlein in *Angriff*, 10 November 1936, see Koestler, *Spanish Testament*, p. 83.
74 *Angriff*, 17 September 1936.
75 *Essener National-Zeitung*, 13 October 1936. Hitler's agent in Spain, Captain Roland von Strunk, protested to Franco, who simply denied that such things were happening. Whitaker, 'Prelude to World War', p. 106.
76 José María Iribarren, 'Notas sobre la gestación y peripecias desdichadas de mi libro *con el General Mola*', unpublished manuscript (Pamplona, 1944), cited in Cacho Viu, 'Los escritos de José María Iribarren, secretario de Mola en 1936', pp. 241–50.
77 'Problemas de la provincia de Toledo y remedios que se proponen', 25 October 1939, AGA, Pres, SGM, caja 228. During the Civil War the Falangist leader in Toledo, José Sainz, boasted of having recorded in a notebook his shooting of 127 'Red' prisoners in a period of four months. Whitaker, 'Prelude to World War', p. 105.
78 This was the so-called 'Instruction Number 1', signed by Mola on 25 May 1936 and carried to the front on the person of rebel officers. See *El Colegio de Abogados de Madrid*, report (Madrid, October 1936); Felipe Bertrán Gúell, *Preparación y desarrollo del alzamiento nacional* (Valladolid, 1939), pp. 119–24; *Franco's Rule: Back to the Middle Ages* (London, n.d. 1938?), p. 154. Also Mola's 'Bando de declaración del estado de guerra, Pamplona, el 19 de julio de 1936', in Mola, *Obras completas* (Valladolid, 1940), p. 1173, calling for 'exemplary punishment . . . without faltering or vacillation'. See also the wartime nationalist circular calling for 'salutory executions', reproduced in Lola Iturbe, *La mujer en la lucha social* (Mexico City, 1974), pp. 183–4.
79 Koestler, *Spanish Testament*, cited in *Franco's Rule*, pp. 154–5.
80 Antonio-Miguel Bernal, 'Resignación de los campesinos andaluces: La resisténcia pasiva durante el franquismo', in David Ruiz et al. (eds.), *España Franquista: causa general y actitudes sociales ante la dictadura* (Castilla-La Mancha, 1993), p. 148; Moreno Gómez, *Córdoba en la posguerra*, especially pp. 3–50. On repression in Jaén, see Francisco Cobo Romero, *La guerra civil y la represión franquista en la provincia de Jaén* (Madrid, 1992). On Málaga, see Encarnación Barranquero Texeira, *Málaga entre la guerra y la posguerra* (Málaga, 1994), pp. 199–228. Prisoners were overwhelmingly landworkers. Eiroa San Francisco, *Viva Franco*, p. 233. See also Manuel Sánchez del Arco, *El sur de España en la reconquista de Madrid* (Seville, 1937).
81 Francisco Moreno Gómez, 'La represión en la España campesina', in J.L. García Delgado (ed.), *El primer franquismo* (Madrid, 1989) p. 192; Pérez Bowie, *El léxico de la muerte*, p. 89. See also R. Gil Bracero, 'La Justicia

Nacional y el Tribunal de Responsabilidades Políticas de Granada', in Ministerio de Cultura, *Justicia en guerra*, pp. 595–610.

82 Surviving records show that 7,679 men and women of the left were shot during the Civil War in Córdoba. 2,306 rightists are recorded as being killed. More than 1,600 men and women were executed, in addition, during the post-war period by the Francoist authorities. Moreno Gómez, *Córdoba en la posguerra* (Madrid, 1990), p. 26. However, many more were also killed and their deaths not recorded, p. 57.

83 Moreno Gómez, 'La represión', pp. 190–9. Further, *La Guerra Civil en Córdoba, 1936–1939* (Madrid, 1985); and also Bernal, 'Resignación', pp. 149–51.

84 See Francisco Gonzálbez Ruiz, *Yo he creido en Franco: proceso de una gran desilusión – Dos meses en la cárcel de Sevilla* (Paris, 1938); *Franco's Rule*, p. 177. See also Antonio Ruiz Vilaplana, *Doy fe . . . un año de actuación en la España nacionalista* (Paris, 1938), pp. 124–34; Ramón-Laca, *Bajo la férula de Queipo*.

85 Bahamonde, *Un año con Queipo*, pp. 124–5.

86 Moreno Gómez, *Córdoba en la posguerra*, especially pp. 10–11.

87 For example, Maeztu, *Defensa de la hispanidad*, p. 216. This was a characteristic of relations between slaves and slaveowners or the colonised and colonisers in North America or Africa. On the perpetuation of the social relations of *latifundismo*, see David Gilmore, 'Carnaval in Fuenmayor: Class Conflict and Social Cohesion in an Andalusian Town', *Journal of Anthropological Research*, 31, 4 (1975), pp. 332–9; Juan Martínez Alier, *Labourers and Landowners in Southern Spain* (Totowa, NJ, 1971).

88 Prologue of Juan Velarde Fuertes in Pascual Carrión, *La reforma agraria de la Segunda República y la situación de la agricultura española*, 2nd edn (Barcelona, 1975), p. 21.

89 For example, Alba, 'De los Tribunales Populares', p. 225.

90 Guzmán de Alfarache, *18 de julio: historia del Glorioso Alzamiento de Sevilla* (Seville, 1937); Rafael de Medina, Duque de Medinaceli, *Tiempo Pasado* (Seville, 1971). On Falangist involvement in purges see, among an ever-mounting quantity of evidence, Moreno Gómez, *La guerra civil*; Juan de Iturralde, *El catolicismo y la cruzada de Franco*, 2 vols. (Bayonne, 1955), vol. II, pp. 107–20; Ian Gibson, *Granada en 1936* (Barcelona, 1986); Herbert Southworth, *AntiFalange: estudio crítico de Falange en la guerra de España* (Paris, 1967); Julián Casanova et al., *El pasado oculto: fascismo y violencia en Aragón, 1936–1939* (Madrid, 1992); Bahamonde, *Un año con Queipo*, pp. 100–1, 113–20.

91 Obsolete rifles were finally distributed after the rising had begun. Braojos, *Sevilla '36*, pp. 183–221.

92 Braojos Garrido, *Sevilla '36*, p. 238.

93 *Franco's Rule*, p. 155. Ian Gibson, *The Assassination of Federico García Lorca* (London, 1979), pp. 61–111; Alberto Reig Tapia, La represión franquista y la guerra civil: consideraciones metodológicas, instrumentalización política y justificación ideológica, PhD thesis (Madrid, 1983), pp. 727–30; Ángel Gollonet Megías and José Morales López, *Rojo y azul en Granada* (Granada, 1937).

94 Frank Kluckhohn, *New York Times*, 11 October 1936.
95 According to the testimony, among others, of the Falangist official Antonio Bahamonde. See *Un año con Queipo*, p. 92. See also *The Times*, 9 December 1936.
96 *The Times*, 12 August 1936; *Franco's Rule*, pp. 145–6. In the province of Córdoba these groups were known as 'Purification Commissions'. Moreno Gómez, *Córdoba en la posguerra*, p. 47. They were packed with the frontmen of the big landowners. On Granada's '*escuadra negra*', see Gibson, *Granada en 1936*, pp. 107–18.
97 For example, Fontana, 'Naturaleza y consecuencias', pp. 20–2.
98 Bahamonde, *Un año con Queipo*, pp. 92, 108.
99 See Manuel Barrios, *El último virrey: Queipo de Llano*, 3rd edn (Seville, 1990).
100 The general belief, even among those civil servants who administer the civil records, is that there were possibly three times as many deaths as have been recorded during this period. Reig Tapia *Ideología*, p. 111. See also Nicolás Salas, *Morir en Sevilla* (Barcelona, 1986), esp. pp. 216–30.
101 Gerald Brenan, *The Face of Spain* ([originally 1950], Harmondsworth, 1965), p. 146. Many of them, and memories associated with them, were unearthed during the transition years of the 1970s. See, for example, 'El pueblo desentierra a sus muertos: casas de Don Pedro, 39 años después de la matanza', *Interviú*, 109 (June 1978), pp. 86–8; 'Solo dejaron los huesos. Albatera (Alicante), ensayo general para el exterminio', *Interviú*, 105 (May, 1978), 40–2; 'Otro "Valle de los Caídos" sin cruz. "La Barranca" fosa común para 2,000 riojanos', *Interviú*, 74 (October 1977), pp. 88–90; 'Jinámar: La sima de los "caídos"; matanza de "rojos" en Canarias', *Interviú*, 66 (August 1977), pp. 24–8; 'El cementario güanche', *Interviú*, 67 (August 1977), pp. 24–7; 'Granada: Las matanzas no se olvidan', *Interviú*, 81 (July 1977), pp. 32–5.
102 José María Iribarren, *Con el General Mola*, p. 187; *Franco's Rule*, p. 187.
103 Salas Larrazábal gives the lower estimate, *Pérdidas*, but see also *Franco's Rule*, pp. 148, 151, and Nicolás Salas, *Sevilla fue la clave* (Seville, 1992), 2 vols. vol. II, pp. 644–55, which gives a figure of 8,000 dead between July 1936 and December 1941.
104 Reig Tapia, *La represión*, p. 710. The Falangist Antonio Bahamonde, from conversations with the authorities involved in the repression, suggested that in Andalucía 150,000 had been killed by 1938. In the city of Seville alone he reckoned that 20,000 had fallen victim to the repression. *Un año con Queipo*, p. 94.
105 Radio broadcast, 19 August 1936. The term 'Marxist' was used as loosely as 'Red' to mean 'Republican'.
106 Gonzálbez Ruiz, *Yo he creído en Franco*, p. 128.
107 See Gibson, *Death of Lorca*, p. 68; Moreno Gómez, *Córdoba*; Bahamonde, *Un año con Queipo*, pp. 123–4; Casanova, *El pasado oculto*, for example. Also Altaffaylla Kultur Taldea, *Navarra 1936; de la esperanza al terror* (Navarre, 1986); Wenceslao Álvarez Oblanca, *La represión de postguerra en León: depuración de la enseñanza, 1936–1943* (León, 1986); Malcolm Muggeridge (ed.), *Ciano's Diplomatic Papers* (London, 1948),

p. 294; see also, 'Matanzas franquistas en Sevilla', *Interviú*, 86 (5–11 January 1978).

108 *Bandos y órdenes dictados por el Excmo. Señor D. Gonzalo Queipo de Llano y Sierra* (Seville, 1937), p. 7; Ramón-Laca, *Bajo la férula*, pp. 20–7.

109 *ABC*, Seville, 26 August 1936.

110 See *Lo que han hecho*, pp. 30, 45–6, 181–2, 199–200; Carlos Fernández, *El alzamiento de 1936 en Galicia* (La Coruña, 1982), pp. 75–83, 89, 100–3. Most executions took place without trial. The authorities pretended that they were defending 'the right to work' by threatening that, 'Anyone who disturbs it, by striking or through a lockout, will be shot without detailing the cause', p. 81. On the general strike called on the island of Mallorca, see Josep Massot i Muntaner, *El primer franquisme a Mallorca* (Barcelona, 1996), pp. 231–6.

111 The provincial gaol in Seville still had 3,441 prisoners in 1942, according to official figures.

112 Hirginio París Eguilaz, *El desarrollo económico español, 1906–1964* (Madrid, 1965), pp. 163–5.

113 1 January 1938, *Palabras*, p. 130.

114 See, for example, Carlos Barciela's Introduction to part 2, vol. III of R. Garrabll, C. Barciela and J. Jiméncz Blanco, *Historia agraria de la España contemporánea* (Barcelona, 1986), pp. 383–413.

115 Preston, *Coming of the Spanish Civil War*, pp. 151–203; Gibson, *Granada en 1936*, pp. 96–118.

116 The first figure was calculated by Ramón Salas Larrazábal in *Pérdidas de la guerra*, p. 208. Ian Gibson estimates the figure to be between 5,000 and 6,000, *Granada en 1936*, p. 126. In July 1936 there were 16,000 affiliates of the anarchist union, the CNT (Confederatión Nacional de Trabajo), in the city of Granada as well as 12,000 of the socialist UGT. The Republican government at first refused to arm the workers as the military rising was unleashed.

117 'Granada: Las matanzas no se olvidan', *Interviú*, 81 (December 1977).

118 Antonio Nadal, *Guerra civil en Málaga* (Málaga, 1984).

119 Larios was replaced by a monument to Labour. Ángel Gollonet Megías and José Morales López, *Sangre y fuego: Málaga* (Granada, 1937), p. 11.

120 Gollonet Megías and Morales López, *Sangre y fuego*, pp. 7–10, 37, 63. The period of 'Red terror' was also seen as a 'purifying of the city's sins', p. 54.

121 Herbert Southworth, *El mito de la cruzada*, pp. 274/5; *AntiFalange*, p. 160; Bahamonde, *Un año con Queipo*, pp. 126–36; Roberto Cantalupo, *Fu la Spagna* (Milan, 1948), pp. 130–45; Barranquero Texeira, *Málaga entre la guerra*, pp. 224–9; Eiroa San Francisco, *Viva Franco*, pp. 244–53; Jonathon Gathorne-Hardy, *The Interior Castle*, pp. 300–17.

122 His report claims that the 'Reds', in the period from 18 July 1936 until the day before the occupation of the city by the Nationalists, 7 February 1937, 'executed or murdered' 1,005 persons. During the first week of Nationalist rule, he claims, 3,500 were executed. In the period from 15 February 1937 to 25 August 1944, 'a further 16, 952 persons have been "legally" sentenced to death and shot in Málaga'. PRO/FO371/39742/C1309/46/41, 31 August 1944.

123 Matilde Eiroa San Francisco has counted 710 executions in prison records during the briefer period from 1939–42, when the initial 'repression of conquest' would already have passed. *Viva Franco*, pp. 246–7.

124 T.C. Worsley, *Behind the Battle* (London, 1939), pp. 179–208. The author estimates that there were 20,000 children on the road to Almería, without counting adults, p. 188.

125 Ibid., p. 204.

126 The majority were or later became ' "honorable businessmen" or state functionaries'. Fernández, *El alzamiento*, p. 98; *Lo que han hecho*, pp. 51/2. For lists of known victims see Fernández, *El alzamiento*, pp. 98–106.

127 See, for example, D. Pastor Petit, *Los dossiers secretos de la guerra civil* (Barcelona, 1978); Joan M. Thomàs, *Falange, guerra civil, franquisme: FET y de las JONS de Barcelona en els primers anys de règim franquista* (Barcelona, 1992); J.M. Fontana Tarrats, *Los Catalanes en la guerra de España* (Madrid, 1952).

128 The Moorish king, Boabdil, who handed Granada to the Spaniards, had 'cried like a woman because he did not know how to die like a man'. Mola, 'El día de la toma de San Sebastián', radio speech, *Obras*, p. 1184. See also, for Boabdil, *Enciclopedia, segundo grado*, p. 233.

129 British Consul in Bilbao to Eden, 11 January 1945, FO371/49575/Z1893/89/41. See also The Autonomous Government of Euzkadi, *Report on the Administration of Justice in The Basque Country During the Civil War* (Paris, 1938), p. 18.

130 Gregorio Morán, *Los españoles que dejaron de serlo* (Barcelona, 1982), p. 123.

131 Juan Pablo Fusi, 'El País Vasco durante la guerra', in *1936–1939, La Guerra de España* (Madrid, 1986). On the exercise of the justice system under the Basque government, see José Luis de la Granja, 'La Justicia en la Euskadi en guerra. La Consejería de Justicia del Gobierno Vasco (1936–37)', in Ministerio de Culturo, *Justicia en Guerra*, pp. 65–85; Sánchez Recio, 'Justicia ordinaria', p. 100, 105–6.

132 Bilbao, 1 July 1937, cited in Fernandez, *Antología*, p. 41.

133 Most of the killings took place 'outside the law'. Autonomous Government of Eustradi, *Report*, pp. 7–15, 17/18. See also Juan de Iturralde, *La guerra de Franco: los vascos y la iglesia*, 2 vols. (San Sebastián, 1978), vol. II, pp. 285–99; Thomas, *Spanish Civil War*, p. 925; Guillermo Cabanellas, *La guerra de los mil días*, 2 vols. (Buenos Aires, 1973), vol. II, p. 861; Tuñón de Lara, *La España del siglo XX* (Paris, 1966), p. 453. Navarre and Alava, the two other provinces of the Basque Country were in insurgent hands from the outset, and yet moderate Basque exiles claimed that thousands here were also executed. Franco, *Palabras* (1938), pp. 75, 87–9.

134 *Lo que han hecho*, pp. 137–40. See also, for example, Casanova et al., *El pasado oculto*; Fernández, *El alzamiento de 1936*. The British Consul in Tenerife reported that there had been 'some hundreds of murders with the presumptive connivance of the military authorities' in his area. PRO/W9548/3921/41, 19 June 1939; 39742/C16811. For repression of the Balearic Islands, see Josep Massot i Muntaner, *El cònsol Alan Hillgarth i les Illes Balears (1936–1939)* (Barcelona, 1995), pp. 174–91; *Els intellectuals*

mallorquins davant el franquisme (Barcelona, 1992), esp. pp. 11–37; *El primer franquisme*, pp. 205–61.

135 *New York Times*, 30 October 1936, cited by Lt Col. The Honorable R.M. Preston, DSO, 'The Ethics of the Spanish Civil War', *The Weekly Review* (1939), p. 29.

136 Whitaker, 'Prelude to World War', p. 104. Whitaker was not escorted by officials, as were most journalists in the Nationalist zone, but went into the field. The first mass execution he witnessed was of 600 prisoners in the main street of the village of Santa Olalla. Also Webb Miller, 'The Little World War in Spain', in *We Cover The World*, p. 423; Southworth, *Guernica*, p. 417. On the mass execution of freemasons during and after the Civil War, see José Antonio Ferrer Benimeli, 'Los masones en la historia contemporánea española', *Historia 16* (November 1977); and 'Franco y la masonería', in Fontana (ed.), *España bajo el franquismo*, pp. 246–68.

137 Many of the women had small children in their care. Many died from lack of food. Mercedes Núñez, *Cárcel de Ventas* (Paris, 1967); *La lutte de femmes sous la terreur de Franco* (Paris, 1947), cited by Fernanda Romeu Alfaro, *El silencio roto. Mujeres contra el franquismo* (Madrid, 1994), p. 41. Official figures on Ventas women's prison are elusive. The number given as held in 'provincial prisons' in Madrid in 1942 is 12,955. There were many other gaols in the province.

138 Di Febo, *Resistencia*, pp. 22/30.

139 Mirta Núñez Díez Balart and Antonio Rojas Friend, 'Víctimas del franquismo en Madrid: Los fusilamientos en el cementerio del este (1939–1945)', in J. Tusell et al., *El régimen de Franco*, (Madrid, 1993), vol. I, pp. 286–7.

140 The Republican informant in touch with the British Foreign Office in early 1941 wrote, 'To the inhabitants of Manuel Becerra Square in Madrid the six lorries which carry off men and women every day to the East Cemetery for execution are a familiar sight.' PRO/FO371/26890/C3986/3/41, March 1941.

141 General Luís Orgaz, General en Jefe del Ejército de Levante, 30 March 1939; circular, Civil Governor, *Boletín Oficial de la Provincia*, 4 April 1939.

142 Ballester, *Quarantena*, p. 15.

143 PRO/FO371/39742/C16811. For more information on Francoist repression in Valencia, see, Vicente Gabarda Ceballan, 'La continuación de la Guerra Civil: la represión Franquista', *Estudis D'Història contemporánea del País Valencià*, 7 (1986), pp. 229–45; and *Els afusellaments al País Valencià (1938–1956)* (Valencia, 1993); 'La represión franquista en el País Valenciano, 1938–1956', in Javier Tusell et al. (eds.), *La oposición al régimen de Franco* (Madrid, 1990), pp. 347–58. These studies support the figures given by British diplomats. The civil registries for the three provinces of Valencia give a total of 4,708 executions for the period from April 1938–December 1956. On Alicante, see J. Martínez Leal and M. Ors Montenegro, 'La represión de postguerra en Alicante (1939–1945)', *Canelobre*, 31–3 (Spring/Summer, 1995).

144 Ballester, *Quarantena*, p. 15. Regime figures show that in 1942 there were

still almost 5,000 prisoners in the Valencia central gaol and more than 3,500 in the notorious prison of San Miguel de los Reyes in the same province. These figures do not give the whole picture. *Anuario estadístico* (Madrid 1942), pp. 1106–9.

145 Declarations to the United Press, 7 November 1938, *Palabras* (1938), p. 285.
146 PRO/FO371/24126/W1215/8/41, January 1939.
147 Josep Pernau, *Diario de la caída de Cataluña* (Barcelona, 1989), p. 219/20; *El Noticiero Universal*, 12 July 1939.
148 Servicio Histórico Militar, *La ofensiva sobre Valencia* (Madrid, 1977), pp. 16–18, cited in Preston, *Franco*, p. 304. PRO/FO371/24160/W9646/ 3921/41, 16 June 1939.
149 *Heraldo de Aragón*, 28 January 1939.
150 'El Tebib Arrumi' (Víctor Ruiz Albéniz), 'El dolor purifica', *Heraldo de Aragón*, 4 February 1939. Cited in Benet, *L'intent franquista*, p. 129. Ruiz was a medical doctor and personal friend of Franco from the days of the Moroccan wars.
151 Ramón Serrano Suñer to *El Noticiero Universal*, 24 February 1939. British diplomats considered that the 'treatment of Catalans is worse than that of victims of the Gestapo and the OVRA'. PRO/FO371/26891/C/1060/3/41, 6 October 1941.
152 Oldemiro Cesar, *A guerra, aquele monstruo . . . Dois meses nas Astúrias entre soldados galegos* (Lisbon, 1937), p. 177.
153 *Catalunya sota el règim franquista: informe sobre la persecució de la llengua i la cultura de Catalunya pel règim del General Franco* (Paris 1973), p. 229.
154 *Catalunya sota el règim franquista*, p. 292. In 1940, González Oliveros became President of the Central Court of Political Responsibilities in Madrid and also served on the regime's 'Commission' charged with 'proving the illegitimacy' of the Popular Front government.
155 *La Vanguardia Española*, 5 August 1939.
156 FO371/W1610/8/41, 24 January 1939.
157 FET y de las JONS, Barcelona, *Informe*, 17 September 1940, AGA, Pres, SGM, caja 30.
158 See 'Informe acerca de FET de las JONS en Cataluña', June 1937; and 'Informe de FET–JONS sobre las delegaciones provinciales de Barcelona, Tarragona, Lérida y Gerona', undated but 1938, AGA, Pres, SGM, caja 31.
159 The three other main legislative planks of the repression were: (1) the Law Against Military Rebellion (28 July 1936); (2) the Law For the Repression of Freemasonry and Communism (March 1940); (3) the Law of the Security of the State (29 March 1941).
160 A detailed exposition on the meaning of 'normality' under the dictatorial judicial system is provided in Bastida, *Jueces y franquismo*.
161 Executions in Catalonia were not limited to Barcelona of course. In the province of Gerona, for example, there were at least 524 executions by the Francoist authorities, the number of recorded killings in the scrupulous study of Solé i Sabaté. *La repressió*, pp. 111–12. Salas Larrazábal's earlier study had recorded only 96. *Pérdidas*, p. 371.

162 Within a few days the Model Prison was overflowing and other sites, like disused factories had to be found. During the period 1939–42 35,000 prisoners passed through the Model Prison. Martín Torrent, *¿Qué me dice usted de los presos?* (Barcelona, 1942), pp. 8/9.

163 Solé i Sabaté, *La repressió*, lists 3,385 executed in Catalonia during the period 1938–53, of which 3,000 took place in 1939 and 1940. These are officially *recorded* executions. The British Consul General in Barcelona confirmed that executions, of which there was no official information available, were taking place throughout the province. Shootings also took place in Falangist headquarters – in Calle Ballester in Barcelona, for example. Víctor Alba, *Sleepless Spain* (London, 1948), p. 109.

164 James W. Cortada, *A City in War: American Views on Barcelona and the Spanish Civil War, 1936–39* (Wilmington, 1985), p. 179. According to the Francoist press, 1,150 Councils of War were held in the city of Barcelona during 1939. Dozens could be tried at once. *El Noticiero Universal*, 1 January 1940.

165 Cortada, *City in War*, p. 205. Count Ciano, after visiting Spain during the summer of 1939, and meeting with Franco and Serrano Suñer, had reported that 150 executions a day were taking place in the city. *Les archives secretes du Comte Ciano, 1936–1942* (Paris, 1948). The correspondent of the London *Times*, Lawrence Fernsworth, reported to the British Parliamentary Committee for Spain that about 2,500 people had been executed in Barcelona by June 1939, a period of only four-and-a-half months. The Committee, misunderstanding the situation, was very concerned by evidence that armed bands of Falangists were carrying out 'reprisals' over the heads of the police and the military authorities. PRO/24160/W9646/3921/41, 16 June 1939; W9033/3921/41, 6 June 1939. Colonel José Ungria, the notorious head of the National Security Service during the Civil War, was, according to a British diplomat, 'a person who makes a very favourable impression on all of us who meet him'. The British believed it unlikely that the Nationalists would use torture 'as the Republicans had done', because 'the military investigation department under Burgos is in the hands of professional soldiers'. PRO/FO371/24126/W1215/8/41, 25 January 1939.

166 José Rodríguez Vega, *Impressions of Franco's Spain* (London, 1943), p. 10.

167 Moreno Gómez, *Córdoba en la posguerra*; Amando de Miguel, *Sociología del franquismo* (Barcelona, 1975); Carles Viver Pi-Sunyer, *El personal político de Franco (1936–1945); contribución empírica a una teoría del régimen franquista* (Barcelona, 1978); Thomàs, *Falange, guerra civil, franquisme*; Barranquero Texeira, *Málaga*; for example.

3   PURIFYING SPAIN (II): DEGENERATION AND TREATMENT

1 See, for example, Franco's declarations, *Palabras* (1938), pp. 48, 139, 243. Also Eloy Montero, *Los estados modernos y la nueva España* (Vitoria, 1939); Giménez Caballero, *Genio de España*; Maeztu, *Defensa de la Hispanidad*; Joaquín de Azpiazu, *El estado católico: líneas de un ideal* (Madrid, 1939); Gay y Forner, *Estampas rojas*; Marqués de Eliseda, *El sentido fascista del Movi-*

miento Nacional (Madrid, 1939); García Morente, *Ideas para una filosofía*, pp. 83–93.

2 Sección Femenina de FET y de las JONS, *Formación política: lecciones para las flechas* (Madrid, n.d), p. 11.

3 Manuel Azaña, 'Reprobación de la política de exterminio', University of Valencia, 18 July 1937.

4 José María Pemán, *Arengas y crónicas de guerra* (Cádiz, 1937), p. 13, Reig, *Ideología*, p. 153.

5 Payne, *Los militares*, p. 368. For comparison with Stalinist Russia, see Gliksman, 'Social Prophylaxis'.

6 Whitaker, 'Prelude to World War', pp. 107–8; *We Cannot Escape History* (New York, 1943), pp. 108–10; Peter Kemp, *Mine Were of Trouble* (London, 1957), pp. 49–50; Foltz, *Masquerade*, p. 116. Aguilera's mother was Scottish and he had been to Stonyhurst and been a keen polo player. He owned great estates near Salamanca and was a personal friend of King Alfonso XIII. The English Catholic writer Arnold Lunn found him 'not only a soldier but a scholar' and had been 'enlightened' by his 'general philosophy'. *Spanish Rehearsal* (London, 1937), pp. 42–108, Southworth, *Guernica*, pp. 50–2. Aguilera insisted that giving sewers to the working class had been the greatest mistake and that all bootblacks in Spain should be shot: 'No need for a trial – his guilt is self-evident in his profession (Kemp, p. 50).

7 Javier Ruiz Almansa, 'Reproductividad neta de las provincias y regiones de España', *Boletín de Estadística* (October–December 1942), pp. 140–59; J.R. Jimeno, 'La natalidad y el futuro desarrollo de la población de España', *Boletín de Estadística* (January–March 1943), pp. 150–73. See also Jeffrey Weeks, *Sex, Politics and Society* (London, 1981), ch. 7; William Schneider, *Quality and Quantity: The Quest for Biological Regeneration in Twentieth-Century France* (Cambridge, 1990); Richard Soloway, *Demography and Regeneration: Eugenics and the Declining Birth-Rate in Twentieth-Century Britain* (London, 1990); Daniel Pick, *Faces of Degeneration: A European Disorder, c.1848–c.1918* (Cambridge, 1989); Dain Borges, ' "Puffy, Ugly, Slothful and Inert"; Degeneration in Brazilian Social Thought, 1880–1940', *Journal of Latin American Studies*, 25 (May 1993), pp. 235–56. On Francoist natalist policy, see Mary Nash, 'Pronatalism and Motherhood in Franco's Spain', in Gisela Bock and Pat Thane (eds.), *Maternity and Gender Politics: Women and the Rise of the European Welfare States, 1880s–1950s* (London, 1991), pp. 160–77.

8 Ortega y Gasset, *España invertebrada*. For Ortega's explicit reference to Darwinism, on this point, see p. 89. *España invertebrada* is saturated with Darwinist references and metaphor. On the 'inferiority' of southerners, see Ortega, *Teoría de Andalucía* (Madrid, 1942), originally published in *El Sol* during April 1927.

9 Tierno Galván, *Costa y el regeneracionismo*, in *Escritos*, p. 152, Lucas Mallada, *Los males de la Patria y la futura revolución española* ([originally 1890], Madrid, 1969), pp. 41, 47; Ricardo Macías Picavea, *El problema nacional: hechos, causas y remedios* (Madrid, 1899), p. 398.

10 Mola, *Obras completas*, p. 1184. Mola was the son of a captain in the Civil Guard.

11 To be performed by a *'limpia casta militar'*. *Laureados de España*, pp. 111–12.

12 Mola, *El pasado, Azaña y el porvenir*, p. 945. A friend declared to the social anthropologist Pitt-Rivers in the early 1950s that 'The modern race is degenerate . . . in the days of our grandfathers there was more manliness than today'. To be *'muy hombre'* was to have an abundance of 'morality'. Julian Pitt-Rivers, *The People of the Sierra* (London, 1954), p. 91.

13 Emilio Mola, *El pasado, Azaña y el porvenir* (originally Madrid, 1934), in *Obras completas* (Valladolid, 1940), p. 319.

14 Gay, *Estampas rojas*, p. 300.

15 Pérez Bowie, 'Retoricismo y estereotipación, rasgos definidores de un discurso ideologizado. El discurso de la derecha durante la guerra civil', in J. Aróstegui, *Historia y memoria*, p. 361; Franco, *Palabras*, pp. 52, 90, for example.

16 Marsé, *Si te dicen que caí*, pp. 151, 231, for example. Visual images repeatedly propagated such ideas. See the 'puffy' bodies and 'orientalised' facial features of milicianos in Francoist propaganda. For example, Sección Femenina, *Calendario*, p. 81; *Quinientas fotos de la guerra* (Valladolid, 1937), pp. 96–7. See fig. 4, p. 63.

17 Probably between 60,000 and 70,000 Moroccans fought for the Nationalists in Spain and losses were heavy. It seems that Africans fought on Franco's side for three main reasons: (1) they were persuaded to a degree that the war was a 'holy crusade' against 'those without God', 'rokhos' or 'Reds'; (2) they lived hard lives and were promised decent pay; (3) the Spanish Republic meant little, since it had done nothing to alter things in Morocco. María Rosa de Madariaga, 'The Intervention of Moroccan Troops in the Spanish Civil War: A Reconsideration', *European History Quarterly*, 22 (1992).

18 García Morente, *Idea de la hispanidad*, pp. 215–17.

19 Juan Goytisolo, *Crónicas sarracinas* (Barcelona, 1982), pp. 29–31. 'Islam . . . is . . . the negative of Europe: what Europe has rejected and at the same time, her temptation . . . that "inner adversary" too close to be tamed, assimilated or reduced.'

20 García Morente, *Idea*, pp. 216–17.

21 See Martín-Santos, *Tiempo de silencio*, p. 129.

22 See, for example, the *Proceedings of the 1st International Congress on Mental Hygiene* (New York, 1930). A Spanish delegation was present at this congress. Eugenics was not a movement exclusively of the Right in Catholic Spain where there was an evident clash between the ideas of creationism and evolutionism. Richard Cleminson, 'Eugenics by Name or by Nature? The Spanish Anarchist Sex Reform of the 1930s', *History of European Ideas*, 18 (1994), pp. 729–40; 'Sanitation, santé et sexualité: quelques concepts anarchistes d'hygiène sociale', unpublished paper, 1995. See also Mary Nash, 'Social Eugenics and Nationalist Race Hygiene in Early Twentieth-Century Spain', *History of European Ideas*, 15 (1992), pp. 741–8.

23 For example, Juan Goytisolo, 'Abandonemos de una vez el amoroso cultivo de nuestras señas de identidad', *El País*, 10 April 1984.

24 See, for example, the section 'La impaciencia patriótica y los nervios en la guerra', Gay y Forner, *Estampas rojas*, pp. 300–6.

25 *Laureados de España*, p. 19.

26 Thomas, *Spanish Civil War*, p. 279. On Franco and regenerationism, see Manuel Vázquez Montalbán, *Los demonios familiares de Franco* (Barcelona, 1978), pp. 10–11, 47–51; 'Franco i el regeneracionisme de dretes', in *L'Avenç*, 165 (December 1992), pp. 8–15.

27 See, for example, Montero, *Los estados modernos*, p. 24.

28 Mola, *El pasado, Azaña y el porvenir*, p. 320.

29 Vicente Gay y Forner, *La revolución nacional-socialista: ambiente, leyes, ideología* (Barcelona, 1934). Gay had been Under-Secretary of Economy, Director General of Industry and Tariffs, and Secretary of the National Assembly during the dictatorship of Primo de Rivera in the 1920s.

30 José Antonio Delgado Iribarren, *Jesuitas en España* (Madrid, 1956), p. 253.

31 Speech, Jaén, 18 March 1940.

32 *La Vanguardia Española*, 4 April 1939. On the centrality of 'work' linked with 'redemption', see El Patronato Central de Redención de Penas por el Trabajo, *La obra de la redención de penas – la doctrina, la práctica, la legislación* (Madrid, 1941).

33 Franco, 19 April 1938. *Palabras* (1938), p. 52.

34 The language of purification and asceticism was likewise employed by Catholic Croats during the Second World War purges in Yugoslavia, but also by Puritans in dealing with indigenous peoples in pushing forward the American frontier. Richard Slotkin, *Regeneration Through Violence: The Mythology of the American Frontier, 1600–1860* (Boston, MA, 1973), p. 5; Richard Drinnon, *Facing West: The Metaphysics of Indian Hating and Empire Building* (New York, 1990), p. xxi. On the Counter-Reformation coupling of purity and enclosure, see Mary Elizabeth Perry, *Gender and Disorder in Early Modern Seville* (Princeton, NJ, 1990), particularly pp. 6–13.

35 Mircea Eliade (ed.), *The Encyclopedia of Religion*, vol. x (London, 1987), pp. 113–15; for example, on the 'chastisement of the flesh' by 'scourging or wounding oneself or by practising other austerities', see *Ejercicios espirituales de San Ignacio de Loyola, en su texto original* (Barcelona, 1892), pp. 57–8.

36 Religious initiatory mortification can often involve fasting. On purging by cutting off superfluous food, see, *Ejercicios*, pp. 57–8.

37 Manuel de Castro Alonso, Archbishop of Burgos, 'Carta pastoral en la Cuaresma de 1937 sobre las enseñanzas de los tiempos presentes', 15 February 1937. See also M. González, 'Lección cuaresmal sobre la tragedia presente: lo que debe resucitar y lo que no debe resucitar en España', *Boletín Obispal de Palencia*, 15 March 1937, cited in Botti, *Cielo*, p. 93.

38 In fact, she probably was of Jewish, *converso*, descent. Teresa was denounced before the Inquisition, though not on account of racial origins. See Otger Steggink, *Tiempo y vida de Santa Teresa* (Madrid, 1968), p. 4; Gareth Alban Davies, 'St Teresa and the Jewish Question', in Trinity and All Saints' College, *Teresa de Jesús and Her World* (Leeds, 1981), pp. 51–74; Enrique Llamas Martínez, *Santa Teresa de Jesús y la Inquisición española* (Madrid, 1972). The first citation in the etymological description of *limpieza*, 'cleanliness', in several reference books, refers to Teresa's letters. For instance, Martín Alonso, *Enciclopedia del idioma* (Madrid, 1958), p. 2574. When aged

only seven Teresa, pursuing a desire for 'martyrdom', ran away from home, hoping to be 'beheaded in the country of the Moors'. E. Allison Peers, *Spanish Mysticism* (London, 1924), p. 99; *Studies of the Spanish Mystics* (London, 1927), vol. I, p. 136; Helmut Hatzfeld, *Santa Teresa de Avila* (New York, 1969), p. 12. On Teresa, 'clean bodies' and 'dirty bodies', see also María José Ruiz Somavilla, *'El cuerpo limpio'; análisis de las prácticas higiénicas en la España del mundo moderno* (Málaga, 1993), especially pp. 75–101; Davies, 'Jewish Question', pp. 63–4.

39 A. Sicroff Albert, *Los estatutos de limpeza de sangre: controversias entre los siglos XV y XVII* (Madrid, 1985). For Richard Ford's comments on 'Bleeding – Heraldic Blood – Blue, Red and Black Blood', see *Gatherings in Spain* ([originally 1846], London, 1923), pp. 276–85. 'Black blood is the Stygian pitch which is found in the carcasses of Jews, Gentiles, Moors, Lutherans, and other combustible heretics, with whose bodies the holy tribunal made bonfires for the good of their souls', p. 283.

40 See di Febo, *La santa de la raza*, pp. 73–4. Teresa was patron of the women's section of the state party, the Sección Femenina. *Formación política*, pp. 15–17, 46.

41 Guillermo Cabanellas de Torres, *Diccionario militar* (Buenos Aires, 1963), vol. III, p. 349. In Luis Martín-Santos' novel, *Tiempo de Silencio*, set during the Franco dictatorship and, therefore, published outside Spain, the narrator reminds us several times of the regime's obsession with cleanliness, purity and *limpieza de sangre*, referring to the Inquisition: p. 74, for example.

42 Agustín Serrano de Haro, *Guirnaldas de la historia: historia de la cultura española contada a las niñas* (Madrid, 1962), p. 94, cited by María Escudero, *The Image of Latin America*, p. 139; *Enciclopedia, segundo grado* (Madrid, n.d.) pp. 225–34. The precise point made by Franco himself in his speech on New Year's Eve 1939, *Mensaje del Caudillo.*

43 On the centrality of racism and sexism to Francoist ideology, see Escudero, *The Image of Latin America*. As we have seen, racial theories have a long tradition, being formulated by many of the regnerationists of the turn of the century and by followers like Ortega y Gasset, whose historical analysis of decline and degeneration rested upon racial characteristics and national 'congenital defects'. Labanyi, *Ironía*, p. 33.

44 For example, *Arriba*, 1, 21 March 1935.

45 Ledesma Ramos, 'España, potencia de Imperio', *La Conquista del Estado*, 1, 8 (1931), p. 1.

46 *Franco's Rule*, p. 147.

47 See, for example, García Piñeiro, *Los mineros asturianos*, p. 183, Borja de Riquer and Joan Culla, *Historia de Catalunya: el franquisme i la transició democràtica, 1939–1988*, vol. III (Barcelona, 1989), p. 38; Doña, *Desde la noche*, pp. 154–5; di Febo, *Resistencia y movimiento*; Alcalde, *Mujeres en el franquismo*; Romeu, *El silencio roto*. Also the radio declarations of Queipo de Llano, *ABC*, 30 August 1936.

48 I. Fernandez de Castro, *De las Cortes de Cádiz al Plan del Desarollo* (Madrid, 1968), p. 226.

49 Exp. 655, ATRP.

50 According to the regime, one could *involuntarily* commit the 'crime' of

'inciting rebellion'. C. Martínez, *Excitación a la rebelión* (Burgos, 1939), p. 53.

51 In some cases virtually an entire family was lost. See, for example, Di Febo, *Resistencia*, p. 107; Barranquero, *Mujer, cárcel, franquismo*, p. 37.

52 Moreno Gómez, p. 23; exp. 658, ATRP, for example.

53 Di Febo, *Resistencia*, pp. 33–8. Some women were imprisoned for the political attitudes of their children. Eiroa San Francisco, *Viva Franco*, p. 261.

54 Di Febo, *Resistencia*, pp. 22–32.

55 Gonzálbez Ruiz, *Yo he creído Len Franco: proceso de un gran derilusión (hedios nuevos y viejas ideas)* (Madrid, 1938), p. 124.

56 'Informe de la Delegación General de Seguridad', 29 April 1942, Toledo, in Fundación Nacional de Francisco Franco (FNFF), *Documentos inéditos* (Madrid, 1994), vol. III, p. 425.

57 Ramón Serrano Suñer, 'Discurso de inauguración, en Barcelona, del V Congreso Nacional de la Sección Femenina de FET–JONS, 11 de enero de 1941', in *De la victoria y la postguerra*, pp. 161–2. The principal method was through courses in *Formación del Espíritu Nacional y Cívica*. See also María Teresa Gallego Méndez, 'Notas sobre el poder, la socialización política y la mujer', in *Nuevas perspectivas sobre la mujer* (Madrid, 1982), pp. 42–9.

58 FET–JONS, DNII, Boletín no. 491, 28 February 1942, AGA, Pres, SGM, caja, 16.

59 See *Lo que han hecho*, pp. 195–6. Official statistics show that there remained 2,971 internees in the provincial prison in La Coruña in 1942.

60 Romeu Alfaro, *El silencio roto*, pp. 40–1. Resistance was also organised inside women's prisons. Di Febo, *Resistencia*, pp. 26–8, 47–61, 87, 122–5; García Madrid, *Réquiem por la libertad*, pp. 91–2; Núñez, *Cárcel de Ventas*.

61 On the anti-Franco guerrilla, see Eduardo Pons Prades, *Guerrillas españolas, 1936–1960* (Barcelona, 1977); F. Aguado Sánchez, *El maquis en España* (Madrid, 1975); Hartmut Heine, *La oposición política* (Barcelona, 1983); *A guerrilla antifranquista en Galicia* (Vigo, 1980); Moreno Gómez, *Córdoba*, pp. 347–536. See also J.P. Chueca Intxusta, 'Mujeres antifranquistas en la retaguardia nacional: el caso de Navarra', in *Las mujeres y la guerra civil*.

62 Di Febo, *Resistencia*, pp. 76–86.

63 See Heine, 'Tipología y características', p. 316.

64 PRO/FO371/73356/Z659/596/41, 15 January 1948. See also Moreno Gómez, *Córdoba en la posguerra*. In Málaga and Granada small tenant farmers caught up in this class conflict between rebellious landless labourers and the state, often fled their properties as a result.

65 J. Prada Rodríguez, 'La mujer y los escapados: aproximación al papel de la mujer como soporte material de la resistencia antifranquista', in *Las mujeres y la guerra civil*, pp. 218–23; Tomasa Cuevas, *Cárcel de mujeres 1939–1945* (Barcelona, 1985), p. 16.

66 For example, Alicia Alted Vigil, 'La mujer en las coordenadas educativas del régimen franquista', and Giuliana di Febo and Marina Saba, 'La condición de la mujer y el papel de la iglesia en la Italia fascista y en la España franquista: ideologías, leyes y asociaciones femeninas', in *Ordenamiento jurídico y realidad social de las mujeres* (Madrid, 1986), pp. 425–37, 439–52.

67 Roca i Girona, *De la pureza*, pp. 48–9; Douglas, *Purity and Danger*, p. 62.

68 Castro, *Mujeres del imperio*, p. 6–7; Jesus Suevos, 'Isabel de Castilla ejemplo y estímulo para las mujeres de la Falange', *IV Consejo-Nacional de la Sección Femenina* (Madrid, 1940).

69 Geraldine Scanlon, *La polémica feminista en la España contemporánea, 1868–1974* (Madrid, 1986), p. 322.

70 'La moralidad pública en España', *Revista Internacional de Sociología*, 2–3, (1943), p. 345. The local boards of the Patronato were composed of the mayor, the parish priest and members of the 'morality section' of Acción Católica. Alicia Alted Vigil, 'Las mujeres en la sociedad española de los años cuarenta', in *Las mujeres y la guerra civil*, p. 295; Roca i Girona, *De la pureza*, p. 38.

71 Carmen Werner Bolín, *Convivencia social: formación familiar y social*, Sección Femenina (Madrid, 1958), pp. 160–1. On the 'impurity' of women, signified in menstruation, see Roca i Girona, *De la pureza*, pp. 48–9.

72 Helen Graham, 'Gender and the State: Women in the 1940s', in Helen Graham and Jo Labanyi (eds.), *Spanish Cultural Studies: An Introduction* (Oxford, 1996), pp. 182–95; Cristina Borderías, 'Evolución de la división sexual del trabajo. Barcelona 1924–1980', PhD thesis (Barcelona, 1984); A. Espina, 'La participación femenina en la actividad económica: el caso español', in R. Conde (ed.), *Familia y cambio social* (Madrid, 1982); Roca i Girona, *De la pureza*, pp. 274–305.

73 For example, J.B. Luis y Pérez, Obispo de Oviedo, *La personalidad de la mujer* (Oviedo, 1933).

74 Gollonet Megías and Morales López, *Rojo y azul en Granada*, pp. 25–7; *Sangre y fuego: Málaga*, pp. 55–6.

75 María del R. Díaz Jiménez, 'Formación de la mujer en la escuela de la nueva españa', *Atenas*, January, 1938, cited in Molero Pintado, *La educación*, p. 448.

76 See, for example, the declarations of General Millán-Astray in Salamanca, 5 December 1936, cited in Fernández, *Antología*, p. 28, for example. Also Eiroa San Francisco, *Viva Franco*, p. 255. *Milicianas* were described as having 'the faces of witches'. *Sangre y fuego*, p. 80, for example.

77 PRO/FO371/26890/C3986/3/41, March, 1941.

78 On 'honour', see Shirley Mangini, *Memories of Resistance: Women's Voices From the Spanish Civil War* (New Haven, CT, 1995), pp. 106–7.

79 See Jesús Fernández Santos, *Cabeza rapada* (Barcelona, 1977); Marsé, *Si te dicen que caí*, pp. 139, 225, 284; Roca i Girona, *De la pureza*, p. 30; Jackson, *Spanish Republic*, p. 377.

80 Moreno Gómez, *Córdoba*, p. 304. The term *'pelandusca'* referred to 'easy women', 'inconstant', 'frivolous' or 'dishevelled'.

81 See di Febo, *Resistencia*, pp. 96–7. *'La pelona'* can also mean 'death' in Spanish, especially in Andalucía.

82 Sheelagh Ellwood, 'Spanish Newsreels 1943–1975; The Image of the Franco Regime', *Historical Journal of Film, Radio and Television*, 7, 3 (1987), p. 230.

83 Romeu Alfaro, *El silencio*, p. 40. Moreno Gómez, p. 22; Carmen Alcalde, *Mujeres en el franquismo: exiliadas, nacionalistas y opositoras* (Barcelona, 1996), p. 42; di Febo, *Resistencia*, pp. 18–20.

84 Legal prostitution was less dangerous to the authorities than illegality and public sexual trade. Brothels and '*casas de tolerancia*' were not prohibited until 1956. Alted Vigil, 'Las mujeres', p. 294. Spanish women imprisoned for political 'crimes' recall how the most disturbing cases they met were those who had resorted to prostitution to live: they were usually half-starved, disease-ridden and extremely frightened. '*Las políticas*' organised protests on their behalf. See, for example, di Febo, *Resistencia*, p. 25. Also Marsé, *Si te dicen que caí*, especially p. 160; J.C. Cela, *La colmena*, ([originally 1951] Barcelona, 1967), p. 29; Rafael Abella, *Por el imperio hacia Dios* (Barcelona, 1978), pp. 130–2; J. Doña, *Desde la noche y la niebla: muýeres en las cárceles franquista* (Barcelona, 1978), pp. 256–7.

85 Decree of Ministry of Justice, 6 November 1941. H. Roldán Barbero, *Historia de la prisión en España* (Madrid, 1985), p. 203.

86 Padre Marcelino Zalba, *La prostitución ante la moral y el derecho* (Madrid, 1942), p. ix.

87 Zalba, *La prostitución*, p. x.

88 The models for Francoist natalist policy was provided by Nazi Germany and Fascist Italy. Severino Aznar, 'El regimen de subsidios familiares, la fraternidad cristiana a las consignas del nuevo estado', in *Revista Internacional de Sociología*, 2/3 (1943), pp. 99–106; Franco, 31 December 1938, *Palabras*, p. 304. Also Gisela Bock, 'Antinatalism, Maternity and Paternity in National Socialist Racism'; Chiara Saraceno, 'Redefining Maternity and Paternity: Gender, Pronatalism and Social Policies in Fascist Italy', in G. Bock and P. Thane, *Maternity and Gender Policies: Women and the Rise of European Welfare States, 1880s–1950s* (London, 1991), pp. 196–212, 233–55.

89 Amando de Miguel, *40 millones de españoles 40 años después* (Barcelona, 1976), p. 94.

90 García Morente, *Ideas para una filosofía*, p. 89.

91 See, for example, Victor María de Sola, *La vida actual en el país de la demencia roja* (Cádiz, 1938); Clarita Stauffer, Auxiliar central de Prensa y Propaganda, 'La mujer y el Marxismo', in Sección Femenina de FET–JONS, *Calendario*, p. 86.

92 'Consideraciones en torno al sentido de la criminalidad Marxista', *Archivo Dirección General de la Guardia Civil*, cited in Eiroa San Francisco, *Viva Franco*, p. 221. He may have been echoing the words of José Pemartín: 'Contagious criminal utopianism . . . impregnated . . . with its vindictive resentments', *Laureados de España*, p. 44.

93 *El Norte de Castilla*, 29 March 1938, in Benet, *L'intent franquista*, p. 130.

94 Francisco Marco Merenciano, 'Nuevas orientaciones sobre higiene mental' [originally 1942], reprinted in *Ensayos médicos y literarios: antología* (Madrid, 1958), pp. 98–9. Marco was director of the state asylum in Valencia. He was a eugenecist who doubted the rationality of psychiatric treatment, since it would allow the 'mentally sick' to breed. *Esquizofrenias paranoides* (Barcelona, 1942).

95 'Creación de un gabinete de investigaciones psicológicas para investigar las raíces bio-psíquicas del Marxismo', Reig, *Ideología*, p. 28.

96 *Semana Médica Española*, 16 September 1939; 8 October 1938, pp. 170–80.

97 Official psychiatry under Franco was effectively controlled from this position, first by Vallejo-Nágera and then by his successor. See Carlos Castilla del Pino, 'La psiquiatría española', in Castilla del Pino (ed.) *La cultura bajo el franquismo* (Barcelona, 1977), p. 88.

98 See Antonio Vallejo-Nágera, *Eugenesia de la hispanidad y regeneración de la raza* (Burgos, 1937); *Política racial del nuevo estado* (San Sebastián, 1938); *La locura y la guerra: psicopatología de la guerra española* (Madrid, 1939); *Psicosis de guerra* (Madrid, 1942).

99 A personal link to Franco was provided by the old friendship that existed between the wives of Vallejo-Nágera and the dictator. Castilla del Pino, p. 86. It was in Germany that Vallejo-Nágera first studied concentration camps.

100 Antonio Carreras Panchón, 'Los psiquiatras españoles y la guerra civil', *Medicina e historia*, 13 (1986), p. 7.

101 Mola, *El pasado, Azaña y el porvenir* (orginally 1934), in *Obras*, p. 945.

102 Bover, *Los soldados*, pp. 6, 44–5. It should not be assumed that the President of the Republic, Manuel Azaña, was simply 'anti-military'. Indeed, he thought, as did others further to the left, that an army could be a force for social and moral improvement or, even 'regeneration'. See Azaña, 'Estudios de política francesa: la política militar', in *Obras*, vol. I; Manuel Espadas Burgos, 'La Institución Libre de Enseñanza y la formación del militar español durante la Restauración', in *Temas de Historia militar* (Madrid, 1983), pp. 413–25.

103 Vallejo-Nágera, *Divagaciones intranscendentes*, pp. 64–5. See also Francisco Peiró, *Sentido religioso y militar de la vida* (Burgos, 1938). On the '*vida-milicia*' as 'the most noble' means to a cultivation of 'the spirit of the race', see also J. López Ibor, *Discurso a los universitarios españoles* (Salamanca, 1938).

104 Vallejo-Nágera, *Divagaciones*, p. 66.

105 Mola, *El pasado, Azaña y el porvenir*, p. 305.

106 Alfonso Iniesta, *Garra Marxista en la infancia* (Burgos, 1939), p. 263.

107 Mola, *El pasado*, p. 321.

108 López Ibor is described by Enrique González Duro, as the main promoter and ideologue of the 'peculiar parapsychiatric venture' to provide a medico-scientific basis for the racial triumphalism of Franco's cause. *Psiquiatría y sociedad autoritaria: España, 1939–1975* (Madrid, 1978), p. 21.

109 Castilla del Pino, *Cultura bajo el franquismo*, p. 83. López Ibor was a Consejero Nacional of the Falange.

110 Mola, *El pasado*, p. 309.

111 Vallejo-Nágera, *Divagaciones*, p. 105; Morodo, *Acción Española: los orígenes ideológicos del franquismo*, pp. 68–71. See among Vallejo-Nágera's articles in the review *Acción Espanola*, 'Psicopatologia de la conducta antisocial', 82–4 (1935–6).

112 Botti, *Cielo y dinero*, pp. 73–82. José Calvo Sotelo, one of the Right's main symbols of capitalist economic development and corporativism, contributed a substantial fortnightly article on 'Politics and Economics' to *Acción Española* in the early 1930s. Eduardo Aunós was another regular contributor. For a view of social Catholicism and corporativism that sees a

contradiction between capitalism and corporativism, see several of the contributions to Tom Buchanan and Martin Conway (eds.), *Political Catholicism in Europe, 1918–1965* (Oxford, 1996), pp. 15, 37, 84, 230–6, for example, and, on the tradition of social Catholicism in Spain, Mary Vincent, 'Spain', pp. 97–128.

113 See Maeztu, editorial, *Acción Española*, 1 (December 1931).

114 Maeztu, *Defensa de la hispanidad*; Botti, *Cielo y dinero*, pp. 24–5, 61. See also Maeztu, *Hacia otra España* (Madrid, 1899).

115 Vallejo-Nágera, cited by Castilla del Pino, *Cultura bajo el franquismo*, p. 90. He professed that, while his ideology was inspired by Nietzsche, his 'psychopathology' was inspired by Thomism (p. 96). See also Marco Merenciano, 'Nuevas orientaciones', in *Ensayos*, p. 116.

116 Iniesta, *Garra Marxista*, p. 267.

117 Vallejo-Nágera, *Eugenesia de la hispanidad*, p. 115; *Divagaciones*, p. 141.

118 Gonzalo de Aguilera to Whitaker, 'Prelude to World War', p. 108. Aguilera was a military attaché to Berlin at the same time as Vallejo-Nágera during the First World War. Like Vallejo-Nágera, he also had experience in the Moroccan campaigns.

119 García Pérez, *Reaccionarios*, pp. 292–310.

120 Iniesta, *Garra Marxista*, p. 276.

121 Pemartín, 'La Cruz Laureada', p. 44.

122 Gonzalo de Aguilera to Whitaker, *Cannot Escape History*, pp. 109–10. He continues, 'You people had better clean up your own houses. If you don't we Spaniards are going to join the Germans and Italians in conquering you all. The Germans have already promised to help us regain our American colonies, which you and your shameful Protestant liberal imperialism stole from us.'

123 'Intelectualidad revolucionaria', *Domingo*, 15 August 1937. Vallejo-Nágera proclaimed his allegiance to Nietzsche for 'the resurrection of the austere (*espartanas*) ideas of the extermination of the inferior organs and psyches, which he calls "parasites of society"'. For development of the critique of 'liberal doctors', see also Marco Merenciano, 'De lo temporal y lo eterno en la moral médica', in *Ensayos médicos y literarios* ([originally January 1940] Madrid, 1958), pp. 117–46.

124 Franco's own belief in a 'Spanish essence' is suggested by the title of the semi-autobiographical film script, *Raza* (Race), which he wrote in 1940, tracing the history of a middle-class Galician family from the imperial collapse of 1898 to the Civil War. See Román Gubern, *Raza: un sueño del general Franco* (Madrid, 1977).

125 Vallejo-Nágera, *Eugenesia de la Hispanidad*, pp. 114–16.

126 Abigail Lee Six, *Juan Goytisolo: The Case for Chaos* (New Haven, CT, 1990), pp. 44, 57, 71.

127 Iniesta, *Garra Marxista*, p. 263.

128 A. Carreras Panchón, 'Los psiquiatras españoles y la guerra civil'.

129 The work of the Italian racial anthropologist Cesare Lombroso, such as *The Criminal Man* (1885) was known in Spain, although it is hard to know whether Mola ever absorbed such studies directly. See the laudatory entry on Lombroso in Espasa Calpe's *Enciclopedia Universal Ilustrada*, vol. XXX

(n.d., but 1920s?), pp. 501–3, for example, and Luis Maristany, *El gabinete del doctor Lombroso (delincuencia y fin de siglo en España)* (Barcelona, 1973); José Luis Peset, *Lombroso y la escuela positivista italiana* (Madrid, 1975); Laura Otis, *Organic Memory: History and the Body in the Late Nineteenth and Early Twentieth Centuries* (Lincoln, NE, 1994), especially pp. 50–2, 67, 75–92.

130 Castilla del Pino, 'La psiquiatría española', pp. 88–90.

131 Vallejo-Nágera, *Divagaciones*, p. 105.

132 Ibid., p. 139. Mola also gloried in the racial virtues of Castilians: 'A strong and warlike people of parched land and fields of gold: a country of snow in which the sun also burns,' *El pasado, Azaña y el porvenir*, p. 1177; as did Franco himself, see Iniesta, *Garra*, p. 282.

133 The notion of a continuing war was prevalent in the first years of Francoism. Emilio Romero, *La paz empieza nunca* (Barcelona, 1958).

134 Italicised in the original.

135 Vallejo-Nágera, *Eugenesia*, pp. 113–19.

136 Vallejo, *Enseñanzas psiquiátricas de la segunda guerra mundial* (Madrid, 1951). According to Vallejo, 'In our war we have seen how many psychopaths [sic] have been excellent soldiers and officials, fanatical partisans of their ideals, for which they have risked their lives repeatedly'. *Psicosis de guerra*, p. 74.

137 Vallejo-Nágera, *La locura*, pp. 228–30.

138 López Ibor, *Neurosis de guerra* (Barcelona, 1942), pp. 8–10; 'El hombre español', in *El español y su complejo de inferioridad*.

139 María Immaculada Pastor i Homs, *La educación femenina en la postguerra (1939–1945); el caso de Mallorca* (Madrid, 1984), p. 92; Gallego Méndez, *Mujer, Falange, franquismo*, p. 79. On educational discrimination against girls, see Alted Vigil, 'La mujer', in *Ordenamiento jurídico*, pp. 425–37.

140 Antonio Nadal Sánchez, 'Experiencias psíquicas sobre mujeres Marxistas malagueñas: Málaga, 1939', in Ministerio de Cultura, *Las mujeres y la guerra civil española*, pp. 340–50. See also 'Psiquismo del fanatismo Marxista: investigaciones psicológicas en Marxistas femeninas delincuentes', *Revista Española de Medicina y Cirugía*, 2, 9 (May 1939); *Semana Médica Española*, 2 September 1939. Approximately 900 women were interned in the women's prison of Málaga from February 1937–1939. Barranquero Texeira, Matilde Eiroa San Francisco and Paloma Navarro Jiménez, *Mujer, cárcel, franquismo: la prisión provincial de Málaga (1937–1945)* (Málaga, 1994), p. 39.

141 Franco's press officer, Captain Rosales, cited in Frances Davis, *My Shadow in the Sun* (New York, 1940), p. 136, Southworth, *Guernica*, pp. 52–3.

142 Gollonet and Morales, *Sangre y fuego*, p. 11–13.

143 For Vallejo-Nágera's ideas of what '*amor libre*' was, and how it related specifically to 'communism', see *Eugenesia*, pp. 72–5. Also José Vicente Puente, *Arriba*, 16 May 1939.

144 'La moralidad pública', *Revista Internacional de Sociología*, 2–3 (1943), p. 345.

145 Vallejo-Nágera, *Eugenesia*. See also Stauffer, 'La mujer y el Marxismo'.

146 Franco, 20 November 1938, *Palabras*, p. 78. *Castidad* can signify both chastity and purity, in terms of morality and of race, in Spanish.

147 Franco, *Palabras del Caudillo (19 abril 1937–7 diciembre 1942)* (Madrid, 1943), p. 13; Padre F. García, Conferencia, V Consejo-Nacional de la Sección Femenina, cited in Marie Aline Barrachina, 'Ideal de la mujer Falangista: ideal Falangista de la mujer', in *Las mujeres y la guerra Civil*, p. 215.

148 Di Febo, 'El "Monje Guerrero"', p. 204–8; Alted Vigil, 'Las mujeres', both in *Las mujeres y la guerra civil*, p. 293; Kurt Baier, 'Autarchy, Reason, and Commitment', *Ethics*, 100 (October 1989), pp. 93–107. On silence, 'enclosing' women and 'hygienic marriage', see Gallego Méndez, 'Notas sobre el poder', in *Nuevas perspectivas sobre la mujer* (Madrid, 1982), p. 48; Isidro Gomá y Tomás, *La familia según el derecho natural y cristiano* (Barcelona, 1946); Antonio García Figar, *Porqué te casas. Para qué te casas. Con quién te casas* (Madrid, 1945); Vallejo-Najera, *Antes que te cases . . .* (Madrid, 1944), which appears to owe something to the ideas of late-sixteenth-century writers like Juan Esteban, *Orden de bien casar y avisos de casados* (originally, Bilbao, 1595) and Fray Luis de Leon, *La perfecta casada* (originally Madrid, 1573), esp. chs. 16 and 17. See also Maeztu, *Defensa de la Hispanidad*, p. 110; Allison Peers, *Spanish Mystics*, vol. I, pp. 297–9; María Angeles Durán, 'Lectura económica de Fray Luis de León', in *Nuevas perspectivas sobre la mujer* (Madrid, 1982), pp. 257–72.

149 Vallejo-Nágera, *Eugenesia*, pp. 131–2. In women there were two 'manifestations of life: interior or spiritual and external or animal'. 'Correct persons . . . hide their animal life' Sección Femenina de FET y JONS, *Formación familiar y social* (Madrid, n.d), p. 9.

150 *Palabras*, p. 34.

151 In calling for a 'modernised Inquisition', as an 'obstacle to the literary poisoning of the masses . . . and the definitive ruin of the spirit of *Hispanidad*', Vallejo-Nágera writes that, 'the blood of inquisitors runs in our veins . . . Inqusitorial chromosomes remain incrusted in our paternal and maternal genes', Vallejo-Nágera, *Divagaciones intrascendentes*, pp. 105–7.

152 See ch. 1 of this study for the explicit connection pointed out by Franco himself.

153 See *The Lancet* 7 January 1939, p. 68.

154 López Ibor, *Discurso a los universitarios*, p. 106.

155 González Duro, *Psiquiatría y sociedad*, pp. 30–1.

156 The wealthy had the option of private consultation and a spell in a 'rest home', of course. These 'sanatorios de reposo' were very different from the state asylums of Francoism. See Enrique González Duro, *Psiquiatría y sociedad*, esp. p. 17.

157 López Ibor, *El español*, pp. 140–1, for example. Vallejo-Nágera, though he was later explicitly anti-Freudian, had commented favourably upon the psychoanalytic revolution prior to the years of Republic and war. See Vallejo-Nágera, 'Locuras curables y locuras incurables', *El Siglo Médico*, 86 (1930), pp. 85–6, cited by Thomas F. Glick, 'Ciencia, política y discurso civil en la España de Alfonso XIII', in Guillermo Gortázar (ed.) *Nación y estado en la España liberal* (Madrid, 1994), p. 267.

158 González Duro, *Psiquiatría y sociedad*, p. 19.

4 THE 'VERTICALISATION' OF SPAIN: THE STATE AND WORK

1 Juan Ignacio Ferreras, 'La generación del silencio: ensayo sobre un novelar de la posguerra española', in Hernán Vidal (ed.), *Fascismo y experiencia literaria: reflexiones para una recanonización* (Minneapolis, 1985), pp. 154–211; Ignacio Soldevila-Durante, 'Consecuencias de la guerra española en la evolución del lenguaje', in *Actas del congreso internacional sobre la guerra civil española, 1977; Historia y literatura* (Montreal/Madrid, 1988), pp. 202–3. See also the Falangist review, *Vértice* (Vertex).

2 José Camilo Cela, *La colmena* ([originally Buenos Aires, 1951] 9th edn, Barcelona, 1967), cited in Herzberger, *Fiction and Historiography*, p. 58, where the regime's 'mythic time' is contrasted with 'common time'. See also the apposite examples from Luis Goytisolo, Carmen Martín Gaite and Rafael Sánchez Ferlosio, pp. 69, 99, 130.

3 Sheilah Wilson, 'Fiestas and Terezín: The Space of Confinement', *Norte*, 8, 4–6 (1972), pp. 97–106. Social space as a focus of historical analysis has been more important to writers in France than in Spain. See, for example, the work of the radical anarchist geographer Elisée Reclus, the existentialist Marxist Henri Lefebvre, or the social theorist Pierre Bourdieu.

4 Arrese, *La revolución social*, p. 206. Arrese was a Falangist 'of the first hour', joining the party in 1933, but also a 'spiritual Catholic'. In the repressive period from 1939–May 1941 he was party chief and Civil Governor in Málaga, resigning in protest against the fall of Serrano Suñer, but straightaway compensated with a ministerial position.

5 Franco, 14 July 1937, *Palabras* (1938), p. 160.

6 Gabriel Ureña, *Arquitectura y urbanística civil y militar en el período de la autarquía (1936–1945)* (Madrid, 1979), pp. 97–102; César Cort, *Campos urbanizados y ciudades ruralizadas* (Madrid, 1941); Juliá et al., *Madrid*, p. 556; Miguel Aparicio, *El sindicalismo vertical y la formación del estado franquista* (Barcelona, 1980).

7 On Franco's own obsession with hierarchy, see his speeches in *Palabras*, pp. 79, 139, 149, 160, 161.

8 López Ibor, 'Experiencias psiquiátricas de guerra', *Revista Española de Medicina y Cirugía de Guerra*, 2, 5 (1939), pp. 82–101.

9 Mircea Eliade, *Sacred and Profane* (London, 1954), pp. 33–4.

10 Juan José López Ibor, 'Experiencias psiquiátricas'; 'El hombre español', in *El español y su complejo de inferioridad* (Madrid, 1951). Also José María Pemán y Pemartín, *El Seneca y sus puntos de vista* (Jeréz de la Frontera, 1953). Franco was explicitly compared to Seneca; for example, José Pemartín, *Laureados de España* (Madrid, 1940), p. 51. On Seneca, Ganivet and stoicism as a central axis of Spanish rightist ideology, see Richards, 'Constructing the Nationalist State: Self-sufficiency and Regeneration in the Early Franco Years', in A. Smith and C. Mar Molinero (eds.), *Nationalism and the Nation in the Iberian Peninsula* (Oxford, 1996), pp. 153–4.

11 González Duro, *Psiquiatría y sociedad autoritaria*, pp. 26/7. González effectively demonstrates how official psychiatry in Spain was one area, among many, where the mentality of war, repression, and cultural closure remained virtually unchanged throughout the entire period of the dictatorship.

12 For example, Juan Antonio Sarazá y Ayustante, *La empresa del movimiento nacional* (Córdoba, 1947).

13 Fenech, *La posición del juez*, pp. 99–100; Sección Feminina de FET–JONS, *Formación política*, p. 94. 'Space', for Falangist ideologues, was a setting for dramatic, 'pure' or 'poetic', acts (not the 'prose' of everyday life), articulating the destiny of the *Patria* as 'unity of experience'. For similar ideas in French intellectual fascism, see Alice Yaeger Kaplan, *Reproductions of Banality: Fascism, Literature, and French Intellectual Life* (Minneapolis, 1986). Franco himself believed in the idea *and* the reality of empire and hierarchy.

14 'Rousseau was a philosopher from Geneva who affirmed . . . that the truth does not exist', Sección Feminina de FET–JONS, *Formación política*, pp. 99–101; article 1 of statutes, Chueca, *El fascismo*, p. 410.

15 *La Vanguardia Española*, 17 August 1939, cited in Benet, *L'intent franquista*, pp. 390/1.

16 See, Franco's speech, 3 October 1942, *Palabras* (1937–43). José Madalena Calvo et al., 'Los lugares de la memoria de la guerra civil en un centro de poder: Salamanca 1936–39', in J. Aróstegui, *Historia y memoria* (Salamanca, 1986), Javier Fernández Delgado, *La memoria impuesta: estudio y catálogo de los monumentos conmemorativos de Madrid, 1939–1980* (Madrid, 1982). On 'sacred space', see, for example, Eliade, *Sacred and Profane*, pp. 20–65.

17 Franco, speech, 24 January 1942.

18 Ureña, *Arquitectura y urbanística*, p. 62.

19 For example, Franco's speeches in *Palabras*, pp. 19, 36, 100, 105. Eliade, *Sacred and Profane*, p. 56.

20 Franco, speech, Burgos, 12 October 1937, *Palabras*, p. 36. See Francisco García Alonso, *Flores de heroismo* (Seville, 1939); A. García Pérez, *Jardines de España* (Tangiers, 1941).

21 Juan Beneyto Pérez, 'La concepción jerárquica de la sociedad en el pensamiento medieval español', *Estudios de historia social de España*, 1 (1949), pp. 555–66; José María Font Rius, *Instituciones medievales españolas: la organización política, económica y social de los reinos cristianos de la Reconquista* (Madrid, 1949).

22 Martínez Tórtola, *La enseñanza*, pp. 65–6; Franco, speech, 1 October 1937, *Palabras*, p. 124. On St James, see *Franco ante el Apóstol Santiago – Visita de S.E. a Santiago de Compostela* (Vigo, 1939).

23 Franco, *Palabras del Caudillo, 1937–1942* (Madrid, 1943), p. 13; Sección Femenina de FET y de las JONS, *Calendario* (Madrid, n.d.); Allison Peers, *Spanish Mystics*, vol. I, pp. 147–229; *Complete Works of St Teresa* (London, 1946), vol. III, pp. xvi–231; H. Thurston and D. Attwater (eds.), *Butler's Lives of the Saints* (London, 1956), vol. IV, p. 117. Medina del Campo was the site of the SF's giant national rally in May 1939 and *Medina* was the title of an SF review. On Francoism's appropriation of 'St Teresa's left hand' as a sign of the miraculous nature of the victory, and the discovery of the 'incorrupt body' of the patron of Madrid, St Isidro, and similar instances, see Di Febo, *La santa de la raza*, pp. 63–71.

24 Juan Antonio Ramírez, 'Imágenes para un pueblo (connotaciones, arquetipos y concordancias en la iconografía de posguerra)', in Antonio Bonet Correa, *Arte del franquismo* (Madrid, 1981), p. 240. See also *Laureados de*

Espana, pp. 50–6; Sección Feminina de FET–JONS, *Formación política,* pp. 73–4. That the Nationalist General Moscardó preferred to have his son killed by the Republicans rather than surrender the Alcázar was seen as as being prophesied in a similar patriotic sacrifice by Guzmán el Bueno in the struggle against the Moors in the reign of Sancho IV. *Enciclopedia,* pp. 230–44. Toledo was to be the site of Franco's new, grandiose Academy of Infantry, which drew upon the 'virile, pure Spanishness' of the place. Gabriel Ureña Portero, 'Emblemática y espíritu de las milicias franquistas', in Bonet, *Arte del franquismo,* p. 262. See fig. 6, p. 69.

25 Sección Feminina de FET–JONS, *Formación política,* pp. 75–6, 111. This particular process was accompanied by several executions of Republican prisoners along the route. Heine, *La oposición política,* p. 44.

26 Only reluctantly, and somewhat in contradiction with the triumphalist rhetoric, were Republican dead permitted a resting place here, although very many families, on both sides, were reluctant. Sueiro, *La verdadera historia*; Aguilar, *Memoria,* pp. 116–30. On plans to construct a 'Monument to the Counter-Reformation', see Angel Llorente, *Arte e ideología en el franquismo (1936–1951)* (Madrid, 1995), p. 78. See fig. 7, pp. 70–1.

27 Aguilar, *Memoria y olvido,* pp. 130–4; 'El Cuartel de la Montaña', *Reconstrucción,* 1, 4.

28 *La Vanguardia Española,* 5 March 1939. Streets and squares were renamed all over the country. Many of them after the leading Francoist generals, including the Caudillo himself, but also after the 'martyrs' of the 'Crusade', like Calvo Sotelo and Maeztu. Names that had been changed in celebration of the Republic in 1931 were again changed. Some of this reclaiming of place appeared as far from subtle allusions to the politics and style of reconquering: in La Coruña, *Fraternity* became *Labour, Equality* became *Justice, Liberty* became *Discipline* and *Primero de mayo* became *Matadero* (slaughterhouse). Fernández, *El alzamiento,* pp. 110–11.

29 Dirección General de Regiones Devastadas y Reparaciones, *La reconstrucción de España: résumen de dos años de labor* (Madrid, 1942). One town 'adopted' was the Basque cultural capital, Guernica, destroyed with huge loss of life in four hours of bombing by Hitler's Condor Legion, directed by Franco's Nationalists, in April 1937. The Franco authorities continued to blame Republicans for raizing their own city to the ground. See 'Estudio de un pueblo adoptado: Guernica', *Reconstrucción,* 1 (April 1940), 22–7. Another example was the town of Brunete, also destroyed during the war, to be rebuilt using the labour of Republican prisoners. *Boletín Oficial de la Dirección General de Prisiones* (Madrid, 1942–3).

30 'Ruinas que ennoblecen', *Arriba* (21 August 1941), in Ureña Portero, *Arquitectura,* pp. 124–5. Actual reconstruction seemed always to begin with churches. See, on Asturias, for example, *Reconstrucción,* 1, 2 (May 1940), pp. 5–17. War ruins have also been interpreted as a physical representation of a constant threat of violence. Antonio Bonet Correa, 'Espacios arquitectónicos para un nuevo orden', in Bonet, *Arte del franquismo,* p. 13.

31 Pedro Bigador, 'Primeros problemas de la reconstrucción de Madrid', *Reconstrucción,* 1 (April 1940), 17.

32 See, for example, Montero, *Los estados modernos*; Juan Beneyto Pérez, *El*

Nuevo Estado Español: el régimen nacional-sindicalista ante la tradición y los demás sistemas totalitarios (Madrid, 1939).

33 See Juan Beneyto, *La identidad del franquismo* (Madrid, 1979), pp. 33–6; Eduardo Aunós Pérez, *La reforma corporativa del estado* (Madrid, 1936); Eliseda, *El sentido fascista del Movimiento Nacional*; Vicente Gay y Forner, *La revolución nacional-socialista: ambiente, leyes, ideología* (Barcelona, 1934). See also *Información* (February 1938), pp. 98–100, 'La lucha contra la crisis mundial – la industria Alemana' in praise of a totalitarian solution to unemployment, etc. See also París Eguílaz, *Resultados de la política económica nacional-socialista* (Madrid, 1940).

34 Antonio Robert, *Un problema nacional: la industrialización necesaria* (Madrid, 1943), and the prologue provided by José María de Areilza; 'El estado y la economía', in *Ciclo de conferencias sobre temas de carácter económico organizado por la Junta de Cultura de Vizcaya y la Cámara Oficial de Comercio, Industria y Navegación de Bilbao* (Bilbao, 1943); and 'La política industrial', in Instituto de Estudios Políticos, *El Nuevo Estado Español: 25 años de movimiento nacional, 1936–1961* (Madrid, 1961). Robert was Chief Engineer of Industrial Studies and Planning in the *Dirección General de Industria*, within the Francoist Ministry of Trade and Industry during the 1940s.

35 Higinio París Eguílaz, *El estado y la economía: política económica totalitaria* (Santander, 1938); *La guerra y los problemas económicos* (Santander, 1939); *Política de creación de trabajo* (Madrid, 1940); *Economía de guerra* (Madrid, 1942); *Política económica nacional* (Madrid, 1943); *Diez años de política económica en España, 1939–1949* (Madrid, 1949); *Problemas económicos de la industrialización* (Madrid, 1952). París was the inspiration behind the creation of the Consejo de Economía Nacional in 1940. See Josep Fontana, 'Reflexiones'. For París' early draft proposals for setting up such a body see his 'Proyecto de Ley creando el Consejo Supremo de Economía', in Fundación Nacional Francisco Franco, *Documentos inéditos*, vol. II, 1, pp. 86–94. He was also instrumental in the preparation of reports by the section of national economy of the *Instituto de Estudios Políticos*, one of the 'think-tank'-like bodies set up under the auspices of the *Movimiento* to bring about the totalitarian ordering of the economy. As well as providing regime ministers with information on detailed economic questions, the Institute also helped shape the main formal contours of economic strategy, reporting on such issues as 'the defence of national industry', 'the new European economic order' and 'forms of state intervention in Italian industry'. 'Relación de los trabajos realizados por la sección de economía nacional del Instituto de Estudios Políticos', 18 November 1941, AGA, Pres, SGM, caja 5.

36 Manuel Fuentes Irurozqui, *Tres ensayos sobre el nuevo orden económico* (Madrid, 1942); *Evolución, presente y futuro del comercio exterior de España* (Madrid, 1942); 'España y el comercio internacional', in *Ciclo de conferencias* (Madrid, 1943); *La economía deformada* (Madrid, 1947); *Economía e industria nacional* (Madrid, 1948).

37 See Areilza, 'El futuro de nuestro pueblo: nacionalsindicalismo', *JONS* (May 1933); 'Estado nacional', *JONS* (September 1933), in Juan Aparicio, *JONS, Antología* (Barcelona, 1939), pp. 253–68. Areilza was appointed

mayor of Bilbao after the fall of the city to Franco in 1937, and was director general in the Ministry of Industry in 1939. Later he was ambassador in Argentina, the US and France.

38 E. Aunós Pérez, *La reforma corporativa del Estado* (Madrid, 1936); *Calvo Sotelo y la política de su tiempo* (Madrid, 1941); *España en crisis (1874–1936)* (Buenos Aires, 1942).

39 Rafael Gay de Montellà, *El Fuero del Trabajo y sistema del estado sindical-corporativo* (Valladolid, 1939); *Autarquía. nuevas orientaciones de la economía* (Barcelona, 1940).

40 Luis Alarcón y de la Lastra, *El triunfo nacional y sus repercusiones en las orientaciones de la industria y el comercio* (Madrid, 1940).

41 Juan Antonio Suanzes, *La marina nacional: dos discursos* (Bilbao, 1938); 'Palabras de . . . a los nuevos ingenieros industriales', *ICE*, supplement 154 (10 November 1946), p. 17; *Situación actual de la economía española* (Madrid, 1948).

42 Azpiazu, *El estado católico: líneas de un ideal* (Madrid, 1939); *Orientaciones cristianas del Fuero del Trabajo* (Burgos, 1939); *Moral profesional económica* (Madrid, 1941); *Los precios abusivos ante la moral* (Madrid, 1941), for example. Azpiazu taught economics and finance from 1918–26 at the Jesuit University of Deusto in Bilbao. In 1946 he helped found and became director of the economic review *Revista del Fomento Social* (Social Development Review), principally concerned with defining the necessary social conditions for economic development.

43 See Montero, *Los estados modernos*. Eloy Montero was a priest, university professor and writer born in Salamanca. Race, economics and morality were his main interests. Among his previous works are *Marruecos: el pueblo moro y el judío* (Madrid, 1911); *El individualismo económico y los modernos exigencias de la justicia social* (Barcelona, 1917); *Neomalthusianismo, eugenesia y divorcio* (Madrid, 1932).

44 Pérez del Pulgar, 'El concepto cristiano de la autarquía'. The views of these influential figures and their contributions to the construction of the Francoist state after the Civil War are discussed at various points in the course of this study.

45 See Montero, *Los estados modernos*, p. 28. See also Matossian, 'Ideologies of Delayed Industrialisation', pp. 217–28; and Ludovico Garruccio, *L'industrializazione tra nazionalismo e rivoluzione: la ideologia politica dei paisi in via di sviluppo* (Bologna, 1969).

46 Montero, *Los estados modernos*, pp. 229–32. The ILE was formally dissolved by a Francoist decree of 17 March 1940, and its facilities confiscated, becoming the Instituto Ramiro de Maeztu. *Boletín del Estado*, 18 May 1940; *Una poderosa fuerza secreta: La institución libre de la enseñanza* (San Sebastián, 1940).

47 Montero, *Los estados modernos*, p. 33.

48 *Los estados modernos*, p. 56.

49 Robert, *Un problema nacional*, pp. 211–12. See H. París Equílaz, *Un nuevo orden económico* (Madrid, 1942). On the example of Japan as a developing authoritarian society see Botti, *El cielo y el dinero*, pp. 104–7. Robert also made a study of rural industrialisation in Japan after journeying there as a

leading member of the Spanish economic mission visiting in 1940. See Robert, *La industrialización rural como remedio al desequilibrio económico entre el campo y la ciudad*, Instituto Nacional de Colonización (Madrid, 1942). Montero, *Los estados modernos*, p. 316.

50 *Los estados modernos*, p. 34.

51 *Los estados modernos*, p. 59. See also Roberto Cantalupo, *La clase dirigente: profundo estudio sobre la ideología del fascismo y la historia contemporánea de Italia* ([Italian original, 1926] Madrid, 1939).

52 Montero, *Los estados modernos*, pp. 64–5.

53 Montero, *Los estados modernos*, p. 248. Also see Ernesto Giménez Caballero, *La nueva catolicidad: teoría general sobre el fascismo en Europa y en España* (Madrid, 1933); Azpiazu, 'Revolución y tradición', *Razón y Fe*, 113 (1938), pp. 18–32; *El estado católico*, esp. pp. 6–34; *Orientaciones cristianas*, esp. pp. 8–24.

54 See the *Fuero del Trabajo*, March 1938; Fernando Díaz Plaja, *La guerra de España en sus documentos* (Madrid, 1986); *Arriba*, 'Meditaciones sobre la autarquía', 24 November 1942; Suanzes, to the Cortes, 3 May 1950; Robert, *Un problema nacional*, pp. 126–7; Ros Hombravella, 'Autárquicos en discusión', *Cambio 16*, 89 (30 July 1973), p. 37.

55 On Ramiro de Maeztu and Acción Española, see Botti, *El cielo y el dinero*, pp. 15, 62–70.

56 See, for example, Antonio de Miguel, Conferencia, in Escuela Superior del Ejército, 30 October 1941, cited in Angel Viñas, 'Autarquía y política exterior en el primer franquismo, 1939–1959', in *Revista de Estudios Internacionales* (January–March, 1980), p. 72; Velasco, 'Sobre una posible caracterización', pp. 399–400.

57 Montero, *Los estados modernos*, p. 68.

58 Marco Merenciano, 'Nuevas orientaciones', p. 96, in *Ensayos*.

59 See Chueca, *El fascismo en los comienzos del régimen de Franco*, pp. 17–50, 294–300.

60 A. Suárez, Colectivo '36, *El libro blanco sobre las cárceles franquistas 1939–1976* (Paris, 1976), p. 46.

61 On the devastating purging of the teaching profession, see Wenceslao Alvarez Oblanca, *La represión de postguerra en León: depuración de la enseñanza, 1936–1943* (León, 1986); Jesús Crespo Redondo et al., *Purga de maestros en la guerra civil: la depuración del magisterio nacional de la provincia de Burgos* (Valladolid, 1987).

62 See announcements of the chief of the occupation forces in Barcelona in *La Vanguardia*, 27 and 28 January 1939.

63 *BOE*, 22 December 1938. Its final report was *Dictamen de la Comisión sobre ilegitimidad de poderes actuantes en 18 de julio de 1936* (Barcelona, 1939). See also Ministerio de Justicia, *Causa general: la dominación roja en España* (Madrid, 1943); Rafael Abella: *Finales de enero*, pp. 18–19.

64 See, for example, the historian Arthur Bryant's preface to *The Second and Third Reports on the Communist Atrocities*, issued on the authority of the Francoist rebels in Burgos (London, 1937).

65 PRO/FO371/24507/C668/40/41.

66 Wilson, 'Fiestas and Terezín', p. 99.

67 For example, Ridruejo, *Escrito en España*, p. 95.
68 *Boletín Oficial del Estado*, 28 July 1939. Fernández Asiaín, *El delito de rebelión militar* (Madrid, 1943), cited in Ballbé, *Orden público y militarismo en la España constitucional*, p. 402; Ignacio Díaz de Aguilar y Elízaga, 'Justicia militar en la España "Nacional" – instituciones', in *Justicia en guerra*, pp. 396–7.
69 Spanish ex-Servicemen's Association, *Franco's Prisoners Speak* (London, 1960); Eiroa San Francisco, *Viva Franco*, p. 230, for example.
70 Cited in Eiroa San Francisco, *Viva Franco*, p. 263. The official records show that of the 124,423 prisoners held in regime gaols at the end of 1942, 80 per cent were detained for 'crimes of rebellion', and only 20,137 were interned for 'common crimes'.
71 Súarez/Colectivo '36, *El Libro blanco*, p. 45.
72 *Informe acerca de FET de las JONS en Cataluña*, June 1937; *Informe de FET-JONS sobre las delegaciones provinciales de Barcelona, Tarragona, Lérida y Gerona*, 1938; AGA, Pres, SGM, caja 31. See also José Lequerica, 'La liberación de Cataluña – un aspecto político', *La Vanguardia*, 12 February 1939, p. 3.
73 *Catalunya sota el règim franquista*, pp. 236–74; Ridruejo, *Escrito en España*, p. 176; Giménez Caballero, *Genio de España*, p. 276; Ruíz Vilaplana, *Doy fe . . . un año de actuación en la España nacionalista* (Paris, 1938), pp. 230–4.
74 Luis Benítez de Lugo, *Responsabilidades civiles y políticas* (Barcelona, 1940).
75 See, for example, the files of the *Tribunal de Responsabilidades Políticas* in the Arxiu General del 'Tribunal de Responsabilidades Politicas' del Tribunal Superior de Justicia de Catalunya (ATRP).
76 This disregarded one of the main postulates of law in the liberal state: *nullum crimen sine lege*. Cano Bueso, *La política judicial*, p. 86. Rather, the imperative was *nullum crimen sine poena*; no crime will remain unpunished.
77 *BOE*, 13 February 1939. Díaz-Plaja, *La guerra de España*, pp. 381–4. See, for example, the report of the Barcelona Tram Company giving to the authorities a full account of a worker's involvement in past strikes. He had later 'directed' the collectivisation of the trams during the conflict. Exp. 343, ATRP. The Law of Political Responsibilities was cosmetically reformed in 1942 but remained in force until a decree of 1966. See Ballbé, *Orden público*, p. 410. The subsequent Ley de Seguridad del Estado (Law of State Security), 29 March 1941, included as offences vague categories such as '*resistencia*' and '*extremista*'.
78 *La Vanguardia Española*, 4 April 1939. See expedientes 654, 656, ATRP.
79 Exps. 339, 444, ATRP.
80 For comparison with the Stalinist legal system and its effect, where 'socially dangerous acts' and any action tending towards the 'weakening' of the government were 'offences', see Gliksman, 'Social Prophylaxis, as a Form of Soviet Terror', in Carl Friedrich (ed.), *Totalitarianism* (New York, 1953).
81 J. Villarroya Font and J.M. Solé i Sabaté, 'El castigo a los vencidos', *Historia 16*, 24, p. 62.
82 Morales Ruiz, *La publicación de la Ley de Represión de la Masonería en la prensa de la España de postguerra (1940)* (Zaragoza, 1992).
83 Franco, 7 November 1938, *Palabras*, p. 285. There were ninety-three such

penal detachments in 1942, employed in digging irrigation channels, reservoirs, railway lines and prisons. Heine, *La oposición política*, p. 46. More than sixty were attached to private companies according to Suárez/Colectivo '36, *Libro blanco*, p. 79. The system was coordinated via the civil governor of each province.

84 Suárez/Colectivo '36, *Libro blanco*, p. 50.

85 El Patronato Central para la Redención de las Penas por el Trabajo, *La obra de la redención de penas*, p. xiii. The project was depicted as a 'scientific revolution' in penal reform. Only prisoners condemned to relatively shorter sentences were eligible, p. 28.

86 This was José Antonio Pérez del Pulgar, the Jesuit priest and author of 'El concepto cristiano de la autarquía', published in 1939. See chapter 1 of the current study.

87 El Patronato, *La obra de la redención*, pp. xiv–xv. Fernández, *Antología*, pp. 484–6. Maeztu, *Hispanidad*, pp. 105–8. See also Roldán Barbero, *Historia de la prisión*, p. 195.

88 El Patronato, *La obra de la redención de penas*. Barcelona provincial prison housed 11,093 prisoners in 1942, according to official records.

89 Di Febo, *Resistencia y movimiento*, pp. 44–6.

90 El Patronato, *La obra*, pp. 27–31. The wives and children of some prisoners in labour batallions were dependent on this paltry income. Exp. 656, ATRP, for example.

91 Eiroa San Francisco, *Viva Franco*, p. 243; Núñez, *Cárcel de Ventas*, p. 17.

92 Martín Torrent, *¿Qué me dice Usted de los presos?*, p. 112.

93 *Redención*, 23 September 1939, cited in Eiroa San Francisco, *Viva Franco*, p. 264.

94 PRO/FO371/24524/C2744/1117/41, 20 February 1940.

95 Javier R. Muñoz, 'La represión franquista: paseos y ejecuciones', in *Historia General de Asturias*, vol. XI (Gijón, 1978); Heine, *La oposición política*, p. 43.

96 El Patronato, *La obra*, pp. 64–5.

97 PRO/FO371/26890/C1371/3/41, 14 March 1941.

98 Confidential circular of under-secretary of the Presidencia del Gobierno issued at request of the Captain General of the 7th military region, 20 May 1943, AGA, Pres, SGM, caja 17.

99 *Alimentación Nacional* (September 1943), p. 9.

100 S.G. Checkland, *The Mines of Tharsis* (London, 1967), pp. 220–9. On the food situation in Huelva, 'bordering on famine', see PRO/FO371/26890/C803/3/41, 18 January 1941; 'Informe sobre la situación de la provincia respecto al abastecimiento de harinas y pan', 29 January 1940, AGA, Pres, SGM, caja 228.

101 At least 421 Republican sympathisers were shot, although popular estimates ranged from 1,200–1,500. Charles E. Harvey, *The Rio Tinto Company: An Economic History of a Leading International Mining Concern* (London, 1981), pp. 270, 286, 290–1. See also Víctor Alba, *Sleepless Spain* (London, 1948) pp. 46–56.

102 PRO/FO371/26890/C3986/3/41, March 1941.

103 El Patronato, *La obra*, p. 30.

104 Letter from the mayor and Party chief in Almadén to the Secretaría General de FET–JONS, 21 February 1940, AGA, Pres, SGM, caja 227. In 1942, official statistics show that Almadén housed 774 prisoners.

105 García Piñeiro, *Los mineros*, pp. 57–61. Records were kept of the past affiliations of each worker by the military authorities in conjunction with the party investigation department.

106 Torres, *Así los viví*, p. 78; Suárez/Colectivo '36, *Libro blanco*, p. 80.

107 *Anuario Estadístico de España* (Madrid, 1942), p. 1099. It is not clear which categories of detainees are included in these figures, however. The official average for the period 1930–4 is calculated as 9,403. By the end of 1942, the prison population, according to the authorities, was still almost 125,000.

108 See Louis Stern, *Beyond Death and Exile: The Spanish Republicans in France, 1939–1955* (Cambridge, MA, 1979); A.A. Bravo-Tellado, *El peso de la derrota 1939–1944; la tragedia de medio millón de españoles* (Madrid, 1974); Llorens, *El exilio*, pp. 99–112; Alcalde, *Mujeres en el franquismo*, pp. 15–30.

109 See Montserrat Roig, *Noche y niebla: los Catalanes en los campos nazis* (Barcelona, 1978); David Wingeate Pike, *In The Service of Stalin: The Spanish Communists in Exile, 1939–1945* (Oxford, 1993), pp. 108–48, 236–78; Eduardo Pons Prades, *Morir por la libertad: españoles en los campos de exterminio nazis* (Madrid, 1995). Also, the moving letters of Pere Vives i Clavé in *Cartes des dels camps de concentració* (Barcelona, 1970) and the Prologue by Agustí Bartra.

110 See, for example, 'Nota del Director General de Prisiones acerca del excesivo numero de presos', in FNFF, *Documentos inéditos*, vol. II, 1, pp. 176–7.

111 FET–JONS, DNII, Murcia, 'Informe – Situación actual', 15 August 1938, AGA, Pres, SGM, caja 4.

112 Koestler, *Spanish Testament*, p. 88.

113 The Minister of Foreign Affairs, Colonel Juan Beigbeder, admitted to the British Ambassador that there were at the beginning of 1940 still 75,000 prisoners awaiting trial, while 100,000 were 'undergoing judicial examination'. PRO/FO371/24524/C1117/41, 17 January 1940. The amnesty anyway only referred to those serving twelve years or less. The vast majority accused of 'military rebellion' were sentenced to periods ranging from twelve years and one day to the death penalty. Republican exiles insisted that the actual number of detainees was three or four times the official figure. PRO/FO371/24524/C2744/1117/41; letter of Manuel Irujo to *The Times*, 20 February 1940. The first substantial reprieve was granted in October 1945 under pressure from the Allied victors after the end of the Second World War. See *BOE*, 19 October 1945. Periodic pardons were decreed until 1971.

114 Alba, *Sleepless*, p. 109.

115 See Ministerio de Industria y Comercio, *Catálogo oficial de la producción industrial de España*, 2 vols. (Madrid, 1938–42), I, p. 170, for example.

116 *Anuario Estadístico de España*, 1948. See also chapter 8.

117 See Michael Richards, 'Autarky and the Franco Dictatorship in Spain, 1936–1945', PhD thesis (University of London, 1995).

118 J.M. de Areilza, 'Directrices de la nueva ordenación económica', p. 482.
119 Gay de Montellà, *Autarquía*, p. 95. Etymologically, 'corporativism' is related to 'bodies'.
120 For example, see Francesc Cambó, *Entorn del feixisme italiana* (Barcelona, 1924); in Spanish, *En torno al fascismo italiano* (Barcelona, 1925), pp. 42–6, 183–5; *Las dictaduras* (2nd edn, Barcelona, 1929); Marqués de Eliseda, *Fascismo, catolicismo, monarquía* (Madrid, 1935); Eduardo Aunós Pérez, *Calvo Sotelo y la política de su tiempo* (Madrid, 1941); José María Gil Robles *No fue posible la paz* (Barcelona, 1968), pp. 150–1; the CEDA leader, Gil Robles' prologue to the Falangist Ramón Ruiz Alonso's *Corporatismo* (Salamanca, 1937).
121 See also Aunós Pérez, *Calvo Sotelo*, p. 136; Gil Robles, *No fue posible*, pp. 150–1; Miguel Sancho Izquierdo, Leonardo Prieto Castro and Antonio Muñoz Casayus, *Corporatismo: los movimientos nacionales contemporáneos* (Zaragoza, 1937), pp. 175–6; José Calvo Sotelo, *Mis servicios al estado: seis años de gestión. Apuntes para la historia* (Madrid, 1931), p. xiii. For Basque industry's favourable comments on the plans for a corporative state, see 'El Proyecto de Ley Sindical', *Información* (30 May 1939), pp. 261–2.
122 'Principios informadores de un programa de Gobierno', *Acción Española*, 3, 43 (1933), pp. 659–68, for example.
123 Enrique Diumaró Mimó, *El problema industrial textil ò el maquinismo y la cuestión social* (Barcelona, 1939), p. 36. Eduardo Aunós Pérez, Primo de Rivera's former Labour Minister, believed, by 1936, that the only way to effective social control was through 'a surgical operation' – indeed, he regretted that this course had not been taken earlier. Aunós Pérez, *España en crisis*, p. 439.
124 *Boletín Oficial del Estado*, 16 and 28 September 1936.
125 Aparicio, *El sindicalismo vertical*, pp. 33–8.
126 Article 30 of party statutes. Also Moret, *ABC político*, pp. 235–8.
127 *BOE*, 10 March 1938; Díaz-Plaja, *La guerra de España*, pp. 304–10. Manuel Ludevid, *Cuarenta años del Sindicato vertical* (Barcelona, 1976), pp. 13–15. The resources of the democratic unions of pre-Civil War Spain were handed over to the Movement, which controlled this syndical system. See also Viñas et al., *Política comercial exterior*, pp. 185, 306, 771. See also *Información* (15 March 1938), pp. 118–20, 125–7. The *Fuero* was known as the Magna Carta of the regime. See David Ruiz, Isidro Sánchez and Manuel Ortiz (eds.) *España Franquista*, p. 15. For Germany's interest, see Hans Erbler, *Spaniens nationalsyndikalistischer verfassungsund sozialbau* (Weimar, 1939). For an example of the rhetoric, see Santiago Montero Díaz, *La política social en la zona Marxista* (Bilbao, 1938); *The Labour Charter for New Spain* (New York, 1938); José Luis de Arrese, *La revolución social de nacional-sindicalismo* (Madrid, 1945). Debate on the nature of the measures to be taken to control labour began in Nationalist circles at an early stage of the Civil War. See the various plans for a '*Carta del Trabajo*', a '*Frente del Trabajo*', and a '*Falange del Trabajo*', as well as a report entitled '*Carta del Trabajo y Vargas*' (Brazil), all prepared from 1937 on. AGA, Pres, SGM, cajas 228, 229 and *Hoy*, 15 March 1938.

128 See Pedro Gual Villalbí, 'Patología y terapeútica de la economía', *La Vanguardia* (6 May 1939), p. 3; Joaquín Garrigues, *Tres conferencias en Italia sobre el Fuero del Trabajo* (Madrid, 1939).

129 Gay de Montellà, *Autarquía*, pp. 95–6.

130 *Enciclopedia*, p. 309.

131 Javier Tusell and Genoveva García Queipo de Llano, 'Fuero del Trabajo: origen y contenido', in *Historia 16, La Guerra Civil*, 20, p. 85.

132 *Fuero del Trabajo*, arts. 1, 3, 5 and 6. Dazí-Plaja, *La guerra de España*, pp. 304–7.

133 See Carles Viver Pi-Sunyer, 'Aproximació a la ideología del franquisme', p. 20.

134 Areilza, Bilbao, 1 July 1937; Fernandez, *Antología*, pp. 41–2.

135 Franco, *Palabras*, pp. 145, 157, 190, 198.

136 Borja de Riquer. 'Dossier: el franquisme i la burguesia Catalana (1939–1951)' *L'Avenç* (January 1979), p. 18.

137 See José María de Areilza, 'Directrices de la nueva ordenación económica', in *Problemas técnicas de importancia económica en la nueva organización de España* (Barcelona, 1940), p. 481.

138 'Autarquía y sindicación – columna de la España de hoy', *Solidaridad Nacional* (4 June 1940); Clavera et al., *Capitalismo español*, pp. 85–9; Lorenzo Espinosa, *Dictadura*, p. 52. See also, for example, *Arriba* (1 April 1948), 'La victoria internal de Franco'. This was a special edition of the Movement's newspaper celebrating the ninth anniversary of Franco's victory in 'the first battle against communism'. According to *Arriba*, 'the industrial intensification achieved in Spain' during these years was 'without precedents'. The editorial stressed the creation of 'more than 50,000 industries' and the growth of total capital of companies from 25,400 million to 45,000 million pesetas. It also boasted that the production of electrical energy had been trebled.

139 M. Valdes Larrañaga, 'Discurso del dia de la Fiesta del Trabajo', July 1940, cited in Chueca, *El fascismo*, p. 87.

140 *Informe acerca.*

141 Ibid.

142 Letter from Niguelas, Granada, to Julián Pemartín, 21 December 1938, AGA, Pres, SGM, caja 12.

143 See Sheelagh Ellwood, *Spanish Fascism in the Franco Era* (London, 1987), p. 62.

144 Wilson, 'Fiestas and Terezín', pp. 97–8.

5   THE POLITICS AND ECONOMICS OF AUTARKY

1 Manuel Fuentes Irurozqui, 'La autarquía y el comercio exterior de España', *Información Comercial Española*, 43 (10 April 1942), p. 2.

2 Juan Velarde Fuertes, 'Política de desarrollo', in Fuentes Quintana, *El desarrollo económico de España* (Madrid, 1963), p. 20, for example. See also Demetrio Carceller, *La situación económica de España* (Madrid, 1943), p. 9. A United Nations resolution in 1946 agreed the withdrawal of ambassadors from Spain. Britain's ambassador was accordingly recalled, but chargés

d'affaires remained and 'normal relations with Spain continued'. PRO/ FO371/96164/WS1016/134, 1951. An ambassador was reappointed in 1950.

3 Hoare to Eden, PRO/FO371/34791/C688/70/41, 11 January 1943.

4 Gabriel Jackson, *Breve historia de la guerra civil española* (Paris, 1974), p. 110.

5 'Informe del Ministro de Hacienda acerca de la posible ayuda norte americana', May 1940, in FNFF, *Documentos inéditos*, vol. II, 1, pp. 199–200.

6 Christian Leitz, *Economic Relations between Nazi Germany and Franco's Spain, 1936–1945* (Oxford, 1996), p. 75.

7 One of the culminating effects was a general strike in Barcelona in 1951, largely caused by the policy of exporting food in order to obtain exchange to purchase industrial plant. See the Falange report, 'Algunas consideraciones políticas a cuenta de los sucesos de Barcelona', AGA, SGM, caja 73.

8 *Boletín Minero e Industrial* (December 1942), pp. 403–5.

9 Clavera et al., *Capitalismo español*, p. 84. See also J. Fontana and J. Nadal, 'Spain, 1914–1970', C.M. Cipolla (ed.), *The Fontana Economic History of Europe*, Vol. VI, pt 2 (London, 1976), p. 504.

10 *Domingo*, 26 March 1939.

11 Carme Molinero and Pere Ysàs, 'Los industriales Catalanes durante el franquismo', *Revista de Historia Económica*, 8, 1 (Winter 1990), pp. 105–29; and *'Patria,* Justian y Fan', *nivells de vida i condicions de treball a Catalunya, 1939–1951* (Barcelona, 1985); Lorenzo Espinosa, *Dictadura y dividendo*; Manuel González Portilla and José María Garmendia, *La posguerra en el País Vasca: Política, acumulación, miseria* (Madrid, 1988).

12 FET–JONS intelligence report, Barcelona, April 1946, AGA, Pres, SGM, caja 16.

13 Losada Malvárez, *Ideología del ejército franquista*, particularly pp. 221–5, 239–55; Ellwood, *Spanish Fascism*, p. 71; Harrison, *An Economic History of Spain* (Manchester, 1978), p. 121; Jérez Mir, *Elites políticas y centros de extracción en España*, pp. 49–175; Gonzàlez, *La economia política*, pp. 26–7.

14 See Clavera et al., *Capitalismo español*, p. 24.

15 For statistics on the devastatingly low wage levels in the 1940s see J.M. Naredo, 'La agricultura española en el desarrollo económico', in R Carballo et al., vol. III of *Historia agraria de la España contemporánea* (Barcelona, 1986), pp. 455–6; José Luis Leal et al., *La agricultura en el desarrollo capitalista español (1940–1970)*, pp. 44–50; Lorenzo Espinosa, *Dictadura*, pp. 16, 119–25; Alba, *Sleepless Spain*, pp. 17–22; Molinero and Ysàs, *'Patria'*, pp. 75–80.

16 See Joaquín Muns, *Industrialización y crecimiento de los paises en desarrollo* (Barcelona, 1972), pp. 87–296; Peter Clark, *Planning Import Substitution* (London, 1970); Celso Furtado, *The Economic Development of Latin America* (Cambridge, 1970); Tom Kemp, *Historical Patterns of Industrialisation* (London, 1978), particularly pp. 88–115.

17 See also Fisher, *Economic Self Sufficiency* (London, 1939), pp. 8–11; P.H. Asher, *National Self-Sufficiency* (London, 1938), pp. 130–8; William Carr, *Arms, Autarky and Aggression: A Study in German Foreign Policy, 1933–1939* (London, 1986), pp. 49–52, 58–62.

18 On ISI in the Spanish case, see Javier Braña, Mikel Buesa and J. Molero, 'El estado en los procesos de industrialización atrasada: notas acerca del caso español (1939–1977)', *El Trimestre Económico*, 197, 50 (January–March 1983); M. Buesa, 'Algunos aspectos de la política económica e industrialización en España (1939–1963)', *Comercio Exterior*, 33, 4 (April 1983); González, *La economía política*, pp. 29, 110; Viñas et al., *Política comercial*, pp. 294, 300, 311, 357. On the development of the economy through autarky during wartime or in preparation for war, see H. París Eguílaz, *El estado y la economía: política económica totalitaria* (Santander, 1939), p. 395. See also Carlos Velasco, 'El origen militar de la autarquía y su significación económica', *Perspectiva contemporánea*, 1 (1988), pp. 117–33.

19 Viñas, *Guerra, dinero, dictadura*, p. 209.

20 See also Velasco, 'Sobre una posible caracterización', p. 394.

21 The *Oxford English Dictionary*, vol. II (Oxford, 1989), p. 795.

22 *Diccionario de la lengua española* (Madrid, 1947), p. 140.

23 Martín Alonso, *Enciclopedia del idioma* (Madrid, 1958), p. 576.

24 See also Max Weber's characterisation of the 'charismatic ruler' in *Economy and Society*.

25 Fenech, *La posición del juez*, p. 98. Also Ramón Serrano Suñer, *Entre el silencio y la propaganda, la historia como fue* (Barcelona, 1977), p. 172. From art. 47 of statutes of FET–JONS, 1937. On Francoism as a regime 'signalled by Providence', see, for example, Eduardo Aunós Pérez (Minister of Justice 1943–5), 'Virtualidad del Caudillo', *La Vanguardia Española*, 1 October 1948.

26 A substantial contribution to the understanding of the first two decades of the dictatorship has been made by Carlo Velasco Murviedro, who, in a series of publications, has demonstrated the many irrational features of autarky. See the following essays: 'Sobre una posible caracterización', pp. 391–406; 'Sucedáneos de posguerra', *Historia 16*, 131 (March 1987), pp. 11–20; 'Las pintorescas ideas económicas de Franco', *Historia 16*, 85 (May 1983), pp. 19–28.

27 See the former's *El nacional-sindicalismo, cuarenta años después* (Madrid, 1972), p. 253; and the latter's *El desarrollo económico español, 1906–1964* (Madrid, 1965), p. 192. See also 'Informe de Higinio París Aguilar [sic] sobre los fallos en la política económica', directed to Franco, 25 September 1940, in FNFF, *Documentos inéditos*, vol. II, 1, pp. 327–70.

28 Viñas, *Guerra, dinero, dictadura*.

29 Hoare to Eden, 11 January 1943.

30 Howard, PRO/FO371/24507/C380/40/41, 2 January 1940.

31 Carlos Velasco Marviedro, 'El pensamiento avtárquicon español como directriz de la política económica (1936–1951)', PhD thesis (Madrid, 1982), pp. 1–93; Chueca, *El fascismo*, pp. 85–6.

32 Viñas, *Guerra*, p. 209.

33 Garruccio, *L'Industrializzazione*, pp. 88–92.

34 Fontana, 'Reflexiones', pp. 25–37; Clavera et al., *Capitalismo español*, pp. 25, 134–5, 154–5; J.J. Castillo, *Propietarios muy pobres* (Madrid, 1979), p. 429; Carlos Velasco Murviedro, 'El pensamiento agrario y la apuesta industrializadora en la España de los cuarenta', *Agricultura y Sociedad*, 23 (1983), pp. 233–72.

35 Herzberger, *Narrating the Past*, pp. 23–4, 46–7. For Franco, the 'problem of civilisation' was to be 'resolved . . . by Castilian spirit', *Palabras*, p. 275.
36 Aparicio, 'Sobre los comienzos del sindicalismo franquista, 1939–1945', in J. Fontana (ed.), *España bajo el franquismo* (Barcelona 1986), pp. 79–81.
37 Franco, *Palabras*, p. 310.
38 Román Perpiña Grau, *De estructura económica y economiá hispana* (Madrid, [1936] 1952), p. 345; Arrese, *La revolución social*, pp. 208–9; Juan Velarde Fuertes, *Política económica de la dictadura* (Madrid, 1968), p. 88; Harrison, *An Economic History*, p. 121; Fontana and Nadal, 'Spain, 1914–70', pp. 482–3; José María de Areilza, 'Directrices de la Nueva Ordenación económica', in *Problemas técnicas de importancia económica en la nueva organización de España* (Barcelona, 1940), pp. 500–2.
39 González, *La economía política*, pp. 30, 45–6, 102.
40 Istituto per gli studi di política internazionale, *La autarquía* (Milan, 1938), pp. 7–17.
41 Ramón Carande, 'Bases de una politica economica de reconstrucción', *Revista de Estudios Políticos*, 1, 1 (1941), pp. 53–6; Istituto, *Autarquía*, p. 19.
42 Juliá et al., *Madrid*, pp. 560–1.
43 See Javier Tusell, 'La autarquía cuartelera: las ideas económicas de Franco a partir de un documento inédito', in *Historia 16*, 115 (1985), pp. 41–9.
44 Franco speech, 18 July 1942, *Palabras*, p. 223.
45 Ramón Garrabou, Joaquim Lleixà and Octavi Pellissa, *Franquisme: sobre resistència i censens a Catalunya (1938–1959)* (Barcelona, 1990), p. 78.
46 Viñas, *Guerra*, pp. 210–13; Juan Pablo Fusi, *Franco*, p. 71.
47 Losada Malvárez, *Ideología*, particularly, pp. 25–34; Gabriel Cardona, *El problema militar en España* (Madrid, 1990); Payne, *Los militares*.
48 No such communist plot existed: communism was an extremely weak political force in Spain prior to the war. The myth of the 'communist plot' of spring 1936 was an invention of Tomás Borrás, a journalist on the conservative Madrid newspaper *ABC*. See Ruiz et al., *España franquista; causa general y actitudes sociales ante la dictatura* (Castilla-La Mancha, 1993), p. 14.
49 Maeztu, *Hispanidad*, p. 297.
50 See Conde de Rodríguez San Pedro, 'Concepto y límites de la autarcía', *Nueva Economia Nacional*, 113 (December 1939), p. 4, cited in Velasco, 'Sobre una posible', p. 397; *España Franquista*, especially pp. 9–24; Lorenzo, *Dictadura*, pp. 52, 66–7.
51 Speech, Madrid, August, 1944, PRO/FO371/39658/C11201.
52 Areilza, 'Directrices', pp. 480–2; *La Vanguardia Española*, 6 March 1940.
53 *Parte*, Barcelona, November, 1946, AGA, Pres, SGM, caja 165.
54 E. Allison Peers, *Studies of the Spanish Mystics*, vol. I (London, 1954), p. 5; Maeztu, *Hispanidad*, pp. 42, 48, 78, 146, 266; Unamuno, *En torno al casticismo*. See also chapter 8.
55 Francisco Moret Messerli, *ABC político de la Nueva España* (Barcelona, 1940). My italics.
56 Manuel-Jesús González, 'La historia económica de España (1939–1959); una interpretación', *Moneda y Crédito*, 143 (December 1977), pp. 60–2; Viñas et al., *Política comercial*, pp. 295–7; Alba, *Sleepless*, p. 36.

57 Fisher, *Economic Self-Sufficiency*, p. 14. On a similar tendency under Primo de Rivera in the 1920s, see Ben-Ami, *Fascism From Above*, p. 261.

58 Carreras, 'Depresión económica', pp. 19–20; Miguel, *España cíclica*, pp. 173–4.

59 Luis Olariaga, 'La economía en la guerra moderna', *Ejército* (May 1940), p. 33.

60 Eiroa San Francisco, *Viva Franco*, p. 145.

61 See Román Perpiña Grau, *De economía hispana* (Barcelona, 1936); *De estructura económica y economía hispana* (Madrid, 1952), p. 345. See also Clavera, *Capitalismo español*, pp. 75–89; Perpiña, *Memorandum sobre la política del carbón* (Valencia, 1935); Jaime Lay, 'España hacia la autarquía', *La Vanguardia Española* (1 July 1939).

62 Thomàs, *Falange*, p. 241.

63 Demetrio Carceller, 'Sentido y Limite de una politica autarquica' *La Vanguardia Española* (27 February 1940); Higinio París Eguílaz, *Política Económica Nacional* (Madrid, 1943), p. 51; José Pemartín, *¿Qué es 'lo nuevo'?* p. 143; José María de Areílza, 'Directrices de la nueva ordenacion economica' in *Problemas técnicas de importancia económica en la nueva organización de España* (Barcelona 1940). Carceller was both a recognised supporter of the Falange and a businessman. He played an important role in persuading business that 'politics had to come before economics'. In the postwar period, though, he was to become one of Spain's richest men, known to the public as 'The Thousand Millions'. Alba, *Sleepless*, pp. 91–6. See also Informe de la Delegación Provincial de Barcelona, 21 November 1940, AGA, SGM, caja 7; Yencken to Eden, 25 September 1943, PRO/FO371/34789/C11098/63/41; J.W. Trythall, *Franco: A Biography* (London, 1970), p. 215; *L'Avenç*, January 1979; Abel Plenn, *Wind in the Olive Trees: Spain from the Inside* (New York, 1946), pp. 142–3; PRO/FO371/89524/WS/1101/12, November 1950; Thomas J. Hamilton, *Appeasement's Child: The Franco Regime in Spain* (New York, 1943), pp. 154–5.

64 At the end of the Civil War, Spain had more than 120 factories specifically dedicated to military production and a further 400 partially so. Jesús Alonso Millán, *Una tierra abierta: materiales para una historia ecológica de España* (Madrid, 1995). See also the writings of military officers in reviews like *Ejército*: Commander Rodrigo García López, 'La fabricación del automóvil en España' (April 1940), p. 73; 'El carburante nacional: diversas soluciones al gran problema actual' (October 1940), p. 65; 'La fabricación del caucho sintético en Alemania' (May 1940), p. 74; Lt Col. Antonio Lafont, 'Industria militar: objeto y misión de las fábricas militares' (December 1940), p. 72; Captain Eduardo Angulo Otaolaurruchi, 'La autarquía en la industria de explosivos militares' (Dec. 1940), p. 75; Commander Juan Priego, 'La interpretación materialista de la guerra' (June 1940).

65 'Financial Report', July 1944, PRO/FO371/39658/C10858.

66 For example, Luis de Alarcón de la Lastra, *El triunfo nacional y su repercusiones en la orientaciones de la industria y el comercio* (Madrid, 1940), p. 18; Antonio de Miguel, Director General de Comercio y Política Arancelaria, Conferencia, *Información Comercial Española* (November 1941).

67 Robert H. Whealey, *Hitler and Spain: The Nazi Role in the Spanish Civil War*

(Lexington, KY, 1989), pp. 6–7, 12, 72–6; John F. Coverdale, *Italian Intervention in the Spanish Civil War* (Princeton, NJ, 1975), pp. 70–2.

68 Rafael Abella, *La vida cotidiana durante la Guerra Civil: (1) la españa nacional* (Barcelona, 1978), p. 226; Serrano Suñer, *Entre Hendaya y Gibraltar*, pp. 62, 175–6; Whealey, *Hitler*, pp. 62, 67; Dionisio Ridruejo, *Casi unas memorias* (Barcelona, 1976), pp. 187–92; Clavera et al., *Capitalismo español*, p. 24; Trythall, *Franco*, p. 215; Ellwood, *Spanish Fascism*, pp. 69, 78–9, 89–90.

69 Franco, *Palabras*, pp. 148, 155, 160, 173, 222/3, 226, 264.

70 Franco, speech, Vigo, 20 August 1942, *Palabras* (1937–1942), p. 230.

71 See the recollections of Franco's first Interior Minister, Serrano Suñer, *Entre Hendaya y Gibraltar*, pp. 33–9; Carande, 'Bases de una política económica de reconstrucción', *Revista de estudios políticos*, 1, 1 (Madrid, 1941).

72 Franco, article, *La Revue Belge*, 15 August 1937.

73 Leitz, *Economic Relations*, pp. 8–52; Viñas et al., *Política comercial*, pp. 146–54.

74 Whealey, *Hitler*, pp. 83/4; Payne, *Franco's Spain*, p. 19.

75 Denis Smyth, 'The Moor and the Money-lender: Politics and Profits in Anglo–German Relations with Francoist Spain, 1936–1940', in Marie-Luise Recker (ed.), *Von der Konkurrenz zur Rivalität: Das britische–deutsche Verhältnis in den Ländern der europäischen Peripherie 1919–1939* (Stuttgart, 1986); Whealey, *Hitler*, p. 89.

76 Raymond Carr, *Civil War in Spain* (London, 1986), p. 216.

77 PRO/FO371/24125/W656/8/41, 28 December 1938.

78 FET–JONS, DNII, Murcia, Boletín no. 871, 15 August 1942, AGA, Pres, SGM, caja 16.

79 FET–JONS, DNII, Murcia, Boletín no. 871, 15 August 1942, AGA, Pres, SGM, caja 16; 100,000 Spanish workers were to be sent according to an agreement between the Nazi Labour Front and the Francoist state syndical organisation made on 22 August 1941. In the end, rather fewer men were dispatched because Spain itself was in so dire a need of skilled labour. See Telegram of Heyden-Rynsch to German Foreign Ministry, 23 August 1939, *Documents on German Foreign Policy, 1918–1945*, Series D, vol. XIII (London, 1951), p. 360; Hoare, *Ambassador*, p. 140.

80 Douglas Little, *Malevolent Neutrality: The United States, Great Britain and the Origins of the Spanish Civil War* (Ithaca, NY, 1985), p. 259. Also Enrique Moradiellos, 'The Gentle General: The Official British Perception of General Franco during the Spanish Civil War', in P. Preston and A.L. Mackenzie, *The Republic Besieged: Civil War in Spain, 1936–1938* (Edinburgh, 1996), pp. 1–19.

81 Roberts to Hodgson, PRO/FO371/22668/W4353/317/41, 25 April 1938; Serrano Suñer, *Entre Hendaya y Gibraltar*, p. 79.

82 Robert Hodgson, *Spain Resurgent* (London, 1953), p. 79; W.L. Kleine-Ahlbrandt, *The Policy of Simmering: A Study of British Policy during the Spanish Civil War* (The Hague, 1962), pp. 100–4.

83 González, *La economia política*, p. 46; Viñas et al., *Política*, p. 103. The US supplied petrol during the period 1939–42, granted a loan to buy cotton, and the telecommunications giant ITT had close links with the regime even

before the end of the Civil War. See Biescas and Fernández, 'La economía autárquica', pp. 69–72; J. Dura, 'Las relaciones hispano–norteamericanas durante la segunda guerra mundial, 1939–1945', *Tiempo de Historia*, 86 (January 1982), pp. 68–83. The British government found itself, at times, having to argue strongly against Spain's 'economic nationalism', forcefully pushing British exports on a somewhat reluctant regime anxious 'to develop certain resources in Spain'. See Carceller's comments in 'Financial Report', July 1944, PRO/FO371/39658/C10858.

84 Hodgson, *Spain*, p. 145. British diplomats had urged recognition of Franco's embryonic state in February 1939, 'before American financiers get in before us'. Maxwell Scott to Cadogan, PRO/FO371/24127/W3291/8/41, 7 February 1939. A further British government loan was agreed in April 1941. Memorandum by Hugh Ellis-Rees attached to Hoare–Eden, 11 January 1943.

85 For a fuller account of this complex process see Preston, *Franco*, pp. 167–73.

86 Tusell, *Franco en la guerra civil*, pp. 57–67.

87 See, for example, Lazúrtegui, 'La progresiva industria del hierro y el acero en Italia – posible fuerte expansión de la de España', *Información* (October 1937), pp. 1029–34; 'El nacionalsocialismo – ideas y realidades – la colaboración italo–germánica – sus finalidades y sus medios', *Información* (15 July 1938), pp. 383–5.

88 Viñas, *Guerra*, p. 205.

89 Interview, United Press, Salamanca, July 1937, *Palabras*, p. 148. Franco also denied that foreign debts had been incurred. *Palabras*, p. 260.

90 *La Vanguardia Española*, 18 July 1939. No mention is made here of the role of Axis military aid in the victory of the 'magnificently equipped' army.

91 See, for example, Ramón de Olascoaga, 'La autarquía económica', *Información* (October 1937), pp. 1027–9; 'El comercio en régimen autárquico', *Información* (November 1937), pp. 1059–61; 'El método para realizar la autarquía', *Información* (15 June 1938), pp. 310–11.

92 *ABC*, Seville, *Palabras*, p. 216.

93 For example, 'Informe Carrero sobre la situación de la flota', in FNFF, *Documentos inéditos*, vol. I, pp. 613–36; Franco, speech, 19 April 1938, *Palabras*, p. 50; *Información* (August 1937), pp. 972–3; (June 1943), pp. 305–7; (July 1943), pp. 330–1; 'El carbón y el hierro así en la lucha militar como en la económica – ¡Alerta España!', José María de Areilza, 'Ante la nueva etapa', *Información* (16 December 1939), p. 698. See also Ramón Carande, 'Bases de una política económica', pp. 71–2.

94 See Franco, *Discursos*, p. 20; interview, January 1938, *Palabras*, p. 225.

95 Viñas, *Guerra*, p. 213.

96 Guillén Salaya, *La economía del porvenir* (Madrid, 1945), p. 188.

97 Viñas, *Guerra*, p. 205; Franco, *Discursos*, p. 20, Burgos 5 June 1939; Marqués de Rozalejo, *La industrialización y el resurgimiento de España: hacia una economía nacional* (Madrid, 1942), p. 18.

98 Mihail Manoilescu, *Teoría del proteccionismo y del comercio internacional* (Madrid, 1943). The first Spanish edition appeared in 1929 and was reissued in 1943, published by the Ministry of Trade and Industry and with

a Foreword written by the influential bureaucrat and economist Manuel Fuentes Irurozqui, who was Inspector General of Trade in the Madrid ministry at the time and a powerful advocate of autarky. Manoilescu's theory pointed to the 'weak productivity of agriculture and great productivity of industry', a similar thesis to Antonio Robert and Higinio París. This analysis was also a prominent feature of thinking on the Spanish left during the Republic and Civil War.

99 Azpiazu, *Orientaciones*, esp. pp. 25–48; Robert, *Un problema nacional*; París Eguílaz, *Política de creación de trabajo*.

100 For eighteenth-century antecedents, see Javier Herrero, *Los orígenes del pensamiento reaccionario español* (Madrid, 1971); Guillermo García Pérez, *La economía y los reaccionarios: la Inquisición y los economistas al surgir la España contemporánea* (Madrid, 1974).

101 See the so-called 'Law for the Defence of Industries of National Interest', October, 1939. 'Concesiones especiales a las industrias que se declaren de "interés nacional"', *Información* (30 November 1939), pp. 657–8.

102 Montero, *Los estados modernos*, pp. 310–12. 'Necesidad de una industrialización nacional', *Información* (August 1943), p. 390. On Robert and 'directed protection', see *Un problema nacional*, p. 214. He claims that 80 per cent of total industrial capitalisation in the years 1940 and 1941 was directed towards those sectors favoured by the state.

103 The most intransigent Franco loyalists clung to autarky as a means to industrialisation until the bitter end. See Luis Carrero Blanco, 'Introducción al estudio de un plan coordinado de aumento de la producción nacional' (1957), printed in Viñas, *Guerra*, pp. 323–8.

104 Irurozqui, preface to Manoilescu, *Teoría del proteccionismo*, pp. xiii–xiv.

105 Franco, speech, Día de la Raza, 12 October 1937, *Palabras* (1938), pp. 35–6.

106 Llibert Ferri et al., *Las huelgas contra Franco, 1939–1956* (Barcelona, 1978), p. 26. By 1948 the situation was more desperate and the regime was willing to amend economic autarky to the extent of receivng Marshall Aid. However, it was not sufficiently ready to liberalise *politically* and aid was witheld. Viñas, *Guerra*, pp. 265–87.

107 PRO/FO371/24507/C380/40/41, 2 January 1940.

108 Franco, *Palabras*, p. 263.

109 *Palabras*, p. 303.

110 See I. Fernández de Castro, *De las Cortes de Cádiz al Plan de Desarrollo* (Madrid, 1968), p. 239; Preston, *Franco*, pp. 297–8; Franco, *Palabras*, pp. 300–10.

111 See *Historia 16*, 115 (November 1985), pp. 44–9.

112 Sevilla Guzmán, 'El campesinado', p. 185.

113 Carlos Barciela, Introduction to part II of R. Garrabou et al. (eds.), *Historia agraria de la España contemporánea* (Barcelona, 1986), vol. III, *El fin del al agricultura tradicional*, pp. 383–413; Roque Moreno Fonseret, *La autarquía en Alicante (1939–1952)* (Alicante, 1995), especially pp. 105–28; Barciela, 'Crecimiento y cambio en la agricultura española desde la Guerra Civil', in A. Carreras, J. Nadal and C. Sudriá (eds.), *La economía española en el siglo*

XX (Barcelona, 1986), pp. 261–4; Lorenzo Espinosa, *Dictadura*, pp. 16, 23, 212; Alba, *Sleepless*, pp. 24–5.

114 A process demanded by Calvo Sotelo prior to the war. See 'Principios informadoras', p. 667. See also INE, *Anuario Estadístico de España*, 1952; González, *La economía política*, pp. 102, 117–20; París Eguílaz, *Factores del desarrollo económico español* (Madrid, 1957), p. 122; J. López de Sebastián, *Política agraria en España, 1920–1970* (Madrid, 1970), p. 102; Manuel Fuentes Irurozqui, *Economía e industria nacional* (Madrid, 1948), p. 102; Leal et al., *La agricultura*, pp. 81–2; 'Folleto de propaganda', in FNFF, *Documentos inéditos*, vol. II, 2, pp. 454–5. It was no coincidence that the journal of the food supply service of the state, the CGAT, carried long articles concerned with industrial aggrandisement. For example, 'La renovación de nuestra flota mercante, la creación de nuevas industrias y la puesta en marcha del plan industrial de España, actuación fundamental del Gobierno en el aspecto comercial e industrial', *Alimentación Nacional* (13 November 1942), pp. 37–42.

115 Juan Sardá, 'El Banco de España (1931–1962)', in *El Banco de España: una historia económica* (Madrid, 1970), p. 460; Miguel, *España cíclica*, pp. 173–4.

116 Miguel, *España cíclica*, pp. 176–7.

117 *Arriba*, 1 April, 1948.

118 Folguera, 'La construcción de lo cotidiano', p. 176.

119 *Información* (March 1944), p. 200.

120 Because of the relatively underdeveloped nature of the Spanish stock market, private banks dominated the financing of economic development in Spain. *Información* (May 1944), p. 398. Garnica was on the board of a great many of the most important industrial concerns in Spain in the early 1940s. PRO/FO371/24125/W952/8141, 11 January 1939; *Información* (15 March 1947), 'Designación de vocales para el Consejo Superior Bancario', pp. 218–19. For a critique of this process by a disillusioned Falangist, see Juan Velarde Fuertes: 'Algunos problemas de la banca privada española', in *Notas sobre política económica española* (Madrid, 1954), pp. 93–8. See also Joaquín Cuesta Garrigos, 'Los grandes bancos españoles: su evolución, 1922–1943', *Moneda y Crédito*, 11 (December 1944); Esteban, 'La política', p. 164. See also Sergio Vilar, *La naturaleza del franquismo*, p. 124.

121 Alfonso Churruca, *Minería, industria, y comercio del País Vasco* (San Sebastián, 1951), p. 113; Payne, *The Franco Regime*, p. 389. The profits of the Banco de Bilbao increased from 16.36 million pesetas in 1940 to 76.84 million in 1950. Over the same period the profits of the Banco Hispano Americano rose from 29.71 million to 122.60 million. Similarly, profits at the Banco de Vizcaya leapt from 16.15 million to 83.09 million, at the Banco Central from 2.99 million to 72.70, and at the Banco Urquijo from 6.99 million in 1942 to 29.33 million in 1950.

122 Esteban, 'La política económica', p. 164.

123 París Eguílaz, *Diez años de política económica en España, 1939–1949* (Madrid, 1949), pp. 217–18.

124 Banco de Bilbao, *Annual Reports and Accounts, 1981* (Madrid, 1982). See also Banco de Bilbao, *Memoria, 1936–41* (Madrid, 1942), pp. 16–17; Banco Hispano Americano, *Memoria, 1936–41* (Madrid, 1942), particularly pp. 9–10; Banco de Vizcaya, *Memoria, 1936–40* (Bilbao, 1941), p. 16; *Memoria, 1941* (Bilbao, 1942), pp. 9–10; and *El Banco de Vizcaya en su cincuentenario* (Bilbao, 1950). The Banco de Bilbao, which always stressed the centrality of the agricultural cycle when reporting its profits and opened many branches in rural areas in this era, announced an annual profit figure of 16.3 million pesetas in 1940, which rose to nearly 29 million four years later. By 1950, the bank was able to declare a profit of 77 million pesetas. The capital of the bank more than trebled over the same period. *Agenda Financiera 1951* (Bilbao, 1951), pp. 47–50. See also Churruca, *Minería, industria y comercio*, p. 110.

125 Brenan, *Face of Spain*, p. 124.

126 See also Bernard Roux, 'Latifundismo, reforma agraria y capitalismo en la Península Ibérica', in *Agricultura y Sociedad*, 23 (April–June, 1982).

127 José Luis Leal et al., *La agricultura en el desarrollo capitalista español, 1940–1970* (Madrid, 1975), pp. 9–21.

128 This is the only possible conclusion from an analysis of the interaction of wages and prices, including an account of the operation of the black market and the tax and public-finance structure, which was a reflection of the social structure as maintained by Francoism. See also Biescas and Tuñon de Lara, *España bajo la dictadura*, p. 42. On fiscal policy specifically see Juan J. Fernandez Caínzos, 'La hacienda pública y la acumulación de capital en España (1939–1959); un ensayo de interpretación', PhD thesis, University of Santiago de Compostela (1980).

129 J.G. Ceballos Teresi, *Economía, finanzas, cambios: historia económica, financiera y política de España en el siglo XX* (Madrid, 1932); R. Canosa, *Un siglo de la banca privada (1845–1945); apuntes para la historia de las finanzas españolas* (Madrid, 1945).

130 Muñoz, *El poder de la banca en España* (Madrid, 1969); Ramón Tamames, *Los monopolios en España* (Madrid, 1967), pp. 13–50.

131 Interview, 14 July 1937, *Palabras*, p. 160.

132 *Memoria de la Junta General de Accionistas del Banco de España* (Madrid, 1942), p. 45. The first advance from the Bank to the Nationalist treasury was effected in Burgos on 28 April 1937 – a credit of 200 million pesetas. There would be five further payments during the year, making a total for 1937 of 2,500 million pesetas. By the end of the war the Bank had paid 10,100 million pesetas over to the Nationalist state.

133 As well as this, support was also provided by American multinationals like Texaco and Ford. PRO FO371/24125/W655/8/41; Jackson, *A Concise History*, pp. 51, 107, 138, 153; Biescas and Fernández, 'La economía autárquica', pp. 71–2; Dura, 'Las relaciones hispano-norteamericanos durante la segunda guerra mundial, 1939–1945', in *Tiempo de Historia*, 86 (January 1982), pp. 68–83.

134 PRO/FO371/22668/W6596/317/41, May and November 1938.

135 For instance, Conxita Mir, 'Personal politic i repressió econòmica: l'actuació del tribunal de responsabilitats polítiques sobre els parlamen-

taris Republicans a Lleida entre 1936 i 1939', in Jaume Barrull Pelegrí, *Violència política i ruptura social a Espanya, 1936–1945* (Lleida, 1994), pp. 117–40.

136 See Muñoz, *El poder de la banca*, pp. 60–9.
137 R. Joseph Harrison, *The Spanish Economy in the Twentieth Century* (London, 1985), p. 122; Muñoz, *El poder*, pp. 60–5; Joan Esteban, 'La política económica', p. 164; González, *La economía política*, p. 33.
138 *Información* (August 1937), pp. 966–7.
139 Juan Velarde Fuertes, 'Sobre la decadencia económica de España', *De Economía*, 6, 25/6 (1953).
140 Leal et al., *La agricultura*, p. 18.
141 PRO/FO371/89524/WS1101/5, April 1950. Carlos Rama, *La crisis española del siglo XX* (Madrid, 1962), p. 350; Llibert Ferri, Jordi Muixi and Eduardo Sanjuan, in *Las huelgas contra Franco, 1939–1956* (Barcelona, 1978), p. 28.
142 FET–JONS, DNII, Murcia, Boletín no. 603, 15 April 1942, AGA, Pres, SGM, caja 16. See also 'Informe sobre el paro existente', June 1939, FNFF, *Documento inéditos*, vol. I, pp. 445–62.
143 Letter of Sanz Orrio, Delegado Nacional de Sindicatos to Secretaría General del Movimiento, 20 February 1950, AGA, SGM, caja 59. For most Spaniards emigration was illegal at this time.
144 PRO/FO371/26890/C3986/3/41, March 1941; Aparicio, 'Sobre los comienzos', p. 85. In some areas the normal daily wage for agricultural labourers was as low as 1.5 pesetas, and even less for women. Alba, *Sleepless*, p. 67.
145 PRO/FO371/89526/Z8037/1103/41, Hankey to Bevin, 7 February 1950.
146 Leal et al., *La agricultura*, pp. 81/2.
147 FET–JONS, DNII, Córdoba, Boletín no. 324, 2 January 1942, AGA, Pres, SGM, caja 16. Given that this was a time of deep economic crisis, this is a quite staggering suggestion.
148 Brenan, *Face of Spain*, p. 71. See also pp. 48–54.
149 Leal et al., *La agricultura*, p. 16; J. Fernández Caínzos, *La hacienda pública*, especially pp. 476, 485–93; Tamames, *Introducción*, p. 424.
150 See R. Alonso González and L. Castañón Súarez, *La contribución excepcional sobre beneficios extraordinarios de guerra* (Lugo, 1939).
151 The pre-Civil War Falange had frequently called for tax reform. Fernández, *La hacienda pública*, p. 122; Ridruejo, *Escrito en España*, p. 26; but in the aftermath of the conflict Falangist militants expected difficulty in making such a law work.
152 M. Tuñón de Lara and J.A. Biescas, *España bajo ia dictadura franquista* (Barcelona, 1980), p. 42.
153 Report 29 January 1942, FNFF, *Documentos inéditios*, vol. III, p. 234.
154 See, for example, the report on industrial opinion in Asturias, 1938, AGA, Pres, SGM, vice-secretario, caja 4. See also Fernández, *La hacienda*, pp. 502–18. The tax reform of the finance minister José Larraz, announced in 1940, did little to alter the pre-1936 situation. *Enmienda presentada al Cortes*, November, 1951, AGA, Pres, caja 72.
155 Payne, *Franco Regime*, p. 389.

156 Antonio Robert, *El Nuevo Estado Español: veintecinco años de Movimiento Nacional (1939–1961)* (Madrid, 1961), pp. 512–13.

157 See, Enrique Fuentes Quintana and Juan Plaza Prieto: 'Perspectivas de la economía española', *Revista de Economía Política* (May/September 1952), p. 99.

158 González, *La economía*, pp. 117, 120; Miguel, *España cíclica*, pp. 172–80; Lorenzo Espinosa, *Dictadura*, pp. 16, 25, 72; Moya, *El poder económico*, p. 107; González Portilla and Garmendia, *La posguerra*, pp. 106–15; Clavera at al., *Capitalismo español*, pp. 107–11; Sima Lieberman, *The Contemporary Spanish Economy: A Historical Perspective* (London, 1982), p. 182.

159 See, for example, the introductory comments of the President of the Bilbao Chamber of Commerce to the centenery exhibition of 1986. Cámara de comercio, industria y navegación de Bilbao, *Exposición centenario (1886–1986)*, p. 10.

6   THE WAGES OF AUTARKY (I): SELF-SUFFICIENCY AND INDUSTRY

1 Franco, Vigo, Galicia, 21 August 1942.

2 Ricardo Carballo, *Capitalismo y agricultura en España: la evolución de las relaciones de producción en el campo* (Madrid, 1978) and *Crecimiento económico y crisis estructural en España (1959–1980)* (Madrid, 1981).

3 See, for example, on the need for a more 'rational' exploitation of national resources, N. Zorrilla, 'Problemas latentes de la economía vizcaína', *Información* (September 1943), pp. 327–8; on prices, *Información* (January 1944), pp. 51–2; on the need for imports to modernise the transport infrastructure and to provide scrap for iron and steel production, 'Unas conclusiones acertadas', *Información* (15 November 1947), pp. 911–12; on calls for a 'normalization' of foreign trade, 'Nuestro comercio exterior', *Información* (15 January 1948), p. 1; on industrial and agricultural disequilibria, 'Imperiosidad de un reajuste en nuestro plantamiento industrial', *Información* (15 January 1948), pp. 2–3. It is not the purpose of this study to deny the evident drawbacks of autarky, but to explain the social and ideological roots of such 'distortions'.

4 Banco de Bilbao, *Un siglo en la vida del Banco de Bilbao* (Bilbao, 1957), pp. 300–28.

5 Alfonso de Churruca, *Minería, industria y comercio del País Vasco* (San Sebastián, 1951), p. 69.

6 See, for example, Jesús Pabón, *Cambó* (3 vols.), vol. II (Barcelona, 1969), ch. 6; Borja de Riquer, *L'ultim Cambó (1936–1947); la drete Catalanista davant la guerra civil i el primer franquisme* (Vic, 1996). Ramón de la Sota had been a personal friend of Alfonso XIII: the industrialist and the monarch used, ocasionally, to take tea together on board the King's yacht. R. Ossa Echarabu, *El Bilbao del novecientos: riqueza y poder de la Ría, 1900–1923* (Bilbao, 1969).

7 Lorenzo Espinosa, *Dictadura*; Pedro Fraile Balbín, *Industrialización y grupos de presión: la economia política de la protección en España, 1900–1950* (Madrid, 1991); Antonio Escudero, 'El "lobby" minero vizcaíno', *Historia Social* 7

(1990), pp. 39–68; José Felix de Lequérica, *La actividad económica de Vizcaya en la vida nacional* (Madrid, 1956); Ossa Echaburu, *El Bilbao de novecientos.*

8 He was also fined the sum of 100 million pesetas for his support of 'separatism'. After Sota's death his family continued legal proceedings to recover some of his assets. In a curious twist, it seems that they were legally represented by Ramón Serrano Suñer, Franco's pro-Axis interior and Foreign Minister in the immediate post-war years, when he had been the fiercest opponent of all 'separatism'.

9 See Lorenzo Espinosa, *Dictadura.*

10 In the 1940s, forty-seven banks were absorbed by the seven main institutions. José Antonio Biescas and Eloy Fernández Clemente, 'La economía autárquica', in *Historia 16, La Guerra Civil,* 24 (1986), p. 78.

11 The *Comisiones Reguladoras de la Producción,* resurrected from the 1920s, and the *Comisiones de Incorporación Industrial* were seen as bodies to organise the resources of the country's main economic centres. See París Eguílaz, *El desarrollo económico español,* p. 162; Alarcón, *El triunfo nacional,* pp. 33–6. A decree issued by the *Junta Técnica del Estado,* on the 21 June 1937, created a Military Commission of Industrial Incorporation and Mobilisation enabling a high level of intervention in industries. Through this organism industry in the Basque country was able to use Nationalist financial resources for technical improvements and the extension of facilities of production. Contacts were also made with Nazi Germany to obtain the resources necessary for the production of artillery equipment. See *Altos Hornos de Vizcaya, Memoria,* 1938.

12 'Informe del Delegado de FET–JONS de Vizcaya', 1 July 1940, AGA, Pres, SGM, caja 23; letter of José Finat, Director General de Seguridad, 1 July 1940, caja 67; Lorenzo Espinosa, *Dictadura;* Santiago Torres, *Así los viví: 50 años de un pueblo y de una empresa* (Bilbao, 1990), pp. 118–19; González Portilla and Garmendia, *La guerra civil en el País Vasco: política y economía* (Madrid, 1988), pp. 79–149.

13 See *Información* (June/July, 1937), pp. 893–4.

14 'En el primer aniversario de la liberación de Bilbao', *Información* (15 June 1938), pp. 301–3.

15 *Información* (15 June 1938), p. 302. See also Altos Hornos de Vizcaya, SA, *Libro del cincuentenario* (Bilbao, 1952), pp. 94–104.

16 Torres, *Así los viví,* pp. 115–16.

17 Alba, *Sleepless,* p. 85.

18 *Información* (15 June 1938), p. 303.

19 Clavera et al., *Capitalismo español,* pp. 96–7, 126–9, 157–8, 207–13; Ridruejo, *Escrito en España,* pp. 102–6; Lorenzo Espinosa, *Dictadura,* pp. 22, 74–7; González Portilla and Garmendia, *La posguerra,* pp. 41, 105, 112–13; José María Marcet Coll, *Mi ciudad y yo: veinte años en una alcaldía 1940–1960* (Barcelona, 1963), p. 163; Harrison, *An Economic History,* p. 131; Jordi Catalán, *La economía española y la segunda guerra mundial* (Barcelona, 1995).

20 Ferri et al., *Las huelgas,* p. 27. See also González and Portilla Garmendia, *La posguerra,* pp. 41, 105, 122–3; Lorenzo Espinosa, *Dictadura,* pp. 22, 74–7,

97, 115; Clavera et al., *Capitalismo español*, pp. 49, 96–7, 126–9, 157–8, 207–8, 212–3; Biescas, 'La economía autárquica'; Viñas et al., *Política comercial*, pp. 249, 256, 260, 300, 325, 412; Serrano Suñer, *Entre Hendaya*, p. 394. The black market allowed room for manoeuvre to Catalan industry too. Marcet Coll, *Mi ciudad y yo*, p. 163; Albert Ribas i Massana, *L'Economía Catalana sota el franquisme (1939–1953); efectes de la política econòmica de postguerra sobre la industria i les finances de Catalunya* (Barcelona, 1978), pp. 155–80; Junta de Ordenación Económico-social de la Provincia de Barcelona, *Plan de ordenación económica y social* (Barcelona, 1947).

21 Lorenzo Espinosa, *Dictadura*, pp. 89–108.

22 Lorenzo Espinosa, *Dictadura*, pp. 173–9. The intervention of the state in the chemical industry had, according to the President of Nitratos de Castilla, produced a situation with 'innumerable possibilities'. Letter of Consejero Delegado del Consejo de Industria, Ministerio de Industria y Comercio, to Director General de Industria, 31 January 1948, AGA, Industria, DGI, Sec. Gen, caja 7105. Sefanitro, for example, although only producing around 14,000 tons of ammonia sulphate in 1951, registering profits of over 10 million pesetas, in the following year produced five times as much. By 1954 profits had hit the 50 million peseta mark. The production of fertilisers, quite essential to the functioning of the economy, formerly supplied through importation, ultimately underwent a dramatic change as a direct result of the encouragement of the state.

23 See Ministerio de Industria y Comercio, *Catálogo oficial de la producción industrial de España* (Madrid, 1938), pp. 21–2. Production was slow at first because of difficulties obtaining production machinery from Nazi Germany, first because of difficulties in obtaining the necessary foreign exchange, and, after 1942, because of the increasing competition for the resources of I.G. Farben, Francoist industries' collaborators in this project, as the German war effort came under increasing strain.

24 Total production in the period 1930–5 was 6.93 million tons, increasing to 10.9 million from 1940–5, and to 12.99 million during the next five years. By a law of 18 June 1942 the company was boosted by an injection of funds from INI. The President of the company was the banker the Marqués de Urquijo. Duro-Felguera, during the first eight post-Civil War years, augmented its total share capital three times. At the end of December 1939, total capital was 77.5 million pesetas. In April 1941, this grew to 125 million, and two years later to 175 million. Finally, in April 1947, capital was increased to 225 million pesetas. This investment growth was a reflection of the company's profit record. The declared annual profit in 1940 was 7.3 million pesetas, more than doubling itself by 1943. By 1950, profits were slightly short of 50 million pesetas.

25 See *BOE*, 15 December 1939. For a typical critique of foreign domination of Spanish industry verging on the xenophobic, see Virgilio Sevillano Carbajál, *¿España de quien?* (Madrid, 1936).

26 Legislation, in October 1939, specifically limited the level of foreign capital invested in companies in Spain to 25 per cent of the total. Originally the plan had been to limit foreign participation to 33 per cent, but it seems that Franco himself insisted on reducing it further. Letter of Alarcón to Minis-

terio de Industria y Comercio, 10 December 1940, AGA, Industria, caja 7177.

27 Juergen B. Donges, *La industrialización en España (1939–1975); políticas, logros y perspectivas* (Barcelona, 1976), pp. 40–4, 48; *Memorias del INI, 1941–1942*, annexe 1, 'Comunicaciones de la Presidencia a los Consejos Técnicos de Marina Mercante, de Electricidad, de Combustibles Líquidos y Lubricantes, Siderúrgico de Combustibles Sólidos y de Investigaciones Mineras' (Madrid, 1942).

28 For a very uncritical account, see A. Ballesteros, *Juan Antonio Suanzes (1891–1977)* (Madrid, 1994).

29 See Manuel Valdes Larrañaga, *De la Falange al Movimiento (1936–1952)*, Fundación Nacional Francisco Franco (Madrid, 1994), p. 8.

30 See Manuel-Jesús González and Pedro Schwartz, *Una historia del Instituto Nacional de Industria (1941–1976)* (Madrid, 1978), pp. 22–37.

31 See Ramón Garriga, *La España de Franco* (Madrid, 1976), p. 385.

32 INI, *Notas en relación con la creación y desenvolvimiento de este Instituto* (Madrid, 1941), pp. 26–7.

33 Trythall, *Franco*, p. 214.

34 See Ministerio de Industria y Comercio, *Catálogo oficial de la producción industrial de España*, vol. I, p. 167.

35 See Lieberman, *Contemporary Spanish Economy*, p. 171; and Whealey, *Hitler*, p. 120.

36 Boletín del Estado, 17 May 1942, Schwartz and González, *Una historia*, p. 19.

37 *BOE*, 30 September 1941.

38 On the *principio de subsidiariedad*, which laid down that public funds were subsidiary to private capital (theoretically, as soon as an economic activity became profitable it would be taken over again by private capital), see José Maravall, *Dictatorship and Political Dissent* (New York, 1978), p. 20; and Germán Fernández Farreras, 'En torno al procedimiento de creación de empresas nacionales: especial referencia al principio de subsidiariedad', *Revista de Administración Pública*, 80 (May–August, 1976).

39 See Pablo Martín Aceña and Francisco Comín, 'El estado en la industrialización española de la posguerra: el Instituto Nacional de Industria', in Leandros Prados de la Escosura and Vera Zamagni (eds.), *El desarrollo económico en la Europa del sur: España e Italia en perspectiva histórica* (Madrid, 1992), pp. 421–43. On the IRI, see Alexander de Grand, 'Cracks in the Facade', *European History Quarterly* 3, (1991), p. 525. There was certainly an element of mimicry in the setting up of the INI. Franco was very impressed with what he perceived had been achieved by the IRI under Mussolini. Schwartz and González, *Una historia*, p. 15. But the creation of such a public body was in no way unusual in Europe during this era, Prados de la Escosura and Zamagni, *El desarrollo*, p. 421.

40 Schwartz and González, *Una historia*, p. 29.

41 The provisions of the law of 24 October 1939, allowing for 50 per cent reductions in taxes for companies of 'national interest' was clarified in 1947 and 1954 specifying that the benefit applied 'to every class of provincial and municipal exaction and imposition'. See *Proyecto de decreto aclarando el de 14*

de mayo de 1947 sobre reducciones tributarias en las empresas de interés nacional, 20 July 1954, AGA, Industria, caja 7126.

42 See Antonio Robert, 'El estado y la economía', in *Ciclo de conferencias sobre temas de carácter económico organizado por la Junta de Cultura de Vizcaya y la Cámara Oficial de Comercio, Industria y Navegación de Bilbao* (Bilbao, 1943).

43 Dirección General de Industria y Comercio, *La política industrial en la Nueva España* (Madrid, 1942), pp. 31–40.

44 Lucas Beltrán Florez, *La industria algodonera española* (Barcelona, 1943), pp. 57–8.

45 This level was second only to investment in the chemical industry – also a leading priority of the Francoist state. See J. Borrell y Macia, *Instalación y modificación de industrias* (Barcelona, 1943).

46 The added motivation for such a venture was that this production would not entail increasing the size of the Barcelona proletariat, since the new factories were to be in the provinces of Santander and Valencia.

47 The company made a profit in 1948 and paid a modest dividend the following year. In 1950, profits reached 13 million pesetas. Banco de Bilbao, *Agenda financiera*, p. 241.

48 *Agenda financiera*, p. 238.

49 *Centro de Estudios Económicos y Sociales*, 'El estado ante el desarrollo económico' (Madrid, 1960).

50 Ministerio de Industria y Comercio, Dirección General de Industria, *La política industrial en la Nueva España* (Madrid, 1942), pp. 9–10.

51 See *Información* (July 1944), p. 2.

52 Fernández Caínzos, 'La hacienda', p. 231.

53 Martín Aceña and Comín, 'El estado en la industrialización', p. 421.

54 See, Fabian Estapé, 'Algunos problemas actuales de la economía española', conferencia inaugural del curso 1958–9, Universidad de Barcelona, in *Apuntes de política económica* (Barcelona, 1973), pp. 17–18; 'Necesidades de vehículos en España', AGA, Pres, SGM, caja 36; Eric Nordlinger, *Soldiers in Politics: Military Coups and Governments* (Englewood, NJ, 1977), pp. 166–70.

55 See, for example, Beltrán Florez, *La industria algodonera española*, pp. 66–74; Martín Aceña and Comín, 'El estado en la industrialización'.

56 The province with the most factories of this sort after Barcelona was Alicante, with 107.

57 *Estadísticas de la Sección de Trabajo de la Industria textil algodonera* (Madrid, 1942).

58 INI, *Breve résumen sobre las finalidades y actuación del INI: años 1941–1946* (Madrid, 1947), p. 71.

59 *Agenda financiera*, p. 242.

60 Banco de Bilbao, *Un siglo en la vida*, p. 63.

61 Ibid. Oriol was a prominent figure within the post-Civil War political structure in Bilbao and was on the board of a great many of the biggest companies. On the centrality of energy generation in the Spanish economy, see Carles Sudriá, 'Un factor determinante: la energía', in Jordi Nadal, et al. (eds.), *La economía española en el siglo XX: una perspectiva histórica* (Barcelona, 1987), especially pp. 330–40.

62 Lorenzo Espinosa, *Dictadura*, p. 139. These were principally the leading figures of the Basque banking community. Victor de Chávarri, Marqués de Triano, was chairman of AHV. Ministerio de Industria, *Catálogo*, p. 63. Pedro Careaga, Conde de Cadagua, was on the board of directors of many manufacturing, chemical and shipping companies, including SEFANITRO and Naviera Aznar. He was also President of the Banco de Vizcaya. The Conde de Arteche, another of the figurehead personalities of the Francoist economic elite, was chairman of Iberduero and President of the Banco de Bilbao. He was on the board of directors of many of the manufacturing, shipping and railway companies of the area in the 1930s and 1940s. In 1946, Franco awarded him the Grand Cross of Isobel la Católica in recognition of his 'economic achievements'. The Caudillo also made him a member of the Francoist pseudo-parliament, the *Cortes*. *Información*, 31 October 1946, p. 964. On 18 July 1950, the occasion of the fourteenth anniversary of the military rising against the Republic, Arteche was ennobled by Franco for his 'untiring labour in the interests of the prosperity of the national industry and economy'. See *Figuras de Hoy* (Madrid, 1956); PRO/FO371/89484/WS/1017/5, Hankey to Younger, 18 July 1950. Lorenzo Espinosa, *Dictadura*, pp. 176–87.

63 See Juan Velarde Fuertes, *Apuntes editados en la Facultad de Ciencias Económicas* (Madrid, 1965); Carlos Muñoz Linares, *El monopolio de la industria eléctrica* (Madrid, 1954); 'La concentración del capital en las sociedades y empresas españolas', *Revista de Economía Política*, 3, 3 (January 1952), 221–59; Fermín de la Sierra, 'La situación monopolista de algunas industrias españolas', *Revista de Economía Política*, 2, 1 (May 1950), pp. 3–37; *La concentración económica en las industrias básicas españolas* (Madrid, 1953). The functions of economic decision-making were carried out within these bodies behind the mask of 'state intervention in the economy', which, in reality, was intervention in the form of social control.

64 Registered profits were 7.61 million pesetas in just the period 1 September–31 December 1944. In 1945, they rose to more than 30 million. By 1947, they had risen to 50 million. By 1950, they were more than 100 million. See *Agenda Financiera*, p. 66.

65 Dirección General de Industria, *La industrialización de la energía eléctrica en España* (Madrid, 1960).

66 See Fomento de la producción nacional, *Homenaje de Cataluña liberada a su Caudillo Franco* (Barcelona, 1940); D. Pastor Petit, *Los dossiers secretos*, pp. 297, 375, 425; Abella, *Finales de enero*, pp. 40–3, 162; Riquer, *Historia*, p. 62.

67 *Información* (31 January 1939), p. 33. For an effusive account of the significance to industrialists of the capture of Catalonia, see the editorial of 15 February 1939, 'La Conquista de Cataluña', pp. 65–6.

68 *Información* (15 April 1939), p. 190.

69 Marcet Coll, *Mi ciudad y yo*, p. 21.

70 Rafael Tasis, 'El paper polític de la burguesía', *La Nostra Revista*, (Mexico) (January/February 1957), republished in *L'Avenç* (January 1979), p. 36.

71 On this relative continuity, see, for example, Xavier Marcet, 'Terrassa, 1939; exploració d'una continuitat,' *L'Avenç*, 126 (May 1989), pp. 56–9; Martí

Marín i Corbera, 'FET y de las JONS a Sabadell, 1939–1945; Els primers temps', *L'Avenç*, 157 (March 1992), pp. 32–9.

72 See Riquer, 'Dossier: el franquisme i la burgesia Catalana'; Albert Ribas i Massana, 'Industrials i banquers', pp. 24–8, *L'Avenç* (January 1979), p. 19.

73 *Informe sobre la situación de Cataluña*, August 1940, AGA, Pres, SGM, caja 30.

74 See Ernest Lluch, *El pensament econòmic a Catalunya, 1760–1840: els orígens ideològics del proteccionisme i la presa de consciència de la burgesia Catalana* (Barcelona, 1973).

75 Thomàs, *Falange, guerra civil*, pp. 42, 99, 239–40, 331.

76 Francesca Minguella, 'El tèxtil cotoner i la metallúrgia Catalana', *L'Avenç* (January 1979), p. 40. For a summary of recent evidence pointing to a lack of discrimination by the state towards Catalan industry, see, for example, Carles Sudrià, 'Catalunya i la política econòmica del primer franquisme: una reconsideració'; Jordi Catalan, 'La política industrial: l'impacte a catalunya'; Jordi Calvet, 'Indústria i burgesia durant la postguerra'; Carme Molinero, 'Les actituds dels industrials Catalans davant la política econòmica del primer franquisme'; all in *L'Avenç*, 149 (June 1991), pp. 24–60. See Ribas i Massana, *L'economia Catalana sota el franquisme (1939–1953)* (Barcelona, 1978), p. 132, for a contrary view.

77 The textile industry benefited from the tranquil labour relations which the regime ensured, but suffered from the difficulties in obtaining raw materials and machinery. However, according to the administration, many factories which had been in a precarious position before the Civil War had recovered and the profit margin was sufficient 'to satisfy the industrialist'. In spite of complaints about the unemployment caused by a lack of raw materials, the state was able to declare that 'we couldn't wish for more than that all industries could be organised in a similar way'. Report, DNII, *Informe sobre Sabadell*.

78 See Clavera et al., *Capitalismo español*, pp. 206–14; Lorenzo Espinosa, *Dictadura*, pp. 29–30, 219–33; Leal et al., *La agricultura*, pp. 16–88.

79 Rafael Tasis. 'El paper polític'.

80 PRO/FO371/89524/WS1101/5, April 1950; Francesc Cabana, *Bancs i banquers a Catalunya: Capitols per una historia* (Barcelona, 1972), pp. 41–54, 249–51.

81 This apparent weakening of Catalan banking within the national panorama was part of a long historical process rather than a result of the Francoist state's anti-Catalan discrimination in the 1940s. See Cabana, *Bancs i banquers a Catalunya*, esp. pp. 300–12; Ribas i Massana, *L'economia Catalana*.

82 *Informe sobre la situación de Cataluña*, August 1940.

83 See José María Lorenzo Espinosa, 'Elecciones sindicales de postguerra en Vizcaya', and Carme Molinero and Pere Ysàs, 'Un instrumento esencial del régimen franquista: la organización sindical', in Tusell et al., *El régimen de Franco* (Madrid, 1993), pp. 89–98; 'Luchas obreras y oposición al franquismo en la Cataluña de postguerra', in Javier Tusell, Alicia Alted Vigil and Abdón Mateos (eds.), *La oposición al régimen de Franco* (Madrid, 1990), 19–27, respectively.

84 See, for example, J. Fernández Casas, 'La disolución de las agrupaciones industriales', *Nueva Economía Nacional,* 97 (15 August 1939). Textile industrialists created several organisations for their activities. In February 1940, the Provincial Syndical Delegate in Barcelona, Pio Irurzún, reminded the Party that any economic association had to be subordinated to the 'discipline of the Movement'. Circular No. 3 of Delegado Sindical Provincial de Barcelona, February 1940, AGA, SGM, caja 30. In 1944, what was effectively a textile employers' consortium (Consorcio de Industriales Textiles Algodoneros, CITA), was created. Although the principal publication of the Barcelona industrialists, *El Trabajo-Nacional,* was not republished after the war until 1943, their main organisation, the Fomento de Trabajo reappeared with a new name, the Servicio Sindical de Alta Cultura Económica. In the industrial town of Terrassa, a centre of textile production in Barcelona, the local industrial institute (Instituto Industrial) continued to have considerable influence. Xavier Marcet i Gisbert, 'La Guerra Civil a Terrassa', in various authors, *Catalunya i la guerra civil, 1936–1939; cicle de Conferències* (Barcelona, 1988), p. 205.
85 See, for example, the comments of the industrialist José María Marcet Coll, *Mi ciudad y yo,* p. 26.
86 Report, *Fracaso de la CNS en Barcelona,* 11 May 1940, AGA, SGM, caja 30.
87 FET–JONS, DNII, Barcelona, Boletín no. 337, 8 January 1942, AGA, SGM, caja 16.
88 FET–JONS, DNII, Barcelona, 'Informe', 11 June 1940, AGA, Pres, SGM.
89 Letter marked 'reservada' of Fermín Sanz Orrio to José Luis de Arrese, 9 May 1945, and *Dictamen sobre la creación de los consorcios de industriales algodoneros y sederos y su incompatibilidad con el sindicato vertical textil,* 12 March 1945, AGA, SGM, caja 41.
90 Ribas i Massana, 'Industrials i banquers', p. 27. PRO/FO371/96165/ XC3526, 'Survey of *cajas especiales* – Special accounts or autonomous bodies', December 1951; letter of José María Fontana, head of the national textile syndicate, to José Solís Ruíz, National Syndical Delegate, 10 July 1952, AGA, SGM, caja 87.
91 FET–JONS, DNII, Barcelona, 'Informe', 20 April 1940, AGA, Pres, caja 30.
92 In July 1939, it came to the attention of the National Delegate of the party investigation department that guarantees of reliability issued to prisoners in some camps, particularly in industrial areas, were only validated if they had the approval of a local individual of 'economic solvency'. Letter of Secretaria Nacional de la DNII, 27 July 1939, AGA, Pres, SGM, caja 7.
93 *Nota Informativa – Sindicatos,* 20 June 1940, AGA, SGM, caja 31.
94 See Botti, *Cielo y dinero,* pp. 73–100, for example.
95 'Informe de FET–JONS sobre las Delegaciones Provinciales de Barcelona, Tarragona, Lérida y Gerona', 1938? AGA, Pres, SGM, caja 31, p. 3.
96 'Informe', p. 4.
97 'Informe', p. 1.
98 Maximiano García Venero, *Falange en la guerra de España: la Unificación y Hedilla* (Paris, 1967), p. 299. Letter of 28 August 1939 to the Secretario-General del Movimiento, AGA, Pres, SGM, caja 31.

99 'Informe político de Barcelona', November 1940, AGA, Pres, SGM, caja 31.

100 'Informe', p. 2.

101 J.M. and J.A. Parpal, *Ferran-Valls Taberner: un polític per a la cultura Catalana* (Barcelona, 1970), p. 262. With the banker Juan March and King Alfonso XIII himself, Ventosa managed to channel $85 million to the insurgent treasury during the Civil War. Jackson, *Breve historia*, pp. 54, 109; Viñas, *Guerra*, 179–188; Plenn, *Wind in the Olive Trees*, pp. 25–7, 142–3; Southworth, *AntiFalange*, p. 186.

102 FET–JONS, Barcelona, 'Informe acerca de FET de las JONS en Cataluña', June, 1937, AGA, Pres, SGM, caja 30.

103 See Juan Claudio Güell Churruca, Conde de Ruisenada, 'Actividad y pensamiento de los tiempos rojos – por que Cataluña tuvo fe en la victoria del Caudillo', *La Vanguardia Española* (1 March 1939). He had been a prominent member of the Nationalist Comisión de Industria y Comercio, a kind of proto-ministry set up in the rebel zone in August 1936. A useful brief summary on Catalan social attitudes to the dictatorship is provided by Borja de Riquer i Permanyer, 'Rebuig, passivitat i suport. Actituts polítiques Catalanes davant el primer franquisme (1939–1950)', in Tusell et al., *La oposición al régimen de Franco* (Madrid, 1990), vol. II, pp. 239–49. For more on the fifth column, see also J.M. Carretero, *La quinta columna* (Madrid, 1940); Manuel Ulibarri, *La quinta columna* (Havana, 1943); *El País Semanal*, 13 February 1977, 'Historia. Quinta Columna: los espías de Franco en la España Republicana'.

104 FET–JONS, Barcelona, 'Informe', 17 September 1940, Secretaría General del Movimiento, AGA, Pres, SGM, caja 30. See also 'Informe sobre varios camaradas que pudieran desempeñar cargos en la organización', 8 May 1940, caja 30.

105 José Bertran y Musitu, a founding leader of the *Lliga Regionalista*, a close associate of Cambó and president of several leading firms in the region, was the director of Franco's counter-espionage organisation in Catalonia during the Civil War and subsequently reorganised the *Somatén*, one of the Barcelona industrial class's parallel police forces. Solé i Sabaté, *La repressió*, p. 55; Pastor Petit, *Los dossiers secretos*, p. 243. The Somatén appeared in several other areas of the country and its reorganisation was formalised by a state decree in July 1945. See also José María March, *El Somatén: su origen y naturaleza, su historia y organización: la salvación de España* (Barcelona, 1923).

106 Expediente 650/'sumarísimo' no. 3062, ATRP.

107 Contacts were maintained through operations of espionage, information and finance for the Francoist cause. 'Informe Confidencial para la Secretaría General del Movimiento' from the Delegación Territorial de Cataluña de FET–JONS, 22 February 1938; 'Informe acerca de FET de las JONS en Cataluña', June 1937, AGA, Pres, SGM, caja 30; Fontana, *Los Catalanes*, pp. 295–305, 308–16.

108 A. Ruiz Vilaplana, *Burgos Justice: A Year's Experience of Nationalist Spain* (1938), pp. 141–2. Also Muniesa, *La burguesía Catalana ante la Segunda República Española, 1931–1936* (2 vols.), vol. I (Barcelona, 1985/6), pp. 260–3.

109 Some Falangists resented the influence in San Sebastián society of old affiliates of the Lliga or Carlists, like José Parellada who was named as President of the Cámara de la Propiedad Urbana de Barcelona, although he had been one of the organisers of the Carlist Servicio de Información during the Civil War. Thomàs, *Falange*, p. 229. Other elite organisations were the Unión Industrial Metalúrgica, the Fomento del Trabajo-Nacional, the Asociación de Banqueros, the Comité Algodonero, the Cámaras de la Propiedad, Industria, Comercio, y Navagación. The representatives of certain of the biggest companies in the city, Aguas de Barcelona, CHADE (Cambó), and Tranvías (the Barcelona tram company), also had influence.

110 PRO/FO371/24125/W585/8/41, January 1939.

111 The *Requeté* was the Carlist militia.

112 'Informe acerca de FET de las JONS'.

113 For example, 'Informe sobre Sabadell', March 1940, AGA, Pres, caja 30.

114 For example, Juan Ventosa Calvell, 'La economía española y la coyuntura mundial', *La Vanguardia Española* (20 February 1940). Ventosa was Finance Minister in the government of General Berenguer in 1930. After the Civil War, he came to Spain, from Belgium, where he had spent most of the conflict, to offer his services to the new government but was apparently told that he was not required in a public role. 'Informe', FET–JONS, DNII, 'oficio' no. 13,510, 9 February, 1940, AGA, Pres, caja 30, citing information supplied by the Delegación Provincial. However, he had been close to Falangists in Burgos during the early war days and was there to salute the first contingent of the party militia dispatched to the front, with arm raised and singing the Falangist anthem, *Cara al Sol*. One of his sons was killed fighting in Franco's army. Another was a post-war city councillor in Barcelona. After the conflict, Ventosa assisted the nascent Francoist regime in having returned to Spain some of the gold reserves sent to France by the Republican authorities during the war. In 1943, he was named by Franco as a member of the dictator's pseudo-parliament the *Cortes*. He contributed to the slow reorientation of economic policy towards a more formal liberal orthodoxy and against extreme state interventionism. This was a slow process, only finally consummated by the major reform of 1959. See, for example, 'La permanencia de las leyes económicas', speech to the Real Academia de Ciencias Morales y Políticas, 29 May 1944 (Madrid, 1944). Also Fontana, *Los Catalanes*, p. 250; Muniesa, *La burguesía catalana*, pp. 261–2; *L'Avenç* (January 1979), p. 18.

115 By 1950, the company was able to announce an annual profit of more than 84 million pesetas. *Agenda financiera*, p. 224.

116 Letter of Sanz Orrio to Ministro Secretario General del Movimiento, 23 September 1942, AGA, SGM, caja 9. The annual profits of the Union Española de explosivos doubled during the 1940s.

117 FET–JONS, DNII, Barcelona, *Boletín* no. 397, 21 January 1942, and *Boletín* 457, 12 February 1942, AGA, SGM, caja 21. On the power of the big companies and distributors to ride roughshod over the syndical organisation, see the party report of 1951 in AGA, SGM, caja 72.

118 FET–JONS, DNII, Barcelona, *Boletín* no. 428, 28 January 1942.

119 See, for example, Fernando Valls y Taberner, 'La falsa ruta', *La Vanguardia*

Española (15 February 1939); 'José Antonio y Cataluña', *La Vanguardia Española* (2 March 1939); and *Reafirmación espiritual de España* (Madrid/ Barcelona, 1939). Before 1936, Valls had been one of the leading figures of the Lliga. With the outbreak of the Civil War he fled to Italy and joined up with the Falangist organisation. In the post-war he became a kind of 'touring ambassador' for Franco. See Muniesa, *La burguesía Catalana*, p. 263. Collaboration was justified philosophically by pointing to the common ideals of spirituality, order and unity as developed by Balmes. See, for example, Valls y Taberner, *Balmes ante el problema constitucional de España* (Vich, 1939).

120 Mateu Pla was a personal friend of the Caudillo, having been a captain stationed at Franco's military headquarters during the conflict. He was also the nephew of the Bishop of Salamanca, Enrique Pla y Deniel, the most explicit supporter within the hierarchy of the Spanish Catholic Church of Franco's 'Crusade' during the Civil War. See Thomàs, *Falange, guerra civil*, p. 331; Preston, *Franco*, pp. 184–5, 188–9.

121 See Riquer and Culla, *El franquisme*, p. 53. On the sense of continuity in power in Barcelona, see Borja de Riquer, 'El "Nuevo Estado" i l'ajunta-ment de Barcelona: la classe política del primer franquisme (1939–1957)', *L'Avenç*, 126 (May 1989), pp. 16–23; Marcet, 'Terrassa'; Carme Molinero and Pere Ysàs, 'Els industrials Catalans durant la postguerra (1939–1951)', *L'Avenç*, 126 (May 1989), pp. 24–9.

122 During the Civil War, Mateu performed some valuable tasks for the Nationalists, entrusted with some 'delicate' missions in both France and Switzerland, both countries in which important Catalan exiles were living for much of the war.

7 THE WAGES OF AUTARKY (II): THE MYTH AND REALITY OF RURAL LIFE

1 Ramón Serrano Suñer, Minister of Interior, 'Discurso pronunciado en la Albufera de Valencia contestando al Presidente de la Federación Sindical de Agricultores Arroceros de España', 23 April 1940, in *De la victoria*, p. 130.

2 Report, 21 March 1942, of Juan de Leyva y Andía, to the Ministry of Agriculture, p. 17, in AGA, Pres, SGM, caja 3; Sanz Orrio, report, October, 1941, p. 6, AGA, Pres, SGM, caja 9. On emigration, see Andres Sorel, *Cuarto mundo: emigración española en Europa* (Madrid, 1974); David Gregory, *La odisea andaluza: una emigración hacia Europa* (Madrid, 1978). On emigration restrictions in the 1940s, see Jesús García Fernández, *La emigración exterior de España* (Barcelona, 1965), especially pp. 15–28.

3 Leyva y Andía, report, p. 16. On the exploitation of small landowners in the post-war years, see also Eduardo Sevilla Guzmán, 'El campesinado en el desarrollo capitalista español (1939–1975)', in Preston, *España en crisis: la evolución y decadencia del régimen de Franco* (Madrid, 1977), pp. 183–216; Antonio Miguel Bernal, 'Riegos: los latifundios del franquismo inicial (1939–1950)'; Eduardo Sevilla Guzmán and Manuel González de Molina, 'Política social agraria del primer franquismo', both in J.L. García Delgado (ed.), *El primer franquismo* (Madrid, 1989), pp. 124–33 and 135–87; Cas-

tillo, *Propietarios muy pobres*. A theory of the apparent dichotomy of eulogising and criticising the peasant is suggested by Matossian, 'Ideologies of
Delayed Industrialization', esp. p. 227.

4 Alejandro López López, *El boicot de la derecha a las reformas de la segunda
república: la minoría agraria, el rechazo constitucional y la cuestión de la tierra*
(Madrid, 1984). Also Aguila Tejerina, *Ideología y fascismo*, pp. 191–4.

5 Castillo, *Propietarios*, pp. 397/8. On the conflictual background of state–
peasant relations, see Jaume Torras, *Liberalismo y rebeldía campesina,
1820–1823* (Madrid, 1976); Josep Fontana, 'Transformaciones agrarias y
crecimiento económico en la España contemporánea', in *Cambio económico y
actitudes políticas en la España del siglo XIX* (Barcelona, 1973); M. Ardit
Lucas, *Revolución liberal y revuelta campesina, 1793–1840* (Madrid, 1977);
Antonio Miguel Bernal, *La lucha por la tierra en la crisis del Antiguo Régimen*
(Madrid, 1979); V. Benítez Fernández, *Carlismo y rebeldía campesina: un
estudio sobre la conflictividad social en Cantabria durante la crisis final del
Antiguo Régimen* (Madrid, 1988).

6 Gay de Montellà, *Autarquía*, p. 21.

7 See Francisco Alburquerque, 'Métodos de control político de la población
civil: el sistema de racionamiento de alimentos y productos básicos impuesto
en España tras la última guerra civil', in Manuel Tuñón de Lara (ed.),
Estudios sobre la historia de España, vol. II (Madrid, 1981), pp. 407–32. See
also, Brenan, *Face of Spain*, p. 217.

8 On the background of rural conflict, see Bernal, *La lucha por la tierra*; Juan
Díaz del Moral, *Historia de la agitaciones campesinas andaluzas – Córdoba*
(Madrid, 1967), for example.

9 Claudio Sánchez Albornoz, *España hace un siglo: una econmía dual* (Barcelona,
1968); José Luis García Delgado, 'Problemas de la industria española: una
visión del conjunto', in Carballo et al., *Crecimiento económico y crisis estructural
en España, 1959–1980* (Madrid, 1980), pp. 407–26; Francisco Alburquerque
and A. Ramos, 'Desarrollo desigual: notas sobre la formación social andaluza',
in Carballo et al., *Crecimiento económico*, pp. 561–78; Cándido Muñóz Cidad
and Laureano Lázaro Araújo, 'El desarrollo desigual en España', in Carballo et
al., *Crecimiento económico*, pp. 579–601. For the industrialists' argument in
favour of some kind of agrarian renovation to facilitate the development of
national industry, see, for example, *El Economista*, 31 July 1943, 2802, p. 857.

10 Jordi Nadal, *El fracaso de la revolución industrial en España, 1814–1913*
(Barcelona, 1975); Carballo et al., 'La formación del capitalismo industrial
en España (1855–1959)', in Carballo et al. *Crecimiento económico*,
pp. 11–63.

11 Fontana, *Cambio económico y actitudes políticas*. On the positive evaluation of
the notion of a 'national essence' see, for example, Unamuno, *En torno al
casticismo*; Maeztu, *Defensa de la hispanidad*; Giménez Caballero, *Genio de
España*; and Ganivet, *Idearium español*.

12 Viñas, *Guerra*, pp. 102–3.

13 See Ernst Bloch, 'Nonsychronism and the Obligation to its Dialectics',
originally published in 1932, as part of *Erbschaft Dieser Zeit*, reprinted in *New
German Critique*, 11 (Spring 1977), and the accompanying introduction,
Anson Rabinbach, 'Unclaimed Heritage: Ernst Bloch's *Heritage of Our Times*

and the Theory of Fascism'; Bloch, 'Efectos políticos de desarrollo desigual', in K. Lenk, *El concepto de ideología* (Buenos Aires, 1971), pp. 109–18.

14 Iniesta, *Garra Marxista*, pp. 267–8, 282. Also, on rural schools, Antonio Molero Pintado, *La educación durante la segunda república y la guerra civil (1931–1939)* (Madrid, 1991), pp. 298–9; 445–7. On the general process of rural decline, see Julio Caro Baroja, *Estudios sobre la vida tradicional española* (Barcelona, 1968), especially pp. 253–74; Víctor Pérez Díaz, *Emigración y cambio social: procesos migratorios y vida rural en Castilla* (Barcelona, 1971), pp. 13–45; 159–225.

15 Gerardo Salvador Merino, Delegado Nacional de Sindicatos, *Pueblo*, 21 June 1941, cited in Castillo, *Propietarios*, p. 429. See also Dionisio Martín Sanz, *Técnica y política agraria* (Madrid, 1946), p. 10. Carlist militia volunteers numbered 62,722 and Falangists totalled 207,933 according to Ricardo de la Cierva, 'The Nationalist Army in the Spanish Civil War', in R. Carr (ed.), *The Republic and the Civil War in Spain* (London, 1971), p. 200. The Minister of Agriculture still talked in the 1950s of this debt to be paid to farmers. Barciela, 'Introducción', p. 391.

16 Aróstegui, 'Sociedad y guerra', in *Historia 16, La Guerra Civil*, 14 (Madrid, 1986), pp. 12–20; Tuñón de Lara and Biescas, *España bajo*, p. 28.

17 Josep M. Bricall, 'La economía española (1936–1939)', in Manuel Tuñón de Lara et al. (eds.), *La guerra civil española 50 años después* (Madrid, 1985), p. 393; Barciela, 'Introducción', pp. 400–1.

18 See Agnes Heller, *Everyday Life* (London, 1984). For example, the declarations of José Antonio Primo de Rivera, *Arriba*, 5 July 1935, cited in Aguila Tejerina, *Ideología y fascismo*, p. 188.

19 On the significance of a 'national humiliation' (1898) and of the 'great event' (i.e.: Franco's victory in the Civil War), in galvanising late-industrialising states, see Garruccio, *L'Industrializzazione*, pp. 65–70, 78–83; Matossian, 'Ideologies of Delayed Industrialisation'.

20 Franco in La Coruña, cited by Iniesta, *Garra Marxista*, p. 278.

21 PRO/FO371/89524/WS1101/7, Foreign Office telegram from Madrid to London, *Monthly Economic Report*, 19 July 1950.

22 Arrese, *La revolución social*, pp. 163, 206–7.

23 Iniesta, *Garra*, p. 279; Arrese, *La revolución social*, p. 207; Aguila Tejerina, *Ideología y fascismo*, pp. 231–41. For example, Manuel Souto Vilas, 'Campo y Ciudad', in JONS, *Antología* (Madrid, 1943), originally published in 1934.

24 Aznar, 'El régimen de subsidios familiares', pp. 102–10; Javier Ruiz Almansa, 'Crecimiento y repartición de la población de España', *Revista Internacional de Sociología*, 1 (1944), 77–105; J. Ros Jimeno, 'La natalidad y el futuro desarrollo de la población de España', *Revista Internacional de Sociología* (Jan–March 1943), p. 1; 'El decrecimiento de la natalidad y sus causas', *Estudios Demográficos* (1945), p. 1. Also Nash, 'Pronatalism and Motherhood'.

25 Leyva y Andía, report, p. 20. The author of this report collaborated with the Director General of the Ministry of Agriculture, Gabriel Bornás Urcullu, and others, on a book in praise of Nazi agrarian policy, *El hombre, la explotación, el mercado: organización de la economía agrícola dirigida en Ale-*

mania (Madrid, 1941). The work had a eulogistic prologue by the Falangist Minister of Agriculture, Raimundo Fernández Cuesta. See Barciela, 'Introducción', p. 389. On peasants and Nazism, including the issues of migration and colonisation, see Corni, *Hitler and the Peasants*, pp. 18–38, 116–42, 220–44; Farquharson, *The Plough and the Swastika*, pp. 141–160, 203–20.

26 Iniesta, *Garra Marxista*, p. 277.

27 Sevilla Guzmán, 'El campesinado'; and Bernal, 'Los latifundios'.

28 Informal report, Toledo, 9 December 1939, AGA, Pres, SGM, caja 228. See also, *Problemas de la provincia de Toledo*, a report on rural Castile which ends with the salute '¡Viva Franco!' and '¡Arriba el campo!' 25 October 1939.

29 On the formal incorporation of smallholders, social Catholic organisations, like the Confederación Nacional Católico-Agraria, by the Falangist national syndical organisation, see Castillo, *Propietarios*, pp. 393–444.

30 Leyva y Andía, report, p. 15; Castillo, *Propietarios*.

31 Informe, DNII, 28 August 1940, AGA, Pres, SGM, caja 30; 'Instrucciones que la secretaría del partido habrá de dar a los Jefes Provinciales para llevar a cabo un mejor aprovechamiento de las tierras improductivas', report, 1940, in FNFF, *Documentos inéditos*, vol. II, 1, pp. 301–4; letter marked 'reservado' from the National Syndical Delegate, Fermín Sanz Orrio, to the Minister Secretary-General of the Movement, Fernández Cuesta, 1 May 1951, on Badajoz, AGA, Pres, SGM, caja 73; Leyva y Andía, p. 21, for example. On the blend of social radicalism and ideological traditionalism in Falangism, see, for instance, Aguila Tejerina, *Ideología y fascismo*, pp. 173–253; Agustín del Río Cisneros, *José Antonio y la revolución nacional* (1st edn, 1949; 4th edn, Madrid, 1968), pp. 271–92; José Antonio Primo de Rivera, *Discursos frente el parlamento* (Barcelona, 1939), pp. 223–39; José-Carlos Mainer, *Falange y literatura* (Barcelona, 1971). See also Manuel Cantarero del Castillo, *Falange y socialismo* (Barcelona, 1973).

32 Levya y Andía, report, p. 4.

33 Moreno Gómez, *Córdoba*; Braojos et al., *Sevilla '36*; Nadal, *Guerra civil en Málaga*; Ortiz Heras, *Violencia política*, pp. 245–307; José Manuel Naredo, 'Antecedentes y características de la sociedad jerárquica que sostiene en Extremadura el expolio, con especial referencia al Plan Badajoz', in *Extremadura saqueada* (Barcelona, 1978); Juan Martínez Alier, *La estabilidad del latifundismo* (Paris, 1978), for example.

34 In the pueblo of Dos Hermanas in Seville, still an important centre of olive production, the olive harvest could not be brought in for lack of labour. Iribarren, *Con el general Mola*, p. 187.

35 PRO/FO371/24160/W9033/3921/41, Paterson to Halifax, 6 June 1939.

36 *Daily Worker*, 20 February 1940.

37 PRO/FO371/26891/C9633/3/41, Hoare to Eden, 28 August 1941. On the background to rural conflict, see Albert Balcells, *El problema agrari a catalunya, 1890–1936; la qüestió rabassaire* (Barcelona, 1968).

38 Hoare to Eden, 28 August.

39 PRO/FO371/C1371/3/41, British Embassy, 14 March 1941.

40 PRO/FO371/26890/C2475/3/41, Hoare telegram, 7 March 1941.

41 Albert Carreras (ed.), *Estadísticas históricas de España, siglos XIX–XX* (Madrid, 1989), pp. 108, 145. All official statistics for the period after 1936

until the 1960s, and particularly those relating to food production, prices and distribution, need to be treated with extreme caution because of the black market. See Carlos Barciela's guide to the sources in the above work, pp. 161–5; and 'Un análisis crítico de las series estadísticas de los precios del trigo entre 1937 y 1980', *Agricultura y Sociedad*, 29 (October–December 1983); 'Introducción', pp. 396–7; J.M. Naredo, 'Reflexiones con vistas a una mejora de las estadísticas agrarias', in the same volume.

42 *Estadísticas históricas*, p. 145. It is striking how official production figures in the 1940s are so uneven from year to year, almost certainly partly a reflection of the extent of the black market.

43 Bricall, 'La economía española', p. 377; *Estadísticas*, p. 144.

44 Areas that had been in Nationalist hands throughout were unaffected. See Jesús González, *La economía política*, p. 128; Leal et al., *La agricultura*, p. 46; Clavera et al., *Capitalismo español*, pp. 166–70; Carlos Barciela, 'Los efectos de la guerra civil sobre la agricultura', *Economistas*, 21 (August–September 1986), pp. 16–18.

45 PRO/FO371/22668/W6677/317/41, 17 May 1938, Hodgson to Howard.

46 For example, *Franquisme*, p. 80; Carlos Tió, *La política de aceites comestibles en la España del siglo XX* (Madrid, 1982), pp. 49–80.

47 Franco, July 1937, *Palabras*, p. 155; Abella, *Finales de enero*, p. 16, for example. The contrast with loyalist Spain was stark. Bricall, 'La economía', p. 378; Edward Malefakis, 'La economía española y la guerra civil', in Nadal et al. (eds.), *La economía española en el siglo XX*, pp. 158–9; Carlos Barciela, 'Producción y política cerealista durante la guerra civil española 1936–1939', in G. Anes et al. (eds.), *Historia económica y pensamiento social* (Madrid, 1983), pp. 671–5.

48 'Ligero informe sobre la situación de los obreros agricultores y ganaderos en esta fecha', AGA, Pres, SGM, caja 8; although other figures show a decline. *Estadísticas históricas*, pp. 111 and 147; Barciela, 'Los efectos', pp. 16–17.

49 Barciela, 'Los efectos', p. 16; González, *La economía política*, p. 90; José Sorní Mañés, 'Aproximación a un estudio de la contrareforma agraria en España', *Agricultura y Sociedad*, 6 (1978).

50 Barciela, 'Producción y política', p. 667; Preston, *Coming of the Spanish Civil War*, p. 39.

51 Barciela, 'Producción y política'.

52 See Dionisio Martín Sanz, *El problema triguero y el nacional sindicalismo* (Valladolid, 1937); Castillo, *Propietarios*, pp. 398–425; Barciela, 'Producción y política', p. 666.

53 Martín Sanz, *El problema*, p. 12. See also Castillo, *Propietarios*, pp. 398, 403.

54 *Boletín Oficial del Estado*, 25 August 1937. See also Leyva y Andía, report, p. 40.

55 Chueca, *El fascismo en los comienzos*; Javier Jiménez Campo, *El fascismo en la crisis de la segunda república* (Madrid, 1979). See also, 'El Servicio Nacional del Trigo', *Alimentación Nacional*, 15 February 1943. Although some historians link Falangism to industrial and urban modernisation. See Ben-Ami, *Fascism from Above*, p. 258.

56 There is no section specifically dedicated to industry, although a chapter

concerning 'the economy, work and the class struggle' does emphasise the syndical system of production and the centrality of private property.

57 Pascual Carrión, *La reforma agraria: problemas fundamentales* (Madrid, 1931); *Los latifundios en España* (Madrid, 1932/1975); Jacques Maurice, *La reforma agraria en España en el siglo XX (1900–1936)* (Madrid, 1975); Edward E. Malefakis, *Agrarian Reform and Peasant Revolution in Spain* (New Haven, CT, 1970); Miguel Artola et al., *El latifundio: propiedad y explotación, siglos XVIII-XX* (Madrid, 1978).

58 Sevilla Guzmán, 'El campesinado', pp. 193–4; Manuel de Torres, 'De los efectos de la intervención en los precios de la producción agraria', *Agricultura*, 95 (March 1940), cited in Barciela, 'Producción y política', p. 674.

59 Arrese, *La revolución social*, p. 209.

60 Preston, *Coming of the Spanish Civil War*, pp. 38–40, 44; Barciela, 'Producción y política', p. 664.

61 Iniesta, *Garra*, p. 282.

62 Franco, in *La Revue Belge*, 15 August 1937, *Palabras*, p. 184. A decree of 23 August 1937 prohibited the augmentation of the area cultivated for wheat. Barciela, 'Producción y política', p. 667.

63 Martín Sanz, *El problema triguero*, p. 14; Moreno Fonseret, *La autarquía*, pp. 131–4; Carlos Barciela, 'La agricultura cerealista en la España contemporánea: el mercado triguero y el Servicio Nacional del Trigo', PhD thesis (Madrid, 1981), p. 19.

64 Aurelio García González and José María Mira Izquierdo, *El trigo, su economía y su legislación actual* (Madrid, 1946), p. 21.

65 A series of commercial treaties with Argentina, the first signed in October 1946, for the importation of food, provided a life-line to the Spanish regime. See Viñas et al., *Política comercial*, pp. 366–74, 454, 545. Biescas, *España bajo*, p. 72.

66 Simón Cano Denia, 'La alimentación nacional', *Revista de Economía Aplicada*, 2 (December 1951), pp. 9–19. Cano reckons that average per person annual consumption of flour in the period 1931–5 at 137,420 kg, and 1941–5 at 90,604 kg. See also Abella, *Por el imperio*, pp. 116–32.

67 Moreno Gómez, *Córdoba*, p. 17.

68 See Fermín Sanz Orrio, critical reports of October 1941 (pp. 6–15) and December 1941 and August 1942, AGA, Pres, SGM, caja 9. The principal recommendations were a more flexible system of rationing, greater imports from abroad, and more control by the state *sindicatos*.

69 For example, 'El estraperlo del mercado libre', *Pueblo*, 23 January 1943.

70 Ridruejo, *Escrito en España*, p. 98; Pitt-Rivers, *People of the Sierra*, p. 21; Marsé, *Si te dicen*, p. 249.

71 Ridruejo, *Casi unas memorias*; Ramón Garriga, *Franco-Serrano Suñer: un drama político* (Barcelona, 1986), p. 178.

72 Cano Denia, 'La alimentación nacional', p. 10; Dirección General de Sanidad, Instituto de Investigaciones Médicas de Madrid, *Estudios de nutrición* (Madrid, 1943). Cano emphasises that consumption of 'hidden produce' was distributed very unevenly. p. 15.

73 Francisco Umbral, *Memorias de un niño de derechas* (Barcelona, 1976), pp. 94–5.

74 'Problemas de la provincia de Toledo', 25 October 1939, AGA, Pres, SGM, caja 228; 'Propuesta de precio del quintal métrico de trigo para la campaña 1942–1943', Delegado Nacional, SNT, 12 March 1942, AGA, Pres, SGM, caja 148, for example. Also Barciela, 'Introducción', p. 390.

75 Joan Clavera, 'El estraperlo en los años cuarenta', *Información Comercial Española*, 514 (1976); Bartolomé Barba, *Dos años al frente del gobierno civil de Barcelona* (Madrid, 1948), pp. 31–3; Pedro Gual Villalbí, *Ante una transformación profunda del concepto del mercado* (Madrid, 1941), pp. 222–6. In Barcelona a leading Falangist described the situation as 'estraperlismo integral', a 'complete' black market. Carlos Trías Bertrán cited in Thomàs, *Falange*, p. 417; Pitt-Rivers, *People of the Sierra*, pp. 19–21.

76 PRO/FO371/26891/C8935/3/41, 31 July 1941.

77 The term originates in a scandal involving the Radical Party in the 1930s and 'fixed' roulette wheels. Subsequently, it came to be applied to clandestine selling of goods at prices above state-fixed levels.

78 PRO/FO371/49575/Z7167/89/41, p. 3.

79 *Boletín Oficial del Estado*, 28 April 1939. See María de los Angeles Arranz Bullido, 'Una aproximación histórica a la política de abastecimientos en los primeros años de la posguerra (1939–1951)', PhD thesis, Universidad Autónoma de Madrid (1986).

80 Certificates of 'good conduct' were already issued by priests in the process of distributing rations and purging of the labour force. For example, A. Alvarez Bolado, 'Guerra civil y universo religioso: fenomenología de una implicación', *Miscelánea Comillas*, 44 (1986), pp. 85, 297–9. See also 'Political responsibilities' files, all of which contained a report from the parish priest. Archive ATRP, for example.

81 Alburquerque, 'Métodos de control', p. 427.

82 Payne, *Franco Regime*, p. 388; Clavera, 'El estraperlo en los años cuarenta', pp. 91–158.

83 See Carlos Barciela, 'El mercado negro de productos agrarios en la posguerra, 1939–1953', in Josep Fontana (ed.), *España bajo el franquismo* (Barcelona, 1986), p. 200; Moreno Fonseret, *La autarquía*, especially p. 153; Sevilla Guzmán and González de Molina, 'Política social agraria del primer franquismo'; Bernal, 'Riegos: los latifundios del franquismo inicial, 1939–1950'; Castillo, *Propietarios*, pp. 398–402; Thomas J. Hamilton, *Appeasement's Child: The Franco Regime in Spain* (New York, 1943), pp. 162–76; PRO/FO371/26891/C9633/3/41, Hoare to Eden, 28 August 1941; 'Folleto de propaganda comunista contra Falange', in *Documentos inéditos*, vol. II, 2, p. 451.

84 See, for example, Moreno Fonseret, *La autarquía*, p. 133, 151, 162, 168–84; Carmen Gutiérrez Castillo, 'Una estimación del mercado negro del aceite de oliva en la postguerra española', in *Agricultura y Sociedad* (October–December, 1983), particularly pp. 153–5; Clavera et al., *Capitalismo español*, p. 48. In 1954, Julian Pitt-Rivers wrote: 'There is no doubt that but for the high prices on the black market during the post-war years (1939–1950), much less land would be tilled than is the case'. *People of the Sierra*, p. 35.

85 See the preamble to Barciela, *La agricultura cerealista*. Barciela's study was

made in spite of the fact that access to records directly related to the SNT was denied by the Spanish Ministry of Agriculture. The archive of the successor organisation to the SNT, SENPA, was firmly closed. Another historian, as well as meeting considerable general resistance to access to the archive of the CGAT, the body organising food distribution, also found, significantly, that all documents referring to the bureaucracy's relations with the military and banks had been destroyed. Arranz Bullido, 'Una aproximación histórica a la política de abastecimientos'.

86 Pitt-Rivers, *People of the Sierra*, p. 20.
87 State-authorised mills were, in many areas, hugely outnumbered by officially 'closed' mills. The two principal mills in Alcalá de la Sierra were owned first by an absentee landowner and second by the head of the state farmers' syndicate. Pitt-Rivers, *People of the Sierra*, pp. 50–2.
88 Goodden to Halifax, PRO/FO371/C758/40/41, 15 January 1940.
89 Gutiérrez Castillo, 'Una estimación del mercado negro', p. 155.
90 Informe, FET–JONS, DNII, Delegación Nacional de Provincias, Bilbao, Boletín 614, 15 April 1942, AGA, Pres, SGM, caja 16.
91 See Ridruejo, *Escrito en España*, p. 102; PRO/FO371/73356/Z5846/596/41, report of FO Research Department, 31 May 1948.
92 FET–JONS, DNII, Barcelona, Boletín no. 643, 30 April 1942.
93 See Samuel Hoare, *Ambassador on Special Mission* (London, 1946), pp. 144–5.
94 *Catalunya sota*, pp. 398–402.
95 'Folleto de propaganda comunista', in *Documentos inéditos*, vol. II, 2, p. 453.
96 José Martí Gómez, *La españa del estraperlo, 1936–1952* (Barcelona, 1995), p. 255.
97 See the bulletins of opposition groups cited in Eiroa, *Viva Franco*, p. 118. Exports to Germany and Italy were up by more than 120 per cent in 1941, compared with 1935, according to official figures, although exports to Britain had slumped to a third of the pre-Civil War level. *Boletín Minero e Industrial*, December 1942, p. 403; Leitz, *Economic Relations*, p. 93; Carlos Barciela, 'Las estadísticas agrarias en España, 1940–1980', in Albert Carreras, *Las estadísticas económicas españolas en los siglos XIX y XX* (Madrid, 1989).
98 Viñas et al., *Política comercial*, pp. 194–215.
99 PRO/FO371/C9633/3/41, 28 August 1941. See also B. Díaz Nosty and D. Sueiro, *Historia del franquismo*, 2 vols., vol. I (Madrid, 1986), p. 233.
100 PRO/FO371/24507/C389/40/41, 4 January 1940. See also Viñas et al., *Política comercial*, particularly pp. 44–50.
101 Report, AGA, Pres, SGM, caja71.
102 PRO/FO371/Z4182/596/41, 1 April 1948. In February, 1940 a report was submitted to the central authorities claiming that serious black market activities were being transacted in the commercialisation of rice produced on land owned by the industrialist and banker Juan March, one of the richest men in Spain. *Nota de la milicia nacional, Jefatura Provincial de FET–JONS*, Málaga, 4 February 1940, AGA, Pres, SGM, caja 228.
103 FET–JONS, DNII, Boletín no. 337, Barcelona, 8 January 1942, no. 643,

Barcelona, 30 April 1942, p. 11, AGA, Pres, SGM, caja 16; DNII, Seville, Boletín no. 366, 13 January 1942, caja 16.

104 The Málaga newspaper *Sur* described 'the most splendid harvest for years', Eiroa San Francisco, *Viva Franco*, p. 105.

105 FET–JONS, DNII, Seville, Informe, no. 366, 13 January 1942, AGA, Pres, SGM, caja 16.

106 PRO/FO371/24507, 29 May 1940. See the note from the Civil Governor of Cádiz on increasing deaths from starvation, 27 October 1941, in Viñas et al., *Política comercial*, p. 318.

107 PRO/FO371/26890/C3986/3/41, March, 1941, p. 9.

108 FET–JONS, DNII, Boletín no. 394, Vizcaya, 21 January 1942, AGA, Pres, SGM, caja 16.

109 Foreign Office Report, May 1948; *Parte*, Barcelona, March, 1948, AGA, Pres, SGM, caja 165; *Informe*, Delegado Provincial de Sindicatos de Barcelona (to Delegado Nacional), 8 February 1950, caja 61; DNII, Oviedo, Boletín no. 627, 15 April 1942, caja 16.

110 FET–JONS, DNII, Boletín no. 552, 15 March 1942, AGA, Pres, caja 16.

111 FET–JONS, DNII, Madrid, Boletín no. 529, 28 February 1942, AGA, Pres, caja 16.

112 PRO/FO371/24507/C40/40/41, Málaga dispatch, 22 December 1939. Also Eiroa, *Viva Franco*, p. 124. Black market prices of food in the period 1939–42 in Málaga were, on average, three times the official levels, pp. 142–3. On the local administration and the black market in nearby Jaén, see the report of 1940 (n.d.), 'Provincia de Jaén', AGA, Pres, SGM, caja 228.

113 Brenan, *Face of Spain*, p. 48. On the extent of the black market within local authorities, see also *Informe*, FET–JONS, DNII, Córdoba, Boletín, no. 324, 2 January 1942, AGA, Pres, caja 16.

114 FET–JONS, DNII, Delegado Provincial de Gerona, 10 October 1940. On Alicante, see Moreno Fonseret, *La autarquía*, pp. 164–5.

115 FO Research Dept, May 1948.

116 Informe de FET–JONS, DNII, Barcelona, 20 April 1940, AGA, Presidencia, caja 30; Marsé, *Si te dicen*, p. 151; Moreno Fonseret, *La autarquía*, p. 165.

117 For example, Doña Jiménez, *Desde la noche y la niebla*, p. 82.

118 Pitt-Rivers, *People of the Sierra*, p. 58.

119 Eiroa San Francisco, *Viva Franco*, p. 258.

120 FET–JONS, DNII, 'Informe', Barcelona, 21 November 1940, p. 37.

121 See also reports of Sanz Orrio, 1941, pp. 3/9, AGA, Pres, SGM, caja 9. Also Josep Pujol Andreu, 'Los precios de los cereales en Cataluña durante los años de autarquía económica: el mercado oficial y el clandestino', *Agricultura y sociedad*, 35 (1985).

122 Ferri et al., *Las huelgas*, pp. 29–34; Alba, *Sleepless*, pp. 74–5; Clavera et al., *Capitalismo español*, p. 158. While black marketeers were reputed always to be fined only 5 or 10 pesetas when they were arrested, individuals found travelling without an authorised safe-conduct pass to do so were punished with a fine of 50 pesetas. FET–JONS, DNII, Gerona.

123 For example, PRO/FO371/26890/C3986/3/41, March 1941; *Informe de la*

Dirección General de Seguridad, León, May 1942, *Documentos inéditos*, vol. III, p. 521. See also Brenan, *Face of Spain*, p. 23; Moreno Gómez, *Córdoba*, p. 305.

124 *Informe, Dirección General de Seguridad*, León, May, 1942, pp. 521–2.

125 Eiroa San Francisco, *Viva Franco*, pp. 120–1.

126 See Barciela, *La agricultura cerealista*, p. 25.

127 Manuel Fuentes Irurozqui, *Abastecimientos, tasas y racionamientos* (Madrid, 1942), pp. 210–11.

128 FET–JONS, DNII, Barcelona, Boletín no. 677, 15 May 1942, Pres, SGM, caja 16.

129 Ellwood, *Spanish Fascism*, p. 137.

130 See Ridruejo, *Escrito en España*, p. 104; Enrique Tierno Galván, *Cabos sueltos* (Barcelona, 1981), pp. 106–7; Enrique González Duro, *Franco: Una biografía psicológica* (Madrid, 1992), p. 248. See also, Moreno Gómez, *Córdoba*, p. 306.

131 Informe, FET–JONS, DNII, Barcelona, 21 November 1940, AGA, Pres, SGM, caja 7; letter from the Falange's Hermandad Provincial de Labradores y Ganaderos to the Congreso Agrario Regional del Duero, Valladolid, 19 May 1945, AGA, Pres, SGM, caja 36. On the phenomenon of the *acaparador*, the merchant/moneylender/landowner who dominated this process of exploitation, see Preston, *Coming of the Spanish Civil War*, p. 39. On the historically unequal effects of agrarian crises, see Gonzalo Anes, *Las crisis agrarias en la España moderna* (Madrid, 1970).

132 For example, FET–JONS, DNII, Barcelona, 'Informe', 28 August 1940, AGA, Pres, SGM, caja 30.

133 PRO/FO371/24507/C758/40/41, pp. 2–4; PRO/FO371/26890/C3986/3/41.

134 'El Servicio Nacional del Trigo'.

135 Arranz Bullido, *Abastecimientos*, pp. 149–55.

136 PRO/FO371/C9633/3/41, 28 August 1941.

137 It was traditional for small producers to hide wheat from the prying eyes of government inspectors, but the impulse to do so became greater in the black market years of the 1940s. See Brenan, *South From Granada*; Pitt-Rivers, *People of the Sierra*, p. 6.

138 PRO/FO371/26890/C3986/3/41, March, 1941.

139 PRO/FO371/26890/C3986/3/41, March, 1941, p. 9.

140 British Embassy report, PRO/FO371/24507/C4786/40/41, 16 May 1940.

141 PRO/FO371/26890/C3986/3/41, March, 1941. Sanz Orrio, report, October, 1941, p. 7, AGA, Pres, caja 9.

142 PRO/FO371/26890/C2855/3/41, 18 March 1941.

143 See the confessions of Angel Zorrilla Dorronsoro, head of the Instituto Nacional de Colonización in 1943, cited in Barciela, 'Introducción', pp. 402–4.

144 Sevilla Guzmán, 'El campesinado', pp. 190–200; Barciela, 'Crecimiento y cambio', pp. 263–4; Alba, *Sleepless Spain*, pp. 24–6; Moreno Fonseret, *La autarquía*, pp. 184–201. See also *Historia y evolución de la colonización agraria en España: políticas administrativa y económica de la colonización agraria, 1937–77* (Madrid, 1990). 'Colonisation', or land settlement, was, in

theory, initiated by a decree of October 1939, 'to carry out in practice the stipulation of ch. 5, art. 6 of the Spanish Labour Charter (Fuero del Trabajo)', which asserts that 'the State aspires to find ways and means to cause the land to pass, on fair terms, into the hands of those who work it directly'.

145 PRO/FO371/73356/Z5846/596/41, 31 May 1948. See the note on land speculation, for example, in Córdoba province, September, 1942, AGA, Pres, SGM, caja 9.

146 See Bernal, 'Los latifundios'; Fontana, 'Reflexiones sobre la naturaleza', pp. 35–6.

147 'Informe sobre la situación de la provincia respecto al abastecimiento de harinas y pan', 29 January 1940, AGA, Pres, SGM, caja 228. See also Huelva FET–JONS, DNII, Boletines, nos. 480, 555, 609, 20 February, 15 March, 15 April 1942, caja 16.

148 PRO/FO371/24507/C758/40/41, 15 January 1940. In Valladolid, for example, a Falangist stronghold.

149 PRO/FO371/24507/C668/40/41, 6 January 1940.

150 PRO/FO371/26890/C1199/3/41, 10 February 1941.

151 See, for example, FET–JONS, DNII, Murcia, Boletín no. 482, 2 February 1942, AGA, Pres, SGM, caja 16.

152 DNII, Murcia, Boletín no. 871, 15 August 1942. Information on epidemics of typhus, diphtheria, smallpox, etc., is provided in PRO/FO371/24507/ C668/40/41, 6 January 1940; C4243/40/41, 19 March 1940; 26890/ C3255/3/41, 2 April 1941; C6035/3/41, 31 May 1941; 26891/C9527/3/41, 19 August 1941.

153 Miguel, España cíclica, pp. 172–3.

154 Letter of Isabel Ruiz de Miralles to the Army Minister, 13 December 1939, AGA, Pres, SGM, caja 227.

155 PRO/FO371/24507/C42/40/41, 27 December 1939; C668/40/41, 6 January 1940; 26890/C4192/3/41, 18 April 1941. Barley was used to manufacture beer while officials complained that people were dying of hunger. 'Problemas de la provincia de Toledo', AGA, Pres, caja 228.

156 Leal et al., La agricultura, pp. 3, 9.

157 PRO/FO371/26891/C9527/3/41, 19 August 1941. At least one regime figure estimated the homeless in Madrid to number 60,000 in 1940. Bigador, 'Primeros problemas', p. 18.

158 Brenan, Face of Spain, p. 50.

159 PRO/FO371/26890/C1371/3/41, 14 March 1941.

160 Comment of Gerald Brenan's chauffeur, Face of Spain, pp. 174–5. Also Manuel Vázquez Montalbán, Crónica sentimental de España (Madrid, 1986), p. 73. The exaggerated Civil War violence of the left had previously been depicted as a 'return to cannibalism' by Francoists. For example, Gay, Estampas rojas, pp. 292–300.

161 PRO/FO371/26890/C2208, 6 March 1941.

162 PRO/FO371/26890/C6120, 7 June 1941. The historian, it seems, will search in vain for photographic evidence of the Spanish famine.

163 PRO/FO371/26890/C803/3/41, 18 January 1941.

164 Letter from the managing director, 2 April 1941, to Ministry of Supply, PRO/FO371/26890/C3689/3/41. The British ambassador reported that in

Seville 'there are well authenticated cases of persons dying in the street from hunger'. Hoare to Ministry of Information, FO371/26890/C2182, 6 March 1941.

165 Hoare to Eden, 22 August 1941, PRO/FO371/26891/C9672/3/41.

166 See González, *La economía política*, pp. 103–20; Clavera et al., *Capitalismo español*, p. 144; Lieberman, *Contemporary Spanish Economy*, p. 182; Lorenzo Espinosa, *Dictadura*, pp. 19, 60–1.

167 Imports of nitrogenous fertilisers fell from 529,000 tons on average per year in the period 1931–5 to 96,200 tons in 1940–4 and 106,000 in 1945–8. Barciela, 'Introducción', p. 388. The state guaranteed to see that a set minimum quantity was consumed nationally at a predetermined price. *BOE*, 25 February 1940, and Dirección General de Industria y Comercio, *La política industrial en la Nueva España*.

168 17 January 1940, AGA, Pres, SGM, caja 227.

169 FET–JONS, DNII, Barcelona, Boletín no. 784 30 June 1942, AGA, Pres, SGM, caja 16. See also Domingo Gallego Martínez, 'Transformaciones técnicas de la agricultura española en el primer tercio del siglo XX', in Garrabou et al., *Historia agraria*, vol. III, pp. 173–200. The willingness of giant chemical companies to sell in the most profitable market is confirmed by the report on the Spanish economy by the Commercial Commissioner of the British Embassy. PRO/FO371/89526/WS1103/2, 15 March 1950, appendix, p. 2. Eiroa San Francisco, *Viva Franco*, p. 118.

170 Boletín al Servicio de la Emigración Española, Mexico 6 June 1940, no. 41, cited in Eiroa San Francisco, *Viva Franco*, p. 118.

171 Jorge Nadal, *La población española (siglos XVI-XX)* (Barcelona, 1966), pp. 167–218; Juan Díez Nicolás, *Tamaño, densidad y crecimiento de la población en España, 1900–1960* (Madrid, 1971); Salustiano del Campo and Manuel Navarro López, *Nuevo análisis de la población española* (Barcelona, 1987); Roser Nicolau, 'Población', in Carreras, *Estadísticas históricas*, pp. 49–90.

172 Informe, '*Paro, crisis industrial, comercial y agrícola en Vizcaya*', May 1949, ACCB. On Málaga, see Eiroa San Francisco, *Viva Franco*, pp. 146/7.

173 See Jaume Barrul, Josep Calvet and Conxita Mir, 'La justicia ordinaria como elemento de control social y de percepción de la vida cotidiana de postguerra: Lleida, 1938–1945', in Tusell et al., *El régimen*, pp. 243/5. Immigrants were also disproportionately represented in local crime figures. The occupation of the city of Lérida, in the spring of 1938, had seen a mass evacuation, turning the place into 'little more than a desert', with 'less than 2,000 civilian inhabitants', according to one observer. *Memoria de la Compañía de Jesús* (1938), cited in J.M. Solé i Sabaté and J. Villarroya, *L'ocupació militar de Catalunya* (Barcelona, 1987), p. 35.

174 See, for example, Pere Ysàs and Carme Molinero, 'La població Catalana a la postguerra: Creixement i concentració', *L'Avenç*, 102 (March 1987); Carles Santacana i Torres, *Victoriosos i derrotats: el franquisme en L'Hospitalet, 1939–1951* (Barcelona, 1994), pp. 73–91; and Santiago Torres, *Así los viví*, p. 105. On the growth of the population of Madrid due to the migration of rural workers from *latifundia* areas, see Folguera, 'La construcción de lo cotidiano durante los primeros años del franquismo',

p. 174; Juliá et al., *Madrid*, pp. 558–9. Under the dictatorship, many peasants who deserted the land found employment with the forces of law. See, for example, the poem 'Quejas de un labrador' ('A Peasant's Complaints'), by 'M. Merayo', which tells of an Estremaduran peasant family of three sons, the first of whom joins the *Policía Armada*, the second becomes a *'carabiñero'*, and the third, a civil guard. A copy is to be found in the archive of the Secretaría General del Movimiento, AGA, Pres, SGM, caja 105.

175 Pedro Bidagor Lasarte, Jefe de la Sección de Urbanismo de la Dirección General de Arquitectura, *El futuro Madrid* (Madrid, 1945), p. 48. This 'vertiginous growth' could 'either be the source of grandeur or ruin'. These claims are based on official statistics. Similar claims of huge growth could be made for other cities, like the main urban centres of Andalusia: Seville, Granada, Málaga and Almería. See *Anuario Estadístico* (1943), p. 44, for example.

176 On the record of Miguel Primo de Rivera as Franco's Minister of Agriculture and the ministry's meagre budget see, for example, Alba, *Sleepless*, pp. 66–9.

177 On paltry ministerial budgets, see Carreras, 'Depresión económica', pp. 20–1; Alba, *Sleepless*, p. 197; Miguel, *España cíclica*, p. 173. PRO/FO371/79719/Z1948/1101/41, January 1949.

178 Letter, Jaén, 27 March 1951, AGA, Pres, SGM, caja 72.

179 Letter to the Ministry of Industry and Commerce, 21 April 1951, AGA, Pres, SGM, caja 72. Emigration was substantial: 10 per cent of the provincial population left in the period 1941–50 and another 10 per cent from 1951–5. See Antonia Muñóz Fernández, 'La emigración en la provincia de Jaén 1900–1955', *Estudios Geográficos*, 81 (November 1960), pp. 455–96.

180 Letter of Delegado Nacional de Sindicatos to Ministro Secretario General del Movimiento, 1 May 1951, AGA, Pres, SGM, caja 73.

181 Arrese, *La revolución social*, pp. 170–1.

182 Enrique Ruíz García, *España hoy: política económica y sociedad en la transición democrática* (Mexico City, 1979), p. 171, cited in Miguel, *España Cíclica*, pp. 177. See also Torres, *Así los viví*, p. 125.

8   AUSTERITY AND RESISTANCE

1 *La Vanguardia Española*, 17 September 1939.

2 Vázquez Montalbán, *Crónica sentimental*, p. 42; also pp. 36, 40–4. On the interpretation of popular post-war songs, see M. Román, *Memoria de la copla: la canción española de Conchita Piquer a Isabel Pantoja* (Madrid, 1993); Manuel Vázquez Montalbán, *Cancionero general, 1939–1971*, 2 vols. (Barcelona, 1972), vol. I; Helen Graham, 'Popular Culture in the "Years of Hunger"', in H. Graham and J. Labanyi (eds.), *Spanish Cultural Studies: An Introduction* (Oxford, 1995), pp. 237–45. See also Carmen Martín Gaite, *Usos amorosos de la postguerra española* (Barcelona, 1987); Sueiro and Díaz Nosty, *Historia del franquismo*, vol. I, p. 226.

3 Franco accused 'Spain's enemies' of *'trading'* with the national essences. For example, *Palabras*, pp. 13–14.

4 See Cela, *La colmena*; the film of Víctor Erice, *El espíritu de la colmena* (1973), cited in Carmelo García Encabo, Reyes Juberías Hernández, and Alberto Manrique Romero, *Cartas muertas: la vida rural en la posguerra* (Valladolid, 1996), pp. 12–13. Also Rikki Morgan, 'Romper los moldes: implicaciones estéticas e ideológicas de *El espíritu de la colmena*', *ACIS* (Journal of the Association for Contemporary Iberian Studies) 6 (spring 1993), pp. 25–32. The beehive in Erice's film is glass and can be looked down on from above, although some people cannot bear to watch. See also Erice and Ángel Fernández Santos, *El espíritu de la colmena* (Madrid, 1976), p. 144; Paul Ilie, *Literature and Inner Exile* (Baltimore, MD, 1980).

5 Roland Barthes (after Theophanes the Hermit), *Sade, Fourier, Loyola* (Paris, 1971), pp. 56–74.

6 Víctor Alba prefers to use the analogy of a *desert*. This reflects some people's own contemporary perceptions, the significant constraints within which the anti-Franco opposition was forced to operate and an overwhelming 'thirst' for freedom and individual control. See Víctor Alba, *La oposición de los supervivientes* (Barcelona, 1978). Also Scheper-Hughes, *Death Without Weeping: The Violence of Everyday Life in Brazil* (Berkeley, CA, 1993), p. 19.

7 Fernando Urbina, 'Formas de vida de la Iglesia en España, 1939–1975', in *Iglesia y sociedad en España, 1939–1975* (Madrid, 1977), pp. 9–65; R. Doucastella, *Análisis sociológico del catolicismo español* (Barcelona, 1967); Lannon, *Privilege*, pp. 22–7, 33–4; Saíz Marín, *El Frente de Juventudes*; Germani, 'La socialización política de la juventud'; Marsé, *Si te dicen*, pp. 80, 81, 127, 176, 202. On the contradiction between the ideology of passivity and submission to be disseminated by the Sección Femenina and the requirement to be *active* in the process, see, for example, Gallego Méndez, *Mujer, Falange y franquismo*; Roca i Girona, *De la pureza*, pp. 23–33, 128–33. Women often emphasised that the SF had more of a religious sentiment than a political one. Antonieta Jarne i Mòdol, *La secció femenina a Lleida* (Lleida, 1991), p. 71. In Badajóz, in 1938, the majority of *camaradas* (comrades) knew nothing of party doctrine and the party lacked funds and facilities. *Memoria*, 26 November 1938, AGA, Pres, SGM, caja 229. Some women joined only to get a party card. FET–JONS, DNII, Boletín 709, 30 May 1942, AGA, Pres, SGM, caja 16. Individuals associated with the regime tried to draw simplistic conclusions from apparent support. For instance, Rafael Calvo Serer, *Política de integración* (Madrid, 1955). Another writer sympathetic to Franco, by looking only at middle-class life, is able to talk of a 'miraculous normalisation' in 1939 and consistently treats persecution in a frivolous way. See Fernando Vizcaíno Casas, *La España de la posguerra (1939–1953)* (Barcelona, 1978), especially pp. 15–29; *Contando los cuarenta* (Madrid, 1972).

8 Vázquez Montalbán, *Crónica sentimental*, p. 56.

9 For example, *Franquisme: sobre resistència i consens*; Roca i Girona, *De la pureza*, p. 32.

10 Expressions of dissent were evident in cinemas, bars, markets, in football crowds or at local folkloric *fiestas* or carnivals. There is very little on much of

these elements of opposition, but see, on cinema, P. Besas, *Behind the Spanish Lens: Spanish Cinema under Fascism and Democracy* (Denver, CO, 1985). On football, particularly as a focus of Catalan and Basque opposition, see Duncan Shaw, *Fútbol y franquismo* (Madrid, 1987). Carnival was suspended by military order in the Nationalist zone in February 1937 and remained outlawed until 1968, although it was frequently celebrated in certain places in spite of this: 'people in Fuenmayor would not give it up, and so they sang their insults from jail . . . No-one could take away carnival from us, not the Pope, not Franco, not Jesus himself'. David Gilmore, *Aggression and Community: Paradoxes of Andalusian Culture* (New Haven, CT, 1987), pp. 99/100; '*Carnaval* in Fuenmayor', p. 344; di Febo, 'La condición de la mujer', in *Ordenamiento jurídico*, p. 449. Much less subversive folkloric activities, traditional dancing and costumes, were, by contrast, encouraged by the regime. For example, Sección Femenina, *Calendario*, pp. 71, 103, 111, 143, 207, 241, 291, 313; Shirley Mangini, *Rojos y rebeldes: la cultura de la disidencia durante el franquismo* (Barcelona, 1987), p. 6. Some local popular traditions were based on folkloric Catholicism which often had relatively little in common with the Catholicism of elites. See Lannon, *Privilege*, pp. 22–7. The local and the popular in traditional piety is emphasised in Vincent, *Catholicism*, pp. 62–81.

11 Garán Encabo et al., *Cartas muertas*, pp. 13–17.

12 Vázquez Montalbán, *Crónica sentimental*, pp. 37–9.

13 Cited in Abella, *Finales de enero, 1939*, p. 14. See also the Primate of all Spain, Cardinal Gomá's Address to the International Eucharistic Conference, Budapest, May 1938.

14 *Mensaje del Caudillo a los españoles, discurso pronunciado por S.E. el Jefe del Estado la noche del 31 de diciembre de 1939* (Madrid, 1940).

15 Iniesta, *Garra Marxista*, p. 275.

16 Reig Tapia, *Ideología e historia*, pp. 137–59.

17 The priority of reconstruction was a thorough purge of society. PRO/FO371/24507/C1092/40/41, 9 January 1940.

18 Report of the British Foreign Office Research Department, PRO/FO371/73356/Z5846/596/41, 31 May 1948.

19 Franco, 18 July 1938. *Palabras*, p. 137.

20 Rodgers to Halifax, 13 February 1939, FO371/24127/W3036/8/41. See also Gaspar Sabater, *En torno a la afirmación española (el espíritu de la nueva generación)* (Madrid, 1943). On Álvarez Arenas' plotting the military rising in Granada in 1936, see Gollonet Megías and Morales López, *Rojo y azul*, p. 33.

21 FET–JONS, DNII, 'Parte Oficial', August, 1946, AGA, Pres, SGM, caja 165; '[the people] will always be able to be asked for sacrifices since it has gone for many years making them'. See also Velasco Murviedro, 'Sobre una posible', p. 401; López Ibor, *Discurso a los universitarios*, p. 99; Gay de Montellá, *Autarquía*, p. x.

22 The Comisario General of Abastecimientos y Transportes, 10 September, 1942, in Benito Cid de la Llave, *Consideraciones sobre el problema del abastecimiento nacional: su origen y causa* (Madrid, 1944), p. 179.

23 Vallejo-Nágera, *Divagaciones intranscendentes*, p. 64.

24 For instance, Roca i Girona, *De la pureza*; J. Cela, *La catira* (Madrid, 1955), p. 384; Allison Peers, *Spanish Mystics*, vol. I, p. 5.

25 See, for example, *Amanecer*, the party newspaper in Zaragoza, 23 December 1939, 'Una nota de la Jefatura Provincial: Justicia Social'. Also FET–JONS, DNII, Murcia, Boletín 501, 28 February 1942; DNII, Barcelona, Boletín 582, 31 March 1942; Boletín 872, 15 August 1942; AGA, Pres, SGM, caja 16; DNII, Barcelona, Informe, April 1940, AGA, Pres, SGM, caja 30.

26 One example were the Navarrese peasants of the Carlist militia. See *Franco's Rule: Back to the Middle Ages* (London, 1938), pp. 133/4; Dionisio Giménez Plaza, 'Navarra, 1936', *Interviú*, 136/7 (November–December, 1978); Blinkhorn, *Carlismo y contrarevolución* (Barcelona, 1979), pp. 348–74.

27 See Bryan S. Turner, *Regulating Bodies: Essays in Medical Sociology* (London, 1992), pp. 177–8. Also, *The Body and Society* (London, 1996), pp. 11, 48–50, 163–6; Pinkus, *Bodily Regimes*; Octavio Paz, *Conjunciones y disyunciones* (London, 1975). See also Max Weber's 'Typology of Asceticism and of Mysticism', in *Die Wirtschaftsethik der Weltreligionen*, trans. H.H. Gerth and C. Wright Mills, *From Max Weber: Essays in Sociology* (London, 1964), pp. 324–7.

28 Among the several studies of the relationship between eras of uncertainty or instability and asceticism, see Susan Ashbrook Harvey, *Asceticism and Society in Crisis: John of Ephesus and The Lives of the Eastern Saints* (Berkeley, CA, 1990); E.R. Dodds, *Pagan and Christian in an Age of Anxiety* (Cambridge, 1965); Peter Brown, *The Body and Society: Men and Women and Sexual Renunciation in Early Christianity* (New York, 1988).

29 Adolfo Maíllo, *Educación y revolución: los fundamentos de una educación nacional* (Madrid, 1943), p. 31. On calls for sacrifice and discipline, see, for example, FET–JONS, Barcelona, 'Informe sobre la situación de Cataluña', August 1940, AGA, Pres, SGM, caja 31; FET–JONS, DNII, Almería, Boletín 602, 15 April 1942, AGA, Pres, SGM, caja 16; FET–JONS, DNII, Barcelona, Informe, 20 April 1940, AGA, Pres, SGM, caja 30; 'Disciplina', editorial, *Arriba* 101 (1939); 'Servicio, disciplina', *Arriba*, 177 (1939); 'Lo militar y lo civil', editorial, *Arriba*, 236 (1939); 'Lo religiosos y lo civil en la Falange', *Arriba*, 264 (1940).

30 Pablo Romero, *Ascetica y mística*; Lamberto de Echeverría, *Ascética del hombre de la calle* (2nd edn, Barcelona, 1956); Di Febo, '"El Monje Guerrero"'; Gabriel Ureña Portero, 'Emblemática y espíritu', in Bonet, *Arte del franquismo* (Madrid, 1981), pp. 261–72; Aguila Tejerina, *Ideología y fascismo*, pp. 205–6; Lorenzo Espinosa, *Dictadura*, pp. 153–4. On the ascetic saints, see Mary Ilford's translation of Walter Nigg, *Vom Geheimnis der Mönche*, *Warriors of God* (New York, 1958). Also Owen Chadwick (ed.), *Western Asceticism* (London, 1958), on the Roman Catholic tradition.

31 Franco, Salamanca, 19 April 1937; Pamplona, November, 1937, *Palabras*, pp. 13/99.

32 Iniesta, *Garra Marxista*, p. 276.

33 Pemartín, *¿Qué es 'lo Nuevo'?*, p. 14, in Di Febo, 'El "Monje Guerrero"', p. 205; P. Antonio García Díaz Figar, *Virtudes militares* (Barcelona, 1941), prologue by Luis Orgaz. (García Díaz was Director Espiritual de la Academia de Alféreces Provisionales de Avila.) Also Ureña Portero, 'Emblemá-

tica', p. 265; 'Catolicismo militante', editorial, *Arriba*, 1371 (1943); Félix G. Olmedo, *Introducción a la vida de San Ignacio de Loyola* (Madrid, 1944); Allison Peers, *Spanish Mystics*, vol. I, pp. 1–30. See also *Cruz y Espada*, the religious review directed at soldiers. San Ignacio de Loyola, 'before all things a soldier', was baptised 'Iñigo'. The Company of Jesus was founded in 1540.

34 Franco, Burgos, 18 July 1938, *Palabras*, pp. 140–1.

35 *Ejercicios espirituales de San Ignacio de Loyola en su texto original* (Barcelona, 1892); *The Spiritual Exercises of St Ignatius Loyola (Commentary by Joseph Rickaby)* (London, 1936). Also Pablo Romero, *Teología ascetica y mística*, p. 20.

36 Marcelino Menéndez y Pelayo, *Heterodoxos*, 6, p. 508; *La mística española* (Madrid, 1956), pp. 401–15, for example. See also Lannon, *Privilege*, pp. 29–30.

37 Peers, *Spanish Mystics*, p. 25.

38 On this distortion, or massification, of Ignatian ascetecism, see Urbina, 'Formas de vida de la Iglesia', pp. 21–6. For the rather unorthodox Cardinal Francesc Vidal y Barraquer's critique of the 'abuses' entailed in this religious patriotism of processions and propaganda, see Ramón Muntanyola, *Vidal y Barraquer, el Cardenal de la Paz* (Barcelona, 1971), p. 422.

39 *Ecclesia*, 7 April 1941, Urbina, 'Formas de vida', p. 12.

40 However, *Ecclesia* is imprecise in defining what was meant by 'spiritual exercises'. *Ecclesia*, 8, 15 April 1941; Urbina, 'Formas de vida', p. 22.

41 *Manresa* (1942), pp. 83–4; *Ecclesia*, 10, 15 May 1941, p. 34, Urbina, 'Formas de vida', p. 24. Manresa was the most important place of Ignatian memory, being the retreat where the saint underwent mystical experiences.

42 José María Llanos, 'Cursos de cristianismo acelerado: ejercicios espirituales', *Hechos y dichos* (August–September 1975), pp. 40–3, Urbina, 'Formas de vida', p. 23.

43 FET–JONS, DNII, Barcelona, 'Informe', 14 March 1951, AGA, Pres, SGM, caja 16.

44 López Ibor, *El español*, pp. 181–2.

45 Barthes, *Sade, Fourier, Loyola*, p. 57.

46 El Tebib Arrumi, *Castilla por España y Cataluña roja, Biblioteca infantil, La Reconquista*, no. 9 (Madrid, 1940), pp. 4–5.

47 For example, Carbonell, *Cartas de combate*, p. 61. Also Pablo Romero, *Teología ascetica*, pp. 83–119.

48 See, for example, Pons Prades, *Guerrillas españolas*; Aguado Sánchez, *El maquis en España*; Heine, *A guerrilla antifranquista en Galicia*; A. Díaz Carmona, *Bandolerismo contemporáneo* (Madrid, 1969); T. Cossías, *La lucha contra el 'maquis' en España* (Madrid, 1956); J.M. Molina, *El movimiento clandestino en España, 1939–1949* (Mexico City, 1976); Fernández Vargas, *La resistencia interior en la España de Franco* (Madrid, 1981), pp. 91–107.

49 As well as unfavourable material and political conditions, Republican parties were left largely leaderless, particularly at a local level, by the repression of the Civil War and its aftermath and by forced exile. Despite this, small groups associated with these parties did continue to trouble the authorities. For example, on PSUC and CNT in Barcelona, see FET–JONS, DNII, Barcelona, 'Parte', August 1945; Boletín 383, 15 January 1942; on anar-

chists 'from Murcia', in the Catalan mining district of Malgrat, see FET–
JONS, DNII, Barcelona, Boletín 784, 30 June, 1942; and formation of
groups of 'libertarian youth' in the Barcelona district of Clot, FET–JONS,
DNII, report, April 1940, AGA, Pres, SGM, caja 30; on 'groups of FAI
militants' in Murcia, FET–JONS, DNII, Boletín 501, 28 February 1942.
On resistance, both 'individual' and 'collective', in the Asturian coal fields,
see García Piñeiro, *Los mineros asturianos*, especially, pp. 200–84. Also
Isidro Guardia Abella, *Otoño de 1941* (Madrid, 1976); Alba, *La oposición de
los supervivientes*; Juan M. Molina, *Noche sobre España* (Mexico, 1958); *El
movimiento clandestino*; *Apuntes para la historia del movimiento obrero español de
la posguerra* (Barcelona, 1977); Fernando Jáuregui and Pedro Vega, *Crónica
del antifranquismo*, vol. I (Barcelona, 1983); Fernández Vargas, *La resistencia
interior*, pp. 109–36.
50 Riquer, 'Dossier: el franquisme', p. 18. Worker protest had already been
organised at the company Moritz in Barcelona during 1940 and a further
strike took place in Mataró in 1942. The CNT organised a stoppage at the
Maestranza de Ingenieros in Cádiz in 1941 and, in Valencia, the cigarette
paper factory at Alcoy saw a major strike. Ferri et al., *Las huelgas*, p. 34.
51 One such reminded workers that 'Falangists and *Requetés* are of one mind
when they carry you off to the Campo de la Bota (the notorious site of
numerous executions in Barcelona) as they were on 19 July 1936'. FET–
JONS, DNII, Barcelona, Boletín 582, 31 March 1942; Boletín 643, 30 April
1942; also calling for sabotage of production and preventing exports to Nazi
Germany, Boletín 784, 30 June 1942; AGA, Pres, SGM, caja 16. Also Alba,
Historia de la resistencia, pp. 15–20, 115–16.
52 The leader of the group in León committed suicide rather than be
captured. Reports were filed on other workers who, among other 'crimes',
were guilty of having participated in the general strike of 1917. FET–
JONS, DNII, Boletín informativo de empresas, no. 440; 'Ferrocarriles
españoles del norte', 29 January 1942; Boletín 400, 21 January 1942;
AGA, Pres, SGM, caja 21. 2,300 workers were employed at the *Norte* works
in 1941; '60 per cent' continually made 'leftist' comments. 'Informe de la
Dirección General de Seguridad', 10 June 1941, FNFF, *Documentos inéditos*,
vol. II, 2, p. 181.
53 FET–JONS, DNII, 'Boletines de información', 439, 29 January 1942; no.
332, 8 January 1942; AGA, Pres, SGM, caja 21.
54 PRO/FO371/26891/C9212/3/41, 9 August 1941, 'Situation in Seville district'. See also Martínez Alier, *Labourers and Landowners*, pp. 177–83.
55 Party investigation bureau complaints of 'go-slows' (or the tactic of '*brazos
lánguidos*') are made in Parte, DNII, Barcelona, November 1946, AGA,
Pres, SGM, caja 165. See also García Piñeiro, *Los mineros asturianos*,
pp. 61–6; for example.
56 García Piñeiro, *Los mineros asturianos*, pp. 205–13.
57 For example, groups of the party 'Old Guard', like the *Guardia de Franco*,
members of the Falange youth front and agents of its intelligence service
were deployed at strategic positions on 14 April 1945. FET–JONS, DNII,
Barcelona, 'Parte', April 1945, AGA, Pres, SGM, caja 165.
58 The clenched-fist salute, rather than the obligatory fascist-style open hand,

was to be seen in certain localities. FET–JONS, DNII, Guipúzcoa, Boletín 671, 15 May 1942; also Barcelona, Boletín 784, 30 June 1942, pp. 5–8; AGA, Pres, SGM, caja 16.

59 FET–JONS, Barcelona, 'Informe: Fracaso de la CNS en Barcelona', 11 May 1940, AGA, Pres, SGM, caja 30.

60 Molinero and Ysàs, 'Luchas obreras', p. 24.

61 FET–JONS, Barcelona, 'Parte', August 1945, AGA, Pres, SGM, caja 165. Riquer, 'Rebuig, pasivitat i suport', p. 191; Carme Molinero and Pere Ysàs, 'Luchas obreras y oposición al franquismo en la Cataluña de posguerra', in Tusell et al., *La oposición al régimen de Franco* (Madrid, 1990) p. 22. See also Ferri, Muixí, and Sanjuán, *Las huelgas contra Franco*, pp. 57–9; Carme Molinero and Pere Ysàs, *L'oposició antifeixista a Catalunya (1939–1950)* (Barcelona, 1981). State syndical officials posted lists of strikers to walls facilitating their detention by the police. Angel Cortes, 'Quan la memoria encara roman fidel', *L'Avenç*, 58 (March 1983), pp. 9–11. Clandestine leaflets pointed out that the Spanish Civil War was effectively 'the first of Hitler's wars of invasion'. Reproduced in FET–JONS, DNII, Barcelona, Boletín 784, 30 June 1942, AGA, Pres, SGM, caja 16, p. 5.

62 In Barcelona, during November and December 1947, there were major strikes and a continual go-slow in textile factories. PRO/FO371/73356/ Z2490/596/41G, 19 March 1948; FO371/89524/WS1101/1, December 1949; FO371/73356/Z4555/596/G, 28 May 1948. On a strike by 2,000 women at the Barcelona textile plant Trinxet Industrial SA for an increase in wages, in September 1949, and the subsequent military occupation of the factory, see the British diplomatic memorandum, PRO/FO371/Z7549/ 10118/41, 4 November 1949. The year 1951 saw a wave of strikes and protests, the most substantial since the 1930s, in Bilbao, Barcelona, Vitoria, Pamplona, Valladolid, Alicante, Madrid and other areas.

63 Molinero and Ysàs, *'Patria, Justicia y Pan'*, pp. 225–6.

64 The general strike was preceded by other localised protests, in Castellar del Vallés, for example. Molinero and Ysàs, 'Luchas obreras', p. 22; Borja, 'Rebuig, passivitat i suport', p. 191; Ferri et al., *Las huelgas*, pp. 78–84; Jaume Fabre, Josep Huertas and Antoni Ribas, *Vint anys de resistència catalana (1931–1959)* (Barcelona, 1978), pp. 196–202; FET–JONS, DNII, Barcelona, 'Parte', September 1945, AGA, Pres, SGM, caja 165. On the response of the *Movimiento* to what was 'one of the worst attacks against our organisation', see FET–JONS, Secretaría General, Circular no. 179, 11 July 1946, AGA, Pres, SGM, caja 41, calling for stern measures and reliance on the already discredited *Sindicatos Verticales*.

65 José María Lorenzo Espinosa, *Rebelión en la ría. Vizcaya 1947; obreros, empresarios y Falangistas* (Deusto, 1988).

66 FET–JONS, 'Nota', Cádiz, 28 May 1942, AGA, Pres, SGM, caja 8; FET– JONS, DNII, Barcelona, 'Parte', June 1946, AGA, Pres, SGM, caja 165; FET–JONS, DNII, Barcelona, 'Nota informativa – Sindicatos', 20 June 1940, AGA, Pres, SGM, caja 31. See also pp. 12–14.

67 The precise motivations of these actions, particularly of PCE and PSUC members joining communist parties after May 1937, are not easy to be precise about. Some evidently sympathised with the Falangist cause. For

example, letter of Delegado Sindical Provincial de Barcelona to Sanz Orrio, July 1946, AGA, Pres, SGM, caja 41. García Piñeiro, *Los mineros asturianos*, pp. 220–1, on socialist miners in Asturias. On CNT infiltration of the syndicates, see FET–JONS, DNII, Barcelona, 'Parte', April 1945, AGA, Pres, SGM, caja 165. Anarchist co-operation with the Falange was often exaggerated by regime conservatives – army, monarchists, etc. – as a way of discrediting the *Movimiento*. For example, a note of a Colonel of Franco's Estado Mayor, forwarded by José María de Areilza to Vice-Secretaria General of the Movement, 30 September 1939, claims some 9,000 old *cenetistas* had infiltrated the Falange. AGA, Pres, SGM, caja 30. See also Balfour, *Dictatorship*, pp. 14–20.

68 Riquer, 'Rebuig, pasivitat i suport', pp. 189–90; FET–JONS, DNII, Granada, Boletín 491, 28 February 1942, for example.

69 PRO/FO371/26890/C3986/3/41, March 1941.

70 García Piñeiro, *Los mineros asturianos*, pp. 216–17, for instance.

71 It seems that the remnants of the PCE and PSUC were first to establish aid networks, based on the pre-existing Socorro Rojo Internacional. But in Barcelona, at least, socialist supporters also subscribed, while the anarchist CNT-FAI was said, by Falangist officials, to have a separate system as did supporters of radical Catalan nationalism through its 'Socorro Rojo del Estat Català', organised by old militants of Francesc Macià's populist party. FET–JONS, DNII, Barcelona, Boletín 677, 15 May 1942, pp. 4–5, AGA, Pres, SGM, caja 16, 52/35.602; PRO/FO371/26890/C3986/3/41, March 1941; Alba, *Historia de la resistencia*, pp. 22–4; Heine, *La oposición*, pp. 63/4.

72 For example, FET–JONS, Barcelona, 'Escrito', September, 1939; 'Informe: fracaso de la CNS en Barcelona', 11 May 1940; AGA, SGM, caja 30; FET–JONS, DNII, Almería, Boletín 602, 15 April 1942; FET–JONS, DNII, Murcia, Boletín 501, 28 February 1942; Boletín 540, 15 March 1942; Barcelona, Boletín 552, 15 March 1942; AGA, Pres, SGM, caja 16; FET–JONS, Barcelona, 'Parte', July 1945; AGA, Pres, SGM, caja 165; 'Informe de la DGS, Valladolid', 4 May 1942, FNFF, *Documentos inéditos*, vol. III, pp. 403–4.

73 Víctor Alba, *Historia de la resistencia antifranquista* (Barcelona, 1978), p. 23; Mirta Núñez Díez Balart and Antonio Rojas Friend, 'Víctimas del franquismo en Madrid: los fusilamientos en el Cementerio del Este (1939–1945)', in Tusell et al., *El régimen de Franco* (Madrid, 1993), p. 286; Suárez/Colectivo '36, *El libro blanco*, pp. 75–7; Doña, *Desde la noche*, pp. 165–6.

74 Carlos Trías, Provincial Head of the State Party in Barcelona, *Informe Político de Barcelona*, AGA, Pres, SGM, caja 31.

75 PRO/FO371/24507/C4243/40/41, 29 May 1940; C2621/40/41, 14 February 1940. From a strategic point of view, according to General Alfredo Kindelán, the Captain-General of Barcelona, it was better to have military forces scattered outside of the urban centre, though easily groupable. The objective was to avoid a situation where the troops would be confined to barracks within the city. The lesson of July 1936 had been learnt: when the military coup which triggered the social revolution in Barcelona broke out the armed forces were successfully confined to their barracks by the actions of the workers of the city.

76 Report of Delegación Provincial de Barcelona, 30 November 1940, SGM, AGA.
77 FET–JONS, DNII, Barcelona, 28 August 1940; Boletín 337, 8 January 1940; AGA, Pres, SGM, caja 30; FET–JONS, Barcelona, 28 October 1940, AGA, Pres, SGM, caja 7.
78 A similar situation was recorded in many other parts of Catalonia, rural and urban. Riquer, 'Rebuig, pasivitat i suport', p. 246.
79 FET–JONS, DNII, Barcelona, report, 21 November 1940.
80 Ibid.
81 Rations of bread were frequently reduced, as low as 150 grams, in particular localities. See, for example, PRO/FO371/79719/Z1948/1101/41, January 1949; 73356/Z1464/596/41, 12 February 1948.
82 Report, FET–JONS, DNII, Barcelona, 17 June 1940, AGA, Pres, SGM, caja 30.
83 *El Caudillo en Cataluña* (Madrid, 1942).
84 FET–JONS, DNII, Barcelona, Boletín no. 489, 20 February 1942, caja 16, p. 21.
85 FET–JONS, DNII, Murcia, Boletín no. 693, 30 May, 1942, caja 16.
86 Cited in Cortada, *A City in War*, p. 191.
87 Hoare to Eden, PRO/FO371/34787/C5724/63/41, 12 May 1943.
88 Report, FET–JONS, DNII, 17 June 1940, AGA, Pres, SGM, caja 30. It was pointed out that, although foreign circumstances remained the same, the situation within Spain was ever worse. Sanz Orrio, report, p. 14.
89 Ibid.
90 For numerous cases, see, for example, FET–JONS, DNII, Barcelona, report, January 1941, AGA, Pres, SGM, caja 51. On politically motivated bank robberies, see, for example, the intelligence report of a raid on the Banco de Vizcaya in Barcelona in the summer of 1945. FET–JONS, Barcelona, 'Parte', 10 August 1945, AGA, Pres, SGM, caja 165.
91 FET–JONS, DNII, Barcelona, Boletín no. 582, 31 March 1942, caja 16, p. 22; DNII, Barcelona, 'Informe', January 1941, caja 51.
92 Ibid.
93 *Auxilio Social* was created by the Nationalists in the winter of 1936 and based on Nazi Germany's Winterhilfswerk. The service was notorious for its corruption, lack of supplies and poor organisation.
94 FET–JONS, DNII, Murcia, Boletines 625, 693, 18 April 1942, 30 May 1942; Alba, *Sleepless*, p. 30. See also FET–JONS, 'Informe sobre San Sebastián', 1940, AGA, Pres, SGM, caja 23; letter of Delegado Nacional de Auxilio Social, 13 November 1941, on corruption in Huelva, AGA, Pres, SGM, caja 4. In Huesca, the Auxilio was 'a comedy' while children died of hunger. Letter to Muñoz Grandes, 17 August 1939, AGA, Pres, SGM, caja 1.
95 DNII, Murcia, Boletín no. 501, 28 February 1942, AGA, Pres, SGM, caja 16. Auxilio's scarce funds were also spent on monuments to the Nationalist 'fallen' during the war. PRO/FO371/C42/40/41, Peterson to Foreign Office, 27 December 1939.
96 FET–JONS, 'Informe sobre Sabadell', March 1940, AGA, Pres, SGM, caja 30; FET–JONS, Barcelona, 'Informe político de Barcelona', November 1940, AGA, Pres, SGM, caja 30. On Granada, DN Provincias, 1940?,

AGA, Pres, SGM, caja 7. Towards the end of 1939 the Interior Minister, Serrano Suñer, apparently called a meeting of heads of Auxilio Social, telling them that mismanagement and speculation so discredited it that Franco was considering replacing it with something else. PRO/FO371/ C389/40/41, Hoare to Foreign Office, 4 January 1940.

97 FET–JONS, DNII, 'Informe', Barcelona, 28 August 1940, caja 30; PRO/ FO371/26890/C3986/3/41, Report, March 1941. ATRP, Exp. 650.

98 *La Vanguardia Española* reported on 4 February 1939 that 28 churches would be re-opened for services on the next day, having undergone some degree of reconstruction. A semblance of pre-1931 normality was to be re-established through the reassertion of the place of the church in everyday life.

99 *Daily Worker*, 20 February 1940.

100 By 1956 there were some 28,000 *chabolas* (self-made shacks) in and on the outskirts of Madrid. The number rose to more than 50,000 in the 1960s and there were still 35,000 in 1973. Juliá et al., *Madrid*, p. 564.

101 A. Cabré and I. Pujades, 'La població de Barcelona i del seu entorn al segle XX', *L'Avenç*, 88 (December 1985), pp. 33–7; Carme Molinero and Pere Ysàs, 'La població Catalana a la postguerra: creixement i concentració', *L'Avenç*, 102 (March 1987), pp. 38–46.

102 Juliá et al., *Madrid*, pp. 560–1.

103 Zalba, *La prostitución*, p. xviii: *El futuro Madrid*, cited in Juliá et al., *Madrid*, pp. 553–4.

104 The real figure was probably considerably greater. See Francesc Candel, *Els altres Catalans* (Barcelona, 1963). For detailed fictional treatments of life in shanty towns, see Juan Goytisolo, *Fiestas* (Paris, 1958); Miguel Delibes, *Diario de un emigrante* (Barcelona, 1958); Antonio Ferrer, *La piqueta* (Barcelona, 1959).

105 According to official figures, between 1943 and 1945 the regime only managed to build 26,000 dwellings and only a total of 70,000 by 1948. PRO/FO371/79719/Z/6901/1101/41, September 1949. Actual homelessness was certainly of even greater proportions. On Barcelona, see particularly, Francesc Martí and Eduardo Moreno, *Barcelona ¿A dónde vas?* (Barcelona, 1974).

106 PRO/FO371/79719/Z/6901/1101/41, September 1949.

107 See Riquer and Culla, *El franquisimo*, pp. 176–7; Informe, 'Algunas consideraciones políticas a cuenta de los sucesos de Barcelona', 14 March 1951, AGA, Pres, SGM, caja 73.

108 Umbral, *Memorias*, pp. 37–40.

109 See the personal testimonies in Eiroa San Francisco, *Viva Franco*, pp. 124–5. Also Marsé, *Si te dicen*, pp. 14/152; Consuelo García, *Las cárceles de Soledad Real* (Madrid, 1982), p. 149.

110 FET–JONS, DNII, Oviedo, Boletín 627, 15 April, 1942, AGA, Pres, SGM, caja 16.

111 FET–JONS, DNII, Boletín 491, 28 February 1942, AGA, Pres, SGM, caja 16. The Governor's house was set alight with the help of local inhabitants and troops were sent from Madrid to put down the unrest. PRO/FO371/26890/C147/3/41, report, 17 February 1941.

112 FO Research Department, FO371/73356/Z5846/596/41, May 1948.

113 Umbral, *Memorias*, p. 32.

114 Vázquez Montalbán, *Crónica sentimental*, pp. 35–7.

115 Umbral, *Memorias*, pp. 32/8.

116 Report, 'Valladolid, Abastos', January 1942, FNFF, *Documentos inéditos*, vol. III, pp. 164–5.

117 For examples, FET–JONS, DNII, Murcia, Boletín 540, 15 March 1942; Boletín 603, 15 April 1942, AGA, Pres, SGM, caja 16; Barcelona, Informe, 28 August 1940, AGA, Pres, SGM, caja 30; Informe 21 November 1940, AGA, Pres, SGM, caja 7.

118 'Blasphemy' had been 'totally suppressed' in Jaén. 'Informe de la DGS', 29 January 1942, FNFF, *Documentos inéditos*, vol. III, p. 234. Other cases of imprisonment of 'women of poor reputation' and 'blasphemy' followed. FET–JONS, DNII, Murcia, Boletines 540, 693, 871 15 March 1942, 30 May 1942, 15 August 1942.

119 Francisco Núñez Roldán, *Mujeres públicas: historia de la prostitución en España* (Madrid, 1995), pp. 189–204. Further, Marse, *Si te dicen que caí*; Umbral, *Memorias*.

120 Nash, 'Pronatalism and motherhood in Franco's Spain', pp. 160–77; Joaquín Arango, 'La modernización demográfica de la sociedad española', in Nadal et al. (eds.), *La economía española*, pp. 218–19. Marriage and fecundity rates appear to have remained well below the levels of the 1930s throughout the 1940s and most of the 1950s. Miguel, *España cíclica*, pp. 180–2.

121 FET–JONS, DNII, Barcelona, Informe, 20 April 1940, AGA, Pres, caja 30; Murcia, Boletín 540, 15 March 1942, AGA, Pres, SGM, caja 16.

122 See, for example, FET–JONS, DNII, Murcia, Boletín no. 540, 15 March 1942; no. 603, 15 April 1942.

123 Iniesta, *Garra Marxista*, p. 264; Arrese, *La revolución social*, p. 164.

124 Zalba, *La prostitución*, pp. xiii–xviii.

125 George Orwell, *Homage to Catalonia* (London 1986), p. 3.

126 Dispatch, DNII, Barcelona, January 1946, AGA, Pres, SGM, caja 165; Ronald Fraser, *In Hiding: The Life of Manuel Cortes* (Harmondsworth, 1972). See also Umbral, *Memorias*, which suggests the problems in analysing social phenomena during the Spanish post-war as economic hardship and psychological responses interacted.

127 Umbral, *Memorias*, p. 70.

128 Alba, *Sleepless Spain*, pp. 185–6. Pilfering from factories was commonplace. For instance, PRO/FO371/73356/Z4555/596/G, 28 May 1948; Balfour, *Dictatorship*, pp. 8–9.

CONCLUSION

1 See the comments of Juan Marsé in Tununa Mercado, 'Juan Marsé: la novela como testimonio de la memoria colectiva', Diorama de la cultura, *El Excelsior*, cited in Mangini, *Rojos y rebeldes*, p. 29.

2 José Asenjo, *Conversación sobre la guerra* (Barcelona, 1978), p. 215, cited in

Eduardo Godoy Gallardo, *La infancia en la narrativa española de posguerra* (Madrid, 1979), p. 22.

3 Carles Santacana i Torres, *Victoriosos i derrotats: el franquisme a L'Hospitalet, 1939–1951* (Barcelona, 1994), p. 113.

4 Mallada, *Los males de la Patria*; Tierno Galván, *Costa y el regeneracionismo*, in *Escritos*, pp. 385–6.

5 For example, FET–JONS, DNII, Huelva, Boletín 480, 20 February 1942, AGA, Pres, caja 16; Barcelona, 'Partes', September 1946; March, September 1947, AGA, Presidencia, caja 165.

6 For example, FET–JONS, DNII, Murcia, Boletín 693, 30 May 1942, AGA, Pres, caja 16.

7 For example, Romeu Alfaro, *El silencio roto*; Marsé, 'La novela como testimonio', in Mangini, *Rojos y rebeldes*, p. 29; Marsé, *Si te dicen que caí*, pp. 275–6.

8 PRO/FO371/49575/Z7167/89/41, Bowker to Eden, 16 June 1945.

Bibliography

(1) PRIMARY PUBLISHED AND UNPUBLISHED SOURCE MATERIAL. (WITH ABBREVIATIONS)

ARCHIVES

Madrid
Archivo General de la Administración (AGA), Alcalá de Henares:
Presidencia del Gobierno (Pres). Secretaria General del Movimiento (SGM).
Ministerio de Industria y Comercio
Archivo Histórico Nacional (AHN)
Causa General. Declaraciones

Bilbao
Archivo de la Cámara de Comercio (ACCB)
Expedientes and Biblioteca
Archive and Library of the Sociedad Bilbaina (ASB)
Archivo del Gobernador Civil (AGC)
Archivo del Centro Industrial de Vizcaya (ACIV)

Barcelona
Arxiu General del 'Tribunal de Responsabilidades Políticas' del Tribunal Superior de Justicia de Catalunya (ATRP)
Arxiu Històric de la Ciutat

London
Public Record Office, Kew (PRO)
Foreign Office Papers

COMPANY REPORTS

Altos Hornos de Vizcaya; Asfaltos y Portland 'Asland'; Banco de Bilbao; Banco Hispano Americano; Banco Urquijo; Banco de Vizcaya; Basconia; Construcciones 'Babcock and Wilcox'; Echevarría SA Euskalduna; Nueva Montaña SA La Papelera Española; Saltos del Duero; Sociedad Española de Construcción Naval.

NEWSPAPERS, PERIODICALS AND OFFICIAL PUBLICATIONS

ABC
Acción Española
El Alcázar
Alimentación Nacional
Anthropos
Anuario Estadístico de España
Anuario Oficial de Estadística
Arriba
Arriba España
L'Avenç
Boletín Minero e Industrial
Boletín Oficial del Estado (BOE)
Chicago Tribune
La Codorniz
La Conquista del Estado
El Correo Catalán
De Economía
Destino
Diario de Barcelona
El Diario Vasco
Domingo
Dyna
Ecclesia
Economía
Economía Mundial
Economía Vascongada
El Economista
Ejército
España Económica y Financiera
Español
Falange Española
Fe y Acción
El Financiero
Fotos
Gaceta de la República
La Gaceta del Norte
Hechos
Heraldo de Aragón
Hierro
Historia 16
Hoy
Información
Información Comercial Española (ICE)
Informaciones
Ingeniería Naval
Interviú

The Lancet
Madrid
Manchester Guardian
Manresa
Moneda y Crédito
New York Herald Tribune
New York Times
El Noticiero Universal
Nueva Economía Nacional
El País
Papers: Revista de Sociología
Pueblo
Qué pasa?
Radio Nacional
Redención
Revista de Economía Política
Revista de Estudios Políticos
Semana Médica Española
Solidaridad Nacional
The Times
El Trabajo Nacional
Unidad: Diario de Combate Nacional-Sindicalista
La Vanguardia Española
Vértice
Ya

PUBLISHED CONTEMPORARY ACCOUNTS, MEMOIRS AND DOCUMENTS

Alarcón y de la Lastra, Luis. *El triunfo nacional y sus repercusiones en las orientaciones de la industria y el comercio* (Madrid, 1940).

Alba, Victor. *Sleepless Spain* (London, 1948).

Albiñana Sanz, José María, *España bajo la dictadura Republicana: crónica de un período putrefacto* (Madrid, 1932).

Alfarache, Guzmán de. *18 de julio: historia del Glorioso Alzamiento de Sevilla* (Seville, 1937).

Alonso, Martín. *Enciclopedia del idioma* (Madrid, 1958).

Alonso González, R. and Castañón Suárez, L. *La contribución excepcional sobre beneficios extraordinarios de guerra* (Lugo, 1939).

Angolotti, Joaquín. 'La minería de Vizcaya y su situación actual', in *Primer Consejo Provincial de Ordenación Económica de Vizcaya* (Bilbao, 1944).

Ansaldo, Juan Antonio. *¿Para qué . . . ? (De Alfonso XIII a Juan III)* (Buenos Aires, 1951).

Aparicio, Juan. *Conquista del estado; antología* (Madrid, 1939).

Arburua, Manuel. *Cinco años al frente del Ministerio de Comercio: discursos y declaraciones, 1951–1956* (Madrid, 1956).

Arcoy Garay, Ricardo. *La idea del imperio en la política y literatura españolas* (Madrid, 1944).

Areilza, José María de. 'El futuro de nuestro pueblo: nacionalsindicalismo', *JONS* (May 1933).

'Estado nacional', *JONS* (September 1933), in Juan Aparicio. *JONS: antología* (Barcelona, 1939).

'Directrices de la nueva ordenación económica', in *Problemas técnicas de importancia económica en la nueva organización de España* (Barcelona, 1940).

'La industria española y la sindicación industrial', *La Vanguardia Española*, 6 March 1940.

Areilza, José María de, and Castiella, Fernando María. *Reivindicaciones de España* (Madrid, 1941).

Arregui Mendia, Antonio. *Orientaciones generales para el desarrollo y prosperidad de la provincia de Vizcaya* (Bilbao, 1934).

Arrese, José Luis de. *El estado totalitario en el pensamiento de José Antonio* (Prologue by Raimundo Fernández Cuesta) ([first published 1938] Madrid, 1945).

La revolución social del nacional-sindicalismo (Madrid, 1940).

Artigas Sanz, Jose Antonio de. *Surco económico en el regazo de España* (Madrid, 1943).

Ascauito, Alfonso de. *España imperio: el nuevo humanismo y la hispanidad* (Avila, 1939).

Asher, P.H. *National Self-Sufficiency* (London, 1938).

Aunós Pérez, Antonio. *Los problemas de la producción en el orden nuevo: ideario político-social* (Barcelona, 1941).

Aunós Pérez, Eduardo. *La reforma corporativa del estado* (Madrid, 1936).

Calvo Sotelo y la política de su tiempo (Madrid, 1941).

España en crisis (1874–1936) (Buenos Aires, 1942).

El general Primo de Rivera (Madrid, 1944).

La política social de la dictadura (Madrid, 1944).

Autonomous Government of Euzkadi. *Report on the Administration of Justice in The Basque Country During the Civil War* (Paris, 1938).

Azaña, Manuel. *Obras completas* (Mexico City, 1968).

Causas de la guerra de España (Barcelona, 1986).

Aznar, Severino. 'El régimen de subsidios familiares, la fraternidad cristiana a las consignas del nuevo estado', *Revista Internacional de Sociología*, 2/3 (1943).

Azpiazu, Joaquín de. *El control obrero en el aspecto cristiano (conferencia en Agrupación Vasca de Acción Social Cristiana)* (Bilbao, 1932).

Deberes de los obreros (Madrid, 1935).

Deberes de los patronos (Madrid, 1935).

El estado católico: líneas de un ideal (Madrid, 1939).

El estado corporativo (Madrid, 1939).

Orientaciones cristianas del Fuero del Trabajo (Burgos, 1939).

Los precios abusivos ante la moral (Madrid, 1941).

Manual de Acción Católica (Madrid, 1941).

Moral profesional económica (Madrid, 1941).

Bahamonde, Antonio. *Un año con Queipo: memorias de un nacionalista* (Barcelona, 1938).

Banco de Bilbao. *Agenda financiera, 1951* (Bilbao, 1951).

Un siglo en la vida del Banco de Bilbao (Bilbao, 1957).

Banco de España. *Ritmo de la crisis económica española en relación con la mundial* (Madrid, 1933).

Banco de Santander. *Aportación al estudio de la historia económica de la Montaña* (Santander 1957).

Bandos y órdenes dictados por el Excmo. Señor D. Gonzalo Queipo de Llano y Sierra (Seville, 1937).

Barba Hernandez, Bartolomé. *Dos años al frente del gobierno civil de Barcelona* (Madrid, 1948).

Barcena y Diaz, Leopoldo. *En defensa de nuestra economía nacional* ([1932]1978).

Barranquero Texeira, Encarnación. *Málaga entre la guerra y la posguerra* (Málaga, 1994)

Beltrán Florez, Lucas. *La industria algodonera española* (Barcelona, 1943).

Beneyto Pérez, Juan. *El Nuevo Estado Español: el régimen nacional-sindicalista ante la tradición y los demás sistemas totalitarios* (Madrid, 1939).

FET–JONS, Antología (Barcelona, 1939).

'La concepción jerárquica de la sociedad en el pensamiento medieval español', *Estudios de historia social de España*, 1 (1949), pp. 555–66.

Benítez de Lugo, Luis. *Responsabilidades civiles y políticas* (Barcelona, 1940).

Bertrán Güell, Felipe. *Caudillo, profetas, y soldados* (Madrid, 1939).

La España de 1936: ruta de la victoria (Madrid, 1939).

Preparación y desarrollo del alzamiento nacional (Valladolid, 1939).

Bertrán y Musitu, José. *Experiencias de los Servicios de Información de la Frontera del Nordeste de España* (Barcelona, 1941).

Biagi, Bruno. *Desarrollos actuales y futuros del corporativismo* (trans. Felipe Ferrer Calbeto) (Cádiz, 1938).

Bidagor Lasarte, Pedro, *El futuro Madrid* (Madrid, 1945).

Bloch, Ernst. 'Nonsynchronism and the Obligation to its Dialectics', *New German Critique*, 11 ([originally 1932] Spring 1977).

'Efectos políticos de desarrollo desigual', in K. Lenk, *El concepto de ideología* (Buenos Aires, 1971).

Bolín, Luis. *Spain: The Vital Years* (London, 1968).

Borkenau, Franz. *The Spanish Cockpit* ([originally 1937] Ann Arbor, MI, 1963).

Borrell y Macia, José. *Instalación y modificación de industrias* (Barcelona, 1943).

El intervencionismo del estado en las actividades económicas, su extensión y límites (Barcelona, 1946).

Bover, José María. *Los soldados: primacias de la gentilidad cristiana* (Barcelona, 1941).

Brenan, Gerald. *The Face of Spain* ([originally 1950] Harmondsworth, 1965).

South From Granada (Cambridge, 1972).

Burgos y Mazo, Manuel de. *¿Quién es España?* (Seville, 1940).

Cabanellas de Torres, Guillermo. *Diccionario militar* (Buenos Aires, 1963).

Calvo Serer, Rafael. *Política de integración* (Madrid, 1955).

Calvo Sotelo, José. *Mis servicios al estado: seis años de gestión: apuntes para la historia* (Madrid, 1931).

El capitalismo contemporáneo y su evolución (Madrid, 1938).

Calzada, Luciano de la. 'El espíritu del 18 de julio como realidad histórica y proyección hacia el futuro', in *La guerra de liberación nacional* (Zaragoza, 1961).

Cambó, Francesc. Prologue to Aunós Pérez, Eduardo, *Problemas de España* (Barcelona, 1922).

Las dictaduras (2nd edn, Madrid, 1929).

Entorn del feixisme italiana (Barcelona, 1924). Spanish version, *En torno al fascismo italiano* (Barcelona, 1925).

Cano Denia, J. 'Beneficios de empresas en 1952', *Revista de Economía Aplicada*, 4 (June 1952), pp. 3–7.

Cano Denia, Simón. 'La alimentación nacional', *Revista de Economía Aplicada*, 2 (December 1951), pp. 9–19.

Canosa, R. *Un siglo de la banca privada (1845–1945): apuntes para la historia de las finanzas españolas* (Madrid, 1945).

Cantalupo, Roberto. *La clase dirigente: profundo estudio sobre la ideología del fascismo y la historia contemporánea de Italia.* ([Italian original, 1926] Madrid, 1939).

Fu la spagna (Milan, 1948).

Capella, Miguel. *La autarquía económica en España* (Madrid, 1945).

Carande, Ramón. 'Bases de una política económica de reconstrucción', *Revista de Estudios Políticos* 1, 1 (1941).

Carbonell, Angel. *Cartas de combate: en defensa de la fe dirigidas a las juventudes cristianas* (Barcelona, 1940).

Carceller, Demetrio. *La situación económica de España* (Madrid, 1943).

Cardell, Carlos, *Antología de José Calvo Sotelo* (Madrid, 1942).

Careaga de Lequerica, Pilar. 'El advenimiento de la república', in *De la Regencia al día de la victoria* (Bilbao, 1956).

Carrero Blanco, Luis. *España y el mar* (Madrid, 1942).

Carrión, Pascual. *La reforma agraria: problemas fundamentales* (Madrid, 1931).

Los latifundios en España (Madrid, [1932]1975).

La reforma agraria de la segunda república y la situación actual de la agricultura española (Prologue by Juan Velarde Fuertes) (Barcelona, 1973).

Castellanos, Pedro. *Policía integral o policía nacional-sindicalista* (Valladolid, 1939).

Castillo, Alberto de. *La maquinista terrestre y marítima: personaje histórico (1855–1955)* (Barcelona, 1955).

Castro Albarrán, D de. 'El Movimiento Nacional Español desde el punto de vista católico', in *Ha hablado la Iglesia* (Burgos, 1937).

Castro, Cristóbal de. *Mujeres del imperio* (Madrid, 1941).

Cereceda, Feliciano, *Historia del imperio español y de la hispandad* (Madrid, 1940).

Cesar, Oldemiro. *A guerra, aquele monstruo . . . dois meses nas Astúrias entre soldados galegos* (Lisbon, 1937).

Churruca, Alfonso. *Minería, industria y comercio del País Vasco* (San Sebastián, 1951).

'El movimiento nacional', in *De la Regencia al día de la victoria* (Bilbao 1956).

Cid de la Llave, Benito. *Consideraciones sobre el problema del abastecimiento nacional: su origen y causa* (Madrid, 1944).

Crisis? Escasez? Especulación? Racionamiento! Consideraciones sobre el problema del abastecimiento nacional, su origen y causas (Madrid, 1944).

Clinton Pelham, G. *Spain: Review of Commercial Conditions* (London. 1951).

Committee of Investigation appointed by the National Government at Burgos. *The Second and Third Official Reports on The Communist Atrocities Committed in Southern Spain from July to October 1936 by the Communist Forces of the Madrid Government* (Preface by Arthur Bryant) (London, 1937).

Conde, Francisco Javier. *Contribución a la teoría del Caudillaje* (Madrid, 1942).

Representación política y régimen español (Madrid, 1945).

Consejo Económico Sindical Nacional. *Veinte años de crecimiento económico* (Madrid, 1960).

Corporativismo Gremial: la organización social en la nueva España (1937).

Cort, César. *Campos urbanizados y ciudades ruralizados* (Madrid, 1941).

Cruz Baños, Ignacio. *Bases para la organización de la propiedad en la Nueva España* (San Sebastián, 1939).

Dávila, Sancho and Pemartín, Julián. *Hacia la historia de la Falange* (Jeréz, 1938).

Delegación oficial del estado en las industrias siderúrgicas. *Memoria* (Madrid, 1944).

Delgado Iribarren, José Antonio. *Jesuitas en España* (Madrid, 1956).

Department of Overseas Trade. *Spain: Review of Commercial Conditions* (London, 1945).

Diccionario de la lengua española (Madrid, 1947).

Dictamen de la Comisión sobre ilegitimidad de poderes actuantes en 18 de julio de 1936 (Barcelona, 1939).

Dirección General de Industria y Comercio. *Avance-resumen de la labor realizada desde Octubre de 1939 a Octubre de 1941 por aplicación del Decreto de 8.9.39 que regula el establecimiento de nuevas industrias* (Madrid, 1941).

La política industrial en la Nueva España (Madrid, 1942).

Memoria-resumen de las actividades desarrolladas por los servicios de industria durante el bienio 1945/6 (Madrid, 1947).

Dirección General de Regiones Devastadas y Reparaciones. *La reconstrucción de España: resumen de dos años de labor* (Madrid, 1942).

Dirección General de Sanidad. *Estudios de nutrición* (Madrid, 1943).

Distrito Minero de Vizcaya, *Memoria estadística* (1940).

Diumaró y Mimó, Enrique. *El problema industrial textil: el maquinismo y la cuestión social* (Barcelona, 1939).

Dominguez Marroquin, Xavier. 'La Falange y sus caídos', in *De la Regencia al día de la victoria* (Bilbao, 1956).

Echeverría, Lamberto de. *Ascética del hombre de la calle* (2nd edn, Barcelona, 1956).

Egert, Franz. *Autarkie* (Berlin, 1934).

Ejercicios espirituales de San Ignacio de Loyola en su texto original (Barcelona, 1892).

Eliseda, Marqués de. *Fascismo, catolicismo, monarquía* (Madrid, 1935).

El sentido fascista del Movimiento Nacional (Madrid, 1939).

Elorduy, Elenterio. *La idea del imperio en el pensamiento español y de otros pueblos* (Madrid, 1944).

Enciclopedia, segundo grado (Madrid, n.d.).

Escagues de Javierre, Isidoro. *La transformación económica de Vizcaya* (Madrid, 1959).

Escobar, Adrián C. *Diálogo íntimo con España: memorias de un embajador durante la tempestad europea* (Buenos Aires, 1950).

Espérabe de Arteaga, Enrique. *La guerra de reconquista española que ha salvado a Europa y el criminal comunismo* (Madrid, 1940).

Eza, Vizconde de. *La agonía del comunismo* (Madrid, 1932).

El progreso social en suspenso (Madrid, 1934).

La economía de España ante la paz (Madrid, 1945).

Fenech, Miguel. *La posición del juez en el Nuevo Estado* (Madrid, 1941).

Fernández Almagro, M. *Política naval de la España moderna y contemporánea* (Madrid, 1946).

Fernández Asiaín, *El delito de rebelión militar* (Madrid, 1943).

Fernandez Baños, Olegario. *Trabajo y capital* (Barcelona, 1940).

Ferrer Calbeto, Felipe. *Nacionalismo económico español* (Madrid, 1934: Cádiz, 1938).

Armas de los imperialismos plutocráticos (Cádiz, 1938).

Nacionalismo en lo económico: ¿simple autosuficiencia o plena autarquía? Libertad y poder nacionales (Conference, Barcelona, July, 1940).

Capacidad económica de España para superar las dificultades del momento actual (Barcelona, 1941).

FET y de las JONS, Organización sindical. *Fichero de historia económico-social* (Madrid, 1957).

FET y de las JONS, *Veinte años de paz: Vizcaya.* (Bilbao, 1959).

Fidalgo, Pilar. *A Young Mother in Franco's Spain* (London, 1939).

Figuras de hoy. (Madrid, 1956).

Fisher, A.G.B. *Economic Self-Sufficiency* (Oxford, 1939).

Foltz, Charles Jr. *The Masquerade in Spain* (Boston, MA, 1948).

Fomento de la producción nacional, *Homenaje de Cataluña liberada a su Caudillo Franco* (Barcelona, 1940).

Fontana Tarrats, J.M. *Los Catalanes en la guerra de España* (Madrid, 1952).

Franco, Francisco. *Palabras del Caudillo (19 abril 1937–31 diciembre 1938)* (Barcelona, 1938).

Mensaje del Caudillo a los españoles, discurso pronunciado por S.E. el Jefe del Estado la noche del 31 de diciembre de 1939 (Madrid, 1939).

Palabras del Caudillo (19 abril 1937–7 diciembre, 1942) (Madrid, 1943).

Franco ha dicho (Madrid, 1947).

Franco in Barcelona (London, 1939).

Franco's Rule: Back to the Middle Ages (London, 1938).

Franco Salgado-Araujo, Francisco. *Mis conversaciones privadas con Franco* (Barcelona, 1976).

Franco Salgado-Araujo, Francisco, and Galinsoga, Luis. *Centinela de Occidente: sembleza biográfica de Francisco Franco* (Barcelona, 1956).

Frentes y Hospitales de Vizcaya, *Seis meses de labor* (Bilbao, 1938).

Fuentes Irurozqui, Manuel. *El comercio exterior del Nuevo Estado, 1936–1940* (Madrid, 1941).

Abastecimientos, tasas y racionamientos (Madrid, 1942).

Evolución, presente y futuro del comercio exterior de España (Publicaciones de la sección de Información y Propaganda del Ministerio de Industria y Comercio (Madrid, 1942).

Tres ensayos sobre el nuevo orden económico (Madrid, 1942).

'España y el comercio internacional', in *Ciclo de conferencias* (Madrid, 1943).

Cinco años de intervención en el comercio español (1939–1944) (Madrid, 1944).

Economía e industria nacional (Madrid, 1948).

El Pensamiento económico de José Antonio Primo de Rivera (Madrid, 1966).

Fuller, J.F.C. *The Conquest of Red Spain* (London, 1937).

Ganivet, Angel. *Idearium Español* (Madrid, 1897).

Antología (Madrid, 1943).

Obras completas (Madrid, 1943).

García Díaz Figar, P. Antonio. *Virtudes militares* (Barcelona, 1941).

García González, Aurelio, and Mira Izquierdo, José María. *El trigo, su economía y su legislación actual* (Madrid, 1946).

García Morente, Manuel. *Ideas para una filosofía de la historia de España* (Madrid, 1943).

Idea de la Hispanidad. I. España como estilo. II. El caballero cristiano. (Madrid, 1947 [1938]).

Garrigues, Joaquín. *Tres conferencias en Italia sobre el Fuero del Trabajo* (Madrid, 1939).

Gay y Forner, Vicente. *Constitución y vida del pueblo español: esudio sobre la etnografía y psicología de las razas de la España contemporánea* (Madrid, 1905).

La revolución nacional-socialista: ambiente, leyes, ideología (Barcelona, 1934).

Estampas rojas y caballeros blancos (Burgos, 1937).

Gay de Montellà, Rafael. *El Fuero del Trabajo y sistema del Estado Sindical-Corporativo* (Valladolid, 1939).

Autarquía. Nuevas orientaciones de la economía (Barcelona, 1940).

Gil Robles, José María. *No fue posible la paz* (Barcelona, 1968).

Giménez Caballero, Ernesto. *Genio de España* (Madrid, 1932).

Ante la tumba del Catalanismo – notas de un viaje con Franco a Cataluña (Barcelona, 1942).

Goicoechea, Antonio. *Discurso ante la Junta General de accionistas del Banco de España (December 1942)* (Madrid, 1942).

Gollonet Megías, Angel and Morales López, José. *Rojo y azul en Granada* (Granada, 1937).

Sangre y fuego: Málaga (Granada, 1937).

Gomá, Cardinal Isidro. *Pastorales de la guerra de España* (Madrid, 1955).

Gonzálbez Ruiz, Francisco. *Yo he creído en Franco: proceso de una gran desilusión (dos meses en la Cárcel de Sevilla)* (Madrid, 1938).

González Oliveros, Wenceslao. *Falange y Requeté orgánicamente solidarios* (Valladolid, 1937).

Gual Villalbí, Pedro. *Política Económica* (Barcelona, 1936).

Ante una transformación profunda del concepto del mercado. (hechos nuevos y viejas ideas) (Madrid, 1941).

Alteraciones en el espíritu y en la estructura de la economía Catalana actual (Barcelona, 1956).

Guillén Salaya. *La economía del porvenir* (Madrid, 1945).

Hamilton, T.J. *Appeasement's Child: The Franco Regime in Spain* (New York, 1943).

Hayes, Carlton. *Wartime Mission in Spain* (London, 1945).

Herce Vales, Fernando and Sanz Nogués, Manuel. *Franco, el reconquistador* (Madrid, 1939).

Herrero Larralda, I. *La política del carbón en España* (Madrid, 1944).

Hoare, Samuel. *Ambassador on Special Mission* (London, 1946).

Hodgson, R. *Spain Resurgent* (London 1953).

Ibarra y Cespedes, Marqués de. *Estudio económico social anterior y posterior a 1931* (Madrid, 1935).

Reconstrucción económica (Madrid, 1939).

Iniesta, Alfonso. *Garra Marxista en la infancia* (Burgos, 1939).

Instituto Nacional de Industria. *Notas en relación con la creación y desenvolvimiento de este Instituto* (Madrid, 1941).

Breve resumen sobre las finalidades y actuación del INI: años 1941–1946 (Madrid, 1947).

Iribarne, J. *Las dos oligarquías capitalistas que devoran a España: el concierto económico de las Vascongadas y la autonomía de Cataluña* (Madrid, 1933).

Iribarren, José María. *Con el General Mola* (Zaragoza, 1937).

Irurzún y Rubio, M. *La política arancelaria nacional* (Barcelona, 1940).

Jimeno, J.R. 'La natalidad y el futuro desarrollo de la población de España', *Boletín de Estadística* (January–March, 1943), pp. 150–73.

Joaniquet, Aurelio. *Calvo Sotelo: una vida fecunda, un ideario político, una doctrina económica* (Santander 1939).

JONS. *Antología* (Prologue by Juan Aparici) (Madrid, 1943).

Jorro y Miranda, J. *La crisis económica mundial y el problema obrero* (Barcelona, 1934).

Junta de Ordenación Económico-Social de la Provincia de Barcelona. *Plan de ordenación económica y social* (Barcelona, 1947).

Kemp, Peter. *Mine Were of Trouble* (London, 1957).

Kindelán, Alfredo. *La verdad de mis relaciones con Franco* (Barcelona, 1981).

Koestler, Arthur. *Spanish Testament* (London, 1937).

Kultur Taldea, Altaffaylla. *Navarra 1936: de la esperanza al terror* (Navarre, 1936).

Labadié Otermín, F. and Cerezo Barredo, G. *Notas al futuro económico de España* (Madrid, 1958).

Laín Entralgo, Pedro. *La generación del noventa y ocho* (Madrid, 1945).

Larráz, José. *El ordenamiento del mercado triguero en España* (Madrid, 1935).

La meta de dos revoluciones (Madrid, 1946).

Laureados de España (Madrid, 1940).

Ledesma Ramos, Ramiro. *Discurso a las juventudes de España* (Madrid, 1954).

Legaz y Lacambra, Luis. *Introducción a la teoría del Estado Nacionalsindicalista* (Barcelona, 1940).

'Libertad política y libertad civil, según Joaquín Costa', *Revista de Estudios Políticos* (September–December 1946).

Legaz y Lacambra, Luis, and Aragon, Bartolomé. *Cuatro estudios sobre sindicalismo vertical* (Zaragoza, 1939).

Lequérica, José Felix de. *La actividad económica de Vizcaya en la vida nacional* (Madrid, 1956).

Les archives secretes du Comte Ciano, 1936–1942 (Paris, 1948).

Leyva y Andía, Juan de, et al. *El hombre, la explotación, el mercado: organización de la economía agrícola dirigida en Alemania* (Madrid, 1941).

Libro de Oro de Bilbao, – album de fotografías del segundo aniversario de la liberación de Bilbao (Bilbao 1939).

Lo que han hecho en Galicia: episodios del terror blanco en las provincias gallegas contados por quienes los han vivido (Paris, 1938).

Lohmann Villena, Guillerno. *Menéndez y Pelayo y la hispanidad* (Madrid, 1957).

López Galua, Enrique. *Futura grandeza de España según notables profecías* (La Coruña, 1941).

López Ibor, Juan José. *Discurso a los universitarios españoles* (Salamanca, 1938).

'Experiencias psiquiátricas de guerra', *Revista Española de Medicina y Cirugía de Guerra*, 2, 5 (1939), pp. 82–101.

Neurosis de guerra (Barcelona, 1942).

El español y su complejo de inferioridad (Madrid, 1951).

López Sáinz, I. 'Algunos datos y sugerencias sobre el suicidio en España', in *IV Congreso nacional de neuropsiquiatría* (Madrid, 1954).

Luis y Pérez, J.B. *La personalidad de la mujer* (Oviedo, 1933).

Llano Gorostiza, Manuel. 'Bilbao: precursor del Alzamiento Nacional', in *De la Regencia al día de la victoria* (Bilbao, 1956).

Macías Picavea, Ricardo. *El problema nacional: hechos, causas y remedios* (Madrid, 1899).

Maeztu, Ramiro de. *Defensa de la hispanidad* (Madrid, 1934).

Maíllo, Adolfo. *Educación y revolución: los fundamentos de una educación nacional* (Madrid, 1943).

Mallada, Lucas. *Los males de la Patria y la futura revolución española* ([originally, 1890] Madrid, 1969).

Manoilescu, Mihail. *Teoría del proteccionismo y del comercio internacional* (Madrid, 1943).

El Partido Unico: institución política de los nuevos regimenes (Prologue by Raimundo Fernández Cuesta) (Zaragoza 1938).

Marcet Coll, José María. *Mi ciudad y yo: veinte años en una alcaldía 1940–1960* (Barcelona, 1963).

Marco Merenciano, Francisco. *Esquizofrenias paranoides* (Barcelona, 1942).

Ensayos médicos y literarios: antología (Madrid, 1958).

Marín Pérez, Pascal. *El caudillaje español: ensayo de construcción históriocojurídica* (Madrid, 1960).

Martín Artajo, Alberto. *La política de aislamiento de España seguida por las naciones aliados durante el quinquenio 1945–1950* (Madrid, 1950).

Martín Sanz, Dionisio. *El problema triguero y el nacional-sindicalismo* (Valladolid, 1937).

Técnica y política agraria (Madrid, 1946).

Martínez, Claudio. *Excitación a la rebelión* (Burgos, 1939).

Matthews, Herbert. *The Yoke and the Arrows* (London, 1958).

Memoria de la Junta General de Accionistas del Banco de España (Madrid, 1942).

Memoria de la V feria de muestras de Bilbao (Bilbao, 1941).

Mendizábal, Alfred. *The Martyrdom of Spain* (London, 1938).

Menéndez y Pelayo, Marcelino. *Historia de los heterodoxos españoles* (Madrid, 1880–2).

Miguel, Antonio de. *El potencial económico de España* (Madrid, 1935).

Millan de Val, F. *La Siderúrgica Española después del movimiento nacional* (Madrid, 1944).

Ministerio de la Gobernación. *La reconstrucción de España: resumen de dos años de labor* (Madrid, 1942).

Ministerio de Industria. *El desarrollo industrial de España, 1939–1958* (Madrid, 1959).

Ministerio de Industria y Comercio. *Catálogo oficial de la producción industrial de España*, 2 vols. (Madrid, 1938; 1938–42).

Ministerio de Industria y Comercio, Dirección General de Industria. *La política industrial en la Nueva España* (Madrid, 1942).

La industrialización de la energía eléctrica en España (Madrid, 1960).

Ministerio de Justicia. *La obra penitenciaria durante el año 1941 – El Patronato Central de Nuestra Señora de la merced para la redención de penas por el trabajo* (Madrid, 1942; 1946; 1947).

Causa general: la dominación roja en España (Madrid, 1943).

Ministerio de Trabajo. *Dos años de actuación* (Madrid, 1943).

Mola, Emilio. *Obras completas* (Madrid, 1940).

El pasado, Azaña y el porvenir (Madrid, 1934) in *Obras completas* (Madrid, 1940).

Montañes, Carlos, E. *Sugerencias para la solución práctica de problemas económico-administrativos de España* (Zaragoza 1937).

Montero, Eloy. *Marruecos: el pueblo moro y el judío* (Madrid, 1911).

El individualismo económico y los modernos exigencias de la justicia social (Barcelona, 1917).

Neomalthusianismo, eugenesia y divorcio (Madrid, 1932).

Los estados modernos y la nueva Espana (Vitoria, 1939).

Montero Díaz, Santiago. *La política social en la zona Marxista* (Bilbao, 1938).

Moret Messerli, Francisco. *ABC político de la Nueva España* (Barcelona, 1940).

Muggeridge, Malcolm (ed.). *Ciano's Diplomatic Papers* (London, 1948).

Muñoz Casayus, Antonio, Prieto Castro, Leonardo and Sancho Izquierdo, Miguel. *Corporatismo: Los movimientos nacionales contemporáneos* (Zaragoza, 1937).

Muñoz Linares, Carlos. 'La concentración del capital en las sociedades y empresas españolas', *Revista de Economía Política*, 3, 3 (January 1952), pp. 221–59.

El monopolio de la industria eléctrica (Madrid, 1954).

Navarro Mora, J.M. 'Conceptos elementales de la autarquía económica', *Moneda y Crédito*, 13 (June 1945), pp. 53–6.

Nordlinger, Eric. *Soldiers in Politics: Military Coups and Governments* (Englewood, NJ, 1977).

Notas sobre política económica española (Madrid, 1954).

Nuñez Morgado, Aurelio. *Los sucesos de España vistos por un diplomático* (Buenos Aires, 1941).

Olariaga, Luis. 'España y la situación económica del mundo', *Economía Española*, 1, 6 (June 1933) pp. 96–118.

Olmedo, Felix G. *Introducción a la vida de San Ignacio de Loyola* (Madrid, 1944).

Ortega y Gasset, José. *España invertebrada: bosquejo de algunos pensamientos históricos* (Madrid, 1921).

Teoría de Andalucía (Madrid, 1942).

Pablo Romero, Juan José de. *Teología ascética y mística* (Soria, 1940).

París Eguílaz, Higinio. *El estado y la economía: política económica totalitaria* (Santander, 1939).

La guerra y los problemas económicos (Santander, 1939).

Política de creación de trabajo (Madrid, 1940).

Resultados de la política económica nacional-socialista (Madrid, 1940).

Economía de guerra (Madrid, 1942).

Un nuevo orden económico (Madrid, 1942).

Política económica nacional (Madrid, 1943).

Diez años de política económica en España 1939–1949 (Madrid, 1949).

'La política económica durante la guerra española de 1936–1939', *Economía* (July–December, 1964).

El desarrollo económico español, 1906–1964 (Madrid, 1965).

Partes Oficiales de Guerra, 1936–1939 (Madrid, 1977).

Patronato Central de Redención de Penas por el Trabajo, El. *La obra de la redención de penas – la doctrina, la práctica, la legislación* (Madrid, 1941).

Peiró, Francisco. *Sentido religioso y militar de la vida* (Burgos, 1938).

Peiró, Joan. *Perill a la reraguarda* (Mataró, 1936).

Pemán y Pemartín, José María. *Arengas y crónicas de guerra* (Cádiz, 1937).

El Séneca y sus puntos de vista (Jeréz de la Frontera, 1953).

Pemartín, José. *Hacia la historia de la Falange* (Jeréz, 1938).

Los orígenes del movimiento (Burgos 1938).

Qué es 'lo nuevo'. Consideraciones sobre el momento español presente (Santander, 1938).

'La Cruz Laureada del Generalísimo Franco', in *Laureados de España* (Madrid, 1940).

Teoría de la Falange (Madrid, 1941).

Peña Boeuf, Alfonso. *Memorias de un ingeniero político* (Madrid, 1954).

Pérez del Pulgar, J.A. 'El concepto cristiano de la autarquía', in *Anales de mecánica y electricidad de los ingenieros del ICAI* (Madrid, 1941).

Pérez Urruti, Manuel. *España en numeros: síntesis de la producción, consumo y comercio nacionales 1940 y 1941* (Madrid, 1942).

Perpiña Grau, Román. *Memorandum sobre la política del carbón* (Valencia, 1935).

Destino hispano: el movimiento: la lucha: la nueva vida (Valencia 1939).

'Economía hispana y orden nuevo', *Anales de Economía*, 1 (April–June, 1941), pp. 219–32.

De estructura económica y economía hispana (Madrid, [1936] 1952).

Prologue to Carrera Pujal, Jaime, *Historia de la economía española* (Barcelona, 1944).

Pique Batlle, Ricardo. *La ficción de los grandes beneficios* (Barcelona, 1947).

Plaza Prieto, Juan. 'El pensamiento económico de José Antonio', *De Economía* (July–August 1950).

Plenn, Abel. *Wind in the Olive Trees: Spain from the Inside* (New York, 1946).

Pradera, Victor. *El Estado Nuevo* (Burgos, 1932).

Primo de Rivera, José Antonio. *Discursos frente el parlamento* (Barcelona, 1939).

Obras completas (Madrid, 1945).

Problemas técnicos de importancia económica en la nueva organización de España (Barcelona, 1940).

Pugés, Manuel. *Como triunfó el proteccionismo en España: la formación de la política arancelaria española* (Barcelona, 1931).

Quinientas fotos de la guerra (Valladolid, 1937).

Ramón-Laca, Julio de. *Bajo la férula de Queipo: como fue gobernada Andalucía* (Seville, 1939).

Recristianización de la cultura española, La (Madrid, 1949).

Redondo, Onésinco. *El estado nacional* (Madrid, 1939).

Ridruejo, Dionisio. *Escrito en España* (Buenos Aires, 1962).

Casi unas memorias (Barcelona, 1976).

Río Cisneros, Agustín del. *José Antonio y la revolución nacional* (Madrid, 1949; 4th edn, Madrid, 1968).

Robert, Antonio. *La industrialización rural como remedio al desequilibrio económico entre el campo y la ciudad* (Instituto Nacional de Colonización, Madrid, 1942).

'El estado y la economía', in *Ciclo de conferencias sobre temas de carácter económico organizado por la Junta de Cultura de Vizcaya y la Cámara Oficial de Comercio, Industria y Navegación de Bilbao* (Bilbao, 1943), pp. 195–218.

Un problema nacional: la industrialización necesaria (Madrid, 1943).

Los países olvidados y la economía de la paz (Madrid, 1944).

'La política industrial', in Instituto de Estudios Políticos, *El Nuevo Estado Español – veinticinco años de Movimiento Nacional, 1936–1961* (Madrid, 1961), pp. 511–24.

Rogers, T.E. *Spain: Economic and Commercial Relations in Spain* (London, 1957).

Ros Jimeno, J. 'La natalidad y el futuro desarrollo de la población de España', *Revista Internacional de Sociología* (January–March 1943).

'El decrecimiento de la natalidad y sus causas', *Estudios Demográficos*, 1 (1945).

Rozalejo, Marqués de. *La industrialización y el resurgimiento de España: hacia una economía nacional* (Madrid, 1942).

Rubio y Muñoz-Bolanegra. *Francisco Franco. III: Pensamiento económico.* (Centro de Estudios Sindicales, Madrid, 1958).

Ruiz, Alonso. *Corporativismo* (Prologue by José María Gil Robles) (Salamanca, 1937).

Ruiz Almansa, Javier. 'Reproductividad neta de las provincias y regiones de España', *Boletín de Estadística* (October–December 1942), pp. 140–59.

'Crecimiento y repartición de la población de España', *Revista Internacional de Sociología*, 1 (1944), pp. 77–105.

Ruiz Vilaplana, Antonio. *Burgos Justice: A Year's Experience of Nationalist Spain* (London, 1938).

Doy fe . . . un año de actuación en la España nacionalista (Paris, 1938).

Sánchez del Arco, Manuel. *El sur de España en la reconquista de Madrid* (Seville, 1937).

Santiago, Eduardo de. *Cuando España renace* (Burgos, 1939).

Sarazá y Ayustante, Juan Antonio. *La empresa del movimiento nacional* (Córdoba, 1947).

Sección Femenina de FET y de las JONS. *Calendario* (Madrid, n.d.).

Formación familiar y social (Madrid, n.d.).

Formación política: lecciones para las flechas (Madrid, n.d.).

Serrano Suñer, Ramón. *De la victoria y la postguerra: discursos* (Madrid, 1941).

Entre Hendaya y Gibraltar (6th edn, Madrid, 1963).

Entre el silencio y la propaganda, la historia como fue (Barcelona, 1977).

Servicio Nacional del Trigo, *Veinte anos de actuación* (Madrid, 1959).

Sevillano Carbajál, Vigiliano. *¿España: de quién?* (Madrid, 1936).

Sierra, Fermín de la. 'La situación monopolista de algunas industrias españolas', *Revista de Economía Política*, 3, 1 (May 1950), pp. 3–37.

'La situación monopolista de la banca privada española', *Revista de Economía Política*, 3, 2 (1951).

La concentración económica en las industrias básicas españolas (Madrid, 1953).

Sierra Bustamente, Ramón. 'El nacionalismo vasco y Catalan', in *De la Regencia al dia de la victoria* (Bilbao 1956).

Sola, Víctor María de. *La vida actual en el pais de la demencia roja* (Cádiz, 1938).

Soler, Alfredo, and Crespo, José. *El comercio exterior de España* (Madrid, 1943).

Soriano, Ramón. *La mano izquierda de Franco* (Barcelona, 1981).

Souto Vilas, Manuel. 'Campo y ciudad', in J. Aparicio, *JONS: antología* ([originally 1934] Madrid, 1943).

Stampa Irueste, F. *El delito de rebelión* (Madrid, 1945).

Stauffer, Clarita. 'La mujer y el Marxismo', in Sección Femenina de FET y de las JONS, *Calendario* (Madrid, n.d.).

Suanzes, Juan Antonio. *La marina nacional: dos discursos* (Bilbao, 1938).

Declaraciones a la prensa sobre la industrialización de España (Madrid, 1948).

Situación actual de la economía española (Madrid, 1948).

La política comercial de España (Madrid, 1950).

La industrialización, obra evidente y preeminente del régimen de Franco (Madrid, 1952).

'Franco y la economía', in *Ocho discursos* (Madrid, 1963).

'El INI en Cataluña', in *Ocho discursos* (Madrid, 1963).

'XX aniversario del INI', in *Ocho discursos* (Madrid, 1963).

Suevos, Jesús. 'Isabel de Castilla ejemplo y estímulo para las mujeres de la Falange', *IV Consejo-Nacional de la Sección Femenina* (Madrid, 1940).

Tallada Paulí, José María. 'Nuestra futura política comercial', *Nueva Economía Nacional* (14 August, 1937).

La política económica en los tiempos de crisis (Barcelona, 1940).

Tasis, Rafael. 'El paper polític de la burguesía', *La Nostra Revista* (January–February, 1957).

Tebib Arrumi, El. (Víctor Ruiz Albéniz). *Castilla por España y Cataluña roja. Biblioteca infantil, La Reconquista*, no. 9 (Madrid, 1940).

Tippetts, Charles Stanford. *Autarchy: National Self-sufficiency* (New York, 1933).

Torrent, Martín. *¿Qué me dice Usted de los presos?* (Alcalá de Henares, 1942).

Tour Du Pin, Marqués de la. *Hacia un orden social cristiano* (Prologue by Eduardo Aunós) (Madrid, 1936).

Tovar, Antonio. *El imperio de España* (Madrid, 1941).

Unamuno, Miguel de. *En torno al casticismo* ([originally 1895], Madrid, 1986).

Universidad de Barcelona, *Aspectos y problemas de la nueva organización de España* (Barcelona, 1939).

Urquijo, Alfonso de. *Cuando empuñamos las armas: la pequeña historia de una familia numerosa entre 1936 y 1942* (Madrid, 1945).

Valle, Luis del. *El estado nacionalista, totalitario, autoritario* (Zaragoza, 1940).

Vallejo-Nágera, Antonio. *Eugenesia de la hispanidad y regeneración de la raza* (Burgos, 1937).

Divagaciones intranscendentes (Valladolid, 1938).

Política racial del nuevo estado (San Sebastián, 1938).

La locura y la guerra: psicopatología de la guerra española (Madrid, 1939).

Psicosis de guerra (Madrid, 1942).

Antes que te cases . . . (Madrid, 1944).

Enseñanzas psiquiátricas de la segunda guerra mundial (Madrid, 1951).

Valls y Taberner, Fernando. *Reafirmación espiritual de España* (Madrid/Barcelona, 1939).

Vázquez de Mella, Juan. *Antología* (Prologue by Juan Beneyto Pérez) (Barcelona, 1939).

Velarde Fuertes, Juan. *Apuntes editados en la Facultad de Ciencias Económicas* (Madrid, 1965).

El nacional-sindicalismo, cuarenta años después (Madrid, 1972).

Ventallo Vergés, Luis, G. *Sentido de lo social y de lo económico en la España del Alzamiento* (Tarrassa, 1948).

Ventosa Calvell, Juan. *La situación política y los problemas económicos de España* (Barcelona, 1932).

Reforma agraria (Barcelona, 1932).

'La permanencia de las leyes económicas' Speech to the Real Academia de Ciencias Morales y Políticas, 29 May 1944 (Madrid, 1944).

Walker, J. *Spain: Review of Economic Conditions* (London 1948).

Werner Bolín, Carmen. *Convivencia social: formación familiar y social* (Madrid, 1958).

Whitaker, John T. 'Prelude to World War: A Witness from Spain', *Foreign Affairs*, 21, 1 (October 1942).

We Cannot Escape History (New York, 1943).

Woolsey, Gamel. *Death's Other Kingdom* (London, 1939).

Worsley, T.C. *Behind the Battle* (London, 1939).

Ygartua y Landecho, Francisco de. 'Calvo Sotelo y el espíritu del 18 de julio', in *De la Regencia al dia de la Victoria* (Bilbao, 1956).

Zalba, Marcelino. *La prostitución ante la moral y el derecho* (Madrid, 1942).

Zulueta, Manuel María de. *Sindicación agrícola – iniciación en su técnica* (Vitoria, 1938).

(2) SECONDARY SOURCE MATERIAL: NON-CONTEMPORARY MONOGRAPHS AND OTHER ACCOUNTS

Abella, Rafael. *La vida cotidiana durante la guerra civil: (1) la España nacional* (Barcelona, 1978).

Por el imperio hacia Dios: Crónica de una posguerra, 1939–1945 (Barcelona, 1978).

La vida cotidiana en España bajo el régimen de Franco (Barcelona, 1985).

Finales de enero de 1939: Barcelona cambia del piel (Barcelona, 1991).

Aguado Sánchez, F. *El maquis en España* (Madrid, 1975).

Aguila Tejerina, Rafael del. *Ideología y fascismo* (Madrid, 1982).

Aguilar Fernández, Paloma. *Memoria y olvido de la guerra civil española* (Madrid, 1996).

Alba, Víctor. *Historia de la resistencia antifranquista* (Barcelona, 1978).

La oposición de los supervivientes (Barcelona, 1978).

'De los Tribunales Populares al Tribunal Especial', in Ministerio de Cultura. *Justicia en guerra. Tornadas sobre la administración de justicia durante la guerra civil española instituciónes y fuentes documentales* (Madrid, 1990).

Sisifo y su tiempo: memorias de un cabreado, 1916–1996 (Barcelona, 1996).

Alburquerque, Francisco. 'Métodos de control político de la población civil: el sistema de racionamiento de alimentos y productos básicos impuesto en España tras la última Guerra Civil', in M. Tuñon de Lara (ed.), *Estudios sobre Historia de España*, vol. II (Madrid, 1981), pp. 407–32.

Alburquerque, Francisco and Ramos, A. 'Desarrollo desigual: notas sobre la formación social andaluza', in Carballo et al., *Crecimiento económico y crisis estructural en España, 1959–1980* (Madrid, 1981).

Alcalde, Carmen. *Mujeres en el franquismo: exiliadas nacionalistas y opositoras* (Barcelona, 1996).

Allison Peers, E. *Studies of the Spanish Mystics* 3 vols. (London, 1927–60).

Alonso Millán, Jesús. *Una tierra abierta: materiales para una historia ecológica de España* (Madrid, 1995).

Alpert, Michael. 'Las relaciones hispano–britanico en el 1940', *Revista de Política Internacional* (September/October 1976), pp. 13–29.

Alted Vigil, Alicia. 'Las mujeres en la sociedad española de los años cuarenta', in *Las mujeres y la guerra civil* (Madrid, 1991) pp. 293–301.

Alvarez, Santiago. *Negrín, personalidad histórica* (Madrid, 1994).

Alvarez Alvarez, Julián. *Burocracia y poder político en el régimen franquista: el papel de los cuerpos de funcionarios entre 1938 y 1975* (Madrid, 1984).

Alvarez Bolado, Alfonso. *El experimento del nacional-catolicismo, 1939–1975* (Madrid, 1976).

'Guerra civil y universo religioso: fenomenología de una implicación', *Miscelánea Comillas*, 44 (1986), p. 85.

Alvarez Oblanca, Wenceslao. *La represión de postguerra en León: depuración de la enseñanza, 1936–1943* (León, 1986).

Alvarez-Uría, Fernando. *Miserables y locos: medicina mental y orden social en la España del siglo XIX* (Barcelona, 1983).

Anderson, Benedict. *Imagined Communities: Reflections on the Origin and Spread of Nationalism* (London, 1983).

Anderson, Charles. *The Political Economy of Modern Spain: Policy-making in an Authoritarian System* (Madison, WI, 1970).

Anes, Gonzalo. *Las crisis agrarias en la España moderna* (Madrid, 1970).

Anes Alvarez, Rafael. 'La Banca y el crecimiento económico en el País Vasco', in *Ekonomiaz* 9/10 (1988), pp. 93–104.

Anthropos, 84 (1988), 'E. Giménez Caballero: una cultura hacista: revolución y tradición en la regeneración de España.'

Aparicio, Miguel, A. *El sindicalismo vertical y la formación del estado franquista* (Barcelona, 1980).

'Sobre los comienzos del sindicalismo franquista, 1939–1945', in Fontana (ed.), *España bajo el franquismo* (Barcelona, 1986), pp. 78–98.

Aragón, Manuel. 'La velada en Benicarló o la agonía Republicana', in *Ínsula* (Barcelona, 1990).

Arango, Joaquín. 'La modernización demográfica de la sociedad española', in Nadal et al. (eds.), *La economía española: una perspectiva histórica* (Barcelona, 1987).

Ardit Lucas, M. *Revolución liberal y revuelta campesina, 1793–1840* (Madrid, 1977).

Aróstegui, Julio. 'Sociedad y guerra', in *Historia 16, La Guerra Civil*, 14 (1986).

'La oposición al franquismo; represión y violencia política', in Tusell et al. (eds.), *La oposición al régimen de Franco* (Madrid, 1990).

'La violencia política en España', *Ayer* (1994), p. 13.

Arranz Bullido, María de los Angeles. 'Una aproximación histórica a la política de abastecimientos en los primeros años de la posguerra (1939–1951)', PhD thesis, Universidad Autónoma de Madrid (1986).

Artís-Gener, Avellí. *La diáspora Republicana* (Barcelona, 1975).

Artola, Miguel et al. *El latifundio: propiedad y explotación, siglos XVIII–XX* (Madrid, 1978).

Balcells, Albert. *El problema agrari a catalunya, 1890–1936: la qüestió rabassaire* (Barcelona, 1968).

Crisis económica y agitación social en Cataluña, 1930–1936 (Barcelona, 1971).

Balfour, Sebastian. *Dictatorship, Workers and the City: Labour in Greater Barcelona Since 1939* (Oxford, 1989).

The End of The Spanish Empire, 1898–1923 (Oxford, 1997).

Ballbé, Manuel. *Orden público y militarismo en la España constitucional 1812–1983* (Madrid, 1985).

Ballester, Josep. *Temps de quarantena (1939–1959)* (Valencia, 1992).

Ballesteros, A. *Juan Antonio Suanzes (1891–1977)* (Madrid, 1994).

Barciela, Carlos. *La financiación del SNT 1937–1971* (Madrid, 1981).

'Producción y política cerealista durante la guerra civil española, 1936–1939', in G. Anes et al., *Histórica económica y pensamiento social* (Madrid, 1983), pp. 649–75.

'Intervencionismo y crecimiento agrario en Espana, 1936–1971', in P. Martín Aceña and L. Prados Escodura, *La nueva historia económica en España* (Madrid, 1985), pp. 285–316.

'Los costes del franquismo en el sector agrario: la ruptura del proceso de transformaciones', in R. Garrabou, C. Barciela and J. Jiménez Blanco (eds.), *Historia agraria de la Espana contemporanea*, vol. III, *El fin de la agricultura tradicional* (Barcelona, 1986), pp. 383–413.

'Crecimiento y cambio en la agricultura española desde la guerra civil', in A. Carreras, J. Nadal and P. Sudriá (eds.) *La economía española en el siglo XX* (Barcelona, 1986).

'El mercado negro de productos agrarios en la posguerra, 1939–1953', in Josep Fontana (ed.), *España bajo el franquismo* (Barcelona, 1986).

'Los efectos de la guerra civil sobre la agricultura', *Economistas*, 21 (August-September 1986).

'La España del "estraperlo"', in José Luis, García Delgado, *El primer franquismo* (Madrid, 1989).

Barral, Carlos. *Años de penitencia* (Barcelona, 1991).

Barranquero Texeira, Encarnación and Eiroa San Francisco, Matilde. 'Hacia la recuperación de la memoria perdida: notas sobre la vida y la muerte en la prisión provincial de Sevilla en 1949', in *Actas del IV congreso sobre el andalucismo histórico* (Seville, 1989).

Barrios, Manuel. *El último virrey: Queipo de Llano* (3rd edn, Seville, 1990).

Barrull Pelegrí, Jaume. *Violència política i ruptura social a Espanya, 1936–1945* (Lleida, 1994).

Barrull Pelegrí, Jaume, Calvet, Josep and Mir, Conxita. 'La justicia ordinaria como elemento de control social y de percepción de la vida cotidiana de postguerra: Lleida, 1938–1945', in Javier Tusell et al., *El régimen de Franco* (Madrid, 1993).

Barthes, Roland. *Sade, Fourier, Loyola* (Paris, 1971).

Bastida, Francisco J. *Jueces y franquismo: el pensamiento político del Tribunal Supremo en la dictadura* (Barcelona, 1986).

Ben-Ami, Shlomo. *Fascism from Above: The Dictatorship of Primo de Rivera in Spain, 1923–1930* (Oxford, 1983).

Benet, Josep. *L'intent franquista de genocidi cultural contra catalunya* (Barcelona, 1995).

Benet, Juan. *Return to Región* (trans. Gregory Rabassa) ([originally 1967] New York, 1985).

'Military Strategy in the Spanish Civil War', in Frieda Brown, et al. (eds.). *Rewriting the Good Fight: Critical Essays on the Literature of the Spanish Civil War* (East Lansing, MI, 1989).

Beneyto, Juan (ed.). *El régimen franquista* (Barcelona, 1978).

La identidad del franquismo (Madrid, 1979).

Benítez Fernández, V. *Carlismo y rebeldía campesina: un estudio sobre la conflictividad social en Cantabria durante la crisis final del Antiguo Régimen* (Madrid, 1988).

Bermejo Merino, Carmen. 'El Tribunal Popular de Cartagena', in Ministerio de Cultura, *Justicia en guerra* (Madrid, 1990).

Bernal, Antonio M. *La lucha por la tierra en la crisis del Antiguo Régimen* (Madrid, 1979).

Economía e historia de los latifundios (Madrid, 1988).

'Riegos: los latifundios del franquismo inicial (1939–1950)', in J.L. García Delgado (ed.), *El primer franquismo* (Madrid, 1989), pp. 124–33.

'Resignación de los campesinos andaluces: la resisténcia pasiva durante el franquismo', in D. Ruiz et al., *España franquista: causa general y actitudes sociales ante la dictadura* (Castilla-La Mancha, 1993).

Berzosa, Carlos. 'La acumulación de capital en el periodo autárquico franquista', in *Negaciones* (May 1977), pp. 197–209.

Besas, P. *Behind the Spanish Lens: Spanish Cinema under Fascism and Democracy* (Denver, CO, 1985).

Biescas, J.A. 'Estructura y coyuntura económicas', in M. Tuñón de Lara and J.A. Biescas, *España bajo la dictadura franquista* (Barcelona, 1980).

Biescas, J.A. and Fernández Clemente, Eloy. 'La economía autárquica', in *Historia 16, La Guerra Civil* 24 (1986), pp. 68–79.

Bilbao, Andrés. 'Fascismo y tecnocracia: carisma y desarrollo capitalista en España', *Sistema*, 26 (1978).

Bilbao entre dos siglos: exposición conmemorativa del centenario de la Bolsa de Bilbao 1890–1990 (Bilbao 1990).

Blanc, Jordi. *Las huelgas en el movimiento obrero español* (Paris, 1966).

Blanc, Xavier. 'La Banca Española', in *Promos*, 41.

Blaye, Edouard de. *Franco and the Politics of Spain* (Harmondsworth, 1976).

Blázquez, Feliciano. *La traición de los clérigos en la España de Franco: crónica de una intolerancia, 1936–1975* (Madrid, 1991).

Blinkhorn, Martin. *Carlismo y contrarevolución* (Barcelona, 1979).

'The Iberian States', in Detlef Muhlberger, *The Social Basis of European Fascist Movements* (London, 1987).

(ed.). *Fascists and Conservatives* (London, 1990).

Bonamusa, Francesc. 'L'administració de justicia a Catalunya, setembre–desembre 1936', *Recerques*, 4 (1974), pp. 191–222.

Bonet Correa, Antonio. *Arte del franquismo* (Madrid, 1981).

Borderías, Cristina. 'Evolución de la división sexual del trabajo. Barcelona 1924–1980: aproximación desde una empresa del sector de servicios. La compañía telefónica nacional de España', PhD thesis (Barcelona, 1984).

Borges, Dain, ' "Puffy, Ugly, Slothful and Inert": Degeneration in Brazilian Social Thought, 1880–1940', *Journal of Latin American Studies*, 25 (May 1993), pp. 235–56.

Botti, Alfonso. *Cielo y dinero: el nacionalcatolicismo en España 1881–1975* (Madrid, 1992).

'Los fantasmas de Clio: a propósito de franquismo y fascismo en la perspectiva de la historia comparada', Anales de la Universidad de Alicante, *Historia contemporánea*, 8/9 (1991/2), pp. 9–34.

Braña, J., Buesa, M. and Molero, J. 'El estado en los procesos de industrialización atrasada: notas acerca del caso espanol (1939–1977)', *El Trimestre Económico*, 197, 50 (January–March 1983), pp. 85–116.

Braojos Garrido, A., Alvarez Rey, L., Espinosa Maestre, F. *Sevilla '36: sublevación fascista y represión* (Seville, 1990).

Bravo-Tellado, A.A. *El peso de la derrota 1939–1944: la tragedia de medio millón de españoles* (Madrid, 1974).

Bricall, J.M. 'La economía española (1936–1939)', in M. Tuñón de Lara et al. (eds.), *La guerra civil española 50 años después* (Madrid, 1985).

'La economía española, 1936–1939', in *Historia 16, La Guerra Civil*, 16 (1986) pp. 6–41.

Broué, Pierre, Fraser, Ronald and Vilar, Pierre. *Metodología histórica de la guerra y revolución españolas* (Barcelona, 1980).

Buchanan, Tom and Conway, Martin (eds.). *Political Catholcism in Europe, 1918–1965* (Oxford, 1996).

Buesa Blanco, Miguel. 'El estado en el proceso de industrialización (1939–1963)', PhD thesis, Madrid (1982).

'Algunos aspectos de política económica e industrialización en España (1939–1963)', *Comercio Exterior*, 33, 4 (April 1983).

'Las restricciones a la libertad de industria en la política industrial española (1938–1963)', *ICE* (February 1984).

Buesa Blanco, Miguel, Braña, Javier and Molero, José, *El estado y el cambio tecnológico en la industrialización tardía* (Madrid, 1984).

Cabana, Francesc. *Bancs i banquers a Catalunya: capitols per una historia* (Barcelona, 1972).

Cabanellas de Torres, Guillermo. *La guerra de los mil días* 2 vols. (Buenos Aires, 1973).

Cabré, A., and Pujades, I. 'La població de Barcelona i del seu entorn al segle XX', *L'Avenç*, 88 (December 1985), pp. 33–7.

Cacho Viu, Vicente. 'Los escritos de José María Iribarren, secretario de Mola en 1936', in *Cuadernos de Historia Moderna y Contemporánea*, 5 (1984), pp. 241–50.

Cámara Villar, Gregorio. *Nacional-catolicismo y escuela. La socialización política del franquismo (1936–1951)* (Jaén, 1984).

'Analizar el franquismo: interpretaciones sobre su naturaleza', in J. Aróstegui (ed.). *Historia y memoria de la guerra civil* (Castilla-León, 1988).

Camilleri, Joseph, Jarvis, A.P. and Paolini, A. *The State in Transition: Reimagining Political Space* (Bouolder, CO, 1995).

Campo, Salustiano del and Navarro López, Manuel. *Nuevo análisis de la población española* (Barcelona, 1987).

Cano Bueso, Juan. *La política judicial del régimen de Franco* (Madrid, 1985).

Cantarero del Castillo, Manuel. *Falange y socialismo* (Barcelona, 1973).

Carballo, Ricardo. *Capitalismo y agricultura en españa: la evolución de las relaciones de producción en el campo* (Madrid, 1978).

Carballo, Ricardo et al. *Crecimiento económico y crisis estructural en España, 1959–1980* (Madrid, 1981).

Caro Baroja, Julio. *Estudios sobre la vida tradicional española* (Barcelona, 1968).

Carr, Raymond. *The Republic and the Civil War in Spain* (London, 1971).

Civil War in Spain (London, 1986).

Carr, Raymond and Fusi, Juan Pablo. *Spain: Dictatorship to Democracy* (London, 1979).

Carreras, Albert. 'La producción industrial española, 1842–1981: construcción de un índice anual', *Revista de Historia Económica*, 2, 1 (1984) pp. 127–57.

'Depresión económica y cambio estructural durante el decenio bélico (1936–1945)', in J.L. Garcia Delgado, *El primer franquismo* (Madrid, 1989).

(ed.). *Estadísticas económicas españolas en los siglos XIX–XX* (Madrid, 1989).

(ed.). *Estadísticas históricas de España, siglos XIX–XX* (Madrid, 1989).

Carreras Panchón, Antonio. 'Los psiquiatras españoles y la guerra civil', *Medicina e Historia*, 13 (1986).

Carrión, Pascual. *La reforma agraria:de la Segunda República y la situación de la agricultura española*, 2nd edn (Barcelona, 1995).

Casanova, Julián, Cenarro, Angela, Cifuente, Julita, Pilar Maluenda, María del and Pilar Salomón, María del. *El pasado oculto: fascismo y violencia en Aragón 1936-1939* (Madrid, 1992).

Castilla del Pino, Carlos. 'La psiquiatría española', in Carlos Castilla del Pino (ed.), *La cultura bajo el franquismo* (Barcelona, 1977).

Castillo, J.J. *Propietarios muy pobres* (Madrid, 1979).

Catalán, Jordi. 'Autarquía y desarrollo de la industria de fábrica durante la segunda guerra mundial: un enfoque comparativo', in J.L. García Delgado, *El primer franquismo* (Madrid, 1989).

La economía española y la segunda guerra mundial (Barcelona 1995).

Catalunya sota el règim franquista: informe sobre la persecució de la llengua i la cultura de Catalunya pel règim del General Franco (Paris, 1973).

Cataluña con Franco (Barcelona, 1984).

Cela, José Camilo. *La colmena* ([originally, Buenos Aires, 1951], Barcelona, 1967).

Chamorro, Santiago, et al. 'Las balanzas de pagos de España del período de la autarquía', *ICE*, 502 (June 1975), pp. 161-84.

Checkland, S.G. *The Mines of Tharsis* (London, 1967).

Chiapuso, Manuel. *El gobierno vasco y los anarquistas: Bilbao en guerra* (San Sebastián, 1978).

Chueca, Ricardo. *El fascismo en los comienzos del régimen de Franco: un estudio sobre FET-JONS* (Madrid, 1983).

Cierva, Ricardo de la. *Francisco Franco: un siglo de España* 2 vols. (Madrid, 1973).

Historia del franquismo: orígenes y configuración (1939-1945) (Barcelona, 1975).

La historia se confiesa (Barcelona, 1976).

Historia ilustrada de la guerra civil española, 2 vols. (Barcelona, 1990).

Los años mentidos: falsificaciones y mentiras sobre la historia de España en el siglo XX (Boadilla del Monte, 1993).

Clark, P.B. *Planning Import Substitution* (London, 1970).

Clavera, Joan. 'Industrialització i canvi de conjuntura a la Catalunya de la postguerra', *Recerques*, 6 (1976).

'El estraperlo en los años cuarenta', *Información Comercial Española*, 514 (1976).

Clavera, Joan et al. *Capitalismo español: de la autarquía a la estabilización (1939-1959)* (Madrid, 1978).

Cobo Romero, Francisco. 'La justicia republicana en la provincia de Jaén durante la guerra civil: la actuación de los Tribunales Especiales populares (1936-1939)', in Ministerio de Cultura, *Justicia en guerra* (Madrid, 1990).

La guerra civil y la represión franquista en la provincia de Jaén (Madrid, 1992).

Collotti, Enzo. 'Cinc formes de feixisme europeu: Àustria, Alemanya, Itàlia, Espanya i Portugal', *Afers*, 25 (1996) pp. 511-24.

Cooper, Norman. *Catholicism and the Franco Regime* (London, 1975).

Corni, Gustavo. *Hitler and the Peasants: Agrarian Policy of the Third Reich, 1930–1939* (Oxford, 1990).

Cortada, J.W. *A City in War: American views on Barcelona and the Spanish Civil War, 1936–39* (Wilmington, DE, 1985).

Coverdale, John F. *Italian Intervention in the Spanish Civil War* (Princeton, NJ, 1975).

Crespo Redondo, Jesús et al. *Purga de maestros en la guerra civil: la depuración del magisterio nacional de la provincia de Burgos* (Valladolid, 1987).

Crozier, Brian. *Franco* (London, 1967).

Cuadernos para el diálogo. XVII Extraordinario, 'Justicia y política' (December 1969).

Cuevas Gutiérrez, Tomasa. *Cárcel de mujeres* 2 vols. (Barcelona, 1985).

Delibes, Miguel. *La censura de prensa en los años 40* (Valladolid, 1985).

Diario 16 (ed. Justino Sinova). *Historia del Franquismo,* 2 vols. (Madrid, 1985).

Díaz, Elias. *Notas para una historia del pensamiento español actual (1939–1973)* (Madrid, 1974).

Díaz Nosty, B. and Sueiro, D. *Historia del franquismo,* 2 vols. (Madrid, 1986).

Díaz-Plaja, Fernando. *La España franquista en sus documentos.* (Barcelona, 1976).

La guerra de España en sus documentos (Madrid, 1986).

La vida cotidiana en la España de la guerra civil (Madrid, 1994).

Díez Nicolás, Juan. *Tamaño, densidad y crecimiento de la población en España, 1900–1960* (Madrid, 1971).

'La mortalidad en la guerra civil española', *Boletín de Demografía Histórica,* 3, 1 (March 1985), pp. 41–55.

Donges, Juergen. B. *La industrialización en España (1939–1975): Políticas, logros y perspectivas* (Barcelona, 1976).

Doña, Juana. *Desde la noche y la niebla: mujeres en las cárceles franquistas* (Barcelona, [1978]1993).

Doucastella, R. *Análisis sociológico del catolicismo español* (Barcelona, 1967).

Douglas, Mary. *Purity and Danger* (London, 1991).

Dura, J. 'Las relaciones hispano–norteamericanas durante la segunda guerra mundial, 1939–1945', *Tiempo de Historia,* 86 (January 1982), pp. 68–83.

Eiroa San Francisco, Matilde. *Viva Franco: hambre, racionamiento, Falangismo, 1939–1942* (Málaga, 1995).

Eisenstadt, S.N. *Max Weber on Charisma and Institution Building* (Chicago, IL, 1968).

Eliade, Mircea. *The Myth of the Eternal Return* (New York, 1954).

Sacred and Profane (London, 1954).

Ellwood, Sheelagh. *Spanish Fascism in the Franco Era* (London, 1987).

Franco (Longman, 1994).

Elorza, Antonio. *La modernización política en España* (Madrid, 1990).

Escudero, Antonio. 'El "lobby" minero vizcaíno', *Historia Social,* 7 (1990), pp. 39–68.

Escudero, María. 'The Image of Latin America Disseminated in Spain by the Franco Regime: Repercussions in the Configuration of a National Identity', PhD thesis, University of California, San Diego (1994).

Esteban, Joan M. 'La política económica del franquismo: una interpretación', in Paul Preston (ed.), *España en crisis* (Madrid, 1977) pp. 147–81.

Fabre, Jaume, Huertas, Josep, M. and Ribas, Antoni. *Vint anys de resistència Catalana (1939–1959)* (Barcelona, 1978).

Fanès, Felix. *La vaga de tramvies del 1951* (Barcelona, 1977).

Farquharson, J.E. *The Plough and the Swastika: The NSDAP and Agriculture in Germany, 1928–45* (London, 1976).

Fava i Compta, M., and Huertas Clavería, J.M. *Conflictos laborales que dejaron huella, 1939–1972* (Madrid, 1974).

Febo, Giuliana di. *Resistencia y movimiento de mujeres en España, 1936–1976* (Barcelona, 1979).

La santa de la raza: un culto barroco en la España franquista (Barcelona, 1988).

'El "monje guerrero": identidad de género en los modelos franquistas durante la guerra civil', in *Las mujeres y la guerra civil* (Madrid, 1991).

Fernández, A. *Emigración Republicana española, 1939–1945* (Madrid, 1972).

Fernández, Carlos. *El alzamiento de 1936 en Galicia* (La Coruña, 1982).

Antología de 40 años, 1936–1975 (La Coruña, 1983).

Fernández Caínzos, J. 'La hacienda pública y la acumulación de capital en España (1939–1959): un ensayo de interpretación', PhD thesis, University of Santiago de Compostela (1979).

Fernández de Castro, I. *De las Cortes de Cádiz al Plan de Desarrollo* (Madrid, 1968).

Fernández de la Mora, Gonzalo. '¿Franco, dictador?', in Fundación Nacional Francisco Franco, *El legado de Franco* (Madrid, 1993).

Fernández Santos, Jesús. *Cabeza rapada* (Barcelona, 1977).

Fernández Vargas, Valentina. *La resistencia interior en la España de Franco* (Madrid, 1981).

Ferrando Badía, Juan. *El régimen de Franco: un enfoque político-jurídico* (Madrid, 1984).

Ferreras, Juan Ignacio. 'La generación del silencio: ensayo sobre un novelar de la posguerra española', in Hernán Vidal (ed.), *Fascismo y experiencia literaria: reflexiones para una recanonización* (Minneapolis, MI, 1985).

Ferri, Llibert, Muixi, Jordi and Sanjuan, Eduardo. *Las huelgas contra Franco, 1939–1956* (Barcelona, 1978).

Fillol, Vicente. *Los perdedores* (Caracas, 1971).

Fioravanti, Eduardo. 'La elite del poder en la España franquista', *Negaciones*, 1 (October 1976), pp. 79–106.

Folguera, Pilar. 'La construcción de lo cotidiano durante los primeros años del franquismo', *Ayer*, 19 (1995), pp. 165–87.

Fontana, Josep. *Cambio económico y actitudes políticas en la España del siglo XIX* (Barcelona, 1973).

'Reflexiones sobre la naturaleza y las consecuencias del franquismo', in Josep Fontana (ed.), *España bajo el franquismo* (Barcelona, 1986).

(ed.). *España bajo el franquismo* (Barcelona, 1986).

Fontana, J. and Nadal, J. 'Spain, 1914–1970', in M. Cipolla (ed.), *The Fontana Economic History of Europe*, vol. VI, pt. 2 (London, 1976).

Fraile Balbín, P. *Industrialización y grupos de presión: la economía política de la protección en España, 1900–1950* (Madrid, 1991).

Fraser, Ronald. *Blood of Spain: The Experience of Civil War, 1936–1939* (London, 1979).

'The Spanish Civil War', in Raphael Samuel, *People's History and Socialist Theory* (London, 1981).

Fundación de Investigaciones Marxistas. *El movimiento guerrillero de los años cuarenta* (Madrid, 1990).

Fundación Nacional Francisco Franco (FNFF). *Documentos inéditos para la historia del Generalísimo Franco*, vols. I–III (Madrid, 1992–4).

Furones Ferrero, Luis. 'Influencias de Angel Ganivet en el pensamiento de José Antonio', *Seminario*, 6.

Furtado, Celso. *The Economic Development of Latin America* (Cambridge, 1970).

Fusi, Juan Pablo. *Franco: Autoritarismo y poder personal* (Madrid, 1985).

'El País Vasco durante la guerra', in *La guerra de España* (Madrid, 1986).

Gabarda Ceballan, Vicente. 'La continuación de la guerra civil: la represión franquista', in *Estudis D'Història contemporánea del País Valencià*, 7 (1986), pp. 229–45.

Els afusellaments al País Valencià (1938–1956) (Valencia, 1993).

Gallego Méndez, M.T. *Mujer, Falange y franquismo* (Madrid, 1983).

Gallo, Max. *Spain under Franco: A History* (London, 1973).

Gamir, Luis. *Política económica de España* (Madrid, 1975).

Garate Cordoba. *Partes oficiales de guerra: los nacionalistas* (Madrid, 1977).

García Barbancho, Alfonso. 'Análisis de la alimentación española', *Anales de Economía*, 18, 66 (September 1960), pp. 73–119, and 67, pp. 271–367.

García Crespo, M., et al. *La economía vasca durante el franquismo, 1936–1980* (Bilbao, 1981).

García Delgado, J.L. *Orígenes y desarrollo del capitalismo en españa: notas críticas* (Madrid, 1975).

'Problemas de la industria española: una visión del conjunto', in Carballo et al., *Crecimiento económico y crisis estructural en España, 1959–1980* (Madrid, 1981).

'Notas sobre el intervencionismo económico del primer franquismo', *Revista de Historia Económica*, 3, 1 (1985).

'La industrialización y el desarrollo económico de España durante el franquismo', in A. Nadal, A. Carreras and C. Sudrià, *La economía española en el siglo XX: una perspectiva histórica* (Barcelona, 1987).

García Encabo, Carmelo, Juberías Hernández, Reyes and Manrique Romero, Alberto. *Cartas muertas: la vida rural en la posguerra* (Valladolid, 1996).

García Fernández, Jesús. *La emigración exterior de España* (Barcelona, 1965).

García Madrid, A. *Réquiem por la libertad* (Madrid, 1982).

García Pérez, Guillermo. *La economía y los reaccionarios: la Inquisición y los economistas al surgir la España contemporánea* (Madrid, 1974).

García Piñeiro, Ramón. *Los mineros asturianos bajo el franquismo (1937–1962)* (Madrid, 1990).

García Venero, Maximiano. *Historia de la unificación* (Madrid, 1970).

Garrabun, Ramón, Barciela, C. and Jiménez, J. *Historia agraria de la España contemporánea* (Barcelona, 1986)

Garrabon, Ramón, Lleixa, Joaquim and Pellissa, Octavi. *Franquisme: sobre resistència i consens a Catalunya (1939–1959)* (Barcelona, 1990).

Garriga, Ramón. *La España de Franco* (Madrid, 1976).

Franco–Serrano Suñer: un drama político (Barcelona, 1986).

Garruccio, Ludovico. *L'Industrializzazione tra nazionalismo e rivoluzione: la ideologia politica dei paesi in via di sviluppo* (Bologna 1969).

Germani, G. 'La socialización política de la juventud en los regimenes fascistas: Italia y España', *Revista Latinoamericana de sociología*, 5 (November 1969).

Gerth, H.H. and Wright Mills, C. *From Max Weber: Essays in Sociology* (London, 1964).

Gibson, Ian. *La represión nacionalista de Granada en 1936 y la muerte de García Lorca* (Paris, 1971).

The Assassination of Federico García Lorca (London, 1979).

Granada en 1936 y el asesinato de Federico García Lorca (Barcelona, 1986).

Queipo de Llano: Sevilla, verano de 1936 (Barcelona, 1986).

Gilmore, David. '*Carnaval* in Fuenmayor: Class Conflict and Social Cohesion in an Andalusian Town', *Journal of Anthropological Research*, 31, 4 (1975), pp. 331–49.

Aggression and Community: Paradoxes of Andalusian Culture (New Haven, CT, 1987).

Giner, Salvador, Sevilla Guzmán, Eduardo and Pérez Yruela, M. 'Despotismo moderno y dominación de clase: para una sociología del régimen franquista', *Papers*, 8 (1978).

Glaser, Herman. *The Cultural Roots of National Socialism* (London, 1978).

Glick, Thomas F. 'Ciencia política y discurso civil en la España de Alfonso XIII', in Guillermo Gortázar (ed.), *Nación y estado en la España liberal* (Madrid, 1994).

Gliksman, Jerzy. 'Social Prophylaxis as a Form of Soviet Terror', in Carl Friedrich (ed.), *Totalitarianism* (New York, 1953).

Gómez Benito, Cristóbal. *Políticos, burócratas y expertos: un estudio de la política agraria y la sociología rural en España (1936–1959)* (Madrid, 1996).

González, Carmela. *The Bitter Fruit of a Broken Tree* (London, 1992).

González, Manuel-Jesus. 'Neomercantilismo en Madrid: dos economistas de la posguerra', *ICE* (1976), 517.

'La historia económica de España, 1939–1959: una interpretación', *Moneda y Crédito*, 143 (December 1977).

La economía política del franquismo (1940–1970): dirigismo, mercado y planificación (Madrid, 1979).

González, Manuel-Jesus and Schwartz, Pedro. *Una historia del Instituto Nacional de Industria (1941–1976)* (Madrid, 1978).

González Calleja, Eduardo, and Limón Nevado, Fredes. *La hispanidad como instrumento de combate: raza e imperio en la prensa franquista durante la guerra civil española* (Madrid, 1988).

González Casanova, J.A. 'El franquismo a diez años vista', *Historia 16*, 10 (November 1985), pp. 35–40.

González Duro, Enrique. *Psiquiatría y sociedad autoritaria: España, 1939–1975* (Madrid, 1978).

Franco: una biografía psicológica (Madrid, 1992).

Historia de la locura en España: del reformismo del siglo XIX al franquismo (Madrid, 1996).

González Portilla, Manuel and Garmendia, José María. *La guerra civil en el País Vasco: política y económia* (Madrid, 1988).

La posguerra en el País Vasco: política, acumulación, miseria (San Sebastián, 1988).

Goytisolo, Juan. *El furgón de cola* (Barcelona, 1976).

'El lenguaje del cuerpo', in *Disidencias* (Barcelona, 1977).

'Remedios de la concupiscencia según Fray Tierno', in *Libertad, Libertad, Libertad* (Barcelona, 1978).

Señas de identidad ([originally, 1966], Barcelona, 1980).

Crónicas saracinas (Barcelona, 1982).

Graham, Helen. 'Gender and the State: Women in the 1940s', in H. Graham and J. Labanyi (eds.), *Spanish Cultural Studies: An Introduction* (Oxford, 1995).

'Popular Culture in the "Years of Hunger"', in H. Graham and J. Labanyi, *Spanish Cultural Studies: An Introduction* (Oxford, 1995), pp. 237–45.

Grand, Alexander de. 'Cracks in the Facade', in *European History Quarterly*, 3 (1991), 3.

Granja Sainz, José Luis de la. 'La historiografía española reciente: un balance', in Carlos Barros (ed.), *Historia a debate*, vol. I (Santiago de Compostela, 1995).

Granjel, Luis. 'La medicina en la guerra', *Historia 16, La Guerra Civil*, 14 (1987).

Gregory, David. *La odisea andaluza: una emigración española hacia Europa* (Madrid, 1978).

Griffin, Roger. *The Nature of Fascism* (London, 1991).

Gubern, Román. *Raza: un sueño del general Franco* (Madrid, 1977).

Gudeman, Stephen. *Economics as Culture: Models and Metaphors of Livelihood* (London, 1986).

Gutiérrez Castillo, Carmen. 'Una estimación del mercado negro del aceite de oliva en la postguerra española', in *Agricultura y Sociedad* (October–December 1983).

Guzmán, Eduardo de. 'Un millón de presos políticos y doscientos mil muertos en España', *Tiempo de Historia*, 41 (April 1978).

Harrison, R. Joseph. *An Economic History of Spain* (Manchester, 1978).

The Spanish Economy in the Twentieth Century (London, 1985).

Harvey, Charles. *The Rio Tinto Company: An Economic History of a Leading International Mining Concern* (London, 1981).

Heine, Hartmut. *A guerrilla antifranquista en Galicia* (Vigo, 1980).

La oposición política al franquismo (Barcelona, 1983).

'Tipología y características de la represión y violencia política durante el périodo 1939–1961', in Tusell et al., *La oposición al régimen de Franco* (Madrid, 1990).

Heller, Agnes. *Everyday Life* (London, 1984).

Hermet, Guy. *Los católicos en la España franquista: (1) los actores del juego político* (Madrid, 1985).

Herrero, Javier. *Los orígenes del pensamiento reaccionario español* (Madrid, 1971).

Herzberger, David. *Narrating the Past: Fiction and Historiography in Postwar Spain* (Durham, NC, 1995).

Historia y evolución de la colonización agraria en España: políticas administrativa y económica de la colonización agraria, 1937–77 (Madrid, 1990).

Iglesia y sociedad en España, 1939–1975 (Madrid, 1977).

Ilie, Paul, *Literature and Inner Exile* (Baltimore, MD, 1980).

Iturbe, Lola. *La mujer en la lucha social* (Mexico City, 1974).

Iturralde, Juan de. *El catolicismo y la cruzada de Franco* (2 vols.) (Bayonne, 1955).

La guerra de Franco: los vascos y la iglesia 2 vols. (San Sebastián, 1978).

Jackson, Gabriel. *The Spanish Republic and the Civil War, 1931–1939* (Princeton, NJ, 1965).

Breve historia de la guerra civil española (Paris, 1974).

La República Española y la Guerra Civil, 1931–1939 (Barcelona, 1976).

Jarne i Mòdol, Antonieta. *La secció femenina a Lleida* (Lleida, 1991).

Jérez Mir, Miguel. *Elites políticas y centros de extracción en España, 1938–1957* (Madrid, 1982).

Jiménez Campo, Javier. *El fascismo en la crisis de la segunda república* (Madrid, 1979).

'Integración simbólica en el primer franquismo, 1939–1945', *Revista de Estudios Políticos*, 2nd series, 14/15 (1980).

Johnson, Richard, McLennon, George and Schwarz, Bill. *Economy, Culture, Concept* (Birmingham, 1978).

Juliá, Santos, Ringrose, David and Segural, Cristina. *Madrid: Historia de una capital* (Madrid, 1995).

Jutglar, Antoni. *Ideologías y clases en la España contemporánea* (Madrid, 1971).

Kaplan, Alice Yaeger. *Reproductions of Banality: Fascism, Literature and French Intellectual Life* (Minneapolis, 1986).

Kemp, Tom. *Historical Patterns of Industrialisation* (London, 1978).

Kleine-Ahlbrandt, W.L. *The Policy of Simmering: A Study of British Policy During the Spanish Civil War* (The Hague, 1962).

Labanyi, Jo. *Ironía e historia en Tiempo de Silencio* (Madrid, 1985).

Laclau, Ernesto. *Politics and Ideology in Marxist Theory* (London, 1977).

Lannon, Frances, *Privilege, Persecution and Prophecy: The Catholic Church in Spain, 1875–1975* (Oxford, 1987).

Lannon, Frances and Preston, Paul (eds.). *Elites and Power in Twentieth-century Spain* (Oxford, 1990).

Las mujeres y la guerra civil española. II Jornadas de estudios monográficos, Salamanca, October, 1989 (Madrid, 1991).

Lash, Scott and Urry, John. *Economies of Signs and Space* (London, 1994).

Leal, José Luis, Leguina, Joaquín, Naredo, José Manuel and Tarrafeta, Luis. *La agricultura en el desarrollo capitalista español (1940–1970)* (Madrid, 1975).

Leitz, Christian. *Economic Relations between Nazi Germany and Franco's Spain, 1936–1945* (Oxford, 1996).

Lieberman, Sima. *The Contemporary Spanish Economy: A Historical Perspective* (London, 1982).

Lifton, Robert Jay. 'Death and History: Ideological Totalism, Victimization, and Violence', in Ernest Menze (ed.). *Totalitarianism Reconsidered* (New York, 1981).

Linz, Juan. 'Una teoría del régimen autoritario. El caso de España', in Manuel Fraga et al., *La España de los años setenta, vol. III: El estado y la política* (Madrid, 1974).

'An authoritarian regime: Spain', in Stanley Payne (ed.), *Politics and Society in Twentieth-century Spain* ([originally 1964] New York, 1976).

Little, Douglas. *Malevolent Neutrality: The United States, Great Britain and the Origins of the Spanish Civil War* (Ithaca, NY, 1985).

Lladó, J.M. and Parpal, J.A. *Ferran-Valls Taberner: un polític per a la cultura Catalana* (Barcelona, 1970).

Llarch, Joan. *Campos de concentración en la España de Franco* (Barcelona, 1978).

Llibert, Ferri, Muixí, Jordi, and Sanjuan, Eduardo. *Las huelgas contra Franco 1939–1956* (Barcelona, 1978).

Llordes, José. *Al dejar el fusil* (Barcelona, 1968).

Llorens, Vicente. *El exilio español de 1939: la emigración Republicana de 1939* (Madrid, 1976).

Lluch, Ernest. *El pensament econòmic a Catalunya, 1760–1840: els origens ideològics del proteccionisme i la presa de consciència de la burgesia Catalana* (Barcelona, 1973).

López de Letona, José María, et al. *La empresa pública industrial en España* (Madrid, 1973).

López López, Alejandro. *El boicot de la derecha a las reformas de la segunda república: la minoría agraria, el rechazo constitucional y la cuestión de la tierra* (Madrid, 1984).

López Rodó, L. *La planificación del desarrollo* (Madrid, 1970).

Lorenzo Espinosa, José María. *Dictadura y dividendo: el discreto negocio de la burguesía vasca (1937–1950)* (Bilbao, 1989).

'Elecciones sindicales de postguerra en Vizcaya', in Tussell et al., *La oposición al régimen de Franco* (Madrid, 1990), vol. II, pp. 51–61.

Losada Malvárez, Juan Carlos. *Ideología del ejército franquista, 1939–1959* (Madrid, 1990).

Luca de Tena, Torcuato. *Franco, sí, pero . . . confesiones profanas* (Barcelona, 1993).

Ludevid, Manuel. *Cuarenta años de sindicato vertical* (Barcelona, 1976).

Madalena Calvo, José, et al. 'Los lugares de la memoria de la guerra civil en un centro de poder: Salamanca 1936–39', in J. Aróstegui, *Historia y memoria* (Salamanca, 1986).

Madariaga, María Rosa de. 'The Intervention of Moroccan Troops in the Spanish Civil War: A Reconsideration', *European History Quarterly*, 22 (1992).

Mainer, José-Carlos. *Falange y literatura* (Barcelona, 1971).

Malefakis, Edward. *Agrarian Reform and Peasant Revolution in Spain* (New Haven, CT, 1970).

Maluquer Sostres, Joaquín. *La política algodonera, 1940–1970* (Barcelona, 1973).

Mangini, Shirley *Rojos y rebeldes: la cultura de la disidencia durante el franquismo* (Barcelona, 1987).

Memories of Resistance: Women's Voices from the Spanish Civil War (New Haven, Ct, 1995).

Maravall, José. *Dictatorship and Political Dissent: Workers and Students in Franco's Spain* (New York, 1978).

Marcet i Gisbert, Xavier. 'La guerra civil a Terrassa', in various authors, *Catalunya i la guerra civil, 1936–1939* (Barcelona, 1988).

Marichal, Juan. *El intelectual y la política* (Madrid, 1990).

Marsé, Juan. *Si te dicen que caí* (Mexico City, 1973).

Martí, Francesc, and Moreno, Eduardo. *Barcelona ¿A dónde vas?* (Barcelona, 1974).

Martí Gómez, José. *La españa del estraperlo, 1936–1952* (Barcelona, 1995).

Martín Aceña, P. and Comín, F. *INI: cincuenta años de industrialización en España* (Madrid, 1991).

'El estado en la industrialización española de la posguerra: el Instituto Nacional de Industria', in Leandros Prados de la Escosura and Vera Zamagni (eds.). *El desarrollo económico en la Europa del sur: España e Italia en perspectiva histórica* (Madrid, 1992).

Martín Gaite, Carmen. *El cuarto de atrás* (Barcelona, 1978).

Usos amorosos de la postguerra española (Barcelona, 1987).

Martín-Santos, Luis. *Tiempo de silencio* (Barcelona, 1962).

Martínez Alier, Juan. *Labourers and Landowners in Southern Spain* (Iotowa, NJ, 1971).

La estabilidad del latifundismo (Paris, 1978).

Martínez Tórtola, Esther. *La enseñanza de la historia en el primer bachillerato franquista, 1938–1953* (Madrid, 1996).

Massot i Muntaner, Josep. *Els intellectuals mallorquins davant el franquisme* (Barcelona, 1992).

El cònsol Alan Hillgarth i les Illes Balears (1936–1939) (Barcelona, 1995).

El primer franquisme a Mallorca (Barcelona, 1996).

Matossian, Mary. 'Ideologies of Delayed Industrialisation: Some Tensions and Ambiguities', *Economic Development and Cultural Change* (April 1958), pp. 217–28.

Matute, Ana María. *Libro de juegos para los niños de los otros* (Barcelona, 1961).

Mayordomo Pérez, Alejandro. *Nacional-catolicismo y educación en la España de posguerra* (Madrid, 1990).

Medina, Rafael de, Duque de Medinaceli. *Tiempo pasado* (Seville, 1971).

Mendizabal, Arantxa, and Serrano, Felipe. 'La politica industrial del franquismo: su influencia en la economía vasca', *Ekonomiaz*, 9/10 (1988) pp. 301–22.

Menze, Ernest (ed.). *Totalitarianism Reconsidered* (New York, 1981).

Mermall, Thomas. *The Rhetoric of Humanism: Spanish Culture after Ortega y Gasset* (New York, 1976).

'La ideología del '98 bajo el franquismo', in J.P Gabriele (ed.), *Divergencias y unidad: perspectivas sobre la generación del '98 y Antonio Machado* (Madrid, 1990).

Miguel, Amando de. *Sociología del franquismo: análisis ideológico de los ministros del régimen* (Barcelona, 1975).

España cíclica: ciclos económicos y generaciones demográficas en la sociedad española contemporánea (Madrid, 1986).

Miguel, Amando de and Oltra, Benjamin. 'Bonapartismo y catolicismo: una hipótesis sobre los orígenes ideológicos del franquismo', *Papers*, 8 (1978).

Miller, Arthur. *The Crucible* (Harmondsworth, 1973).

Ministerio de Cultura. *Justicia en guerra: jornadas sobre la administración de justicia durante la guerra civil española* (Madrid, 1990).

Mir, Conxita. 'Personal politic i repressió econòmica: l'actuació del tribunal de responsabilitats polítiques sobre els parlamentaris Republicans a Lleida entre 1936 i 1939', in Jaume Barrull Pelegrí, *Violència política i ruptura social a Espanya, 1936–1945* (Lleida, 1994), pp. 117–39.

Miralles, Ricardo. 'La crisis económica de los años treinta en el País Vasco', in *Ekonomiaz*, 9/10 (1988), pp. 277–300.

Molero Pintado, Antonio. *La educación durante la segunda república y la guerra civil (1931–1939)* (Madrid, 1991).

Molinero, Carme, and Ysàs, Pere. *'Patria, Justicia y Pan': nivells de vida i condicions de treball a Catalunya, 1939–1951* (Barcelona, 1985).

'La població Catalana a la postguerra: creixement i concentració', *L'Avenç*, 102 (March 1987).

'Luchas obreras y oposición al franquismo en la Cataluña de postguerra', in J. Tusell et al., *La oposición al régimen de Franco* (Madrid, 1990).

'Los industriales catalanes durante el franquismo', *Revista de Historia Económica*, 8, 1 (Winter, 1990), pp. 105–29.

'Un instrumento esencial del régimen franquista: la organización sindical', in J. Tusell et al., *El régimen de Franco* (Madrid, 1993).

Montero, José R. *La CEDA: el catolicismo social y político en la II República* (Madrid, 1977).

Moradiellos, Enrique. 'The Gentle General: The Official British Perception of General Franco during the Spanish Civil War', in P. Preston and A.L. Mackenzie (eds.), *The Republic Beseiged: Civil War in Spain, 1936–1939* (Edinburgh, 1996), pp. 1–19.

Morales Ruiz, Juan José. *La publicación de la Ley de Represión de la Masonería en la prensa de la España de postguerra (1940)* (Zaragoza, 1992).

Morán, Gregorio. *Los españoles que dejaron de serlo* (Barcelona, 1982).

Moreno Fonseret, Roque. *La autarquía en Alicante (1939–1952)* (Alicante, 1994).

Moreno Gómez, Francisco. *La guerra civil en Córdoba 1936–1939* (Madrid, 1985).

Córdoba en la posguerra (Córdoba, 1987).

'La represión en la España campesina', in J.L.García Delgado (ed.), *El primer franquismo* (Madrid, 1989), pp. 189–207.

Moreno Luzón, José Javier. 'El estudio de los apoyos sociales del franquismo: una propuesta metodológica', in Santiago Castillo (ed.), *La historia social en España: actualidad y perspectivas* (Madrid, 1991).

Morgan, Rikki. 'Romper los moldes: implicaciones estéticas e ideológicas de *El espíritu de la colmena*', *ACIS*, 6 (spring, 1993), pp. 25–32.

Morodo, Raul. *Acción Española: orígenes ideológicas del franquismo* (Madrid, 1980).

Morse, Jonathon. *Word By Word: The Language of Memory* (Ithaca, NY, 1990).

Moya, Carlos. *El poder económico en España (1939–1970): un análisis sociológico* (Madrid, 1975).

Señas de Leviatán: estado nacional y sociedad industrial: España 1936–1980 (Madrid, 1984).

Muniesa, Bernat. *La burguesía Catalana ante la Segunda República Española*, 2 vols. (Barcelona, 1985/6).

Muns, Joaquín. *Industrialización y crecimiento de los paises en desarrollo* (Barcelona, 1972).

Muntanyola, Ramón. *Vidal y Barraquer, el Cardenal de la Paz* (Barcelona, 1971).

Muñoz, Javier R. 'La represión franquista: paseos y ejecuciones', in *Historia general de Asturias*, vol. XI (Gijón, 1978).

Muñoz, Juan. *El poder de la banca en España* (Madrid, 1969).

Muñoz Cidad, Cándido and Lázaro Araújo, Laureano, 'El desarrollo desigual en España', in R. Carballo et al., *Crecimiento económico y crisis estructural en España, 1959–1980* (Madrid, 1980).

Muñoz Fernández, Antonia. 'La emigración en la provincia de Jaén 1900–1955', in *Estudios geográficos*, 81 (November 1960), pp. 455–96.

Myro Sanchez, R. *El INI en la industria española: especialización sectorial, eficacia económica y rentabilidad* (Madrid, 1981).

Nadal, Antonio. *Guerra civil en Málaga* (Málaga, 1984).

Nadal, Jordi. *El fracaso de la revolución industrial en España, 1814–1913* (Barcelona, 1975).

Nadal, Jordi, Carreras, Albert, and Sudrià, Carles (eds.). *La economia española en el siglo XX: una perpesctiva histórica* (Barcelona, 1987).

Nadal, Jorge. *La población española (siglos XVI–XX)* (Barcelona, 1966).

Nadal Sánchez, Antonio. 'Experiencias psíquicas sobre mujeres Marxistas malagueñas: Málaga, 1939', in *Las mujeres y la guerra civil española* (Madrid, 1991).

Naredo, J.M. 'Antecedentes y características de la sociedad jerárquica que sostiene en Extremadura el expolio, con especial referencia al Plan Badajoz', in *Extremadura saqueada* (Barcelona, 1978).

'La incidencia del "estraperlo" en la economía de las grandes fincas del Sur', *Agricultura y Sociedad*, 19 (1981).

'La agricultura española en el desarrollo económico', in R. Carballo et al., *Historia agraria de la España contemporánea*, vol. III (Barcelona, 1986).

Nash, Mary. 'Pronatalism and Motherhood in Franco's Spain', in Gisela Bock and Pat Thane (eds.), *Maternity and Gender Politics: Women and the Rise of the European Welfare States, 1880s–1950s* (London, 1991).

'Social Eugenics and Nationalist Race Hygiene in Early Twentieth-century Spain', *History of European Ideas*, 15 (1992), pp. 741–8.

Navarro Sandalinas, Ramón. *La enseñanza primaria durante el franquismo (1936–1975)* (Barcelona, 1990).

Nuevas perspectivas sobre la mujer (Madrid, 1982).

Núñez, Diego. *El darwinismo en España* (Madrid, 1969).

Núñez, Mercedes. *Cárcel de Ventas* (Paris, 1967).

Núñez Díez Balart, Mirta and Rojas Friend, Antonio. 'Víctimas del franquismo en Madrid: los fusilamientos en el Cementerio del Este (1939–1945)', in Tusell et al., *El régimen de Franco* (Madrid, 1993).

Núñez Roldán, Francisco. *Mujeres públicas: historia de la prostitución en España* (Madrid, 1995).

Olsson, G. 'Towards a Sermon on Modernity', in M. Billinge, D. Gregory and R. Martin (eds.), *Recollections of a Revolution: Geography as Spatial Science* (London, 1984).

Ordenamiento jurídico y realidad social de las mujeres (Madrid, 1986).

Oroñóz, Javier. *Transformaciones del sistema capitalista y evolución de la formación social española (1939–1979)* (San Sebastián, 1980).

Ortiz Heras, Manuel. *Violencia política en la II República y el primer franquismo: Albacete, 1936–1950* (Madrid, 1996).

Ossa Echarabu, R. *El Bilbao del novecientos: riqueza y poder de la ría, 1900–1923* (Bilbao, 1969).

Otis, Laura. *Organic Memory: History and the Body in the Late Nineteenth and Early Twentieth Centuries* (Lincoln, NE, 1994).

Pabón, J. *Cambó*, 3 vols. (Barcelona, 1952–69).

Palafox, Jordi. 'Contradicciones del capitalismo español durante la depresión económica de los años treinta', *ICE*, 514 (June 1976), pp. 110–17.

'La gran depresión de los años treinta y la crisis industrial española', *Investigaciones económicas*, 11 (1980).

Atraso económico y democracia: la segunda república y la economía española, 1892–1936 (Barcelona, 1991).

Palomino, Angel. *Caudillo* (Barcelona, 1992).

Pámies, Teresa. *Cuando éramos capitanes* (Barcelona, 1974).

Papers. Revista de sociología, 8 (1978), 'El régimen franquista.'

Pasamar Alzuria, Gonzalo. *Historiografía e ideología en la postguerra española: la ruptura de la tradición liberal* (Zaragoza, 1991).

Pasamar Alzuria, Gonzalo and Peiró Martín, Ignacio. *Historiografía y práctica social en España* (Zaragoza, 1987).

Passerini, Luisa (ed.). *Memory and Totalitarianism* (Oxford, 1992).

Pastor i Homs, María Immaculada. *La educación femenina en la postguerra (1939–45): el caso de Mallorca* (Madrid, 1984).

Pastor Petit, D. *Los dossiers secretos de la Guerra Civil* (Barcelona, 1978).

Payne, Stanley. *Politics and the Military in Modern Spain* (Stanford, CA, 1967).

Franco's Spain (London, 1968).

'Spanish Fascism in Comparative Perspective', in Henry Turner (ed.), *Reappraisals of Fascism* (New York, 1975).

The Franco Regime 1936–1975 (Madison, WI, 1987).

'Political Violence During the Spanish Second Republic', *Journal of Contemporary History*, 25 (1990).

Pérez Bowie, José Antonio. *El léxico de la muerte durante la guerra civil española* (Salamanca, 1982).

'Retoricismo y estereotipación: rasgos definidores de un discurso ideologizado: el discurso de la derecha durante la guerra civil', in Julio Aróstegui, *Historia y memoria de la guerra civil* (Salamanca, 1988).

Pérez Díaz, Víctor. *Emigración y cambio social: procesos migratorios y vida rural en Castilla* (Barcelona, 1971).

Pernau, Josep. *Diario de la caída de Cataluña* (Barcelona, 1989).

Petschen, Santiago. *La iglesia en la España de Franco* (Madrid, 1977).

Pick, Daniel. *Faces of Degeneration: A European Disorder, c.1848–c.1918* (Cambridge, 1989).

Pike, David Wingeate. *In The Service of Stalin: The Spanish Communists in Exile 1939–1945* (Oxford, 1993).

Pinkus, Karen. *Bodily Regimes: Advertising under Italian Fascism* (Minneapolis, MI, 1994).

Pitt-Rivers, Julian. *People of the Sierra* (London, 1954).

Plata, Gabriel. 'Joaquin Adán: de los proyectos regeneracionistas a la lucha contrarevolucionaria, 1931–1936', *Muga*, 72 (March 1990), pp. 66–9.

Plaza Prieto, Juan, et al. *El ahorro y la formación de capital en España (1939–1968)* (Madrid, 1971).

Pons Prades, Eduardo. *Los derrotados y el exilio* (Barcelona, 1977).

Guerrillas españolas, 1936–1960 (Barcelona, 1977).

Morir por la libertad: españoles en los campos de exterminio nazis (Madrid, 1995).

Prados de la Escosura, Leandros and Zamagni, Vera (eds.). *El desarrollo económico en la europa del sur: España e Italia en perspectiva histórica* (Madrid, 1992).

Preston, Paul. *España en crisis: la evolución y decadencia del régimen de Franco* (Madrid, 1977).

The Coming of the Spanish Civil War (London, 1978).

'War of Words: The Spanish Civil War and the Historians', in Preston (ed.). *Revolution and War in Spain, 1931–1939* (London, 1984).

The Politics of Revenge: Fascism and the Military in Twentieth-century Spain (London, 1990).

Franco: A Biography (London, 1993).

Preston, Paul and McKenzie, Anne L. (eds.). *The Republic Besieged: Civil War in Spain, 1936–1938* (Edinburgh, 1996).

Rabinbach, Anson. 'Unclaimed Heritage: Ernst Bloch's *Heritage of Our Times* and the Theory of Fascism', *New German Critique*, 11 (spring 1977).

Raguer, Hilari. 'La "cuestión religiosa"', Santos, Juliá. (ed.), *Política en la segunda república, Ayer*, 20 (1995).

Rama, Carlos. *La crisis española del siglo XX* (Madrid, 1962).

Ramírez Jiménez, Manuel, et al. *Las fuentes ideológicas de un régimen: España, 1939–1945* (Zaragoza, 1978).

Reig Tapia, Alberto. 'La represión franquista en la guerra civil', *Sistema*, 33 (November, 1979).

'La represión franquista y la guerra civil: consideraciones metodológicas, instrumentalización política y justificación ideológica', PhD thesis, Madrid (1983).

Ideología e historia: sobre la represion franquista y la guerra civil (Madrid, 1984).

Violencia y terror: Estudios sobre la guerra civil española (Madrid, 1990).

Franco 'Caudillo': mito y realidad (Madrid, 1995).

Ribas, Massana, Albert. *L'economía Catalana sota el franquisme (1939–1953)* (Barcelona, 1978).

L'economía Catalana sota el franquisme (1939–1953): efectes de la política económica de postguerra sobre la industria i les finances de Catalunya (Barcelona, 1978).

Richards, Michael. '"Terror and Progress": Industrialisation, Modernity, and the Making of Francoism', in H. Graham and L. Labanyi (eds.), *Spanish Cultural Studies: An Introduction* (Oxford, 1995), pp. 173–82.

'Autarky and the Franco Dictatorship in Spain, 1936–1945', PhD thesis, University of London (1995).

'Civil War, Violence and the Construction of Francoism', in P. Preston and A.L. McKenzie (eds.), *The Republic Beseiged: Civil War in Spain, 1936–1939* (Edinburgh, 1996).

'Constructing the Nationalist State: Self-sufficiency and Regeneration in the Early Franco Years', in A. Smith, and C. Mar Molinero (eds.), *Nationalism and the Nation in the Iberian Peninsula* (Oxford, 1996), pp. 149–67.

Riquer, Borja de. 'Dossier: el franquisme i la burguesía Catalana (1939–1951)', *L'Avenç* (January 1979).

'Rebuig, passivitat i suport: actituts polítiques Catalanes davant el primer franquisme (1939–1950)', in Javier Tusell et al., *La oposición al régimen de Franco* (Madrid, 1990), vol. II, pp. 239–49.

L'ultim Cambó: la Crete catalanista davant la guerra civil i el primer franquisme (Vic, 1996).

Riquer, Borja de and Culla, Joan. *A historia de Catalunya: el franquisme i la transició democratica ,1939–1988)*, vol. VII (Barcelona, 1989).

Rivera Blanco, Antonio. 'La recomposición del poder local franquista en una ciudad de provincias: Vitoria', in Ruiz-Manjon Cabeza et al., (eds.), *Los nuevos historiadores ante la guerra civil española* (Granada 1990).

Roca i Girona, Jordi. *De la pureza a la maternidad: la construcción del género femenino en la postguerra española* (Madrid, 1996).

Rodriguez, Angel, and D'alos-Moner, Raimon. *Economía y territorio en Cataluña: los centros de gravedad de población, industria y renta* (Madrid, 1978).

Roig, Montserrat. *Noche y niebla: los Catalanes en los campos nazis* (Barcelona, 1978).

Roldán, S. and García Delgado, J.L., *La formación de la sociedad capitalista en España, 1914–1920* (Madrid, 1973).

Roldán Bárbero, H. *Historia de la prisión en España* (Madrid, 1985).

Román, M. *Memoria de la copla: la canción española de Conchita Piquer a Isabel Pantoja* (Madrid, 1993).

Romeu Alfaro, F. *El silencio roto: mujeres contra el franquismo* (Madrid, 1994).

Roseberry, W. 'Political Economy', *Annual Review of Anthropology*, 17 (1989), pp. 161–85.

Roux, Bernard. 'Latifundismo, reforma agraria y capitalismo en la Peninsula Ibérica', in *Agricultura y Sociedad*, 23 (April–June, 1982).

Ruiz, David, Sánchez, Isidro, and Ortiz, Manuel. (eds.) *España franquista: causa general y actitudes sociales ante la dictadura* (Castilla-La Mancha, 1993).

Ruiz Rico, Juan José. *El papel político de la iglesia católica en la España de Franco, 1936–1971* (Madrid, 1977).

Ruiz Somavilla, María José. *'El cuerpo limpio': análisis de la prácticas higiénicas en la España del mundo moderno* (Málaga, 1993).

Saez Alba, A. *La otra 'cosa nostra': la Asociación Católica Nacional de Propagandistas* (Paris, 1974).

Saíz Marín, J. *El Frente de Juventudes: política de juventud en la España de la postguerra (1937–1960)* (Madrid, 1988).

Salas, Nicolás. *Morir en Sevilla* (Barcelona, 1986).
Sevilla fue la clave 2 vols. (Seville, 1992).
Salas Larrazábal, R. *Pérdidas de la guerra* (Barcelona, 1977).
Los datos exactos de la guerra civil (Madrid, 1980).
Sánchez, José María. *The Spanish Civil War as a Religious Tragedy* (Notre Dame, IN, 1987).
Sánchez Albornoz, Claudio. *España hace un siglo: una economía dual* (Barcelona, 1968).
Sánchez Albornoz, Nicolás (ed.). *The Economic Modernization of Spain* (New York, 1987).
Sánchez Ayuso, Manuel. 'Industrialización y financiación de la economía española, 1939–1959', in *Anuario de ciencia económica* (Madrid, 1973).
Sánchez López, R. *Mujer española: una sombra de destino en lo universal* (Murcia, 1990).
Sánchez Recio, Glicerio. 'Los tribunales populares y su actuación durante la guerra civil en el País Valenciano', in *Historia y memoria de la guerra civil* (Salamanca, 1986).
'Justicia ordinaria y justicia popular durante la guerra civil', in Ministerio de Cultura, *Justicia en guerra* (Madrid, 1990).
'En torno al régimen franquista: revisión de una antigua polémica', Anales de la Universidad de Alicante, *Historia Contemporánea*, 8/9 (1991/2), pp. 9–34.
Santacana i Torres, Carles. *Victoriosos i derrotats: el franquisme a L'Hospitalet, 1939–1951* (Barcelona, 1994).
Sardá, Juan. 'El Banco de España (1931–1962)', in *El Banco de España: una historia económica* (Madrid, 1970).
Saz Campos, Ismael. 'El franquismo: ¿régimen autoritario o dictadura fascista?', in Javier Tusell et al. (eds.). *El régimen de Franco (1936–1975)* (Madrid, 1993).
Scanlon, Geraldine. *La polémica feminista en la España contemporánea, 1868–1974* (Madrid, 1986).
Scheper-Hughes, Nancy. *Death Without Weeping: The Violence of Everyday Life in Brazil* (Berkeley, CA, 1993).
Schneider, William. *Quality and Quantity: The Quest for Biological Regeneration in Twentieth-century France* (Cambridge, 1990).
Schweitzer, Arthur. *The Age of Charisma* (Chicago, IL, 1984).
Servicio Histórico Militar. *La ofensiva sobre Valencia* (Madrid, 1977).
Sevilla Guzmán, Eduardo. 'El campesinado en el desarrollo capitalista español (1939–1975)', in P. Preston (ed.) *España en crisis* (Madrid, 1977), pp. 183–215.
Sevilla Guzmán, Eduardo and González de Molina, Manuel. 'Política social agraria del primer franquismo', in García Delgado, J.L. *El primer franquismo* (Madrid, 1989), pp. 135–87.
Sevilla Guzmán, E. and Giner, S. 'Absolutismo despótico y dominación de clase: el caso de España', *Cuadernos de Ruedo Ibérico*, 43/45 (Paris 1975).
Shaw, Duncan. *Fútbol y franquismo* (Madrid, 1987).
Sicroff Albert, A. *Los estatutos de limpieza de sangre: contoversias entre los siglos XV y XVII* (Madrid, 1985).
Sinova, Justino. *La censura de prensa durante el franquismo* (Madrid, 1989).

Si, Abigail Lee. *Juan Goytisolo: The Case for Chaos* (New Haven, CT, 1980).

Smyth, Denis. *Diplomacy & Strategy of Survival: British Policy and Franco's Spain 1940–41* (Cambridge, 1986).

'The Moor and the Money-lender: Politics and Profits in Anglo–German Relations with Francoist Spain, 1936–1940', in Marie-Luise Recker (ed.), *Von der Konkurrenz zur Rivalität: Das britische–deutsche Verhältnis in den Ländern der europäischen Peripherie 1919–1939* (Stuttgart, 1986).

Solé i Sabaté, Josep María. *La repressió franquista a Catalunya, 1938–1953* (Barcelona, 1985).

Solé i Sabaté, J.M., and Villarroya i Font. J. *Catalunya sota les bombes* (Barcelona, 1986).

La repressió a la reraguarda de Catalunya (1936–1939) (Barcelona, 1989).

L'Ocupació militar de Catalunya (Barcelona, 1987).

Soloway, Richard. *Demography and Regeneration: Eugenics and the Declining Birth-rate in Twentieth-century Britain* (London, 1990).

Sopeña Monsalve, Andrés. *El flórido pensil: memoria de la escuela nacional-católica* (Barcelona, 1994).

Sorel, Andrés. *Cuarto mundo: emigración española en Europa* (Madrid, 1974).

Soriano, Antonio. *Exodos: historia oral del exilio repúblicano en Francia, 1939–1945* (Barcelona, 1989).

Sorní Mañés, José. 'Aproximación a un estudio de la contrareforma agraria en España', *Agricultura y Sociedad*, 6 (1978).

Soucy, Robert. 'The Nature of Fascism in France', *Journal of Contemporary History*, 1, 1 (1966), pp. 27–55.

Southworth, Herbert. *El mito de la cruzada de Franco* (Paris, 1963).

Antifalange: estudio crítico de Falange en la guerra de España (Paris, 1967).

'La Falange: un análisis de la herencia fascista española', in P. Preston (ed.), *España en crisis* (Madrid, 1977).

Guernica! Guernica! A Study of Journalism, Diplomacy, Propaganda and History (Berkeley, CA, 1977).

Stern, Louis. *Beyond Death and Exile: The Spanish Republicans in France, 1939–1955* (Cambridge, MA, 1979).

Suárez A./Colectivo '36. *El libro blanco sobre las cárceles franquistas 1939–1976* (Paris, 1976).

Suárez Fernández, Luis. *Francisco Franco y su tiempo*, 8 vols. (Madrid, 1984).

Sueiro, Daniel. *La verdadera historia del valle de los caídos* (Madrid, 1976).

Tamames, Ramón. *Los monopolios en España* (Madrid, 1967).

La república. La era de Franco (Madrid, 1973).

Estructura económica de España (Madrid, 1974).

Taussig, Michael. *The Devil and Commodity Fetishism in Latin America* (North Carolina, 1980).

Taya, Regina. 'Sobre la intervenció estatal i el creixement industrial a Espanya de 1939 a 1966', in *Economía crítica: una perspectiva Catalana* (Barcelona, 1973).

Tello Lázaro, José Angel. *Ideología y política. La iglesia católica española, 1936–1959* (Zaragoza, 1984).

Terrón Montero, Javier. *La prensa en España durante el régimen de Franco: un intento de análisis político* (Madrid, 1981).

Tezanos, Jose Felix. 'Notas para una interpretación sociológica del franquismo', *Sistema*, 111, 23 (1978).

Thomas, Hugh, *The Spanish Civil War* (Harmondsworth, 1979).

Thomàs, Joan M. *Falange, guerra civil, franquisme: FET y de las JONS de Barcelona en els primers anys de règim franquista* (Barcelona, 1992).

Tierno Galván, Enrique. *Escritos (1950–1960)* (Madrid, 1971).

Cabos sueltos (Barcelona, 1981).

Tió, Carlos. *La política de aceites comestibles en la España del siglo XX* (Madrid, 1982).

Torres, Santiago. *Así los viví: 50 años de un pueblo y de una empresa* (Bilbao, 1990).

Tortella, Gabriel. 'Sobre el significado histórico del franquismo', *Revista de Occidente*, 59 (1986), pp. 104–14.

Trythall, J.W. *Franco: A Biography* (London, 1970).

Tuñón de Lara, Manuel. *La España del siglo XX* (Paris, 1966).

Poder y sociedad en España, 1900–1931 (Madrid, 1992).

Turner, Bryan S. *Regulating Bodies: Essays in Medical Sociology* (London, 1992).

Turner, Terence. 'Production, Exploitation and Social Consciousness in the "Peripheral Situation"', *Social Analysis*, 19, pp. 91–115.

Tusell, Javier. 'La autarquía cuartelera: las ideas económica de Franco a partir de un documento inédito', *Historia 16*, 115 (1985).

La dictadura de Franco (Madrid, 1988).

Franco en la guerra civil: una biografía política (Barcelona, 1992).

Tusell, Javier and García Queipo de Llano, Genoveva. 'Fuero del Trabajo: orígen y contenido', in *Historia 16, La guerra civil*, 20.

Tusell, Javier, Vigil, Alicia Alted and Mateos, Abdón (eds.). *La oposición al régimen de Franco* (Madrid, 1990).

Tusell, Javier, Sueiro, Susana, Marín, José María and Casanova, Marina (eds.). *El régimen de Franco (1936–1975)* (Madrid, 1993).

Umbral, Francisco. *Memorias de un niño de derechas* (Barcelona, 1976).

La derechona (Barcelona, 1997).

Urbina, Fernando. 'Formas de vida de la Iglesia en España, 1939–1975', in *Iglesia y sociedad en España, 1939–1975* (Madrid, 1977).

Ureña Portero, Gabriel. *Arquitectura y urbanística civil y militar en el periodo de la autarquía (1936–1945)* (Madrid, 1979).

Valdes Larrañaga, Manuel. *De la Falange al Movimiento (1936–1952)* (Madrid, 1994).

Vázquez Montalbán, Manuel. *Cancionero general, 1939–1971*, 2 vols. (Barcelona, 1972).

Los demonios familiares de Franco (Barcelona, 1978).

Crónica sentimental de España (Madrid, 1986).

Barcelonas (Barcelona, 1987).

'Franco i el regeneracionisme de dretes', *L'Avenç*, 165 (December 1992), pp. 8–15.

Velasco Murviedro, Carlos. 'Las pintorescas ideas económicas de Franco', *Historia 16*, 85 (May 1983), pp. 19–28.

'El pensamiento autárquico español como directríz de la política económica (1936–1951)', PhD thesis (Madrid, 1982).

'El pensamiento agrario y la apuesta industrizadora en la España de los cuarenta', *Agricultura y Sociedad*, 23 (1983), pp. 233–72.

'Sobre una posible caracterización de la autarquía española (1939–1945)', in Manuel Tuñón de Lara (ed.), *Estudios sobre la historia de España*, Homenaje M.Tuñón de Lara, vol. II (Madrid, 1981), pp. 391–406.

'El ingenierismo como directríz básica de la política economía durante la autarquía', *ICE*, 606 (1984).

'Sucedáneos de posguerra', *Historia 16*, 131 (March 1987), pp. 11–20.

'El origen militar de la autarquía y su significación económica', in *Perspectiva Contemporánea*, 1 (1988), pp. 117–33.

Vida cotidiana en la España de los 40, La (Madrid, 1990).

Vilanova, Antonio. *Los olvidados: los exiliados españoles en la segunda guerra mundial* (Paris, 1969).

Vilar, Pierre. *Spain: A Brief History* (London, 1977).

La guerra civil española (Barcelona, 1986).

Vilar, Sergio. *La naturaleza del franquismo* (Barcelona, 1977).

Villanueva Edo, Antonio. *Historia Social de la tuberculosis en Bizkaia* (Bilbao 1989).

Villarroya i Font, J. and Solé i Sabaté, J.M. 'El castigo a los vencidos', *Historia 16*, 24 (1986), pp. 54–66.

Vincent, Mary. *Catholicism in the Second Spanish Republic: Religion and Politics in Salamanca, 1930–1936* (Oxford, 1996).

Viñas, Angel. 'La administración de la política económica exterior de España, 1936–1979', in *Cuadernos económicos de ICE*, 13 (1980), pp. 157–247.

Guerra, dinero, dictadura: Ayuda fascista y autarquía en la España de Franco (Barcelona, 1984).

Viñas, Angel, Viñuela, J., Eguidazu, F., Pulgar, C.F., and Florensa, S. *Política comercial exterior en España (1931–1975)* (Madrid, 1979), 3 vols.

Viver Pi-Sunyer, Carles. *El personal político de Franco (1936–1945): contribución empírica a una teoría del régimen franquista* (Barcelona, 1978).

'Aproximació a la ideología del franquisme en l'etapa fundacional del règim', *Papers*, 14 (1980).

Vives i Clavé, Pere. *Cartes des dels camps de concentració* (Barcelona, 1970).

Vizcaíno Casas, F. *Contando los cuarenta* (Madrid, 1972).

La España de la posguerra (1939–1953) (Barcelona, 1978).

Weber, Max. *Economy and Society* (New York, 1968).

Weeks, Jeffrey. *Sex, Politics and Society* (London, 1981).

Whealey, Robert H. *Hitler and Spain: The Nazi Role in the Spanish Civil War* (Lexington, KY, 1989).

Wilson, Sheilah. 'Fiestas and Terezin: The Space of Confinement', in *Norte*, V8, 4–6 (1972), pp. 97–106.

INDEX

abortion, 54, 167
Acción Católica, 153, 154, 164
Acción Española, 16, 58
Africanista generals, 34, 35
agrarian myth, 17, 18
agriculture, 105, 108, 128–9, 130, 171
  food production, 132–46
  protectionism, 132–3
  reform, 104, 106, 129, 131, 146
Aguilera, Gonsalo de, 47
air strikes, 40, 41
Alarcón y de Lastra, Luis de, 74, 75
Albacete, 145
Alicante, 117
Almadén, 83
Altos Hornos de Vizcaya (AHV), 112–13
anarchists, 21, 87
anarchy, 67, 68
Andalusia, 20, 37, 38, 39, 40, 101, 130
anti-clerical violence, 31
'Anti-Spain', 4, 7, 9, 21, 27, 49, 93, 156
Areilza, J. M. de, 42, 74, 86, 92, 97
Argentina, 92
army, *see* military, the
ascetism, 50, 152–6, 172
Asturias, 30, 31, 72, 81, 113, 157
austerity, 152–6
autarky, 2–3, 4, 26, 30, 65, 75, 76, 80,
  86–7, 106, 109, 114, 126, 147, 150
  and civil war, 99–105, 171
  definition of, 94
  economic, 99–109, 172–3
  political and cultural origins, 91–9
  and resistance, 156–69
  as social quarantine, 22–5, 174
  and wheat prices, 133, 134–5
  see also self-sufficiency
authority, 22, 33, 76, 77, 151
autonomism, 19, 20
Auxilio Social, 164
Axis powers, 91, 100, 102, 137, 144, 162
Azaña, President Manuel, 32, 60, 61

Badajóz, 35, 142
banks, 106, 107, 110, 113, 117, 120
Barcelona, 19, 21, 29, 32, 43, 44, 45, 46,
  73, 74, 77, 78, 79, 80, 86, 87, 101,
  117, 124, 125, 126, 130, 131, 132,
  136, 137, 138, 139, 144, 151, 153,
  154, 168
  bread shortages, 162
  defiance in, 158
  fall of, 118
  first strike under Franco, 86, 156
  Franco's visit to, 162–3
  general strike (1951), 158
  industry, 119–23
  population growth, 165
Basque country, 19, 20, 21, 41–2, 83,
  111–18, 157, 158
Benet, Juan, 29, 35
Bilbao, 42, 74, 83, 86, 87, 101, 102, 110,
  111–12, 118, 130, 145
black market, 55, 108, 109, 113, 134,
  135, 136, 138–40, 143, 156, 165,
  166
body, 7, 152, 153; *see also* social conflict,
  medicalisation of
Bonapartism, 15
Brenan, Gerald, 33, 108
Britain, 59, 91, 92, 95, 101, 102, 109, 118
Burgos, 45, 101, 124, 145

Cádiz, 37, 138
Calvo Sotelo, J., 77, 85
Cambó, Francesc, 74, 111, 122–3
capital accumulation, 105–6, 133, 172
capitalism, 15, 58, 59, 72, 76, 122, 129,
  156
Carceller, Demetrio, 97, 99, 100, 106, 117
Carlists, 16, 34, 124, 125
Cartagena, 162
Castile, 20, 48, 72, 73, 95, 129, 156
Catalonia, 21, 43–6, 77, 78, 79, 118–26,
  130, 131, 156

Catholicism, 7, 12, 15, 16, 17, 18–19, 21,
    27, 56, 58, 71, 81, 86, 95, 98, 128,
    171–2
  and austerity, 152–6
  and fascism, 65, 76, 172
  and purification, 46, 49, 50–1
  and racism, 60
  and women, 53–4
Centrales Nacional Sindicalistas (CNS),
    85, 121, 122, 138, 157
'charismatic authority', 11–12
Christianity, 7, 11, 20, 23, 24, 28, 49, 50,
    54, 64, 68, 73, 80, 168
cities, 73–4, 129, 130, 145
Civil War, 9, 12, 17, 25, 28, 150, 170, 171,
    172
  and autarky, 99–105
  business elites, 123
  consequences of, 11
  executions in, 30
  historiography, 9, 10, 27, 30
  nationalist martyrs of, 73
  role of violence in, 35, 62
  social purpose of, 20–1, 34–5
class structure, 15, 26, 68, 156
clergy, 16
'closed space', 1, 4, 28, 67, 88
colonial campaign, 28, 34
'colonisation' programme, 141–2
common graves, 38
communism, 16, 17, 35, 39, 42, 44, 47, 59,
    71, 79–80
concentration camps, 43, 50, 57, 83, 84
Confederación Española de Derechas
    Autónomas (CEDA), 19, 40
consumption, domestic, 98–9, 127–8, 134,
    168–9
Córdoba, 30, 36, 37, 39, 139
corporativism, 58, 76, 84–7, 115
Correa Veglison, Antonio, 137
corruption, 137, 139, 149
Cortes (1943), 13
Councils of War, 38
criminality, 56, 64, 78, 79, 159, 163
Cuba, 48
culture, 26, 28, 68, 93, 95

Darwinism, 16
deaths, registration of, 30–1, 38
'defeated, the', 4, 18, 24, 25, 26, 28, 29,
    93, 109, 149–50, 159–60, 173
degeneration, 3, 16, 48, 49, 60, 61, 66
Díaz Criado, Captain Manuel, 38
dictatorship, theories of, 14–15
discipline, 57, 86, 151, 152
disease, 142–3, 146

dissent, 26, 88, 156 see also resistance
divorce, 54

economic development, 11, 15, 76, 92–3,
    103–4, 109
  and repression, 22–5, 40
economics, see political economy
education, 13, 54, 75, 77, 78, 105
Eguílaz, H. P., 74, 94–5
elites, 10, 11, 15, 16, 17, 19, 20, 22, 23,
    40, 75, 87, 93, 106, 107, 109
  and autarky, 95–6, 110, 174
  in Catalonia, 123–6
  in post-war period, 160, 164
  and repression, 25, 46
  and rural areas, 127
empire, idea of, 16, 17, 51–2, 68
employers, 121–2, 125–6, 158, 172
employers' organisations, 85
eugenics, 49, 57, 58–60, 66
everyday life, 24, 57, 158
'evil', 7, 18, 27
executions, 30, 35, 36, 37, 38, 39, 40, 41,
    43, 46, 82
extermination, 10, 17, 28, 31, 32, 33, 38,
    39, 40, 44, 47

Falange, 16, 19–20, 27, 34, 42, 47, 52, 53,
    76, 93, 94, 117, 120, 126, 140, 156,
    172
  attitude to violence, 3, 4, 28
  as coloniser, 28
  in historiography, 14
  ideology, 17, 28, 51, 68, 77, 81, 95, 121,
    122, 152, 161–2
  in post-war period, 158, 159, 160,
    161–2, 167
  and purges, 37, 38, 40, 41, 45, 46
  role of, 9, 85, 86, 87, 124, 125
  and rural areas, 130, 132
families, 30, 36, 52–4, 164, 167, 170
family, role of, 64–5, 77, 86
famine, 141, 143–4; see also starvation
fantasy, 170, 172
farms, 130–1, 141–2
fascism, 14, 15, 16, 17, 19, 20, 34, 49–50,
    59, 65, 76, 85, 92, 95, 102, 119, 172
feminism, 16
fertiliser industry, 113, 125, 144
FET y de las JONS, 68, 78, 79, 84, 86,
    123, 144
finance, 105–9, 123
food, 80, 81, 101–2, 108, 127, 132–41,
    144–6, 157, 159, 162, 164, 165–6
forced labour, 73, 80, 83, 101, 112
foreign debt, 101, 112

foreign exchange, 98, 113
foreign influences, 9, 19, 23, 27, 45, 47,
    58, 59, 60, 65, 96–7, 128, 129, 130
France, 59, 83, 92, 95, 101, 109, 118
Franco, General Francisco, 12, 14, 22, 33,
    34–5, 40, 42, 43, 45, 50, 73, 79, 86,
    103, 150–1, 162–3
  appointed Head of State, 102
  and autarky, 96
  character of, 60–1, 152
  historiography of, 7, 9
  rural policies, 129, 134
Francoism
  and autarky, 95–9
  and change, 11, 13–14
  contradictions in, 17–18
  definition of, 11–15
  economic policy, 22–5
  historiography, 7, 9–10, 13–15, 29
  ideology of, 16–19, 50, 62, 96–7
  and Ignatius, 153–6
  mythology of, 16–17
  and role of women, 52–6, 64
  and rural areas, 129
  social base of, 19–22
  use of terror by, 27, 29, 30–4
freemasonry, 75, 79–80
Fuertes, J. V., 94

Galicia, 30, 39, 41, 42, 83, 142
gamekeepers, 37
Gay y Forner, Vicente, 49–50
Germany, 92, 100, 101, 102, 107, 112,
    116, 119, 137, 138, 144, 158, 161–2,
    171, 172; see also Nazism
Gerona, 139
Giral, José, 32
God, 23, 50, 68, 94
Gonzáles Oliveros, W., 44–5
'good', 7, 18
Granada, 39, 40, 87
guerillas, 53, 149, 166, 173
Guipúzcoa, 157–8

health, 60–2; see also social conflict,
    medicalisation of
hierarchy, 67, 68, 69, 74, 76, 84, 86, 96, 97
historiography, 156
  exculpatory tone of, 15
  and Francoism, 7, 9–10, 13–15, 27
  Marxist, 15
  of political relations, 14
history, 29, 67, 71, 77
Hitler, Adolf, 49
Hodgson, Robert, 102, 131
horizontalism, 67, 68, 72

housing, 105, 146, 164–5
Huelva, 142

Iberduero, 118
ideas, 26, 27, 156, 171
identity, 24, 168–9
ideology, 14, 15, 16–19, 27, 28, 93, 95, 97
import substitution (ISI), 94, 116, 144
imports, 92
industrialisation, 11, 17, 24, 75, 76, 92, 93,
    96, 98, 99–100, 104, 105, 106, 108,
    109, 110, 128, 143
industry, 110–26, 145, 168
Institute of National Industry (INI),
    114–17
internalisation, 26, 28, 30, 65, 95, 173
iron and steel industry, 112–13
iron ore, 112
Isabella, Queen, 9
isolation, 30, 46, 91, 92, 96, 97, 152, 155,
    161, 170
Italian fascism, 10, 14, 15, 17, 31, 74, 75,
    76
Italy, 43, 44, 92, 100, 107, 109, 112, 116,
    119, 137, 138, 171, 172

Jaén, 145–6
Jews, 9, 49, 50, 51, 57
judiciary, 13, 45
justice, 20, 27, 32, 45, 79, 124
Juventud de Acción Popular (JAP), 19,
    40
Juventudes Socialistas Unificadas (JSU),
    159

La Coruña, 39, 41, 53, 145
labour, control of, 84–8, 98, 108
land, 17, 18, 36, 37, 110, 114, 141–2
landowners, 36–7, 40, 106, 108, 109,
    124, 127, 128, 130–1, 132, 141,
    142–3
Las Palmas, 145
law, 13, 27, 45, 54, 77–80
Lerroux, Alejandro, 21
liberalism, 3, 16, 18, 22, 23, 36, 47, 59, 69,
    73, 75, 92, 97, 116, 129
Linz, Juan, 13
List, Friedrich, 96
Lliga Regionalista, 74, 120, 122, 123, 124,
    125
local administration, 13, 38, 120
López Ibor, Juan José, 58, 61, 68
Lorca, F. G., 40
loss, 28, 170
Loyola, San Ignacio de (1491–1556), 62,
    153–5

Madrid, 32, 35, 55, 57, 58, 73, 74, 96,
    101, 105, 115, 118, 129, 130, 132,
    133, 157, 159, 160
  black market, 138, 139
  food shortages, 143–4, 166
  repression in, 42–3, 44
  social problems, 165
  unemployment, 108
Maeztu, Ramiro de (1875–1936), 58–9,
    80, 97
Majorca, 62, 141
Málaga, 40–1, 55, 62, 81, 138–9
malaria, 142–3
Mallada, Lucas, 48, 170
Martín Sanz, D., 132, 133
Marxism, 9, 15, 35, 39, 44, 45, 46, 56, 57,
    62, 64, 84, 157, 158, 161, 165
material deprivation, 23, 24, 28, 29, 37,
    40, 88, 108, 151, 152, 163–4
material goods, 23–4
Mateu Pla, Miguel, 126
May Day celebrations, 157, 158
memory, 29, 30, 40, 170
mental illness, 56
middle-classes, 21, 34, 40, 67, 75, 85, 105,
    111, 119, 120, 123, 125, 128, 143,
    163, 164, 172; see also petit
    bourgeoisie
migration, internal, 144–5
militarism, 16, 49, 57–8, 171
military, the, 14, 17, 20, 33, 35, 38, 99,
    160
military expenditure, 99, 145
military rebellion, justification of, 77, 78
military virtues, 62, 152
miners, 81–3, 112, 145, 157
mining, 101, 112, 113
minorities, 17
modernisation, 58, 68, 95, 104, 146
modernity, 10–11, 58, 59
Mola, General, 32, 34, 35–6, 38, 42, 48,
    57, 61, 64, 128
monarchism, 14, 16
Montalbán, Manuel Vázquez, 10
Moors, 49, 50, 51, 57, 72
morality, 23, 26, 27, 36, 54, 55–6, 57, 58,
    65, 98, 156, 166–8
Moroccan campaigns, 35
Murcia, 39, 84, 101, 108, 142–3, 164
mysticism, 86, 147, 153–5, 172
myths, 7, 15, 16, 17, 95, 116

nationalism, 11, 12, 15, 16, 17, 19, 35, 74,
    92, 100, 171, 172
  economic, 94–6
Nationalist government, 33–4, 77, 102, 118

National-Syndicalism, 86, 87, 120–1, 122,
    125, 160, 163
Navarra, 45, 141
Navy, 115, 145
Nazism, 10, 14, 15, 17, 31, 35, 49–50, 74,
    75, 83, 91, 100, 101, 102
Negrín, Juan, 32–3

olive oil, 137, 138, 146
organicism, 18, 65, 84
Oriol, J. M., 118
Osaba, Luis Campos, 189

'Pact of Hunger', 37
Pamplona, 34
pathology, see social conflict,
    medicalisation of
Patria, 9, 13, 17, 18, 22, 23, 25, 31, 34, 46,
    49, 57, 58, 60, 62, 86, 126, 127
peasantry, 16, 17, 19, 36, 37, 42, 48, 93,
    104, 117, 127, 129, 130, 132, 133
  and food production, 140, 141
  moral qualities of, 152
  starvation, 142
  support for Franco, 128
Peiró, Joan, 32
penitence, 23
Perpiñá Grau, R., 99
petit bourgeoisie, 19, 20, 21
physical survival, 24, 29
places, sanctification of, 72–3
pluralism, 13, 14, 18, 33, 34
political discrimination, 78–80
political economy, 1, 15, 93–9, 156, 172
Pontevedra, 41
Popular Front, 20, 31, 36, 77, 82, 85,
    128
popular justice, 27, 32
popular songs, 148, 166
population decline, 56
population growth, 145, 165
poverty, 98, 108, 129, 132, 152, 163, 166,
    170
power, 96
press, 10, 77
Prieto, Indalecio, 32
Primo de Rivera, J. A., 73, 75, 111
prisons, 43, 53, 55, 73, 78, 80–1, 83, 84,
    115, 139, 159
private sphere, 24, 29, 173
property, 21, 45, 86, 93, 111, 125
prostitution, 55–6, 64, 167
protectionism, 93, 94, 95–6, 104, 126,
    132–3, 173
psychiatry, 16, 56–66
public sector, 98–9

punishment, 23, 26, 30, 33, 45, 52, 53, 54, 55, 78, 80–1, 172
purges, 34–46, 71, 77, 151
purification, 1, 4, 10, 14, 17, 27, 28, 30, 33, 34, 43, 46, 47, 62, 65, 73, 86, 96, 149, 174
  brigades, 38
  and post-war reconstruction, 49–50, 154, 156
  and women, 52–6
'purity', 14, 17, 18, 49–51, 60, 65, 72, 73, 148, 156, 172, 173

Quart, Pere, 29
Queipo de Llano, General, 38, 39, 40, 64, 101

racism, 47, 48, 51, 57, 58, 59, 60–2, 64, 115
Rada, Colonel Ricardo, 136–7
rape, 52
rationality, 17, 23, 59
reconstruction, 4, 49
regeneration, 3–4, 16, 17, 18, 30, 47, 48, 64, 68, 95, 115
regionalism, 122; see also separatism
religion, 7, 12, 14, 16, 23, 54, 64, 68, 81, 153–6, 171–2
repression, 10–11, 13, 14, 21–2, 34–46, 68, 77, 150, 160, 161, 168, 172
  analysis of, 30–4
  and economic policy, 22–5
  methods of, 28, 146
  purpose of, 26–7, 31–2, 47, 50
  scale of, 30–1
  of women, 52–6
  see also violence
Republic Second, 7, 9, 11, 13, 34, 77, 104, 173
  economic decline, 110
  lack of purpose, 33–4
Republican movement, 19, 20, 21, 36
  divisions in, 33–4
  violence by, 27, 31, 32, 33
resistance, 24, 39, 53, 81, 88, 141, 144, 147, 149, 150, 173
  and autarky, 156–69
  economic protest, 159–60
  popular, 158–9, 166, 169
  working-class, 156–8
revolutionaries, 21
Ridruejo, Dionisio, 134
right-wing movements, 19–21
Rio Tinto mines, 82–3, 101
Robert, Antonio, 74, 109
Ruisenada, Conde de, 123

rural areas
  and Civil War, 131–2
  contradictions in, 129
  and food production, 132–46
  impact of Francoism on, 127
  and urban areas, 128–30, 146
Russia, 17, 23, 56, 76

Sabadell, 161, 162
sacrifice, 23, 24, 50, 86, 88, 95, 98, 109, 146, 151, 152, 153
Saint Teresa of Ávila, 50–1, 54, 73
Salamanca, 142, 145
salvation, 50
San Sebastián, 41–2, 124–5, 126
sanctification, 72–4
Sant Quirze del Vallés, 161
Santander, 112, 166
savings, 105–6
science, 59–60, 75
segregation, 96
self-denial, 151–2
self-sufficiency, 1, 2–3, 4, 26, 30, 59, 65, 71, 84, 86, 147, 148, 151, 152, 173, 174
  and economic policy, 91–9, 103–5, 109
  as economics and repression, 22–5
  and finance, 105–9
  and food production, 132–46
  and industry, 110–26, 145
  see also autarky
separatism, 42, 44, 45, 78, 122
Serrano Suñer, R., 44
Servicio Nacional del Trigo (SNT), 132, 133, 134, 136, 137, 141
Seville, 29, 37–8, 39, 40, 52, 130, 137, 144, 153, 157
sex, 64, 65, 167
shaving, 55
shipbuilding, 115
silence, 4, 147, 148, 150, 170
smallholders, 129, 130, 133, 141, 152
social change, 11, 13–14
social conflict, medicalisation of, 3, 7, 9, 10, 11, 16, 18, 20, 22–3, 26, 34, 35, 44, 46, 47–50, 56–7, 61, 64, 152, 171, 174
social relations, 67, 94, 151
social revolution, 13
socialism, 75, 76, 96–7; see also communism
Sociedad Anónima Cros, 125
Socorro Rojo (Red Aid), 159
Sota, Ramón de la, 111
space, closure of, 67, 68, 71, 88

Spain
    compared to Germany and Italy, 171
    democracy in, 10
    historic destiny of, 9
    identity, 24,, 25, 26, 28
    rural–urban conflict, 128–9
    society, 13, 14, 15, 19–22, 69
    spirit of, 9, 11, 16–17, 23, 103
    uniqueness of, 23
    and world economy, 103–4
Spaniards, 47–8, 51, 58–9, 68, 92, 151,
    169
Spanish Communist Party (PCE), 21
'Spanish essence', 3, 7, 22–3, 48, 60, 62,
    128, 155
'Spanishness', 16, 98
spiritual training, 153–5
starvation, 92, 108, 127, 142, 143, 166,
    167, 173; see also famine
starvation wages, 24, 37, 108
state, 11, 12, 13, 20, 21, 23, 25, 69, 71–2,
    74, 75–6, 97, 98, 102–3, 168
    and finance, 105–9
    and industry, 113–18, 125–6
    and labour, 84–8
strikes, 39–40, 86, 156, 157, 158
Suanzes, J. A., 75, 103, 114–15, 116, 145
suffering, 50
suicide, 11
symbolism, 12, 16, 17, 65, 72–3; see also
    myths

taxation, 108–9, 114
technology, 24
terror, 27, 29, 30–4, 35ff., 135, 156, 174;
    see also repression; violence
textile industry, 116, 117, 120, 158, 161,
    162
Tharsis mines, Huelva, 81–2
Toledo, 36, 73, 129
torture, 11
totalitarianism, 76–8, 84–8, 94, 102, 104
trade, 91–2, 101–2, 103
trade unions, 39, 74, 76, 84, 85, 86–7, 128,
    157, 158
Traditionalists, 125

unemployment, 104, 108, 145, 146, 164,
    166
United States, 92, 101
unity, 18–19, 20
urbanisation, 128–30, 145, 146, 165

Valencia, 43, 137, 145, 159, 160
Valladolid, 73, 117, 142, 157
Valle de los Caídos, 73
Vallejo-Nágera, Antonio (1889–1960),
    57–62
Ventosa, Juan, 123
verticalism, 67, 68, 69, 71, 74, 84–8
Vigo, 42
Vilar, Pierre, 33
violence, 1, 2, 10–11, 12, 21, 23, 24, 53,
    74, 151, 171, 174
    aim of, 26–7, 31–2, 61, 66
    cult of, 20
    Falange and, 4
    justification for, 19, 26, 49
    myths of, 95
    and purges, 34–46
    and regeneration, 3
    by Republicans, 27, 31, 32
    studies of, 15
    see also repression
Vizcaya, 111–12, 136, 138

wages, 24, 37, 84, 106, 108, 121, 143, 158,
    160, 163
war, 2, 4, 12, 62, 153, 171; see also violence
Weber, Max, 11, 12
wheat, 40, 92, 127, 131, 132, 133, 134,
    136, 137, 142
Whitaker, John, 42
women, 16, 43, 51, 52–6, 62, 64, 65, 108,
    124, 139, 149, 158, 159, 164, 166,
    167, 172, 173
work, 80–4, 86, 108, 146, 151, 158, 163–4,
    168
working class, 9, 17, 20, 21, 24, 26, 29, 33,
    48, 53, 54, 76, 93, 98, 101, 105, 108,
    128, 129, 154
    Falange and, 121–2, 126, 160–1
    and food shortages, 137, 143, 144,
    145–6, 164, 165–6, 172
    identity, 168–9
    repression of, 34, 36, 37, 41, 81–4, 161
    resistance, 39–40, 156–8, 173
    state control of, 84–8
World War II, 91–2, 94, 100, 158
Worsley, T. C., 41

Yagüe, General Juan, 35

Zaragoza, 39, 125

Lightning Source UK Ltd.
Milton Keynes UK
UKOW050956020112

184622UK00001B/274/A